Core-Plus
Mathematics
Project

Contemporary Mathematics in Context

A Unified Approach

Core-Plus Mathematics Project

Contemporary Mathematics in Context

A Unified Approach

Arthur F. Coxford
James T. Fey
Christian R. Hirsch
Harold L. Schoen
Gail Burrill
Eric W. Hart
Ann E. Watkins
with
Mary Jo Messenger
Beth Ritsema

Janson Publications, Inc.
Chicago, Illinois

The Core-Plus Mathematics Project curriculum was developed at Western
Michigan University in collaboration with the University of Iowa, the
University of Maryland, and the University of Michigan. This material is based
upon work supported by the National Science Foundation under Grant No.
MDR-9255257.

Any opinions, findings, and conclusions or recommendations expressed in this
material are those of the authors and do not necessarily reflect the views of the
National Science Foundation.

Photo Acknowledgements

Illustration credits are given on page 554 and constitutes a continuation of the
copyright page.

In addition, Janson Publications would like to thank the following for providing
photographs of Core-Plus students in their schools. Many of these photographs
appear throughout the text.

Janice Lee, Midland Valley High School, Langley, SC

Steve Matheos, Firestone High School, Akron, OH

Ann Post, Traverse City West Junior High School, Traverse City, MI

Alex Rachita, Ellet High School, Akron, OH

Judy Slezak, Prairie High School, Cedar Rapids, IA

The Core-Plus Mathematics Project

Library of Congress Cataloging-in-Publication Data

Contemporary mathematics in context: a unified approach/Arthur F. Coxford…[et al.].

    p.   cm.

At head of title: Course 1. Core-Plus Mathematics Project.

Includes indexes.

ISBN 0-939765-91-8

1. Mathematics. I. Coxford, Arthur F. II. Core-Plus Mathematics Project.

QA39.2.C663   1997

510--dc20   96-29041

                                     CIP

Printed in the United States of America

9 8 7 6   1 2 3 4 5 6 7 8 9

Design Malcolm Grear Designers

Core-Plus Mathematics Project

Project Director
Christian R. Hirsch
Western Michigan University

Project Co-Directors
Arthur F. Coxford
University of Michigan
James T. Fey
University of Maryland
Harold L. Schoen
University of Iowa

Curriculum Developers
Gail Burrill
University of Wisconsin-Madison
Eric W. Hart
Western Michigan University
Ann E. Watkins
California State University, Northridge

Professional Development Coordinator
Beth Ritsema
Western Michigan University

Advisory Board
Diane Briars
Pittsburgh Public Schools
Jeremy Kilpatrick
University of Georgia
Kenneth Ruthven
University of Cambridge
David A. Smith
Duke University
Edna Vasquez
Detroit Renaissance High School

Curriculum Development Consultants
Alverna Champion
Grand Valley State University
Cherie Cornick
Wayne County Alliance for Mathematics and Science
Edgar Edwards
(Formerly) Virginia State Department of Education
Richard Scheaffer
University of Florida
Martha Siegel
Towson State University
Edward Silver
University of Pittsburgh
Lee Stiff
North Carolina State University

Technical Coordinator
Wendy Weaver
Western Michigan University

Evaluation Coordinator
Steve Ziebarth
University of Iowa

Collaborating Teachers
Emma Ames
Oakland Mills High School, Maryland
Laurie Eyre
Maharishi School, Iowa
Cheryl Girardot
Sitka High School, Alaska
Annette Hagelberg
West Delaware High School, Iowa

Michael J. Link
Central Academy, Iowa
Mary Jo Messenger
Howard County Public Schools, Maryland
Valerie Mills
Ypsilanti High School, Michigan
Marcia Weinhold
Kalamazoo Area Mathematics and Science Center, Michigan

Graduate Assistants
Diane Bean
University of Iowa
Judy Flowers
University of Michigan
Chris Rasmussen
University of Maryland
Rebecca Walker
Western Michigan University

Production and Support Staff
Lori Bowden
Michelle Magers
Cheryl Peters
Jennifer Rosenboom
Kathryn Wright
Western Michigan University

Software Developers
Jim Flanders
Colorado Springs, Colorado
Eric Kamischke
Interlochen, Michigan

Core-Plus Mathematics Project

Special thanks are extended to the students and teachers at these field-test schools

Ann Arbor Huron High School
Ann Arbor, Michigan

Ann Arbor Pioneer High School
Ann Arbor, Michigan

Arthur Hill High School
Saginaw, Michigan

Battle Creek Central High School
Battle Creek, Michigan

Bedford High School
Temperance, Michigan

Bloomfield Hills Andover High School
Bloomfield Hills, Michigan

Bloomfield Hills Middle School
Bloomfield Hills, Michigan

Brookwood High School
Snellville, Georgia

Caledonia High School
Caledonia, Michigan

Centaurus High School
Lafayette, Colorado

Clio High School
Clio, Michigan

Davison High School
Davison, Michigan

Dexter High School
Dexter, Michigan

Ellet High School
Akron, Ohio

Firestone High School
Akron, Ohio

Flint Northern High School
Flint, Michigan

Goodrich High School
Goodrich, Michigan

Grand Blanc High School
Grand Blanc, Michigan

Grass Lake Junior/Senior High School
Grass Lake, Michigan

Gull Lake High School
Richland, Michigan

Kalamazoo Central High School
Kalamazoo, Michigan

Kelloggsville Public Schools
Wyoming, Michigan

Knott County Central High School
Hindman, Kentucky

Loy Norrix High School
Kalamazoo, Michigan

Midland Valley High School
Langley, South Carolina

Murray-Wright High School
Detroit, Michigan

North Lamar High School
Paris, Texas

Okemos High School
Okemos, Michigan

Portage Northern High School
Portage, Michigan

Prairie High School
Cedar Rapids, Iowa

San Pasqual High School
Escondido, California

Sitka High School
Sitka, Alaska

Sturgis High School
Sturgis, Michigan

Sweetwater High School
National City, California

Tecumseh High School
Tecumseh, Michigan

Tecumseh Middle School
Tecumseh, Michigan

Traverse City East Junior High
Traverse City, Michigan

Traverse City High School
Traverse City, Michigan

Traverse City West Junior High
Traverse City, Michigan

Vallivue High School
Caldwell, Idaho

West Hills Middle School
Bloomfield Hills, Michigan

Ypsilanti High School
Ypsilanti, Michigan

Contents

Preface

Contemporary Mathematics in Context provides a common core of broadly useful mathematics for all students. It was developed to prepare students for success in college, in careers, and in daily life in contemporary society. The series builds upon the theme of *mathematics as sensemaking*. Through investigations of real-life contexts, students develop a rich understanding of important mathematics that makes sense to them and which, in turn, enables them to make sense out of new situations and problems.

Each course in the *Contemporary Mathematics in Context* curriculum shares the following mathematical and instructional features.

- *Multiple Connected Strands* Each year the curriculum features four strands of mathematics, unified by fundamental themes, by common topics, and by habits of mind or ways of thinking. Developing mathematics each year along multiple strands helps students develop diverse mathematical insights and nurtures their differing strengths and talents.

- *Mathematical Modeling* The curriculum emphasizes mathematical modeling and modeling concepts including data collection, representation, prediction, and simulation. The modeling perspective permits students to experience mathematics as a means of making sense of data and problems that arise in diverse contexts within and across cultures.

- *Access* The curriculum is designed so that core topics are accessible to all students. Differences in student performance and interest can be accommodated by the depth and level of abstraction to which common topics are pursued, by the nature and degree of difficulty of applications, and by providing opportunities for student choice of homework tasks and projects.

- *Technology* Numerical, graphics, and programming/link capabilities such as those found on many graphics calculators are assumed and capitalized on. This technology and/or computer software permits the curriculum and instruction to emphasize multiple representations (numerical, graphical, and symbolic) and to focus on goals in which mathematical thinking, rather than mere computation, is central.

- *Active Learning* Instruction and assessment practices are designed to promote mathematical thinking through the use of engaging problem situations. Both collaborative groups and individual work are used as students explore, conjecture, verify, apply, evaluate, and communicate mathematical ideas.

Mathematical Content

Each course of *Contemporary Mathematics in Context* features important mathematics drawn from four "strands."

The Algebra and Functions strand develops student ability to recognize, represent, and solve problems involving relations among quantitative variables. Central to the development is the use of functions as mathematical models. The key algebraic models in the curriculum are linear, exponential, power, and periodic functions (including trigonometric functions) and combinations of these various types. Modeling with systems of equations, both linear and nonlinear, also is developed.

The primary goal of the Geometry and Trigonometry strand is to develop visual thinking and ability to construct, reason with, interpret, and apply mathematical models of patterns in visual and physical contexts. Specific activities include describing patterns with regard to shape, size, and location; representing patterns with drawings, coordinates, or vectors; and predicting changes and invariants in shapes and patterns.

The primary role of the Statistics and Probability strand is to develop student ability to analyze data intelligently, to recognize and measure variation, and to understand the patterns that underlie probabilistic situations. Graphical methods of data analysis, simulations, sampling, and experience with the collection and interpretation of real data are featured.

The Discrete Mathematics strand develops student ability to model and solve problems involving sequential change, decision-making in finite settings, and relationships among a finite number of elements. Topics include matrices, vertex-edge graphs, recursion, voting methods, and systematic counting methods (combinatorics). Key themes are existence (Is there a solution?), optimization (What is the best solution?), and algorithmic problem-solving (Can you efficiently construct a solution?).

These four strands are connected within chapters by fundamental ideas such as: symmetry, recursion, function, data analysis and curve-fitting. The strands also are connected across chapters by mathematical habits of mind such as: visual thinking, recursive thinking, searching for, and describing patterns, making and checking conjectures, reasoning with multiple representations, inventing mathematics, and providing convincing arguments. The strands are linked further by the fundamental themes of data, representation, shape, and change. Important mathematical ideas are continually revisited through this attention to connections within and across strands, enabling students to develop a robust understanding of mathematics.

Active Learning and Teaching

The manner in which mathematical ideas are developed can be as important as the mathematics to which students are introduced. *Contemporary Mathematics in Context* features multi-day lessons centered on big ideas. Lessons are organized around a four-phase cycle of classroom activities designed to engage students in investigating and making sense of problem situations, in constructing important mathematical concepts and methods, and in communicating orally and in writing their thinking and the results of their efforts. Most classroom activities are designed to be completed by students working together collaboratively in heterogeneous groupings of two to four students.

The launch phase promotes class discussion of a situation and of related questions to think about, setting the context for the student work to follow. In the second or explore phase, students investigate more focused problems and questions related to the launch situation. Next is a class discussion in which students summarize concepts and methods developed in their groups, providing an opportunity to share their progress and their thinking. Finally, students are given a task to complete on their own, reinforcing their initial understanding of a concept or method.

Each lesson also includes tasks to engage students in Modeling with, Organizing, Reflecting on, and Extending their mathematical knowledge. These MORE activities are central to the learning goals of each lesson and are intended primarily for individual work outside of class. Selection of activities for use with a class should be based on student performance and the availability of time and technology. Students can exercise some choice of tasks to pursue, and at times they can be given the opportunity to pose their own problems and questions to investigate.

Multiple Approaches to Assessment

Assessing what students know and are able to do is an integral part of *Contemporary Mathematics in Context*. Initially, as students pursue the investigations that make up the curriculum, the teacher is able to assess informally student performance in terms of process, content, and disposition. At the end of each investigation, the "Checkpoint" and class discussion provide an opportunity for the teacher to assess the levels of understanding that the various groups of students have reached. Finally, the "On Your Own" problem situation as well as the tasks in the MORE sets provide further opportunities to assess the level of understanding of each individual student. Quizzes, in-class exams, take-home assessment activities, and extended projects are included in the teacher resource materials.

Acknowledgements

Development and evaluation of the student text materials, teacher resource materials, student assessments, and calculator software for *Contemporary Mathematics in Context* was funded through a grant from the National Science Foundation to the Core-Plus Mathematics Project (CPMP). In addition to the NSF grant, a series of grants from the Dwight D. Eisenhower Higher Education Professional Development Program has helped to provide professional development support for Michigan teachers involved in the testing of each year of the curriculum.

As seen on page v, CPMP has been a collaborative effort that drew on the talents and energies of teams of mathematics educators at several institutions. This diversity of experiences and ideas has been a particular strength of the project. Special thanks is owed to the support staff at these institutions, particularly at Western Michigan University.

From the outset, our work has been guided by the advice of an international advisory board consisting of Diane Briars (Pittsburgh Public Schools), Jeremy Kilpatrick (University of Georgia), Kenneth Ruthven (University of Cambridge), David A. Smith (Duke University), and Edna Vasquez (Detroit Renaissance High School). Preliminary versions of the curriculum materials also benefited from careful reviews by the following mathematicians and mathematics educators: Alverna Champion (Grand Valley State University), Cherie Cornick (Wayne County Alliance for Mathematics and Science), Edgar Edwards (formerly Virginia State Department of Education), Richard Scheaffer (University of Florida), Martha Siegel (Towson State University), Edward Silver (University of Pittsburgh), and Lee Stiff (North Carolina State University).

Again, our gratitude is expressed to the teachers and students in our 42 evaluation sites listed on page vi. Their experiences using pilot- and field-test versions of *Contemporary Mathematics in Context* provided constructive feedback and improvements. We learned a lot together about making mathematics meaningful and accessible to all students.

Finally, a very special thanks to Barbara Janson for her interest and encouragement in publishing a core mathematical sciences curriculum that breaks new ground in terms of content, instructional practices, and student assessment and to Eric Karnowski for his careful editorial work.

To the Student

This book, *Contemporary Mathematics in Context*, may be quite different from other math textbooks you have used. With this text, you will learn mathematics by doing mathematics, not by studying "worked out" examples. You will investigate important mathematical ideas and ways of thinking as you try to understand and make sense of realistic situations. Because real-world situations and problems often involve data, shape, change, or chance, you will learn fundamental concepts and methods from several strands of mathematics. In particular, you will develop an understanding of broadly useful ideas from algebra and functions, from statistics and probability, from geometry and trigonometry, and from discrete mathematics. You also will see connections among these strands—how they weave together to form the fabric of mathematics.

Because real-world situations and problems are often open-ended, you often will find that there is more than one correct approach and more than one correct solution. Therefore, you will often be asked to explain your ideas. This text will provide you help and practice in communicating clearly about mathematics.

Because the solution of real-world problems often involves teamwork and the use of technology, you often will work collaboratively with a partner or in small groups as you investigate realistic and interesting situations. You will find that 2 or 4 students working collaboratively on a problem can often accomplish more than any one of you would working individually. As you work through the investigations in the text, you will use a graphing calculator or computer as a tool to help you understand and make sense of the situations. If you need help using a graphing calculator, appropriate Technology Tips are referenced in the context where a particular capability is first needed.

You're going to learn a lot of useful mathematics in this course—and it's going to make sense to you. You're going to learn a lot about working cooperatively and communicating with others as well. You're also going to learn how to use technology tools intelligently and effectively. You'll have plenty of opportunities to be creative, too, so let your imagination lead you and enjoy.

Chapter

Patterns in Data

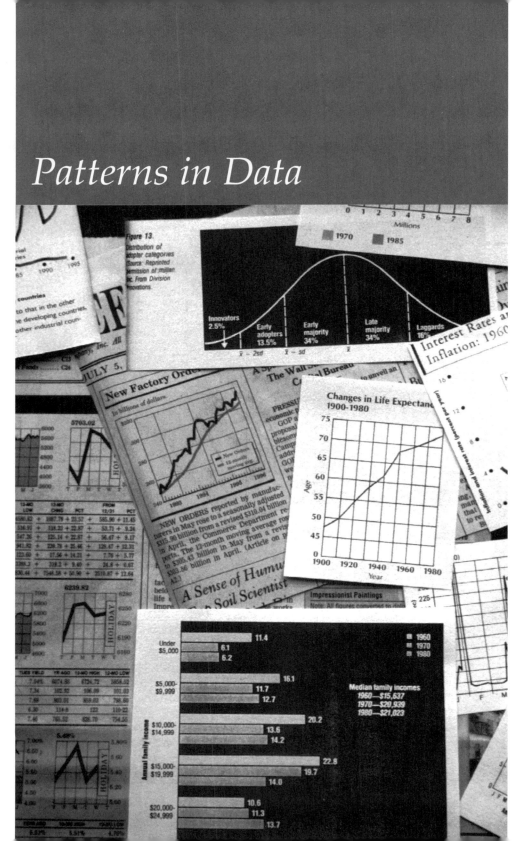

1 *Exploring Data*

The main theme of this text is that mathematics provides a powerful way of making sense of the world in which you live. Contemporary mathematics is rooted in the study of patterns involving data, shape, change, and chance—aspects of situations you experience every day. It involves investigating and expressing relationships among these patterns in ways that make sense to you. Once understood, the patterns and relationships can be applied in a variety of ways to other common and complex situations.

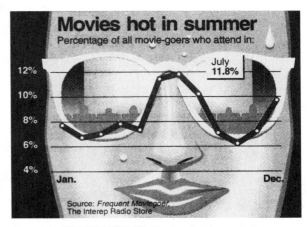

Copyright 1994, USA TODAY. Reprinted with permission.

For example, patterns in data are used to make decisions that affect you every day. As a class, consider the kinds of data that are collected by the movie industry and by clothing manufacturers.

Think about this situation

a Examine the data on movie attendance.
  – How could theater owners use this information?
  – How could movie makers use this data?
  – How could you use this information?

b How do you think a T-shirt manufacturer decides how big to make a size "large" T-shirt?

Decisions that are made based on data are only as good as the data itself. It is therefore very important that data collected be appropriate and accurate.

Investigation 1.1

Collecting and Analyzing Data

As you use this text, besides working as a whole class and individually, you often will work in pairs and in small groups. It is important that you have confidence in one another, share ideas, and help each other when asked. When working in groups, assigning specific jobs to group members helps the work run smoothly. Here is one way to do that.

Role	Responsibility
Coordinator	Obtains necessary resources. Recommends data gathering methods and units of measure appropriate for the situation. Communicates with other coordinators or the teacher on behalf of the group.
Measurement Specialist	Performs the actual measurements as needed.
Recorder	Records measurements taken and shares information with other groups.
Quality Controller	Carefully observes the measuring and recording processes and suggests when measurements should be double-checked for accuracy.

Work with your teacher to do the following.

– Form into groups of 4 people each if possible.

– Assign each group member one of the above roles.

Complete the data-gathering activities that follow by working together in your small groups. Each group will need a measuring tape or a measuring stick and a string.

Project 1

1. a. Measure, in centimeters, the height and armspan of each person in your group. Record your data on a table like the one shown here.

Student Name	Height	Armspan

b. What one height would be most typical or representative of your group?

c. Do you think your typical group height would be the same as the typical height of the entire class? Explain your reasoning.

d. How much variation is there in the armspans of your group?

e. Do you think the amount of variation in armspans of your class would be less than or greater than the variation in your group? Explain your reasoning.

2. a. Combine your data for heights and armspans with that of other groups and record it in another table. Call it the Class Data Table.

b. Use the Class Data Table to find a typical height for the entire class. Do you still agree with your answer to activity 1.c?

c. After examining the Class Data Table, do you still agree with your response to activity 1.e?

3. On the basis of the data from your class, does there seem to be a relationship between height and armspan?

Project 2

Before starting this next project, everyone in your group should change roles. One way to arrange this is to have each group member pass his or her job to the student on the left. Project coordinators should decide together on a common unit of measure and method to be used by every group.

1. Measure the circumference (distance around) of the thumb and wrist of each person in your group. Record your data in a table like the one shown here.

Student Name	Thumb Circumference	Wrist Circumference

2. Combine your data of thumb and wrist circumferences with that of other groups and record it in the Class Data Table. Again, record all measurements in the same unit.

3. Based on the class data, what relationship, if any, do you see between the wrist and thumb size of a person?

4. In the novel *Gulliver's Travels*, the Lilliputians made clothes for Gulliver. They estimated that twice around the thumb is once around the wrist and twice around the wrist is once around the neck.

   a. Does the first part of this statement seem true for your class data? Why or why not?

   b. Describe how you could check the second part of the Lilliputians' statement.

Project 3

Rotate group jobs before beginning the following project. Common units of measure for every group should be decided upon by the project coordinators. Agreement should also be reached on a method for measuring stride length.

1. a. Determine the shoe length and stride length for each person in your group. Record the data in a table like the one shown here.

Student Name	Shoe Length	Stride Length

   b. Why do you think you were asked to determine shoe length rather than shoe size?

2. a. Combine your data for shoe lengths and stride lengths with that of other groups and record it in the Class Data Table.

b. What is the smallest shoe length in the class? What is the largest shoe length?

c. Does there appear to be a relationship between shoe length and stride length?

Keep your class data from Projects 1, 2, and 3. You will need them later in this chapter.

Checkpoint

 What kinds of relationships did you look for in the data from the three projects?

 What pitfalls are possible when you generalize results from a small sample of people, such as your group, to a larger population, such as your class?

 How well did your group cooperate in completing these projects? Write one comment about each group member in the following form.

We appreciated it when ...

✓ **Each person from your group should be prepared to report to the whole class on the group's responses to these questions.**

On Your Own

Determine the thumb dominance of a sample of your family or friends by having each person fold their hands on top of a desk with fingers interlocked. The dominant thumb (right or left) is on top of the other.

a. Record your finding for each person in a table along with information on his or her hand dominance (left-handed or right-handed).

b. Does there appear to be a relationship between hand dominance and thumb dominance? If so, write a sentence describing the relationship.

c. How confident are you in your conclusion?

d. What might you do to have more confidence in your conclusion?

Investigation 1.2

Describing Patterns in Data

To learn from one another in investigating situations, it is important that your group work together as a team. Following the guidelines below will help your group work well together. It will also help you build skills that have become very important for people who work in fields such as health care, business, and industry.

Group Guidelines

- Each group member contributes to the group's work.
- Each member of the group is responsible for listening carefully when another group member is talking.
- Each member of the group has the responsibility and the right to ask questions.
- Each group member should help others in the group when asked.
- Each member of the group should be considerate and encouraging.
- Work together until everyone in the group understands and can explain the group's results.

1. How well did your group work together in completing the projects in the last investigation? In your group, discuss responses to the following questions.

   a. How could your group encourage everyone to contribute ideas?

   b. How could your group ensure that everyone listens while someone is talking?

   c. How could your group ensure that each person understands and agrees with the group's decisions?

In this investigation, you will continue to collaborate with one another in small groups. The activities will not require taking and recording measurements. Nevertheless, it is helpful if each group member has an assigned role at the beginning. Roles often used by groups of four people are described below. When working in groups of three, the roles of quality controller and coordinator can be combined. Decide on a role for each member of your group.

Role	Responsibility
Reader	Reads and explains the questions or problems on which the group will be working.
Recorder	Writes a summary of the group's decisions and ideas, and reads them back to the group to ensure agreement and accuracy. Shares group's summary with other groups or the entire class.
Quality Controller	Monitors the group's results and makes sure that the group produces high quality work of which they can be proud.
Coordinator	Keeps the group on track and makes sure everyone is participating. Communicates with the teacher on behalf of the group.

Making sense of information and data is a common feature of many careers. It is also important for a thorough understanding of radio, television, and newspaper reports. Several of those reports include information gathered from opinion polls or surveys. As an example, consider the following report of a survey of the pop music industry.

The *Los Angeles Times* once asked 25 important people in the pop music industry to determine the pop world's "hottest properties." Among the 25 people were the presidents of Motown Records and Capitol Records. The artists and groups were ranked by giving 10 points for each first-place vote, 9 points for a second-place vote, and so on. The following is the list of the twenty artists and groups who received the most points.

Rank	Artist	Points	Rank	Artist	Points
1	U2	165	11	En Vogue	30
2	R.E.M.	95		Janet Jackson	30
3	Pearl Jam	83	13	Madonna	29
4	Metallica	81	14	Michael Jackson	27
5	Garth Brooks	75	15	Bruce Springsteen	22
6	Whitney Houston	69	16	Michael Bolton	20
7	Guns N' Roses	54		Mariah Carey	20
8	Boyz II Men	44		Red Hot Chili Peppers	20
9	Arrested Development	40		Nirvana	20
10	Nine Inch Nails	38	20	George Michael	18

Source: Hilburn, Robert. 1993. Who are pop's hottest properties? *Los Angeles Times Calendar*, Feb. 7.

2. In your group, discuss each of the following questions. Record the answer that your group decides is the best response.

   a. U2 could have received its 165 points by getting 15 first-place votes, a second-place vote, and a fifth-place vote. Find two other ways that U2 could have received its 165 points.

   b. What is the largest possible number of points an artist or group could have received?

   c. How popular are these artists and groups today? Does your group believe that these record executives were good at predicting "pop's hottest properties?" Give some evidence to back up your position.

   d. Does it appear that the rankings of the 25 executives were a lot alike, or do you think there was substantial disagreement in their rankings?

3. Students in one class at City High were asked to *describe* the distribution of points for the top 20 artists and groups.

   Joshua's response: "U2 was highest with 165 points and George Michael was last with 18 points. My favorite singer, Mariah Carey, came in tied for 16th place. I don't think that is an accurate assessment of how 'hot' she is. She definitely will be a bigger star than some of those rated above her."

   Sarah's response: "U2 was much higher than the other artists and groups. The next highest group, R.E.M., received an average ranking of less than 4 from the 25 raters. Most of the artists and groups received low scores, under 40 points."

   a. Whose response does your group think was the most complete and helpful? Why?

   b. What would you do to improve the response that you chose as the best?

4. When asked to *describe* the distribution of points for the top 20 artists and groups, Paul and María first made a **stem-and-leaf plot** like the one shown here.

   a. In your group, discuss the organization of this stem-and-leaf plot. Is the plot an accurate display of the data in the chart? If not, explain how to correct it.

Stem	Leaf
1	8
2	0 0 0 0 2 7 9
3	0 0 8
4	0
5	4
6	9
7	5
8	1 3
9	5
10	
11	
12	
13	
14	
15	
16	5

1 | 8 represents 18

Paul's description: "Based on the stem-and-leaf plot, most artists and groups were ranked low. Only one of the artists and groups was high."

María's description: "You can see in the stem-and-leaf plot that there were a whole bunch in the 20s. The rest were spread out."

b. What are the strengths and weaknesses of Paul's response?

c. What are the strengths and weaknesses of María's response?

d. As a group, write what you think would be a better response than either Paul's or María's. Compare your response with that of other groups.

5. Fifteen students from the Student Council at City High ranked their top ten artists and groups from the *Los Angeles Times'* list in a similar manner. Their results are shown in the chart below. Make a stem-and-leaf plot for these data.

Rank	Artist	Points
1	Pearl Jam	105
2	R.E.M.	102
3	Boyz II Men	98
4	Arrested Development	87
5	Metallica	59
	Red Hot Chili Peppers	59
7	U2	56
8	Nine Inch Nails	55
9	Guns N' Roses	52
10	Janet Jackson	48

Rank	Artist	Points
11	Whitney Houston	41
12	En Vogue	33
13	Mariah Carey	11
14	Garth Brooks	7
15	Madonna	5
16	Michael Jackson	4
17	Bruce Springsteen	2
18	Nirvana	1
19	Michael Bolton	0
	George Michael	0

6. Students were asked to make a stem-and-leaf plot for the Student Council rankings and to *compare* the plot to the one in activity 4.

Desmond's response: "The new stem-and-leaf plot has more ratings in the middle of the plot."

Regina's response: "They both have a gap. The new plot has a cluster of groups ranked high."

a. What are the strengths and weaknesses of Desmond's response?

b. What are the strengths and weaknesses of Regina's response?

c. As a group, write what you think would be a better response than either Regina's or Desmond's. Compare your response to that of other groups.

7. For homework, students at City High were asked to *explain why* stem-and-leaf plots are helpful in understanding data such as that from the *Los Angeles Times*.

> *Cecilia wrote this explanation:* "Stem-and-leaf plots help you understand the information because you can see quickly how the data is spread out or clumped together. You can see any gaps where there are no data. By using the numbers instead of tally marks or Xs, you can still read the number of points that the judges assigned. Since these data sets are small, the stem-and-leaf displays were concise, easy to make, and easy to read."

Ms. Thomas, the mathematics teacher, decided that Cecilia's explanation was excellent, so she gave her 5 points, the maximum points possible.

> *Here is Jesse's explanation:* "The stem-and-leaf plot has the stems on the left and the leaves on the right. For the numbers that have two digits, the tens digit is the stem and the ones digit is the leaf. For numbers that have three digits, the hundreds and tens digits together are the stem and the ones digit is the leaf. The numbers are in order from smallest at the top to largest at the bottom."

As a group, use Cecilia's response as a guide to evaluate Jesse's explanation on a scale of 1 to 5, with 5 being the top score. Explain why you assigned the score you did.

Checkpoint

a What are the important features of a good response when you are asked to *describe* something?

b What are the important features of a good response when you are asked to *explain* your reasoning?

c What are the important features of a good response when you are asked to *compare* two or more things?

✓ *Each person from your group should be prepared to share your group's characteristics of good descriptions, explanations, and comparisons.*

On Your Own

a. Make a stem-and-leaf plot of the heights reported in the Class Data Table.

b. Write a description of the information you can see from looking at your plot.

By now you may be wondering: "What's all the fuss about writing good explanations? This is a math course!" Being able to describe your conclusions and explain your reasoning is important for at least two reasons: (1) it helps you better understand your own thinking and the mathematics you are studying; and (2) it is a skill, like teamwork, that businesses and industries look for in new employees.

The final activity in this lesson will help you and your group become more familiar with these new aspects of doing mathematics.

Reassign your group roles. Study the chart below giving average monthly earnings in 1990 for adults in the United States.

Does Education Pay?
Average Monthly Earnings (Adults 18 and Over)

Level of Education	Average Monthly Earnings
No high school diploma	$856
High school diploma only	1357
Vocational degree	1568
Associate degree	1879
Bachelor's degree	2489
Master's degree	3211
Doctorate degree	4545
Professional degree (*e.g.* medicine)	5554

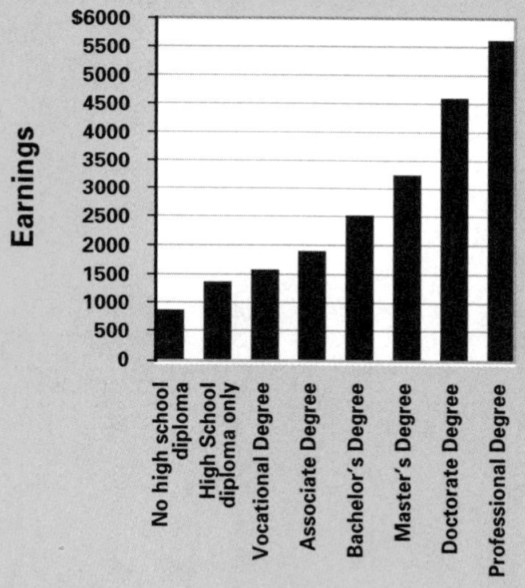

Source: Bureau of the Census, *Statistical Abstract of the United States: 1994* (114th edition.) Washington, DC, 1994.

8. Discuss each question and then come to a single response that each member of your group agrees with and understands.

   a. On the average, what would a U.S. worker make in a year, if the person was not a high school graduate?

   b. On the average, how much more per year would a person with a high school diploma only earn than a person who did not have a high school diploma?

9. Now it's your turn. Write a question that interests your group and can be answered using these data. Write the answer to your question, too.

10. **a.** From which level of education to the next is the largest jump in average monthly earnings?

    b. Did you use the table or *bar graph* in answering part a? Explain why you chose the display you did.

11. Write a summary of the conclusions you can draw using the information in the table and the graph.

Checkpoint

> **a** Compare the information shown in the table and the bar graph. In what ways is the graph better than the table for displaying the data on average monthly earnings? In what ways is it worse?
>
> **b** How could your analysis of this data be used to plan for your own future?
>
> **c** How has your group work improved since the first day of class? How could you further improve your group work next time?
>
> ✓ *Be prepared to share your group's responses with the whole class.*

In this lesson, you have reviewed how to make stem-and-leaf plots and how to measure lengths and record your results efficiently. You also have begun to learn how to analyze and write descriptions of distributions of data. In the next lesson, you will learn more about plotting and describing distributions.

On Your Own

a. Over a lifetime, how much more money could a person expect to earn with a bachelor's degree than with a high school diploma? Assume the retirement age is the traditional 65 years.

b. Find one example of how working in groups (teamwork) is used in business or industry. Write a brief summary of your findings.

2 *Shapes and Centers*

Everyday, people are bombarded by data on television, on radio, in newspapers, and in magazines. For example, states release report cards for schools and statistics on crime and unemployment; cities are rated to determine the "best places to live"; sports writers report batting averages and select the top NFL quarterback; and consumers shop for "best buys." Making sense of data is important in everyday life and in most professions today. Read carefully the following news story.

AAA revs up car list
GM, Toyota each hold three spots

From wire reports

The American Automobile Association picked three General Motors cars for its list of the best 1993 models, topping Ford and Chrysler combined. Toyota also had three models on the list, but two were from its pricey Lexus line.

GM's winners were the Geo Prizm LSi in the $10,000–$15,000 range, the Oldsmobile Eighty Eight LS $20,000–$25,000 and the Cadillac Seville STS, $40,000–$45,000.

The 34-million member AAA used a 10-point scale to evaluate 121 cars in 20 categories. The top score of 177 went to the Lexus LS 400 at $45,000–$50,000.

The Dodge Intrepid ES displaced Honda Accord at $15,000-$20,000. Ford Escort LX tied with Toyota Tercel for under $10,000.

Other winners: Saab 9000 CS Turbo, $25,000–$30,000; Lexus SC 300, $30,000–$35,000; BMW 525i Touring station wagon, $35,000–$40,000 and Mercedes-Benz 400SEL, $50,000 plus.

To make their ratings, the staff of the American Automobile Association identified the 20 characteristics that they felt were most important to consider when buying a car. Groups of three to six staff people tested the cars for a two-week period. They rated them on each of the categories using a scale of 1 to 10. Ratings of 1 to 5 are negative; 6 to 10 are positive. The results are summarized in the following table.

American Automobile Association Ratings of 1993 Cars
($15,000 to $20,000 Price Range)

Car	Acceleration	Transmission	Braking	Steering	Ride	Handling	Driveability	Fuel Economy	Comfort	Interior Layout	Driving Position	Instrumentation	Controls	Visibility	Entry/Exit	Quietness	Cargo Space	Exterior	Interior	Value
Chrysler LeBaron GTC Convertible	8	7	9	8	6	7	8	7	6	6	8	8	6	6	7	6	4	9	7	7
Chevrolet Camaro	10	8	10	9	6	10	8	5	7	5	8	9	9	5	6	6	6	8	8	8
Chevrolet Lumina	9	9	8	8	7	8	8	5	7	8	8	7	7	8	9	6	7	8	6	8
Chrysler Concorde	8	9	9	9	9	8	9	6	9	10	10	9	8	8	10	7	8	9	9	9
Dodge Intrepid	7	8	10	9	9	9	9	6	9	10	10	9	8	8	10	8	8	9	9	9
Ford Probe	9	9	10	9	6	9	9	7	7	5	8	9	9	7	5	7	7	7	7	7
Ford Taurus	8	7	8	8	8	8	9	6	8	8	8	8	7	7	8	7	8	8	7	9
Honda Accord	8	6	9	9	8	8	8	7	8	8	9	9	9	8	8	8	8	8	9	8
Honda Civic del Sol	8	9	8	9	7	8	8	8	8	7	9	9	9	7	6	6	5	8	8	8
Plymouth Laser	9	6	8	9	6	10	8	6	7	6	8	9	9	5	5	5	4	8	8	8
Mazda Miata	8	9	9	8	5	9	9	8	8	7	8	9	9	7	6	5	2	9	7	9

A rating of 1 is the lowest. A rating of 10 is the highest.

Think about this situation

Suppose your family wants to buy a used 1993 car that originally sold for between $15,000 and $20,000.

a According to the article, which car did the American Automobile Association (AAA) think was best? Do you think there are any important characteristics that they have omitted?

b There is so much information in the table above that it is difficult to see which car might be best. Discuss with your class how you could organize or summarize this information to make it more useful in deciding which car to buy.

c Based on the rating table, do you agree with the conclusions drawn by AAA and reported in the article? Why or why not?

Investigation 2.1 Shapes of Distributions

1. With your small group, select one of the cars that you would like to study more carefully.
   a. If you were a dealer selling the car you selected, what feature(s) would you stress? Why?
   b. If you were the manufacturer of the car, what feature(s) would you try to improve? Why?
   c. Using the scale of 1 to 10, what overall rating would you assign the car? Explain your reasoning.

An examination of any of the columns of the table reveals that the ratings vary from car to car. The ratings are all 8 or 9 in steering, but vary from 5 to 10 in entry/exit. The pattern of variation or **distribution** of the ratings is best seen in a plot.

2. Examine this **number line plot** of the AAA ratings of *acceleration*. Describe the overall shape of the distribution by answering the following questions:
   a. What is the lowest rating? What is the highest rating? What cars are associated with these ratings?
   b. Are there any **outliers**—unusually high or low ratings that lie away from the other ratings?
   c. Does the plot have one or more peaks?
   d. Does the plot appear **symmetric**— right and left sides look almost like mirror images of each other? If not, does the plot appear to be stretched more to the higher or lower ratings?

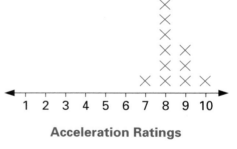

Acceleration Ratings

   e. Do you see any gaps in the overall pattern of the plot?
   f. Where is the center of the distribution?
   g. How spread out are the ratings?

Once a distribution is displayed in a plot, you can describe its important features by discussing questions similar to those in activity 2. The key questions are summarized in the handout, "Describing Distributions."

3. a. Make a number line plot of the *entry/exit* ratings.
   b. In what ways is the distribution of *entry/exit* ratings like that of the *acceleration* ratings? In what ways is it different?
   c. Part of your group should make a number line plot of the *transmission* ratings. The rest of your group should prepare a plot of the *braking* ratings. Compare the two distributions in terms of the key questions for describing distributions.

Number line plots can be used to get a quick visual display of data. They enable you to see any patterns or unusual features in the data. They are most useful when working with small sets of data. **Histograms** can be used with data sets of any size. In a histogram, the **horizontal axis** is marked with a numerical scale. The **vertical axis** represents counts or frequencies. (Note that neither of these two last characteristics are true of the bar graph near the end of Lesson 1.)

4. Examine this histogram of the ratings for the Chrysler LeBaron convertible.

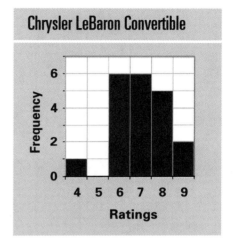

Chrysler LeBaron Convertible

   a. What does the bar at 9 represent?

   b. Why is there no bar at 5?

   c. Describe the distribution of the ratings.

5. a. Make a number line plot and a histogram of the ratings for the Dodge Intrepid.

   b. What does the height of a bar on the histogram tell you? Give an example.

   c. Describe the distribution of these ratings.

   d. How is the histogram of the ratings for the LeBaron convertible like the one for the Intrepid? How is it different?

6. The percentage of families with children under 18 who live below the poverty level vary from state to state. Shown below is a histogram of these percentages for the fifty states. The frequency, or number of states, is on the vertical axis.

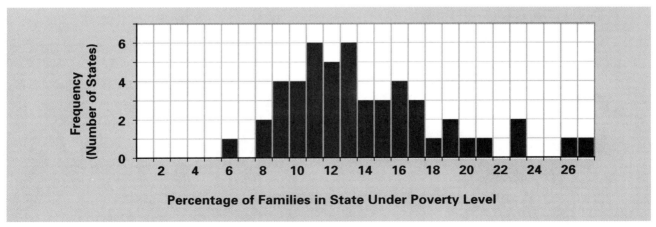

Source: *The Universal Almanac 1996*, Kansas City, MO: Andrews and McMeel, 1996.

a. What does the bar above 16% represent?

b. What is the percentage of families with children under 18 who live in poverty in the state with the largest percentage?

c. What is the percentage in the state with the smallest percentage?

d. How many states have 20% or more of the families with children under 18 living in poverty?

e. Describe the distribution of these percentages.

Checkpoint

a When would you prefer to make a histogram rather than a number line plot?

b Make a sketch of what you think the histogram of the ages of all women married last year in the United States might look like. Describe this distribution.

c How might the histogram of the ages of all men married last year in the United States compare to that of the women?

✓ *Be prepared to share your group's thinking and results with the whole class.*

On Your Own

The two histograms below show the performance of a social studies class at Central High School on a quiz and on a retake of the quiz. The quiz scores were grouped into intervals of size 5. *A score on the edge of a bar is counted in the bar on the right.*

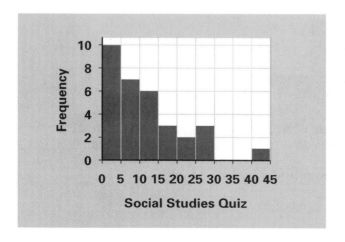

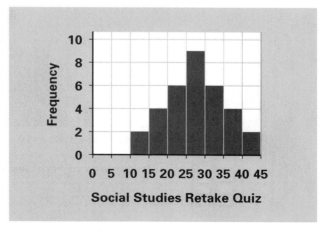

a. How many students took the quiz? How many scored above 30?

b. Where is each distribution centered? What conclusion can you draw by comparing the two histograms?

c. Do either of the plots show gaps in the distribution of scores?

d. Which of the distributions is approximately symmetric? Would you expect the data to have this shape? Why or why not?

e. Which of the distributions is stretched to the right or left? What might account for the distribution having this shape?

Investigation (**2.2**) **Producing Plots with Technology**

In the previous investigation, you learned that the shape of a distribution can reveal certain features of the data: where the data are centered, how much the data vary, whether there are gaps or clusters in the data, and the existence of outliers or other unusual values. Some distributions are **approximately normal**, where most of the data are centered around one point and the distribution tapers off on both sides. Normal distributions are symmetric—the two halves look like mirror images of each other. Some distributions have the data stretched more towards the right. These distributions are said to be **skewed to the right**. Some distributions have the data stretched more towards the left. These distributions are said to be **skewed to the left**. (See the diagram below.)

| **Approximately normal** | **Skewed to the right** | **Skewed to the left** |

Producing a graphical display is the first step toward understanding data. You can use computer software or a graphing calculator to produce various plots of data. This generally requires the following three steps.

– Enter the data into an array or list(s). Be sure to clear any previous unwanted data.

– Set a *viewing window* for the plot. This is usually done by specifying the minimum and maximum values and scale on the horizontal (*x*) axis. Depending on the nature of the data, you may also need to specify the minimum and maximum values and scale on the vertical (*y*) axis. Some technological tools have automatic scaling for data plots.

– Select the type of plot desired.

Examples of the screens involved are shown here. Your calculator or software may look different.

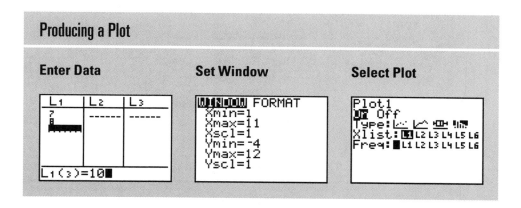

In this investigation, you will learn how to produce and analyze a histogram on your graphing calculator or computer.

1. a. Produce a histogram of the AAA ratings for the Dodge Intrepid. The "Technology Tips" handout could be helpful.

   b. Most calculators and software can display values along a graph, using a feature such as "Trace." Use the trace feature to move along the graph.

      – What information is given for each bar?

      – If a value occurs on the edge of a bar, in what bar is it counted?

   c. Use the trace feature to find how many ratings of 8 there are.

   d. Describe the overall shape of the distribution of ratings.

   e. What is the most common rating? How can you tell from the histogram?

   f. Change the "Xscl" value to 2. What does this do to the histogram? Why? Does it change the basic shape of the histogram? (Software and calculators vary. Your teacher may give you different instructions.)

   g. Experiment with other widths for each bar. Which value seems to be the best for displaying these data?

2. Divide the remaining ten cars listed on page 15 among your group.

   a. Individually, make a histogram of the ratings for each of your cars using your calculator or computer. Make a sketch of each histogram.

b. With your small group, examine the overall shape of the distributions of car ratings.

– For which cars is the distribution of ratings almost symmetric? Explain how you can tell.

– Which cars have a distribution that is skewed? What does this tell you about the ratings for that car?

– Which distribution is spread out the most? The least? What does it mean if the ratings for a car have a large spread?

c. For which car is the distribution of ratings centered at the highest value?

d. Based on the histograms, select the top four cars you would consider buying. How did the plots help you make your choice?

Histograms can help you see the shape of a distribution. Choosing the width of the bars (Xscl) determines the number of bars. If the data set is small, histograms with different numbers of bars can give different visual impressions. When you explore the following data set you will examine several possible histograms and decide which you think is best. You also may come to better understand the nutritional differences among what may be some of your favorite foods.

The table on the following page gives nutritional information about fast foods. Total calories, amount of fat in grams, amount of cholesterol in milligrams, and amount of sodium (salt) in milligrams are provided. Foods are organized according to type of meat: burgers, chicken, and roast beef.

3. As a group, examine the data in the table. What information do you find surprising or interesting?

4. Many people order chicken in fast food restaurants because they believe it will have less fat than a hamburger. Does it appear from the table that they are right or wrong? Explain your response.

5. a. Make a histogram of the total calories data for the fast foods listed. Use Xmin = 150, Xmax = 1000, Ymin = -4, Ymax = 12, and Yscl = 1. Experiment with different choices of Xscl. Which value of Xscl gives a good picture of the distribution?

b. Why isn't 198 the best value to use for Xmin?

c. Describe the pattern of the data that you can see from the histogram. Consider the usual features such as the spread, approximate location of the center, symmetry or skewness, gaps, and any unusual values.

How Fast Foods Compare

Company	Fast Food	Total Calories	Fat (Grams)	Cholesterol (mg)	Sodium (mg)
McDonald's	McLean Deluxe	350	12	60	670
Wendy's	Single (plain)	350	15	70	510
McDonald's	Quarter Pounder	420	21	70	690
McDonald's	Big Mac	530	28	80	960
Burger King	Hamburger Deluxe	344	19	43	496
Wendy's	Big Bacon Classic	640	36	110	1500
Burger King	Whopper	640	39	90	870
Hardee's	Big Burger	590	35	120	1150
Burger King	Double Whopper w/Cheese	960	63	195	1420
Hardee's	Grilled Chicken	290	9	65	860
Hardee's	Chicken Fillet	420	15	50	1190
Wendy's	Grilled Chicken	290	7	55	720
Wendy's	Chicken (regular)	450	20	60	740
Burger King	BK Broiler Chicken	550	29	80	480
McDonald's	McChicken	510	30	50	820
McDonald's	Chicken McNuggets (6)	300	18	65	530
Burger King	Chicken Sandwich	710	43	60	1400
Kentucky Fried Chicken	Lite'n Crispy (4 pieces)	198	12	60	354
Kentucky Fried Chicken	Original Recipe (4 pieces)	248	15	90	575
Kentucky Fried Chicken	Extra Crispy (4 pieces)	324	21	99	638
Arby's	French Dip	475	22	55	1411
Arby's	Regular Roast Beef	388	19	43	1009
Arby's	Super Roast Beef	523	27	43	1189

Source: *McDonald's Nutrition Facts*, McDonald's Corporation, 1995; *Good Nutrition News from Wendy's*, Wendy's International, Inc., 1994; *Nutritional Information*, Burger King Corp., 1996; Hardee's Nutritional Informations, 1996; *KFC Nutrition Facts*, KFC, 1995; *Comprehensive Guide of Quality Ingredients*, Arby's, Inc., 1995

6. a. Make a histogram of the amount of cholesterol. Use $Ymin = -4$, $Ymax = 10$, and $Yscl = 2$. Experiment with your own values of $Xmin$, $Xmax$, and $Xscl$. Which values give a good picture of the distribution?

   b. Describe the histogram of the amount of cholesterol in fast foods.

   c. Change the maximum y value to 5. Is this a good choice? Why or why not?

Checkpoint

   a What does the shape of a distribution tell you about the data?

   b If you are producing a histogram with your calculator or computer, how will you decide on the best choice of width for the bars?

   c How will you decide on a reasonable value for the maximum y value?

   ✓ *Be prepared to share your group's thinking on ways of producing and interpreting histograms.*

In this investigation, you have learned how to make histograms using technology. It takes a lot of practice to be able to set the viewing window efficiently. You will get more practice in later investigations.

On Your Own

Consider the data on the amount of fat in the fast foods.

a. Which fast food item has the least amount of fat? Which has the greatest amount?

b. Use your calculator or computer to produce a histogram of these data. Set $Ymin = -4$ and $Yscl = 1$.

   – How can you use the numbers from part a to determine $Xmin$, $Xmax$, and $Xscl$?

   – What procedure can you use to find a good value for $Ymax$?

c. Write a short description of the histogram so that a person who had not seen the histogram could draw an approximately correct sketch of it.

Modeling Organizing Reflecting Extending

Modeling

These activities provide opportunities for you to use the ideas you have learned in the investigations. Each activity asks you to model and solve problems in other situations.

1. Ratings of automobile characteristics such as comfort or visibility are subjective. They are based on how the rater feels about the characteristic. Other ratings such as acceleration or fuel economy can be based on more objective measures. The table below gives data on the mileage (miles per gallon) for city and highway driving of the rated cars.

	LeBaron	Camaro	Lumina	Concorde	Intrepid	Probe	Taurus	Accord	del Sol	Laser	Miata
City (mpg)	21	17	17	18	20	21	19	22	29	20	24
Highway (mpg)	28	25	26	26	28	26	27	28	33	25	30

   a. Make a number line plot of the city mileage of the tested cars.

   b. Make a similar display of the highway mileage of the rated cars.

   c. Compare your plots for parts a and b. How are they similar? How are they different? The handout, "Describing Distributions," may be helpful here.

   d. Would a stem-and-leaf plot of the highway mileage data reveal more or less information about the distribution than your number line plot? Explain your reasoning.

2. Refer to the armspan data in the Class Data Table prepared in Lesson 1.

   a. Use your calculator to produce a histogram of the armspans of all the students in your class.

   b. Describe the distribution of armspans.

   c. Enter the armspans of all the males in your class in one list and the armspans of all the females in your class in a different list. Produce and make sketches of separate histograms for the armspans of females and of males. Use the same viewing window for each plot.

   d. How is the histogram of the armspans for females like the one for males? How is it different?

   e. Suppose armspan is one of the characteristics you will use in sizing rain ponchos for sale to students in your school. Describe how you would use the histograms to help make decisions about the range of measurements that correspond to the sizes small, medium, large, and extra large.

3. Worker compensation is a major factor in the economic competitiveness of companies in world markets. The following table gives hourly compensation costs (in U.S. dollars) for production workers from selected countries. Hourly compensation costs include not just hourly salary, but also vacation, holidays, benefits such as insurance, and other costs to the employer.

Hourly Compensation Costs for Production Workers
(Selected Countries, 1992)

Country	1992	Country	1992
Australia	$12.94	Netherlands	20.72
Austria	19.65	New Zealand	7.91
Belgium	22.01	Norway	23.20
Canada	17.02	Portugal	5.01
Denmark	20.02	Singapore	5.00
Finland	18.69	South Korea	4.93
France	16.88	Spain	13.39
Germany	25.94	Sweden	24.23
Hong Kong	3.89	Switzerland	23.26
Ireland	13.32	Taiwan	5.19
Italy	19.41	United Kingdom	14.69
Japan	16.16	United States	16.17
Mexico	2.35		

Source: *The Universal Almanac 1994*. New York: Andrews and McMeel, 1993.

a. How do you think the U.S. Bureau of Labor Statistics might have determined the estimate of hourly compensation costs for production workers in the United States?

b. What was the average cost to the employer of a production worker in Switzerland in 1992? What is the yearly cost if the worker is paid for 52 weeks, 40 hours each week? Would the worker actually receive this amount? Explain.

c. Make a histogram of the hourly compensation costs shown in the previous chart. Make each bar represent an interval of $2. Write a summary of the information conveyed by the histogram.

d. How does hourly compensation in the United States compare to that of the other countries?

e. Experiment with changing the widths of the bars and redrawing the histogram. Use 5, 10, and 1 for the widths. Compare your results. Which width reveals the most information about the distribution of compensation costs?

4. In the early part of this century, the United States was viewed as a "melting pot" for people immigrating from countries with differing cultures. More recently, cultural diversity has come to be viewed by many as a strength of this country. One measure of this diversity is the variety of languages spoken in this country.

   The following table gives the 25 most commonly spoken languages in the United States after English, the number of Americans 5 years or older who speak each language, the percent change from 1980 to 1990, and the state with the highest percent of speakers.

Languages in the United States

Language	Number of Speakers in 1990	Percent Increase Since 1980	State with Highest % of Speakers	Language	Number of Speakers in 1990	Percent Increase Since 1980	State with Highest % of Speakers
Spanish	12,339,172	50.1	New Mexico	Hindi	331,484	155.1	New Jersey
French	1,702,176	8.3	Maine	Russian	241,798	38.5	New York
German	1,547,099	-3.7	North Dakota	Yiddish	213,064	-33.5	New York
Italian	1,308,648	-19.9	New York	Thai/Lao	206,266	131.6	California
Chinese	1,249,213	97.7	Hawaii	Persian	201,865	84.7	California
Tagalog	843,251	86.6	Hawaii	French Creole	187,658	654.1	Florida
Polish	723,483	-12.4	Illinois	Armenian	149,694	46.3	California
Korean	626,478	127.2	Hawaii	Navajo	148,530	20.6	New Mexico
Vietnamese	507,069	149.5	California	Hungarian	147,902	-17.9	New Jersey
Portuguese	429,860	19.0	Rhode Island	Hebrew	144,292	45.5	New York
Japanese	427,657	25.0	Hawaii	Dutch	142,684	-2.6	Utah
Greek	388,260	-5.4	Massachusetts	Mon–Khmer	127,441	676.3	Rhode Island
Arabic	355,150	57.4	Michigan				

Source: *USA Today,* April 28, 1993. Copyright 1993, USA TODAY. Reprinted with permission.

a. What is the most common language, other than English, spoken in the United States? What does its percent increase tell you? Which state has the highest percentage of speakers of this language? What might explain this fact?

b. Which language had the largest *percent* increase in number of speakers? Which language had the largest increase in the *number* of speakers of the language?

c. What does the -19.9% for Italian mean? What might account for this and other negative percent increases?

d. How many people in the United States spoke Japanese in 1980? How many people spoke Spanish in 1980?

e. Make a histogram that displays the number of speakers of the different languages. What does the height of a bar tell you? Write three sentences explaining to some adult in your home what the plot tells you.

f. Your histogram includes only the top 25 languages. Draw a sketch of what you think a histogram would look like if it included the top 50 languages. Explain why you think your sketch is reasonable.

Organizing

These activities will help you organize the mathematics you have learned in the investigations and connect it with other mathematics.

1. Copy this number line plot of the acceleration ratings. Transform it into a histogram by drawing bars around the Xs. You will also need to add a vertical axis with a frequency scale.

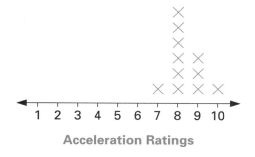

Acceleration Ratings

2. The two histograms below both represent the heights of the ninth-grade soccer team at Greendale High School.

   a. How do the histograms differ?

   b. How many students were between 64 and 65 inches tall?

   c. Compare how well the two plots convey information about the data.

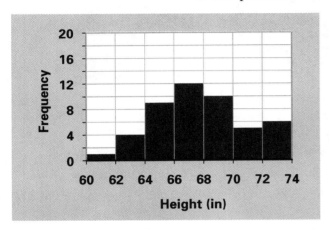   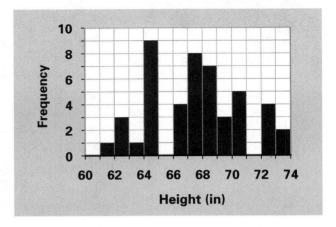

3. Make a sketch of what you think the histograms of the following distributions would look like. Classify each of the distributions as skewed to the right, skewed to the left, approximately normal, or rectangular-shaped.

   a. The last digits of the phone numbers of students in your school

   b. The heights of adult women

   c. The weights of adult men

   d. The age of all people who died in the United States last week

4. Describe a situation different from those in this investigation which would yield data whose distribution is

   a. skewed to the right.

   b. skewed to the left.

   c. approximately normal.

   d. rectangular-shaped.

5. Sketch a distribution of scores that might be described as follows.

   "The distribution ranges from 10 to 100 and is skewed to the left with most of the data clustered between 60 and 90. No one received a score in the 30s. About $\frac{2}{3}$ of the scores are greater than 50."

Reflecting

These activities will help you think about what the mathematics you have learned means to you. These activities also will help you think about what you do and do not understand.

1. What kinds of graphical representations of data are most common in your social studies textbook? In your science textbook? What have you learned in these two investigations that might be of help to you in these other courses?

2. In the book *On the Shoulders of Giants*, one author describes *data* as "numbers with a context." What do you think the author means by this statement?

3. Ask two adults what factors they would take into account when buying a car. Would they make use of comparison tests and ratings published in automotive or consumer magazines? Summarize what they say.

4. As you saw in Investigation 2.2, fast foods vary considerably in the amounts of calories, fat, cholesterol, and sodium they contain. People concerned about their health may prefer foods lower in calories, fat, cholesterol, and sodium. Which of the foods listed in the table in that investigation seem to best satisfy these conditions?

5. **a.** What did you find most interesting in this investigation?

   b. What, if anything, seemed to cause you difficulty? How did you overcome the difficulty?

Extending

Activities in this section provide opportunities for you to explore the mathematics you are learning further or more deeply.

1. With a partner, choose a topic from the list below and survey at least 30 people for their response.
   - Amount of money people carry with them
   - Time it takes to get to school each day
   - Number of hours per week spent on the phone
   - Number of hours per week spent watching television
   - Number of miles driven per week
   - Amount of money spent per week
   - Number of hours spent participating in athletics per week

   Make a number line plot or histogram of your data. Write a paragraph describing the topic you investigated and the results. Do you think the answers given were accurate? Explain.

2. Making sense of data is a skill that is becoming more and more important for a thorough understanding of news reports. Read the news story below.

From sea to sea, garbage washes up

By Anita Manning
USA TODAY

Here's a word to remember when you go to the beach this summer. Plastics.

"The story is the same from the Mediterranean to the Pacific, down to the Caribbean," says Lisa Younger of the Center for Marine Conservation. "There's trash on the beach, and the majority of it is plastic."

International laws prohibit dumping plastic at sea and regulate the dumping of other debris, yet the problem persists, says Younger.

The Washington, D.C.-based group, which released its 1991 international beach cleanup study Thursday, proposes improved U.S. Coast Guard enforcement of the laws and a "watchdog campaign" that asks passengers and cruise line employees to report violations.

"We're feeling we need to do more than talk about it," she says. "We need to take action."

Plastic found includes fishing equipment, garbage bags and packaging materials. And this year, the cleanup found debris—59 pieces—from 15 cruise ship lines.

Royal Caribbean had the most, with 24 pieces, followed by Carnival, with 10 pieces.

Royal Caribbean spokesman Lloyd Axelrod called the amount "very infinitesimal" but says, "any trash is too much. We're doing everything we can to make sure nothing gets into the water."

Seagoing vessels aren't the only source of trouble. Litter tossed on the streets inland washes down storm drains and toward the ocean.

"It's everybody's prob-

lem—the beachgoer, the person who tosses a cigarette butt out a car window. It's touching everyone," Younger says.

Dick Doher, sanitation superintendent for Atlantic Beach, N.C., believes: "If the beach looked trashy, people wouldn't want to come."

"Plastics thrown overboard look like food to sea turtles, and it can kill them," says Jody Merrit, superintendent of Fort Macon State Park, N.C.

But things are getting better. Richard Pasco, coordinator of South Bay Naturists, has been cleaning up his favorite Santa Cruz, Calif., beach for five years. In the past, he and 20 to 30 volunteers have hauled out "as much as two tons of trash." "Last year we were down to half a ton," Pasco says. "I'm real pleased."

a. Who collected the information and how?

b. What is the major type of debris on beaches? What are some of the items made from this material that show up on beaches?

c. The article indicates that 219,468 pieces of glass were collected in the cleanup. What do you think about this fact?

d. Make a plot that will display the number of individual items collected.

e. Describe what the article tells you about the change in the debris on beaches from 1988 to 1991.

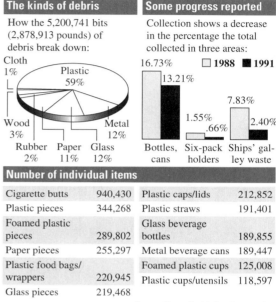

Cleaning up the beaches

Plastics continue to top the list of beach debris collected in the annual coastal cleanup coordinated by the Center for Marine Conservation. Some findings:

The kinds of debris

How the 5,200,741 bits (2,878,913 pounds) of debris break down:

Cloth 1%
Plastic 59%
Wood 3%
Metal 12%
Rubber 2%
Paper 11%
Glass 12%

Some progress reported

Collection shows a decrease in the percentage the total collected in three areas:

☐ 1988 ■ 1991

16.73% 13.21% Bottles, cans
1.55% .66% Six-pack holders
7.83% 2.40% Ships' galley waste

Number of individual items

Cigarette butts	940,430	Plastic caps/lids	212,852
Plastic pieces	344,268	Plastic straws	191,401
Foamed plastic pieces	289,802	Glass beverage bottles	189,855
Paper pieces	255,297	Metal beverage cans	189,447
Plastic food bags/wrappers	220,945	Foamed plastic cups	125,008
Glass pieces	219,468	Plastic cups/utensils	118,597

Source: Center for Marine Conservation

3. Some graphing calculators and computer software have an option that sorts data stored in a list. Explore the sorting capabilities of your calculator or software.

a. How might you use these capabilities to help find the middle value for a list of data? The most common value?

b. Share your findings with the class.

Investigation 2.3 Measures of Center

In Lesson 1 you collected and analyzed data about some of the physical characteristics of your class, such as height and stride length. Human services agencies often contract with research groups to conduct large survey studies of behavior patterns of various segments of the population. Data from such surveys are used to help shape policies and programs. The results of a survey on adolescent behavior presented in the *Washington Post* in December 1992 are summarized on the following page.

Adolescents At Risk

The Carnegie Council on Adolescent Development warns of the risks faced by adolescents in this country, many of whom spend much of their discretionary time engaged in unproductive and unsupervised activities. Among the findings:

– Nearly 30 percent of eighth graders spend at least two hours at home alone after school. The poorest children were most likely to spend more than three hours home alone.

– Teenagers spend an average of 5 minutes a day in one-on-one interaction with their fathers, one study found, and about 20 minutes of such time with their mothers.

– Teenagers watch television an average of about 21 hours a week.

– They devote 5.6 hours weekly to homework.

– They read for pleasure 1.8 hours a week.

Source: *The Washington Post*, Dec. 10, 1992. ©1992, The Washington Post. Reprinted with permission.

Think about this situation

a The article says that adolescents "devote 5.6 hours weekly to homework." What exactly do they mean by this?

b Do you believe the report accurately reflects adolescent behavior?

c How could information like this be collected? Which of the information seems almost impossible to get?

Among the characteristics of adolescent behavior not reported by the *Washington Post* were eating habits, such as the average number of hamburgers consumed each week. If you eat a hamburger, you consume more than just bun, beef, and toppings. Reproduced below is information from Investigation 2.2 on the cholesterol in burgers and in chicken from fast food restaurants.

Cholesterol (mg)

Burgers	60	70	70	80	43	110	90	120	195	
Chicken	65	50	55	60	80	50	65	60	60	90	99

A quick scan of the data in the table suggests that the distributions of amount of cholesterol are somewhat different. A *back-to-back stem-and-leaf plot* is often a good way to compare the shapes of two distributions.

1. a. Copy the stems at the right. Put the leaves for the chicken entrees to the right of the stems and put the leaves for the burgers to the left of the stems.

b. In general, is there more cholesterol in a burger or in a chicken entree? Explain your reasoning.

Cholesterol		
Burgers		**Chicken**
	4	
	5	
	6	
	7	
	8	
	9	
	10	
	11	
	12	
	13	
	14	
	15	
	16	
	17	
	18	
	19	

5 | 6 represents 56 mg.

2. When asked to find a "typical" amount of cholesterol in a burger, Meliva, Kyle, and Yü responded with different answers.

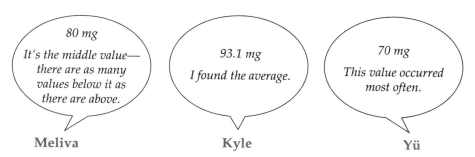

80 mg
It's the middle value—there are as many values below it as there are above.

Meliva

93.1 mg
I found the average.

Kyle

70 mg
This value occurred most often.

Yü

a. If Meliva, Kyle, and Yü continued their same line of thinking, what would each say about the amount of cholesterol in a "typical" chicken entree?

b. Did any one of the three give a better answer than the other two? Why or why not?

c. Whose answer could help you determine if most burgers have 93.1 mg of cholesterol or more? Explain your reasoning.

d. Why is Kyle's answer larger than Meliva's?

Checkpoint

> **ⓐ** Compare a stem-and-leaf plot to a histogram. How are they alike and how are they different?
>
> **ⓑ** How does a back-to-back stem-and-leaf plot help you compare two distributions?
>
> **ⓒ** Describe three methods of estimating a typical or representative value for a distribution.
>
> ✓ *Compare your thinking and descriptions with those of other groups.*

Summaries that describe a typical or representative value for a distribution are called **measures of center**. You may already be familiar with three measures of center.

- The **median** is the midpoint of an *ordered* list of data—half the values are at or below it and half are at or above it.
- The **mode** is the value that occurs most frequently.
- The **mean**, or arithmetic average, is the sum of the values divided by the number of values.

On Your Own

a. By comparing means, would you conclude there is more cholesterol in the burgers or in the chicken selections? Does the same conclusion hold if you compare medians? Modes?

b. For a popular CD, what does the median price in the stores in your area tell you? The mode price? The mean price? Which piece of information about the distribution would you rather know? Why?

The mean lies at the "balance point" of the number line plot, histogram, or stem-and-leaf plot. That is, if the histogram were made of bricks stacked on a light tray, the mean is where you would place one hand to hold the tray so the tray would balance.

3. The histogram at the right shows the ages of the Best Actress winners at the annual Academy Awards (Oscars). Estimate the mean age of the winners.

Source: From a student project in the class of Gretchen Davis, Santa Monica High School, Santa Monica, CA.

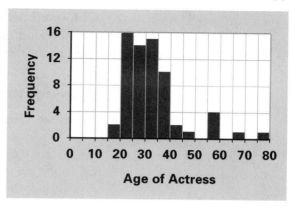

4. The histogram below shows 40 pieces of data.

   a. How many 5's are there in this set of data?

   b. What is the mode of this set of data?

   c. Find the median of this set of data. Locate the median on the horizontal axis of the histogram.

   d. Find the area of the bars to the left of the median.

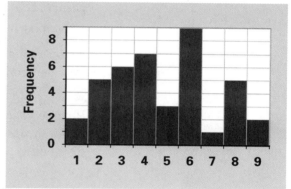

   e. Find the area of the bars to the right of the median.

   f. What do you conclude about the location of the median on a histogram?

   g. Estimate the mean of the distribution by estimating the balance point of the histogram.

   h. Find the mean of the data using your calculator or computer. How close was your estimate in part g?

5. Once data have been entered into your calculator or computer, you can calculate measures of center quickly.

   a. Use your calculator or computer to find the mean and median for the amount of cholesterol in the chicken items. The "Technological Tip" handout may be helpful. Mark the mean and median on the stem-and-leaf plot you prepared in activity 1.

   b. With a partner, explore other ways of calculating the mean number of milligrams of cholesterol on your calculator or computer using sorted lists.

c. Most technological tools have no operation for calculating the mode of a distribution. Explain how sorting data would make the process of determining a mode easier.

d. Using data lists on your calculator or computer, find the minimum and the maximum amounts of cholesterol in the chicken items.

6. a. Find the mean and median of the following set of data.

$$1, 2, 3, 4, 5, 6, 70$$

b. Change the outlier, 70, in the data set in part a to 7 and find the mean and median of the new set of data.

c. Did the mean or the median change the most? Explain why this is the case.

d. Is the mean or the median more **resistant to outliers**? That is, which tends to change the least if an outlier is added to the set of data?

e. Is the mode resistant to outliers? Why or why not?

7. Describe a situation where it would be better if the teacher uses the median test score when computing your grade. Describe a situation where the mean is better.

8. a. Refer to your histograms of the total calories and amounts of cholesterol and fat for the fast foods in Investigation 2.2. Find the mean and median of each distribution. Divide up the work within your group.

b. Using different colored pencils or pens, locate and label the mean and median on the horizontal axis of each histogram.

c. Write down any observations you can make about connections between the shape of the distribution and the locations of the mean and the median. Test your observations using the data on the amount of sodium in the fast foods listed and with at least two sets of data that you make up yourselves.

Checkpoint

> **a** What are the advantages and disadvantages of each measure of center for summarizing a set of data?
>
> **b** Describe how to find or estimate the mean, median, and mode from a histogram.
>
> ✓ *Be prepared to share your group's thinking with the whole class.*

On Your Own

The table below gives the percentage of households who own their own home in countries in North America where this information is available.

Country	Percentage Who Own Home	Country	Percentage Who Own Home
Barbados	70.7	Jamaica	46.7
Belize	58.8	Mexico	61.1
Canada	62.6	Panama	75.5
Dominica	66.4	Saint Kitts-Nevis	56.7
Grenada	74.5	St. Vincent/Grenadines	72.1
Guatemala	64.7	Trinidad/Tobago	63.6
Haiti	73.2	United States	64.2

Source: *United Nations Statistical Chart on World Families*, New York: United Nations, 1993.

a. Describe two ways of finding the median of this set of data. Use what you believe to be the easier method and find the median.

b. Describe two ways of finding the mean of this data set. Find the mean using what you believe to be the easier method. Are there any outliers in this data set that might affect the mean? If so, how do they affect the mean?

c. Write a sentence or two reporting the median of this set of data. Explain what the median tells you about home ownership.

Modeling Organizing Reflecting Extending

Modeling

1. Listed below are fast growing franchises in the U.S. based on the number of new franchise units added in 1994.

Fast-Growing Franchises

Company	Type of Business	Minimum Start-up Costs
Subway	submarine sandwiches	$43,000
Choice Hotels Intl.	hotels and motels	1,500,000
McDonald's	hamburgers	400,000
7-Eleven Convenience Stores	convenience stores	12,500+
Burger King Corp.	hamburgers	73,000
Dunkin' Donuts	doughnuts	181,600
The Historical Research Center	misc. retail products	20,000
Hardee's	hamburgers	497,200
Tower Cleaning Systems	commercial cleaning	1,190
Coverall North America, Inc.	commercial cleaning	350
Mail Boxes Etc.	postal and business services	68,500
Re/Max Intl. Inc.	real estate services	60,000
Jackson Hewitt Tax Service	income tax services	13,000
GNC Franchising, Inc.	health food stores	73,700
Jani-King	commercial cleaning	2,400+
Furniture Medic	cabinet refacing	5,600
Baskin-Robbins USA Co.	ice cream	80,200
Play It Again Sports	sports equipment and apparel	94,000
Super 8 Motels	hotels and motels	300,000
Futurekids	children's computer learning centers	45,000
Merry Maids	residential cleaning	6,950
Arby's Inc.	misc. fast food	525,000
Super Coups	direct-mail advertising	3,470
Great Clips Inc.	hair care	55,600
Pretzel Time	pretzels	112,700

Reprinted with permission from *Entrepreneur Magazine*, January 1995.

a. What kinds of businesses occur most often in this list? What are some possible reasons for their popularity?

b. Make a graph that would be appropriate for displaying the distribution of minimum start-up costs.

c. Describe the shape of the distribution.

d. Why might a measure of center of minimum start-up costs be somewhat misleading to a person who wanted to start a franchise? (Hint: What franchises are these?)

2. Juanita, a recent high school graduate seeking a job at United Tool and Die, was told that "the average salary is over $21,000." Upon further inquiry, she obtained the following information about the number of employees at various salary levels.

Type of Job	Number Employed	Individual Salary
President/owner	1	$200,000
Business manager	1	60,000
Supervisor	2	45,000
Foreman	5	26,000
Lathe & drill operator	50	16,000
Secretary	2	14,000
Custodian	1	9,000

a. How many employees earn $45,000?

b. How many people are employed by this company? To compute the mean salary, how many salaries would you have to add up? Is the reported average salary correct?

c. Which measure of center is the most important for Juanita to know?

d. Suppose the president's annual salary is increased by $5000. How will this change affect the mean? The median? The mode?

e. In a different company of 54 employees, the median salary is $24,000, the mode is $18,000, and the mean is $26,000. What is the total payroll?

3. The following table gives the number of accidental deaths and the death rate by nation for one year. The information was obtained from the World Health Organization.

Nation	Accidental Deaths	Accidental Death Rate Per 100,000 Population
Australia	5751	34.8
Austria	3792	49.7
Bulgaria	3865	43.0
Canada	9152	35.3
Costa Rica	902	31.5
Cuba	8278	81.5
Czechoslovakia	8769	56.1
Denmark	2598	50.7
Ecuador	4968	48.7
England, Wales	11,529	22.8
France	33,101	59.2
Greece	4243	42.4
Hungary	8130	76.9
Iceland	85	33.6
Japan	31,049	25.4
Netherlands	3464	23.5
Norway	1953	46.4
Poland	20,538	54.1
Portugal	4640	45.0
Switzerland	3302	49.7
United States	97,100	39.5
West Germany	20,070	32.3
Yugoslavia	9325	39.6

a. Study the numbers in the table and write down at least two observations.

b. Which country had the fewest number of accidental deaths? What might explain this?

c. What was the rate, per 2,000,000 people, of accidental deaths in the Netherlands?

d. Using the data provided, estimate the populations of the United States and Cuba in the year shown.

e. Use the histogram shown here to help describe the distribution of the number of accidental deaths.

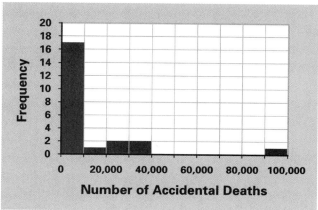

f. Does it make sense to find an average number of accidental deaths? Why or why not?

g. Locate the position of the United States on the histogram. How does it compare to the other countries? What might explain the large number of accidental deaths in the United States?

4. a. A histogram of the rate of accidental deaths per 100,000 population is shown at the right. What observations can you make from it?

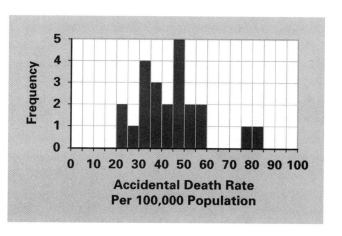

b. How does the histogram of the rates of accidental deaths compare to the histogram of the actual deaths in part e of Modeling task 3? Explain any difference.

c. Find the median rate of accidental deaths per 100,000 population for 1989. Write a sentence describing what the median tells you.

d. List the five nations that had the greatest number of accidental deaths.

List the five nations that had the greatest rate of accidental deaths per 100,000 population. Compare the two lists. What might explain the differences?

5. For each of the following four distributions:

– Estimate the mean and median. Which is larger?

– Write a sentence describing what the median tells about the data.

– Write a sentence describing what the mean tells about the data.

a. The distribution represents the percentage of the population that is between the ages of 5 and 14 for a selected set of countries.

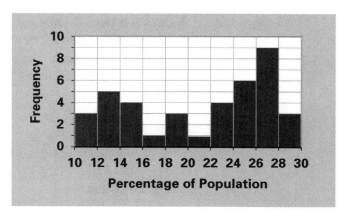

b. The distribution represents the reported sales, in millions of dollars, from clothing and accessories stores in each state and the District of Columbia in one year.

Source: U.S. Bureau of the Census, *Statistical Abstract of the United States: 1995* (115th edition.) Washington, DC, 1995.

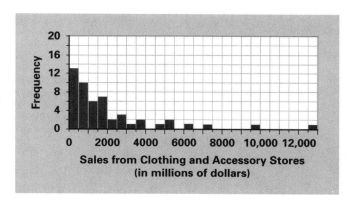

c. The distribution is the amount paid, in thousands of dollars per year, by various companies for local television advertising.

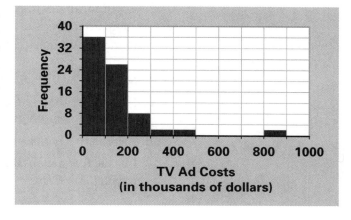

d. The distribution represents the vertical jump, in inches, of basketball players in the NBA draft.

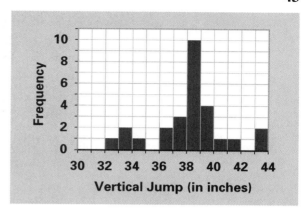

Organizing

1. Use the fifteen numbers below for parts a through e.

13, 23, 20, 14, 27, 21, 29, 31, 12, 10, 11, 21, 5, 19, 36

Create a new data set from the one above by adding or deleting just one number so that the new data set will have

a. a mean larger than the median

b. a median of 20.5

c. no mode

d. a median of 20

e. a mean of 25

2. For each situation below, find five whole numbers between 1 and 10 inclusive that illustrate the situation. You may repeat numbers in each set.

a. The mean and median of the set are the same.

b. The mean is less than the median of the set.

c. The set has the largest possible mean. What is the median of this set? What is the mode of this set?

d. A mode exists, and the mean, median, and mode are all the same, but the shape of the distribution is different from that in part c.

e. Exchange papers with a classmate. If you have different sets, do both of your sets illustrate the same situation?

3. Matt received an 80 and an 85 on his first two English tests this quarter.

a. If a grade of B requires a mean of at least 85, what must he get on his next test to earn a B grade?

b. Suppose, on the other hand, that a B requires a median of at least 85. What would Matt need on his next test to earn a B grade?

4. a. Describe the characteristics of a histogram whose mean and median are nearly the same.

   b. Describe the characteristics of a histogram whose mean is greater than its median.

   c. Describe the characteristics of a histogram whose mean, median, and mode are nearly the same.

   d. Which of your descriptions fit the following graph?

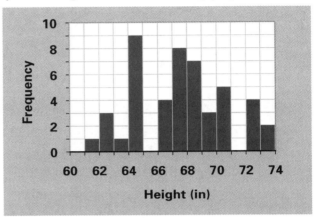

Reflecting

1. The National Longitudinal Survey of Youth asked Americans in their thirties about jobs they held between their 18th and 30th birthdays. The mean number of jobs was 7.5 and the median was 7.0. The mean number of years they worked between these two birthdays was 8.6 and the median was 9.4.

   a. Why is the mean number of jobs higher than the median number of jobs?

   b. Why is the mean number of years worked less than the median number of years worked?

2. You have seen in this investigation that each measure of center has certain advantages and disadvantages.

   a. Which measure of center will always be the same as one of the pieces of data? Explain your answer.

   b. Which measure of center will be most affected by extreme values in the data? Explain your reasoning.

3. Describe how you could find the median height of students in your mathematics class by making at most two measurements.

4. The median is typically reported when giving a measure of center for house prices in a region and for family incomes. Why do you think this is the case?

Extending

1. The planning committee for a class party decided to show a movie. They asked sixteen students to rank the following movies from 1 to 5 (1 was their least favorite movie and 5 was their favorite). The rankings for the males and the females were recorded separately.

Movie	Females' Rankings					Males' Rankings				
	1	2	3	4	5	1	2	3	4	5
The Net	//	//	/	//	/	//	/		/	////
Apollo 13	///		///	/	/	///	///	/	/	
Clueless	/	/	///	///		/	///	///	/	
Aladdin	/	///			////	/	/	//	//	//
Addams Family	/	//	//	/	//	/		/	////	//

a. Using the total number of points, which movie would be the overall favorite?

b. Using the mean for each movie, find the group favorite using
   - just the females
   - just the males
   - all the students

c. Is there any difference in the outcome using the means instead of total points? Why or why not?

d. Which movie do you think the students should rent for the class party? How did you decide? Do you think your method was fair?

2. Suppose that a survey of a small number of families counted how many children were in each family. The results are recorded in the table.

Number of Children	Number of Families
0	15
1	22
2	36
3	21
4	12
5	6
7	1
10	1

a. Make a histogram of the distribution. Estimate the average number of children per family from the histogram.

b. Calculate the average number of children per family. You can do this on some calculators and spreadsheet software by entering the number of children in one list and the number of families in another list. The following instructions work with some calculators. Your calculator or computer may work differently.

  – Enter the data in lists L1 and L.

  – While still in the lists, position the cursor on top of L3 and type $\boxed{L1}$ $\boxed{\times}$ $\boxed{L2}$ and then press $\boxed{ENTER}$. What appears in list L3?

  – Using list L3, find the average number of children per family.

c. Find the average number of children for the families in your class. How is the distribution from your class sure to be different from the one above?

3. Get a set of weights and a meter or yard stick. Experiment by placing several weights at various positions on the meter stick and finding the balance point. Explain how this experiment can be used to justify the statement: "The mean of a set of data is the balance point of the distribution."

4. Many people who have dropped out of the traditional school setting can earn an equivalent to a high school diploma. A GED (General Educational Development Credential) is given to a person who passes a test for a course to complete high school credits. There were 498,000 people who received GEDs in the year shown here. The break-down by age of those receiving GEDs was as follows:

Age	19 yrs and under	20–24 yrs	25–29 yrs	30-34 yrs	35 yrs and over
% completing GED	35%	26%	13%	10%	16%

Source: *Digest of Education Statistics, 1995.* Washington, DC: U.S. Department of Education, 1995.

a. Find a way to estimate the mean age of someone who receives a GED.

b. Explain how you arrived at your estimate.

c. Find a way to estimate the median age.

d. Explain how you arrived at your estimate.

3 *Variability*

Whenever two people observe an event, they are likely to see different things—just ask a police officer who has tried to collect evidence at the scene of an accident or a crime. In fact, there is **variability** in nearly everything; no two leaves or snowflakes are exactly alike. If two people measure something to the nearest millimeter, they probably will get two different measurements. If two people conduct the same experiment, they will get slightly different results. Because variability is so common, it is important that you begin to understand what causes variability and how it can be measured and interpreted.

The following plots show the mean heights of boys and girls from birth to age 14.

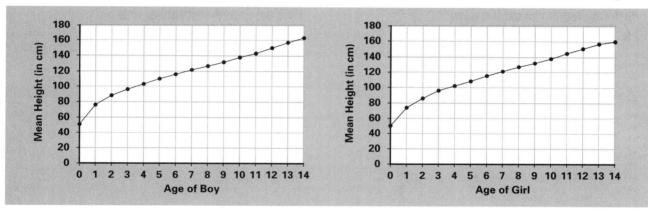

Think about this situation

Refer to the plots above, if necessary.

a Is it reasonable to call a 14-year-old boy "taller than average" if his height is 165 cm? Is it reasonable to call a 14-year-old boy "tall" if his height is 165 cm? What additional information about 14-year-old boys would you need to know to be able to say that he is "tall"?

b How tall would a 14-year-old girl have to be before you would be willing to call her "tall"? Do you have enough information to make this judgment?

c The average heights come from a physician's handbook. If you were a physician, what other information would you need to know in order to decide if a child was growing normally?

Investigation 3.1 Measuring Variability: The Five-Number Summary

If you are in the 40th **percentile** of height for your age, that means that 40% of people your age are shorter than you are and 60% are taller. Shown here are physical growth charts for boys and girls, 2 to 18 years in age. The charts were developed by the National Center for Health Statistics.

The curved lines for the height (top) and weight (bottom) tell a physician what percentile a boy or girl is in. The percentiles are the small numbers 5, 10, 25, 50, 75, 90, and 95 towards the right end of the curved lines. For example, suppose John is a 17-year-old boy who weighs 60 kg or 132 pounds. John is in the 25th percentile of weight for his age. Twenty-five percent of 17-year-old boys weigh less than John and 75% weigh the same or more than John. John's height is 180 cm or almost 5'11". He is in the 75th percentile of height for his age.

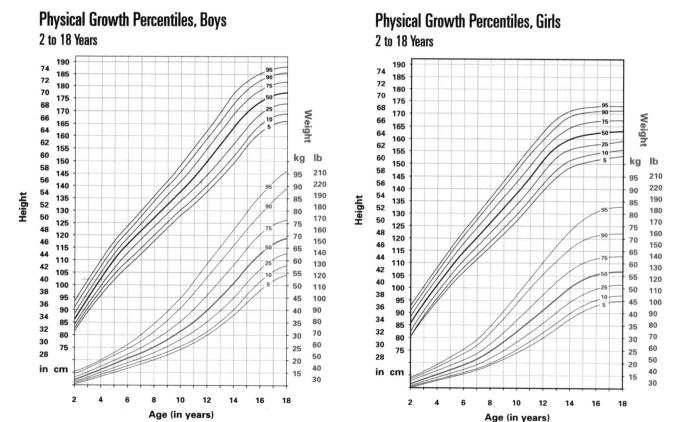

Physical Growth Percentiles, Boys
2 to 18 Years

Physical Growth Percentiles, Girls
2 to 18 Years

Adapted from: Hamill PVV, Drizd TA, Johnson CL, Reed RB, Roch AF, Moore WM: Physical growth: National Center for Health Statistics percentiles. AM J CLIN NUTR 32:607-629, 1979. Data from the National Center for Health Statistics (NCHS), Hyattsville, MD. Used with permission of Ross Products Division, Abbott Laboratories, Columbus, OH 43216 from NCHS Growth Charts ©1982 Ross Products Division, Abbott Laboratories

1. Based on the information given about John, how would you describe John's general appearance?

2. Obtain copies of the NCHS growth charts from your teacher. With your group, spend some time learning to read the charts. They contain an amazing amount of information!

   a. What is the approximate percentile for a 9-year-old girl who is 128 cm tall?

   b. About how tall does a 12-year-old girl have to be so that she is taller than 75% of the girls her age?

   c. How tall would a 14-year-old boy have to be so that you would consider him "tall" for his age? How did you make this decision?

   d. How tall would a 14-year-old girl have to be so that you would consider her "tall" for her age? How did you make this decision?

   e. What is the 25th percentile in height for 4-year-old boys? The 50th percentile? The 75th percentile?

   f. How can you tell from the height and weight chart when children are growing the fastest? When is the increase in weight the greatest for girls? For boys?

3. a. What is another name for the 50th percentile?

   b. The 25th percentile is sometimes called the **lower quartile**. Estimate the lower quartile of height for 6-year-old girls.

   c. The 75th percentile is sometimes called the **upper quartile**. Estimate the upper quartile of height for 6-year-old girls.

The quartiles together with the median give some indication of the center and spread of a set of data. A more complete picture of the distribution of a set of data is given by the **five-number summary:** the **minimum value**, the **lower quartile** (Q_1), the **median** (Q_2), the **upper quartile** (Q_3) and the **maximum value**.

4. From the charts, estimate the five-number summary for 13-year-old girls' heights and for 13-year-old boys' heights. Some estimates will be more difficult than others. Explain how you arrived at the numbers you gave.

The distance between the first and third quartiles is called the **interquartile range (IQR)**. The IQR is a measure of how spread out or variable the data are. The distance between the minimum value and the maximum value is called the **range**. The range is another, typically less useful, measure of how variable the data are.

5. a. What is the interquartile range of the heights of 13-year-old girls? Of 13-year-old boys?

   b. What happens to the interquartile range of heights as children get older?

   c. In general, do boys' heights or girls' heights have the larger interquartile range or are they about the same?

   d. What happens to the interquartile range of weights as children get older?

6. Can you estimate the range of the heights of 18-year-old boys? Why is the interquartile range more informative than the range?

For the children's heights, you were able to estimate quartiles from the chart. Next you will learn how to compute them from sets of data.

When you explored the AAA ratings for cars in Investigation 2.1, you saw variability in the ratings of each car. Below are the ratings for the Civic del Sol and the Laser and their corresponding histograms.

Civic del Sol Ratings

8, 9, 8, 9, 7, 8, 8, 8, 8, 7,
9, 9, 9, 7, 6, 6, 5, 8, 8, 8

Laser Ratings

9, 6, 8, 9, 6, 10, 8, 6, 7, 6,
8, 9, 9, 5, 5, 5, 4, 8, 8, 8

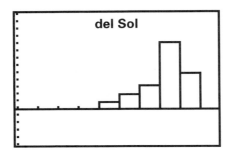

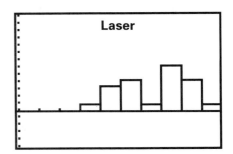

7. Which of the cars has greater variability in its ratings? Explain your reasoning.

8. a. Put the ratings for the Civic del Sol in an ordered list and find the median. Mark the position of the median on your ordered list.

   b. How many ratings are on each side of the median?

   Once the data are ordered, you can divide them into quarters to find the quartiles.

   c. Find the midpoint of each half of the ratings for the Civic del Sol. Mark the positions of the quartiles on your ordered list of the ratings.

   d. What fraction or percentage of the ratings is less than or equal to the lower quartile?

   e. What fraction or percentage of the ratings is greater than or equal to the upper quartile?

9. a. You can find the five-number summary quickly using technology. Find the five-number summary for the Laser's ratings using your calculator or computer software. The "Technology Tip" handout may be useful.

   b. What is the 25th percentile of the ratings for the Laser? The 75th percentile?

VARIABILITY

51

Checkpoint

a Will the range be changed if an outlier is added to a data set? Will the interquartile range be changed?

b Why does the interquartile range tend to be a better measure of variability than the range?

c If you get 75 points out of 100 on your next math test, can you tell what your percentile is? Explain.

d Give an example of when you would want to be in the 10th percentile rather than in the 90th.

e Give an example of when you would want to be in the 90th percentile rather than in the 10th.

✓ *Be prepared to share your group's thinking and examples with the rest of the class.*

On Your Own

The ratings for the Intrepid are reproduced below.

Acceleration	Transmission	Braking	Steering	Ride	Handling	Driveability	Fuel Economy	Comfort	Interior Layout	Driving Position	Instrumentation	Controls	Visibility	Entry/Exit	Quietness	Cargo Space	Exterior	Interior	Value
7	8	10	9	9	9	9	6	9	10	10	9	8	8	10	8	8	9	9	9

a. Find the five-number summary for the Intrepid. What is the interquartile range?

b. Refer to your results in activity 8 and activity 9. Of the ratings for the Intrepid, the Laser, and the del Sol, which has the greatest interquartile range? What would this tell you as a possible buyer?

Investigation **3.2** | Picturing Variability

Your heart continually pumps blood through your body. This pumping action can be felt on the side of your neck or your wrist where an artery is close to the skin. The small swelling of the artery as the heart pushes the blood is called your *pulse*.

1. a. Take your pulse for 60 seconds. Record the pulse rate (number of beats per minute) for each member of your group.

   b. Record your data with that of other groups on the Class Data Table you started in Lesson 1.

   c. Find the five-number summary for your class data.

The five-number summary can be displayed in a **box plot**. To make a box plot of your pulse rates, first make a number line. Below this line draw a box from the lower quartile to the upper quartile; then draw line segments connecting the box to each extreme (the maximum and minimum values). Draw a vertical line in the box to indicate the median. The segments at either end are often called **whiskers**, and the plot is sometimes called a *box-and-whiskers plot*. Here are the results for one class.

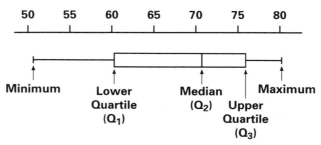

2. a. Is the distribution represented by the sample box plot above skewed to the left or to the right, or is it symmetric?

   b. Draw a box plot of the pulse rates for your class.

   c. Is the distribution of pulse rates for your class skewed to the left or to the right, or is it symmetric?

   d. What is the length of the box for your class data? What is the mathematical term for this length?

3. Box plots are most useful when comparing two or more distributions.

   a. How do you think box plots of class pulse rates before and after exercising would compare?

   b. Have some members of your group do some sort of mild exercise for a short time. Take your pulse immediately afterwards. Record it on the Class Data Table.

c. Combine your new data with that of other groups.

d. Construct a box plot of the new pulse rates. Place it below your first box plot.

e. How are the box plots different? Write a summary of your conclusions about pulse rates of the class before and after exercise.

f. What other plot could be used to compare the two distributions? Make this plot. Can you see anything interesting that you could not see from the box plots?

You can produce box plots with technology by following a procedure similar to that when making histograms. After entering the data and specifying the viewing window, select box plot as the type of graph desired.

4. Refer to the ratings for the Civic del Sol and Laser given in Investigation 3.1.

a. Using your calculator or computer software, make a box plot of the ratings. The "Technology Tip" handout may be useful.

b. Use the trace feature to find the five-number summary for the Civic del Sol. Compare the results with your computations in activity 8, Investigation 3.1.

c. Draw the box plot below a histogram of the Civic del Sol's ratings. Use the same scale for both.

d. How does the box plot compare to the histogram?

e. Produce a box plot of the ratings for the Laser. Draw the box plot below a histogram of the Laser's ratings. Use the same scale for both.

f. Compare the box plots for the Civic del Sol and the Laser. What do the different lengths of the boxes tell you about the variability in their AAA ratings? Is either distribution skewed? Symmetric?

Reproduced below are the ratings for the LeBaron, Camaro, and Miata.

LeBaron Ratings	Camaro Ratings	Miata Ratings
8, 7, 9, 8, 6, 7, 8, 7, 6, 6,	10, 8, 10, 9, 6, 10, 8, 5, 7,	8, 9, 9, 8, 5, 9, 9, 8, 8, 7,
8, 8, 6, 6, 7, 6, 4, 9, 7, 7	5, 8, 9, 9, 5, 6, 6, 6, 8, 8, 8	8, 9, 9, 7, 6, 5, 2, 9, 7, 9

5. Produce box plots for the LeBaron, Camaro, and Miata ratings. Draw each box plot below a corresponding histogram. Divide up the work among your group. Including the Civic del Sol and the Laser, your group now has five different box plots to compare.

   a. Use the box plots to determine which of the five cars has the largest interquartile range.

   b. Which cars have almost the same interquartile range? Does this mean their distributions are the same? Explain your thinking.

   c. Why does the Miata have no whisker at the upper end?

   d. Why is the lower whisker for the Miata so long?

   e. Based on the box plots, which of the five cars seems to have the best ratings? How did the plots help you make your decision?

Checkpoint

> **ⓐ** How does a box plot convey how close together data are in a distribution?
>
> **ⓑ** What does a box plot tell you that a histogram does not?
>
> **ⓒ** What does a histogram tell you that a box plot does not?
>
> ✓ *Be prepared to share your group's thinking about the usefulness of box plots.*

In this investigation you have learned how to display the five-number summary on a box plot. Box plots can be used to compare several distributions. Some computer software and graphing calculators allow you to display several box plots on the same screen.

On Your Own

Refer to the data on the amount of fat in the fast foods listed in Investigation 2.2. Produce a box plot of these data.

a. What is the five-number summary of these data?

b. What is the interquartile range for these data, and what information does it tell you?

c. Where is the Burger King Double Whopper with cheese located on the plot?

d. Choose a single item (such as your favorite, if you have one) and describe its relation to the other foods in the list in terms of fat content.

Modeling **O**rganizing **R**eflecting **E**xtending

Modeling

1. The table below gives the percentile ranks of recent SAT mathematics scores for national college-bound seniors. The highest possible score is 800 and the lowest possible score is 200. Only scores that are multiples of 50 are shown in the table, but other scores are possible.

SAT Math Score	Percentile	SAT Math Score	Percentile	SAT Math Score	Percentile
750	99	550	70	350	16
700	96	500	57	300	6
650	90	450	42	250	1
600	82	400	28	200	0

Source: *Digest of Education Statistics, 1995*. Washington, DC: U.S. Department of Education, 1995.

a. What percentage of students get a score lower than 650 on the mathematics part of the SAT?

b. What is the lowest score you could get on the mathematics part of the SAT and still be in the top 30% of those who take the test?

c. Estimate what score you would have to get to be in the top half of the students who take this test.

d. Estimate the 25th and 75th percentiles and the interquartile range. In a sentence or two, explain what this interquartile range means.

e. What do you think is the range of scores on a SAT test for a given year?

2. Refer to the height data in the Class Data Table prepared in Lesson 1.

    a. Produce a box plot of these data.

        – Make a sketch of the plot. Write the five-number summary at the appropriate places.

        – Mark where your height would be on the plot.

        – If your teacher's height was added to the data, how would that change the box plot?

    b. Produce separate box plots for the heights of females and of males in your class. Put these on the same screen as the first plot, if possible.

    c. What is the median height for the class? For females? For males?

    d. Which of the three height data sets: total class, females, or males, has the largest interquartile range? What does this tell you about the distribution of heights?

3. The following table gives the price and size of shampoos as reported in *Consumer Reports*.

    a. The cost per ounce is missing for Prell Normal and for Finesse Regular. Compute those values.

    b. Organize the data in the "Cost per Oz." column by making a stem-and-leaf plot.

    c. At about what percentile is Johnson's Baby Shampoo? Your favorite shampoo?

    d. Are there any outliers in the cost-per-ounce data?

    e. Examine the stem-and-leaf plot and make a sketch of what you think the box plot of the same data will look like. Then, make the box plot, either by hand or using technology, and check your sketch.

    f. What information about shampoos can you learn from the stem-and-leaf plot that you cannot from the box plot? What information about shampoos can you learn from the box plot that you cannot from the stem-and-leaf plot?

    g. Which shampoo would you label as a "good buy"? Explain your reasoning.

    h. Why is it more reasonable to plot the cost-per-ounce data than the price data?

Shampoos Labeled "for Normal Hair"	Price	Size Oz.	Cost per Oz.
Denorex Medicated Regular	$ 6.32	8	$ .79
Paul Mitchell Shampoo Three	5.07	8	.63
Johnson's Baby	2.89	15	.19
Faberge Organics Normal	1.31	15	.09
Jhirmack Fabulously Clean All Hair Types	4.09	11	.37
Paul Mitchell Awapuhi	3.93	8	.49
Bio Pure Jojoba with Keratin	3.25	16	.20
Halsa Balanced Care	2.42	15	.16
Pantene Normal	3.84	7	.55
Redken Glypro-L	6.25	9	.69
Finesse Regular	3.48	15	
Revlon Flex Normal to Dry	2.03	15	.14
Alberto VO5 Normal	1.30	15	.09
Tegrin Medicated Advanced Formula	5.72	6.6	.87
Paul Mitchell Shampoo One	3.55	8	.44
Ivory Free Normal	1.90	15	.13
Salon Selectives Level 5	2.39	15	.16
Prell Normal	3.46	15	
Agree New Advanced Regular	2.95	15	.20
Head & Shoulders Concentrate Normal to Dry	3.54	5.5	.64
Head & Shoulders Normal to Dry	4.26	15	.28
Safebrands Normal	2.89	16	.18
Vidal Sassoon Normal	3.54	11	.32
Selsun Blue Dandruff Regular	5.69	7	.81
Neutrogena All Hair Types	5.08	6	.85
Prell Concentrate Normal to Dry	3.29	7	.47
Nexxus Therappe	8.05	16	.50
Suave Normal to Dry	1.21	16	.08
Avon Simply Brilliant Normal	1.99	15	.13
Silkience Regular/Frequency	3.22	15	.21
White Rain Regular	1.28	15	.09

Source: *Consumer Reports*, June 1992

4. The following table indicates the percentage of the population in each state who speaks a language other than English at home. Only people aged 5 years and older were included.

State	% Who Speak Other Languages	State	% Who Speak Other Languages	State	% Who Speak Other Languages
Alaska	12.1	Kentucky	2.5	North Dakota	7.9
Alabama	2.9	Louisiana	10.1	Ohio	5.4
Arkansas	2.8	Massachusetts	15.2	Oklahoma	5.0
Arizona	20.8	Maryland	8.9	Oregon	7.3
California	31.5	Maine	9.2	Pennsylvania	7.3
Colorado	10.5	Michigan	6.6	Rhode Island	17.0
Connecticut	15.2	Minnesota	5.6	South Carolina	3.5
DC	12.5	Missouri	3.8	South Dakota	6.5
Delaware	6.9	Mississippi	2.8	Tennessee	2.9
Florida	17.3	Montana	5.0	Texas	25.4
Georgia	4.8	Nebraska	4.8	Utah	7.8
Hawaii	24.8	New Hampshire	8.7	Virginia	7.3
Iowa	3.9	New Jersey	19.5	Vermont	5.8
Idaho	6.4	New Mexico	35.5	Washington	9.0
Illinois	14.2	Nevada	13.0	Wisconsin	5.8
Indiana	4.8	New York	23.3	West Virginia	2.6
Kansas	5.7	North Carolina	3.9	Wyoming	5.7

Source: U.S. Bureau of the Census, *Statistical Abstract of the United States: 1994* (114th edition.) Washington, DC, 1994.

a. What percent of the population in your state speaks a language other than English at home?

b. Make a box plot of the data for the states that are on the edge of the U.S. That is, Alaska, Hawaii, and any state that touches an ocean, Canada, or Mexico. (See the following map.)

c. Below the box plot of the boundary, or "edge" states, make a box plot of the percentages for the remaining interior states.

d. Put a star on the appropriate box plot to show where your state would appear in the box plot. Write a sentence describing how your state fits into these data.

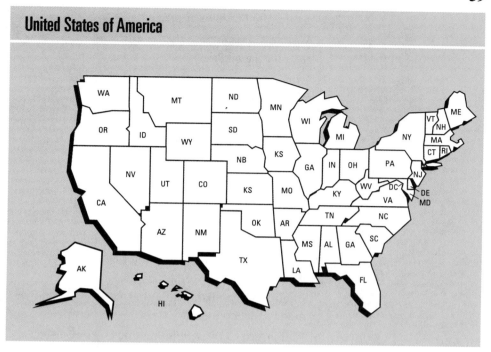

United States of America

e. Describe the differences between the two box plots. Why do you think there are these differences?

f. What other plot could be used to compare the two distributions? Make this plot that shows the two distributions. Can you see anything interesting that you could not see from the box plots?

Organizing

1. Below is a box plot and a histogram for the Ford Probe, created from the data in Investigation 2.1. What is missing from the box plot of the Probe? Why? Does the histogram give you a clue that this would happen?

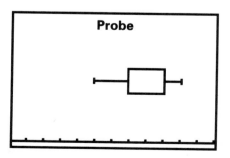

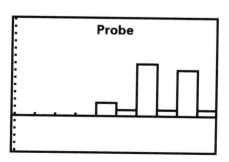

2. Consider the box plot at the right.

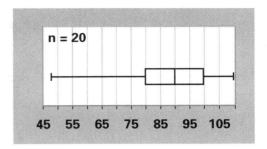

   a. What do you suppose the "n = 20" on the plot means?

   b. How many values are between 50 and 80? Between 80 and 100? Greater than 80?

   c. Is it possible for the box plot to represent the data below? Explain your reasoning.

   50, 60, 60, 75, 80, 80, 82, 83, 85, 90, 90, 91, 91, 94, 95, 95, 98, 100, 106, 110

   d. Create a data set that could be represented by this box plot.

3. The box plots below represent the amount of money (in dollars) carried by all of the people surveyed in four different places at a mall.

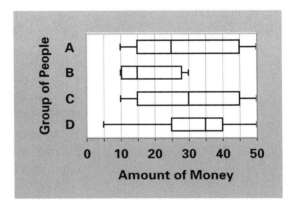

   a. Which group of people has the smallest range in the amounts of money? The largest?

   b. Which group of people has the smallest interquartile range in the amounts of money? The largest?

   c. Which group of people has the largest median amount of money?

   d. Which group of people has the most symmetric distribution of amounts of money?

   e. Which group of people do you think might be high school students standing in line for tickets at a movie theater on Saturday night? Explain your reasoning.

   f. Match each box plot above with the histogram that seems most appropriate.

   i.

   ii.

   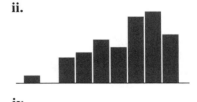

   iii.

   iv.

   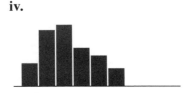

4. Draw histograms that might describe the same data sets as those represented by these box plots.

a.

n = 20

0 10 20 30 40 50

b.

n = 20

0 20 40 60 80 100

Reflecting

1. Describe two ways to use your calculator or computer to produce the five-number summary for a data set. Which do you prefer? Why?

2. Suppose when you finished activity 1 of Investigation 3.2, you found that your pulse rate was below the lower quartile. What does this mean?

3. In what situations would you use a histogram to display data? A box plot?

4. Why is the word "quartile" a good name for the 25th, 50th, and 75th percentiles? What do you suppose a "decile" is?

5. Is a maximum always an outlier? Is an outlier always a maximum or minimum? Explain your answers.

Extending

1. The histogram below displays the results of a survey filled out by varsity athletes in football and women's and men's basketball from the Detroit, Michigan area. These results were reported in the school newspaper.

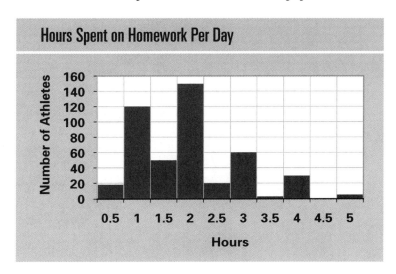

a. Estimate the median and the quartiles. Draw a box plot that also might represent the data.

b. What is an unusual feature of this distribution? What do you think is the reason for this?

c. Write a paragraph describing how many hours a typical student athlete from that area and in these sports spends doing homework.

2. If your family has records of your growth, plot your own growth in height on a copy of the appropriate National Center for Health Statistics growth chart. What percentile are you in now for your age? How much has the percentile varied over your lifetime?

3. These box plots represent the scores of 80 men and 80 women on a performance test. List the characteristics you know will be true about a box plot for the combined scores of men and women. For example, what will the minimum be?

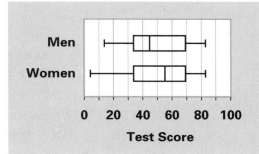

4. An **outlier** can be defined formally as any value in a data set larger than

$$Q_3 + 1.5 \times (Q_3 - Q_1)$$

or smaller than

$$Q_1 - 1.5 \times (Q_3 - Q_1).$$

a. Refer to the data on the number of calories in the fast foods listed in Investigation 2.2.

- Calculate the mean and the median for this data set. Which is larger? Why?

- Determine whether this set of data has any outliers. If so, remove the outlier(s) from the data set. Calculate the mean and median for the new data set. Compare the two means and the two medians.

b. Jolaina found outliers by using the box plot. She measured the length of the box and marked off 1 box length to the right of the original box and 1 box length to the left of the original box. If any of the values extended beyond these new boxes, these points were considered outliers. Jolaina had a good idea but made one mistake. What was it?

Outliers

Investigation 3.3 MAD About the Mean

In the last investigation, you examined the variability within a set of data by looking at graphical displays such as stem-and-leaf plots, histograms, and box plots and by computing the interquartile range. You may have found box plots particularly useful in displaying the difference in variability between two or more distributions. In this investigation, you will learn about the MAD, another measure of variation.

1. As a class activity, your teacher will look at a watch with a second hand and say "start." After a certain length of time he or she will say "stop."

   a. Write down on paper your (individual) estimate of how many seconds passed between the "start" and the "stop." It's not fair to look at your watch!

   b. Your teacher will tell you how many seconds it actually was. How far off was your estimate? Make a stem-and-leaf plot of the *errors* made by your class. Don't use negative numbers. An error of 6 seconds too long and an error of 6 seconds too short will both go on the stem-and-leaf plot as 6.

   c. Find the average error for students in your class.

   d. Try the experiment again with a different length of time. Is the new average error larger or smaller than before? Why is this the case?

2. Next, as a class choose one pair below for which you do not know the answers, but have a way to find them.

   – Length of your book in inches and height of the doorway in inches.

   – Your teacher's height in centimeters and your principal's height in centimeters.

   – The number of students who were absent from your school last Tuesday and the number of students who were absent last Friday.

   – The cost of running the athletic program at your school and the profit from tickets and concessions.

   a. Each member of your class should make his or her own estimate of the two values.

   b. Your teacher will help you get the correct answers. How far off were you from the correct answers? Make a back-to-back stem-and-leaf plot of the *absolute value* of the errors (record both -5 and 5 as 5) you and your classmates made in estimating the two values. Which of the two estimates seems to have the largest errors?

c. Find the average error for each estimated value. What does the average error tell you about the goodness of the estimates of each value?

d. For which value was the average error the smallest? Give a possible reason for this.

3. Refer to your Class Data Table prepared for Lesson 1.

a. Calculate the mean height for your group.

b. How much does each member of your group vary from the mean height?

c. On average, how much did the members of your group differ from the mean? How did you find this average?

d. Compare your results with each of the other groups. Which group had the greatest variability among its members? Which one had the least?

The average of the distances from the mean that you found in activity 3 is called the **mean absolute deviation** or **MAD**.

4. Each of the two data sets below has a mean of 10 and a range of 16.

Data Set 1	Data Set 2
2, 4, 6, 8, 10, 12, 14, 16, 18	2, 2, 2, 2, 10, 18, 18, 18, 18

a. Which of the two data sets has values that vary more from the mean? Explain.

b. Check your answer to part a by computing the MAD for each data set.

5. What is the MAD for each data set below? Explain how to get the answer without doing any calculations.

a. 4, 4, 4, 4, 4, 4, 4, 4

b. 5, 5, 5, 5, 5, 5, 15, 15, 15, 15, 15, 15

6. Long Life batteries have a mean life of 12 hours with a MAD of 1 hour. Power Plus batteries have a mean life of 15 hours with a MAD of 10 hours. They cost the same.

a. Give an example of a situation where you would prefer to use Long Life batteries.

b. Give an example of a situation where you would prefer to use Power Plus batteries.

7. The Emperor is a type of hog for which the mean weight is 120 pounds with a MAD of 15 pounds. Squealer is a type of pig for which the mean weight is 133 pounds with a MAD of 30 pounds. The Emperor weighs 150 pounds and Squealer weighs 163 pounds. Is it the Emperor or Squealer who has the nickname "Porky" among his animal friends? Explain your reasoning.

Checkpoint

a Why is it important to measure variability?

b Describe two ways of measuring and reporting variability in a data set.

c Which would you expect to have a smaller mean absolute deviation, the distribution of current prices of blue jeans or the distribution of current prices of new compact disks? Explain your reasoning.

✓ *Be prepared to share your group's descriptions and thinking with the entire class.*

Measures of center, such as the mean and median, and measures of variability, such as the mean absolute deviation and the interquartile range, are called **summary statistics**. They provide a quick summary of a set of data. However, they are most informative when accompanied by an appropriate graphical display.

On Your Own

At exactly the same instant, Tony and Jenny checked the time on the clocks and watches at their houses. The times on Jenny's ten clocks were 8:16, 8:10, 8:14, 8:16, 8:12, 8:15, 8:13, 8:17, 8:15, and 8:22.

a. Calculate the mean time on Jenny's clocks. Calculate the mean absolute deviation.

b. Tony had the same mean on his ten clocks as Jenny did, but his mean absolute deviation was 10 minutes. Find an example of ten times that could be the times on Tony's clocks.

c. What do the mean and the MAD tell you about how useful it is to look at a clock at Tony's house and at Jenny's house?

Investigation (3.4) Transforming Measurements

Calculating the mean absolute deviation (MAD) for a set of data can be tedious and time consuming. In this investigation you will first learn how to compute the MAD on your calculator or computer. You will then explore how transformations such as changing from inches to centimeters affects the mean and the MAD.

1. **a.** Each member of your group should measure the length of a desk or table to the nearest tenth of a centimeter. Do your measurements independently without others watching or knowing your measurement. Get results from classmates so that your group has a total of at least ten measurements.

   b. Make a number line plot of the measurements.

   c. Enter the data into a list on your calculator or spreadsheet software and calculate the mean. Mark the mean on the number line plot.

   d. Compute the mean absolute deviation of the measurements. Use the "Technology Tip" handout, if necessary.

   e. What do the mean and MAD tell you about the accuracy of your measurements?

2. Suppose that a group of 10 students would have collected the same measurements that your group did in activity 1, except the end of their ruler was damaged. Consequently, each of their measurements is exactly 2 cm longer than those collected by your group.

   a. What do you think they got for their mean and mean absolute deviation?

   b. **Transform** the data in the calculator or computer list by adding 2 cm to each of your measurements. The "Technology Tip" on transforming a list can help you.

   c. Describe how a number line plot of the transformed data would compare to the plot you made in part b of activity 1.

   d. Compute the mean and mean absolute deviation of the transformed measurements.

   e. In what way is the mean of the transformed measurements related to the original mean?

   f. In what way is the mean absolute deviation of the transformed measurements related to the original mean absolute deviation?

3. a. Use your calculator or computer to change each measurement in activity 1 from centimeters to inches. To do this, divide each measurement by 2.54.

b. Predict what the new mean and the mean absolute deviation will be for the measurements in inches.

c. Compute the mean and the mean absolute deviation of these new transformed measurements.

d. In what way is the mean of the transformed measurements related to the original mean?

e. In what way is the mean absolute deviation of the transformed measurements related to the original mean absolute deviation?

f. Suppose that one student mistakenly multiplied by 2.54 when transforming the measurements. What do you think this student got for the mean and mean absolute deviation of the transformed measurements? Check your prediction.

4. The summer of 1995 was unusually hot in the midwest United States. In July, the mean daily high temperature in Chicago was 88.1° Fahrenheit. The mean absolute deviation was 5.5°. In most countries, other than the United States, temperature is measured in degrees Celsius. Temperature C in degrees Celsius is related to temperature F in degrees Fahrenheit, by the rule $C = \frac{5}{9}(F - 32)$ or $\frac{5}{9}F - \frac{160}{9}$.

a. The temperature in Chicago on July 13 reached a high of 104° Fahrenheit. Express this temperature in degrees Celsius so that it would be better understood by a visitor from Canada.

b. Suppose you want to calculate the mean daily high temperature for July and the mean absolute deviation in degrees Celsius. Do you need to know the July daily high temperatures in Chicago? Explain your reasoning.

c. What are the mean daily high temperature and the mean absolute deviation in degrees Celsius?

Checkpoint

ⓐ What is the effect on the mean of transforming a set of data by adding or subtracting the same number to each value? What is the effect on the mean absolute deviation? Explain why this is the case.

ⓑ What is the effect on the mean of transforming a set of data by multiplying or dividing each value by the same number? What is the effect on the mean absolute deviation?

✓ ***Be prepared to share your group's thinking with the class.***

On Your Own

In the Amar family, the mean age is 30 with a MAD of 15 years.

a. What will be their mean age in 5 years? Their MAD in 5 years?

b. What is their mean age now in months? Their MAD in months?

c. Find possible ages for the six people in the Amar family. The six ages should have a mean of 30 and a MAD of 15.

  – Find the mean and MAD of your six possible ages *in 5 years*. Was your prediction in part a correct?

  – Find the mean and MAD of your six *current* ages in months. Was your prediction in part b correct?

Modeling Organizing Reflecting Extending

Modeling

1. Find a thick book, preferably one that other members of your class are using also. Measure the thickness of a piece of paper in this book in the following way. Compress more than a hundred pages from the middle of the book and measure the thickness in millimeters to the nearest tenth of a millimeter. Divide by the number of sheets of paper. Round to four decimal places.

   a. How can you determine the number of sheets of paper from the page numbers?

   b. Repeat your measurement ten times, taking a different number of pages each time. Place your measurements on a number line plot.

   c. What is the mean of your measurements? What is the mean absolute deviation of the measurements?

   d. How would you report to a supervisor how thick a piece of paper is?

2. Lynn and Seung are members of their high school track team. Their times in seconds for the last seven 50-meter races are given in the table.

Lynn	5.8	6.4	6.3	6.3	6.1	6.0	6.6
Seung	5.6	6.7	6.3	5.7	6.1	6.8	5.5

a. Using what you have learned in this investigation, summarize the times for Lynn and for Seung.

b. If only one of them can be entered in the final conference race, which one would you choose? Defend your choice using statistics.

c. Compare your choice with those made by others in your group. As a group, decide which of the two to select for the race and be ready to explain your choice to the class.

3. News accounts suggested that the inauguration of President Clinton marked the beginning of government by an unusually young President. Refer to the table below on ages of U.S. Presidents at inauguration and at death.

President	Age at Inauguration	Age at Death	President	Age at Inauguration	Age at Death
George Washington	57	67	Grover Cleveland	47	71
John Adams	61	90	Benjamin Harrison	55	67
Thomas Jefferson	57	83	Grover Cleveland	55	71
James Madison	57	85	William McKinley	54	58
James Monroe	58	73	Theodore Roosevelt	42	60
John Quincy Adams	57	80	William H. Taft	51	72
Andrew Jackson	61	78	Woodrow Wilson	56	67
Martin Van Buren	54	79	Warren G. Harding	55	57
William H. Harrison	68	68	Calvin Coolidge	51	60
John Tyler	51	71	Herbert C. Hoover	54	90
James K. Polk	49	53	Franklin D. Roosevelt	51	63
Zachary Taylor	64	65	Harry S. Truman	60	88
Millard Fillmore	50	74	Dwight D. Eisenhower	62	78
Franklin Pierce	48	64	John F. Kennedy	43	46
James Buchanan	65	77	Lyndon B. Johnson	55	64
Abraham Lincoln	52	56	Richard M. Nixon	56	81
Andrew Johnson	56	66	Gerald R. Ford	61	
Ulysses S. Grant	46	63	James E. Carter, Jr.	52	
Rutherford B. Hayes	54	70	Ronald W. Reagan	69	
James A. Garfield	49	49	George H.W. Bush	64	
Chester A. Arthur	50	56	William J. Clinton	46	

Source: *The World Almanac and Book of Facts 1996*. Mahwah, NJ: World Almanac, 1995.

a. Select the measure that is the most appropriate to use to examine the media's description of the Clinton presidency: the interquartile range, the mean absolute deviation, or Clinton's percentile. Compute that measure.

b. Make an appropriate graphical display of the ages at inauguration and another for ages at death. Which distribution appears to have greater variability?

c. Find the mean and mean absolute deviation of the age of presidents at inauguration and at death.

d. Which distribution has the greater mean absolute deviation? Is this finding consistent with your answer to part b?

e. How many mean absolute deviations is President Clinton's age at inauguration from the mean?

4. The table below shows the total points scored during the first 8 years of the NBA careers of high-scoring athletes. In their eighth year, one played for the Lakers, the other for the Bulls.

Lakers Star		Bulls Star	
Year	Points Scored	Year	Points Scored
1970	2361	1985	2313
1971	2596	1986	408
1972	2822	1987	3041
1973	2292	1988	2868
1974	2191	1989	2633
1975	1949	1990	2752
1976	2275	1991	2580
1977	2152	1992	2541

a. Which player had the higher mean number of points per year?

b. What summary statistic could you use to measure consistency in a player? Which player was more consistent according to your measure?

c. On the basis of mean points scored per year and consistency, who was the better scorer? Explain.

d. Can you think of possible reasons why the player for the Bulls scored so much lower in 1986? Should his performance for that year be ignored? If so, would your answer to part b be different? Explain.

e. Compute the mean absolute deviation for the Bulls player with and then without the points scored in 1986. Is the MAD sensitive to outliers?

Organizing

1. Refer back to "On Your Own" in Investigation 3.3.

    a. Subtract the mean from each of the times on Jenny's clocks, giving the difference as a positive or negative number.

    b. Find the average of the differences. What happened? What might explain this fact?

    c. Explain how the calculation of the mean absolute deviation overcomes the difficulty in part b.

2. Refer to your measurement work of Investigation 3.4 on transformed data.

    a. Find the median and interquartile range for the original measurement data.

    b. Find the median and interquartile range after each measurement is transformed to inches.

    – How do the median and interquartile range of the transformed data compare to those of the original data?

    – In general, what is the effect on the median and interquartile range if you divide each value in a data set by the same number?

    c. Investigate the effect that multiplying each value in a data set by the same number has on the median and interquartile range. What can you conclude?

    d. Find the median and interquartile range after adding 2 cm to each original measurement.

    – How do the median and the interquartile range of the transformed data compare to those of the original data?

    – In general, what is the effect on the median and interquartile range of adding the same number to each value of a data set? Explain your reasoning.

    e. Suppose the same number is subtracted from each value in a data set. How do you think the median and interquartile range of the transformed data compares to that of the original data? Explain your reasoning.

3. Find two different data sets so that the interquartile range (IQR) of the first data set is larger than the IQR of the second and the mean absolute deviation of the second is larger than the mean absolute deviation of the first.

4. For parts a through d, use the data set of 1, 2, 3, 6, and 23.

    a. Compute the mean absolute deviation from the mean.

    b. Compute the *median* absolute deviation from the mean.

    c. Compute the mean absolute deviation from the *median*.

    d. Compute the median absolute deviation from the median.

    e. Which is larger, the mean absolute deviation from the median or the mean absolute deviation from the mean? Test other data sets to see if your answer holds for all of them.

Reflecting

1. Describe a situation in which the interquartile range would be a better measure of variability than the MAD. Describe a situation in which the mean absolute deviation would be preferable.

2. Comment on the statement, "If two sets of data have the same mean and the same mean absolute deviation, they have the same distribution."

3. Describe a situation in science class for which the concept of mean absolute deviation might be important.

4. At this point, what are the things you understand about variability? What do you feel you do not understand?

Extending

1. The **standard deviation** is another way of measuring the amount of variation about the mean. It is found by computing the average of the *square* of the distance between each data point and the mean. Then, the *square root* ($\sqrt{}$) of this number is calculated. The ratings for the Chrysler LeBaron convertible reported in Lesson 2 were

   8, 7, 9, 8, 6, 7, 8, 7, 6, 6, 8, 8, 6, 6, 7, 6, 4, 9, 7, and 7.

   These ratings have a mean of 7.

   a. List the distance from the mean of 7 for each rating.

   b. Square each distance. (That is, multiply each distance by itself: $1 \times 1 = 1$, $0 \times 0 = 0$, and so on.) Find the total of these squared distances, then divide by the number of ratings (20) to find the average of the squared distances.

   c. Finally, calculate the square root of this number using your calculator or computer software. You have calculated the standard deviation of the ratings for the LeBaron convertible.

   d. Compute the standard deviation for a car that appears to have little variability in its ratings. Compare it with the standard deviation for the LeBaron.

   e. Compute the mean absolute deviation of the ratings for the LeBaron and for your other car. Is there much difference between the standard deviation and the mean absolute deviation in these cases?

2. Suppose the AAA raters changed their minds and gave the Chrysler LeBaron convertible a "7" on Cargo Space instead of the "4" it originally received.

    a. How do you think the new mean and the new standard deviation will compare to the original mean and standard deviation?

    b. You can find the mean and standard deviation quickly using technology. In the calculator display at the left, the mean is $\bar{x}$. The standard deviation is σx. The letter n indicates the number of data points used in the calculations. These are standard mathematical notations. Use your calculator or computer to find the mean and standard deviation of the adjusted LeBaron data and check your prediction from part a.

```
1-Var Stats
x̄=7
Σx=140
Σx²=1008
Sx=1.213953957
σx=1.183215957
↓n=20
■
```

3. The symbol Σ (Greek letter "sigma") means to add the values indicated. Σx is a mathematical shorthand for indicating the *sum of all the data points x*.

    a. The data set below represents the amount of change carried by the 28 students in a first-hour science class. Enter the data into your calculator and find the *one-variable statistics* Σx and Σx^2. Explain in terms of the data what Σx and Σx^2 represent.

Amount of Change

$.00	.25	.07	.00	.00	.35	.00	1.70	.00	.85
.35	.25	.00	.50	1.00	1.55	.50	.00	.00	.85
1.30	.00	.65	.25	.15	.90	3.35	.00		

    b. Write an expression using Σ notation which represents the mean of this data set.

    c. Which of the expressions below represents the standard deviation for this set of data?

      i. $\sqrt{\dfrac{\Sigma(x-\bar{x}^2)}{28}}$ **ii.** $\sqrt{\dfrac{\Sigma(x-\bar{x})^2}{28}}$ **iii.** $\dfrac{\sqrt{\Sigma(x-\bar{x})^2}}{28}$

    d. Which of the following represents the mean absolute deviation for this set of data? (Note: $|x|$ means the absolute value of x; for example, $|-5|=5$ and $|3|=3$.)

      i. $\dfrac{\Sigma|x-\bar{x}|}{28}$ **ii.** $\dfrac{|\Sigma(x-\bar{x})|}{28}$ **iii.** $\dfrac{\Sigma|x|-\bar{x}}{28}$

4. If the data are available, get the heights of the players on sports teams at your school. Analyze these data with appropriate graphical displays, measures of center, and measures of variability. Write a report on the differences in the teams.

4 *Relationships and Trends*

The article that accompanied the guide to the American Automobile Association's auto test ratings as reported in Lesson 1 stated:

Each vehicle must make compromises between power and fuel efficiency, ride and handling, cargo space and interior room, price and value.

If you want to find a car with the combination of two characteristics, it may be necessary for you to compromise. Suppose you are interested primarily in interior layout and cargo space for the cars in the $15,000–$20,000 range tested by the AAA. Examine the ratings of the tested cars on these two characteristics.

Car	Interior Layout	Cargo Space
Chrysler LeBaron GTC Convertible	6	4
Chevrolet Camaro	5	6
Chevrolet Lumina	8	7
Chrysler Concorde	10	8
Dodge Intrepid	10	8
Ford Probe	5	7

Car	Interior Layout	Cargo Space
Ford Taurus	8	8
Honda Accord	8	8
Honda Civic del Sol	7	5
Plymouth Laser	6	4
Mazda Miata	7	2

A rating of 1 is the lowest. A rating of 10 is the highest.

Think about this situation

a According to the table above, do the cars with the best interior layout also have the best cargo space?

b Do the cars with the worst interior layout also have the worst cargo space?

c In general, does it look like cars with better interior layouts have better cargo space and cars with poorer interior layouts have poorer cargo space?

d Does there have to be a compromise between interior layout and cargo space?

Investigation 4.1 — Scatterplots

A **scatterplot** helps make comparisons like those in "Think about this situation." On the following scatterplot, the *horizontal axis* (called the **x-axis**) represents the ratings for interior layout, and the *vertical axis* (called the **y-axis**) represents the ratings for cargo space. (It doesn't really make any difference in this case which characteristic goes on which axis. However, class discussion will be easier if everyone does it the same way.)

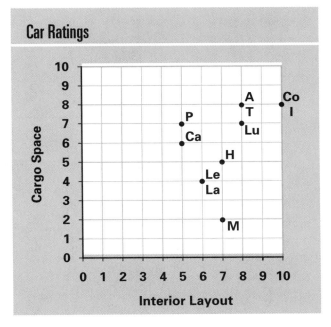

1. a. What does the point P in the plot represent? What does point M represent?

b. How many cars had a 7 rating for interior layout? Name the cars and indicate which points represent them on the plot. How could you verify your answers?

c. Name the cars that had a 6 rating for cargo space.

d. How many cars had the same ratings for both characteristics? Where are the points that represent them located on the plot?

e. What point would represent a car with the highest possible ratings on both characteristics? What point would represent a car with the lowest possible rating on each characteristic?

f. In an **ordered pair** such as (7, 2), the **first coordinate**, 7, represents the value on the *x*-axis. The **second coordinate**, 2, represents the value on the *y*-axis. Which car is represented by the point (7, 2)? By the point (5, 6)?

g. What ordered pair would represent the ratings of the Probe? The Lumina?

2. Now look at the line on the scatterplot below.

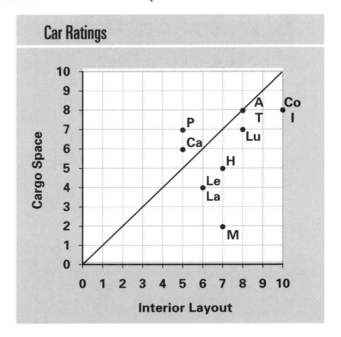

a. What is true of every ordered pair on the line? If *x* represents interior layout ratings and *y* represents cargo space ratings, what equation could be used to describe all ordered pairs on the line?

b. How many cars have a *higher* rating for interior layout than they do for cargo space? Where are the points that represent these cars located on the plot?

c. Describe the location of the points that represent the cars for which $x < y$.

d. Which car or cars are the best considering *both* interior layout and cargo space? Explain why you chose the car or cars you did.

e. Which car ranks lowest considering *both* characteristics? Where is the point that represents that car on the plot? Explain how you selected this car.

Both the Concorde and Intrepid are made by the Chrysler Corporation. They are manufactured on the same chassis (frame, wheels, and machinery). You might expect the ratings of the two cars across all tested characteristics to be similar. Are they?

Car	Acceleration	Transmission	Braking	Steering	Ride	Handling	Driveability	Fuel Economy	Comfort	Interior Layout	Driving Position	Instrumentation	Controls	Visibility	Entry/Exit	Quietness	Cargo Space	Exterior	Interior	Value
Concorde	8	9	9	9	9	8	9	6	9	10	10	9	8	8	10	7	8	9	9	9
Intrepid	7	8	10	9	9	9	9	6	9	10	10	9	8	8	10	8	8	9	9	9

3. Use your calculator or computer to make a scatterplot to help you compare the ratings. The "Technology Tip" handout may be helpful.

   a. Examine the scatterplot for the Concorde and Intrepid. Does your scatterplot show only 9 points? If so, why? If not, describe what your calculator or computer does to display more than one point in the same location.

   b. Trace the plot to display the coordinates of the points as they were entered in the lists.

   – For how many categories were the two cars rated exactly the same?
   – Is it easier to answer this question by using the plot or the table? Why?

   c. Now produce the graph of the line $y = x$ on your calculator or computer. Trace along the line and observe the readout of the coordinates. What do you notice?

   d. Which car had more ratings which were greater than the other car's ratings? How can you tell from the plot?

   e. Where are all of the points located for which $x > y$? In words, describe what $x > y$ means for this situation.

   f. In what category did both cars rate the lowest? How can you tell from the plot?

   g. Are the ratings of the Concorde and Intrepid similar? Is it easier to answer this question by using the plot or the table? Explain your reasoning.

4. Now refer to the resting pulse rates and exercising pulse rates for your class as recorded in the Class Data Table.

   a. On graph paper or using your calculator, make a scatterplot with the *x*-axis representing resting pulse rates and the *y*-axis representing exercising pulse rates. Draw in the $y = x$ line to help you compare the pulse rates.

   b. Write down at least four observations about your scatterplot.

   c. Which student is the farthest vertical distance from the line $y = x$?

Checkpoint

Suppose a scatterplot is made of the average 1980 and 1990 temperatures for 50 major world cities. The horizontal axis represents the average temperature in 1980 and the vertical axis represents the average temperature in 1990.

  ⓐ What does a point on the plot represent?

  ⓑ Where are the points located that represent cities that had the same average temperature in 1980 and 1990?

  ⓒ How could you use the line $y = x$ to determine if temperatures generally increased from 1980 to 1990?

  ⓓ Is it always helpful to draw in the line $y = x$ on a scatterplot? Why or why not?

  ✓ *Be prepared to share your group's responses with the whole class.*

In this investigation you have learned how to use the $y = x$ line to help interpret scatterplots. You should know where a point lies if $x < y$ and where a point lies if $x > y$.

On Your Own

The table below gives the cost of movies produced by Carolco Pictures and the total box office income from those movies.

Movie	Cost (millions)	Box Office Income (millions)
Terminator 2	90.0	52.9
The Doors	29.0	35.0
L.A. Story	20.0	28.0
Jacob's Ladder	27.8	26.0
Narrow Margin	21.0	10.6
Air America	35.0	30.5
Total Recall	60.1	118.3
Mountains of the Moon	20.0	3.3
Music Box	18.0	5.4
Johnny Handsome	20.0	6.6
Deepstar Six	9.0	8.6
Iron Eagle II	15.5	10.5
Red Heat	32.0	35.0
Rambo III	58.0	53.75

Source: *The Wall Street Journal,* July 1991

a. Make a scatterplot with cost on the *x*-axis and income from the box office on the *y*-axis. Draw in the line $y = x$.

b. For how many movies is the cost greater than the income from the box office? Where are the points that represent these movies on the plot? Which **inequality** describes these points: $x < y$ or $x > y$?

c. Use the plot to determine which movie has the greatest income from the box office. Where is the point representing that movie located on the plot? What are its coordinates?

d. Which movie had the greatest loss? The greatest profit? How does the plot help you find the answer?

e. Does there appear to be a relation between the cost of making these movies and the income they generate? Explain.

Investigation (4.2) Plots Over Time

In this unit you have displayed and summarized data in a variety of ways. You explored how those different ways helped you make sense out of situations ranging from sports and entertainment to worker salaries and best buys. Sometimes people are interested in a particular situation at a particular moment in time; for example, the present win/loss record of a school team. On another occasion they may be interested in the win/loss record of the team over the last several years. There are many such situations in the world of business in which trends over time are of particular interest. For example, trends in life expectancy are very important to the insurance industry.

The plot below shows the life expectancy at birth for people born in the United States between 1920 and 1990. It is called a **plot over time**.

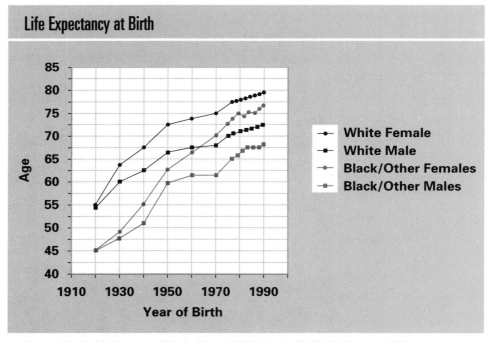

Source: *The World Almanac and Book of Facts 1996*. Mahwah, NJ: World Almanac, 1995.

1. a. What is the life expectancy of a black female born in 1920?

  b. Which group had the greatest increase between 1940 and 1950? How can you see this from the plot?

  c. What happened to the life expectancy of males born between 1960 and 1970?

d. Where is the only place in the plot that two lines cross? Describe what is happening there.

e. According to the plot, what is your life expectancy?

f. Describe the trends in the plot. From the evidence in the plot, how high do you think life expectancies will be for children born in the year 2000?

Analyzing the track record of appliances or automobiles over time can help consumers make wise decisions. For example, information on frequency and kinds of repair on earlier models together with ratings of cars can help you decide on the model and year for your used car purchase.

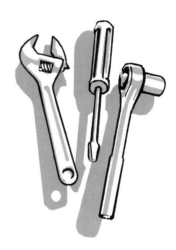

2. Each year, *Consumer Reports* provides a rating of repair records. The table below contains those ratings for several cars. A rating of 5 represents few problems, and 1 represents many problems. Of course, it is expected that older cars will have more problems. The ratings include categories such as paint, rust, brakes, clutch, ignition system, suspension, and transmission.

Average Repair Ratings

Car Model	Year							
	88	89	90	91	92	93	94	95
Accord	3.13	3.56	3.88	4.19	4.50	4.63	4.63	4.94
Taurus	1.79	2.07	2.50	2.71	3.21	3.50	4.07	4.43
Camaro	1.64	1.86		2.36		3.93	3.88	4.29
Civic	2.69		3.25	3.88	4.38	4.50	4.75	4.94
LeBaron	2.00		3.00	3.07	3.50	4.14	4.07	

a. What does a rating of 4.14 for the 1993 LeBaron indicate about the repair records for that LeBaron?

b. Which 1989 car had the fewest problems?

3. Plotting an event over time allows you to see trends and make comparisons. The horizontal axis usually represents time. In this plot, the horizontal axis indicates the model year and the vertical axis gives the repair ratings for the Honda Accord.

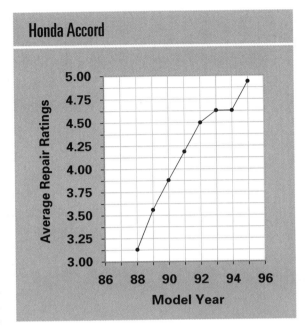

a. Use the plot shown here to estimate the average repair rating for Honda Accords built in the model year 1989.

b. Between which model years was there the greatest change in the ratings? How does the plot help you see that change?

c. Describe the change in the ratings for the Accord over the 8-year span.

d. How could you use the plot to estimate the overall average rating of the Accord across the 8 model years?

e. If you were considering buying an Accord, how could you use this information to help make your decision?

4. As you might expect by now, you can use your calculator or computer to make a plot over time. Produce a plot over time of the Accord repair ratings for the model years from 1988 to 1995. The "Technology Tip" handout may be helpful.

a. How does the plot on your calculator or computer compare to the one in activity 3? Trace along the plot and check the coordinate readouts against the data table.

b. Change Ymin to 0 and Ymax to 5.

– Does the new plot change your perception (visual impression) of the amount of change in the ratings?

– What happens if you set the *x*-axis to begin at 0 and end at 100 with a scale of 5?

– Use the automatic scaling option for statistical plots, if your tool has one. How did this alter your plot?

c. Compare the average repair ratings for the Accord and the Civic (another car manufactured by Honda Motor Corporation) by using two plots over time.

d. Change Ymin to 0 and Ymax to 5 with Yscl = 1. How does this change your perception of the two sets of ratings?

e. What would happen to the plots and your perception of the change in ratings over the years if you changed the minimum value of *x* to 60 and the maximum value of *x* to 100? Do you think this is a reasonable way to represent the data? Why or why not?

Checkpoint

a Describe a plot over time.

b What information can you learn from a plot over time?

c How can you use a plot over time to find the time period when the least change occurs? The most?

d How can the scale on the axes affect your interpretation of a plot over time?

✓ *Be prepared to share your group's thinking on the interpretation of plots over time.*

On Your Own

The data below give the number of cassette tapes, record albums (LPs), and compact disks (CDs) that were sold each year from 1983, when CDs became generally available, until 1992.

Year	Cassette Sales (in thousands)	LP Sales (in thousands)	CD Sales (in thousands)
1983	236,800	209,600	800
1984	332,000	204,600	5,800
1985	339,100	167,000	22,600
1986	344,500	125,200	53,000
1987	410,000	107,000	102,100
1988	450,100	72,400	149,700
1989	446,200	34,600	207,200
1990	442,200	11,700	286,500
1991	360,100	4,800	333,300
1992	366,400	2,300	407,500

Source: *The Universal Almanac 1994*. New York: Andrews and McMeel, 1993.

a. Produce a plot over time of the sales of the CDs, making appropriate choices for the viewing window. Describe any pattern you observe from the plot.

b. On the same display, make plots over time of the sales of cassettes and of LPs. Use different marks, if possible. Change your viewing window if necessary. Describe what happened to cassette, LP, and CD sales from 1983 to 1992.

Modeling Organizing Reflecting Extending

Modeling

1. Refer to the height and armspan measurements in the Class Data Table you prepared in Lesson 1.

   a. Make a scatterplot of the heights and armspans of the students in your class.

   b. Draw in the $y = x$ line.

   - Do the points fall near this line?

   - Are more points above this line or below it?

   - If the point representing Wayne's measurements is below the line, what do you know about his height and armspan?

   - Which inequality describes points that are below the line: $x < y$ or $x > y$?

   c. Describe the relationship shown on your scatterplot.

   d. The **centroid** of a scatterplot is the point $(\bar{x}, \bar{y})$ where $\bar{x}$ is the mean of the x values and $\bar{y}$ is the mean of the y values. Find the centroid and mark it on your scatterplot.

   e. Are there any points close to $(\bar{x}, \bar{y})$? If so, what can you say about the students represented by those points?

2. Refer to the thumb circumference and wrist circumference measurements in your Class Data Table.

   a. Make a scatterplot of the thumb circumference (on the x-axis) and wrist circumference (on the y-axis) of the students in your class.

   b. Describe the relationship shown on your scatterplot.

   c. Do the points fall near the $y = x$ line? Draw in a line that the points seem to fall near. What is the relationship between x and y on this line?

   d. Find the centroid $(\bar{x}, \bar{y})$ and mark it on your scatterplot.

   e. Are there any points close to $(\bar{x}, \bar{y})$? If so, what can you say about the students represented by those points?

3. The following table gives data about the life expectancy (at birth) for people living in the Americas, their (average) daily calorie supply, and the infant mortality rate.

Region/Country	Life Expectancy at Birth (years)		Daily Calorie Supply	Infant Mortality per 1,000 births
	1970	1992		
Antigua/Barbuda	67	74	—	20
Argentina	67	71	3,113	29
Bahamas	65	70	—	25
Barbados	69	75	—	10
Belize	—	69	—	41
Bolivia	46	60	1,916	82
Brazil	59	66	2,751	57
Canada	73	78	3,482	7
Chile	62	72	2,581	17
Colombia	59	69	2,598	37
Costa Rica	67	76	2,808	14
Dominica	—	72	—	18
Dominican Republic	59	68	2,359	53
Ecuador	58	67	2,531	53
El Salvador	58	66	2,317	46
Guatemala	53	65	2,235	58
Guyana	65	65	—	48
Haiti	48	55	2,013	93
Honduras	53	66	2,247	49
Jamaica	67	74	2,609	15
Mexico	62	70	3,052	35
Nicaragua	54	67	2,265	53
Panama	66	73	2,539	21
Paraguay	65	67	2,757	47
Peru	54	65	2,186	52
St. Kitts & Nevis	—	71	—	34
St. Lucia	62	72	—	17
St. Vincent & the Grenadines	63	71	—	20
Surinam	64	69	—	37
Trinidad & Tobago	66	71	2,853	18
United States	71	76	3,671	9
Uruguay	—	74	2,653	20
Venezuela	65	70	2,582	33

Source: *The Universal Almanac 1996*, Kansas City, MO: Andrews and McMeel, 1995.

a. Study the numbers carefully and write a brief summary of your observations.

b. Prepare an appropriate graphical display to compare the life expectancy in 1970 with that in 1992. Describe how life expectancy in the Americas has changed between these years.

c. Which country is farthest from the line $y = x$? What can you say about that country?

d. Make an appropriate graphical display of the infant mortality rate. Describe any patterns or clusters you see and give some possible reasons for their occurrence.

4. The following plot shows how long the average American had to work (before taxes) to earn enough to purchase a half gallon of milk or a pound of hamburger.

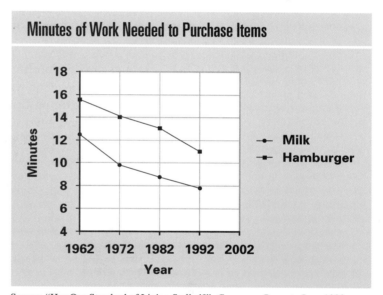

Source: "Has Our Standard of Living Stalled?", *Consumer Reports*, June 1992.

a. How many minutes did the average American have to work to buy a half gallon of milk in 1972?

b. Describe the change in the number of minutes someone had to work to buy a half gallon of milk from 1962 to 1992.

c. Starting at 1962, during what ten-year period was there the greatest change in the number of minutes of work needed to buy a half gallon of milk? How can you tell this from looking at the plot?

d. How does the change over time in the minutes of work needed to buy a pound of hamburger compare with that for a half gallon of milk?

e. Estimate the difference in the minutes of work needed in 1972 to buy the two items.

f. Do you think it ever took more minutes of work to buy a half gallon of milk than a pound of hamburger? How can you use the plot to answer the question?

g. Copy the plot above, keeping everything the same except double the distance between 4 and 18 on the *y*-axis. How does this change your perception of the decrease in the number of minutes of work needed to buy a half gallon of milk?

h. Which changed more over the years—the minutes of work needed to buy a pound of hamburger or the minutes of work needed to buy a half gallon of milk? Explain your answer.

i. Can we conclude that the price of a half gallon of milk decreased from 1962 to 1992? Explain.

5. The Nielsen ratings provide information on the percentage of U.S. households with televisions that are tuned into various programs. The plot below shows the average per game ratings for professional football (NFL) and college football televised between 1980 and 1990. The rating of 17.6 for NFL games in 1980 means that, on the average, 17.6% of all households with televisions watched the NFL game that was being broadcast.

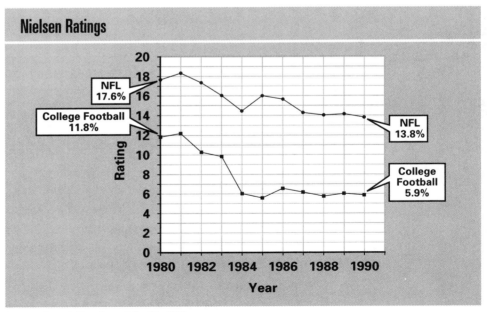

Source: *Detroit Free Press*, May 12, 1992

a. Did the NFL and college football have their highest reported rating in the same year? Their lowest?

b. Estimate the Nielsen rating for NFL games in 1986.

c. In what year did the NFL have the largest increase in ratings from the previous year?

d. For how many years during the period 1980–1990 was the Nielsen rating for NFL games above 15?

e. Overall, what trend do you see in NFL viewing over the period 1980–1990?

f. In what years did college football have an increase in ratings from the previous year?

g. In what year did college football ratings experience their sharpest decline?

h. Overall, what trend do you see in college football viewing over the period 1980–1990?

i. What, if anything, can you say about college football viewership in 1994? Explain your reasoning.

j. Did professional football or college football suffer the greater loss of viewership during the 1980s? Explain the basis for your conclusion.

Organizing

1. The following table contains the average high and low temperatures in January and July for selected cities around the world. A scatterplot of the average maximum temperatures in January and July is shown below.

a. How many cities have nearly the same maximum temperature in January as in July? Which cities are these?

b. What is true about the cities represented by points located below the line? Where are these cities located geographically?

c. What was the change in temperature for the city represented by point *B*? Which city does *B* represent?

d. Which city had the greatest change from January to July? Use the plot to find your answer and explain how it helps.

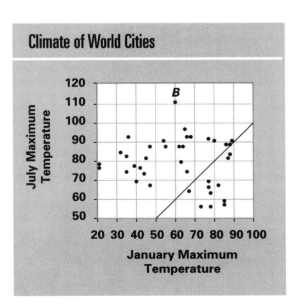

   e. Which of the following describe the region on the plot that contains the points representing cities warmer in January than in July? Here, J stands for the temperature in January and U stands for the temperature in July.

$$J > U \quad J < U \quad J = U \quad U = J \quad U > J \quad U < J$$

       Shade in that region on a copy of the graph.

   f. Select a point in the shaded region and verify that it does represent a city that is warmer in January than in July.

Climate of Selected World Cities

City	January Temp. (in °F) Max.	Min.	July Temp. (in °F) Max.	Min.	City	January Temp. (in °F) Max.	Min.	July Temp. (in °F) Max.	Min.
Accra, Ghana	87	73	81	73	Istanbul, Turkey	45	36	81	65
Amsterdam, Netherlands	40	34	69	59	Jerusalem, Israel	55	41	87	63
Athens, Greece	54	42	90	72	Kabul, Afghanistan	36	18	92	61
Auckland, New Zealand	73	60	56	46	Karachi, Pakistan	77	55	91	81
Baghdad, Iraq	60	39	110	76	Lagos, Nigeria	88	74	83	74
Bangkok, Thailand	89	67	90	76	Lima, Peru	82	66	67	57
Beirut, Lebanon	62	51	87	73	London, UK	44	35	73	55
Berlin, Germany	35	26	74	55	Madrid, Spain	47	33	87	62
Bogota, Columbia	67	48	64	50	Manila, Philippines	86	69	88	75
Bombay, India	88	62	88	75	Melbourne, Australia	78	57	56	42
Budapest, Hungary	35	26	82	61	Mexico City, Mexico	66	42	74	54
Buenos Aires, Argentina	85	63	57	42	Montreal, Canada	21	6	78	61
Cairo, Egypt	65	47	96	70	Moscow, Russia	21	9	76	55
Calcutta, India	80	55	90	79	Nairobi, Kenya	77	54	69	51
Cape Town, S. Africa	78	60	63	45	Osaka, Japan	47	32	87	73
Casablanca, Morocco	63	45	79	65	Paris, France	42	32	76	55
Dublin, Ireland	47	35	67	51	Santiago, Chile	85	53	59	37
Geneva, Switzerland	39	29	77	58	Sao Paulo, Brazil	77	63	66	53
Hanoi, Vietnam	68	58	92	79	Seoul, South Korea	32	15	84	70
Hong Kong	64	56	87	78	Taipei, Taiwan	66	53	92	76

Source: *The Universal Almanac 1996*. Kansas City, MO: Andrews and McMeel, 1995.

2. Refer to the temperature chart in Organizing task 1.

   a. Make a scatterplot of the maximum (on the *x*-axis) and the minimum (on the *y*-axis) temperatures for January. Leave room to the left and below it to complete part c.

   b. Which city has the largest range in temperature for the month of January?

   c. Below the scale on the *x*-axis, make a box plot of the maximum temperatures for January. To the left of the scale on the *y*-axis, make a box plot of the minimum temperatures for January.

   d. Describe the variability in minimum temperature in January.

   e. Describe what information the box plots add to the scatterplot.

   f. Explain why you do or do not find this new type of plot useful.

3. For each statement, sketch a plot over time in one-year increments that illustrates the statement.

   a. The cost of a compact disk of new releases is increasing every year.

   b. The cost of a delivered cheese pizza is increasing every year by approximately the same amount.

   c. There is no predicting the cost of a stereo; some years it is up and others it is down.

   d. The annual cost of electricity is decreasing.

4. The table below gives the amount of daylight in minutes for Kalamazoo, Michigan on the first day of each month in one year.

Month	Daylight	Month	Daylight	Month	Daylight
Jan.	545 min.	May	846 min.	Sept.	791 min.
Feb.	597 min.	June	908 min.	Oct.	703 min.
Mar.	675 min.	July	917 min.	Nov.	617 min.
Apr.	764 min.	Aug.	869 min.	Dec.	555 min.

   a. Prepare a plot over time of these data. Code January as 1, February as 2, and so on.

   b. Describe the pattern you see in the plot.

   c. Use your plot to estimate the number of minutes of daylight on October 15.

   d. Explain how you could use your plot to estimate the number of minutes of daylight for any day of the year. How confident would you be of your estimate?

Reflecting

1. Suppose you were given a plot of the sales of various brands of athletic shoes with the 1990 sales on the horizontal axis and the 1994 sales on the vertical axis. Each point represents the number of sales for a specific brand of athletic shoe. If the point representing your favorite brand lies below the line $y = x$, what can you conclude?

2. To answer a question, Toni and David each made a scatterplot of a set of data. Toni indicated that the area containing the correct points for the question was *above* the line $y = x$. David maintained the area was *below* the line $y = x$. Is there any way they could both be correct? Explain your reasoning.

3. Suppose you are studying a plot over time.

   a. How does the plot help you to see the range of the values over time?

   b. How does the plot help you to see the variability in the values over time?

   c. How can you detect possible extreme changes from the plot?

   d. How might you estimate the median y value?

   e. How might you use the plot to predict the value at a time in the future?

4. Refer to the plot of average repair ratings for the Accord (Investigation 4.2). Is the point (89.5, 3.72) on the plot? What, if anything, does this point represent?

5. How do you decide whether to use your calculator or computer or to use paper and pencil to produce a graphical display of data?

6. Look at a local newspaper over a week's time. Keep a record of the types of plots used to display data. Write a brief summary of your findings.

Extending

1. The following table gives the population (in thousands) of selected major cities in the United States for 1980 and 1990.

   a. Enter the data for the populations of the cities in 1980 and 1990 in your calculator or computer. Use List 1 for the 1980 data and List 2 for the 1990 data. Produce a scatterplot of the data.

   b. Overall, would you say the population in the cities increased or decreased? How can you tell this from the plot?

   c. Find the differences between the populations by subtracting the 1980 data from the 1990 data. Make a box plot of the differences. How can you tell from the box plot whether, overall, the population in the cities has increased or decreased?

Major U.S. Cities: Population 1980-90

City	1980	1990	City	1980	1990
Topeka, KS	119	120	Berkeley, CA	103	103
St. Petersburg, FL	239	240	Aurora, CO	159	222
Reno, NV	101	134	Atlanta, GA	425	394
Newark, NJ	329	275	Anchorage, AK	174	226
Milwaukee, WI	636	628	Anaheim, CA	219	266
Louisville, KY	299	270	Allentown, PA	104	105
Independence, MO	112	112	Albuquerque, NM	332	385
Honolulu, HI	365	377	El Paso, TX	425	515
Hartford, CT	136	140	Oklahoma City, OK	404	445
Gary, IN	152	117	Portland, OR	368	437
Chattanooga, TN	170	152	St. Louis, MO	453	397
Cleveland, OH	574	506	San Francisco, CA	679	724
Boise City, ID	102	126			

Source: *The Universal Almanac 1996,* Kansas City, MO: Andrews and McMeel, 1995.

d. Use your calculator or computer to find the mean change. How does this relate to your earlier conclusion on population change?

2. Collect at least 20 ordered pairs of data from a situation of your choice in which the line $y = x$ would make sense. Make a scatterplot and write a paragraph describing the observations you can make from your plot. Be prepared to share your plot and observations with the class.

3. The following data are the number of immigrants to the United States, in millions, during the 1900s.

Decade	1910s	1920s	1930s	1940s	1950s	1960s	1970s	1980s
Immigrants	5.8	4.1	0.5	1.0	2.5	3.8	7.0	9.5

Source: *Urban Institute*

Make a plot over time of the number of immigrants since 1900. Describe the change in the pattern of immigration. What might have caused the fluctuations?

5 *Looking Back*

In this chapter you have worked together in groups to make sense of situations and solve problems. You have learned how to analyze data using graphical displays such as histograms, box plots, and scatterplots. You have used visual patterns in data and summary statistics such as the median and interquartile range to describe distributions, to make decisions, to make comparisons, and to make predictions. The three activities in this final lesson give you an opportunity to pull together the ideas you have developed in the chapter.

1. In Project 3 of the first lesson, you collected data about the shoe length and stride length of the members of your class. Refer to those measurements in the Class Data Table. Working together as a group, construct appropriate plots and use the statistics you have learned to answer the following questions.

   a. How do the distributions of shoe lengths and stride lengths compare?

   b. Is there more variability in shoe length or in stride length?

   c. Is there a relationship between shoe length and stride length?

   d. Write a paragraph describing what you have learned about shoe lengths and stride lengths of the students in your class. (You may need to compute some additional summary statistics or make additional plots to illustrate your points.)

   e. Compare your work here to your work in the first lesson. What are the most important things you have learned about analyzing data?

2. Recently *Car and Driver* magazine set out to identify the best car priced under $10,000 in three distinct categories: "Most Fun to Drive," "Best People Mover," and "Best Value." The 12 cars tested and their ratings are summarized in the table at the top of the next page. Each car included air conditioning, a rear defroster, and an AM/FM radio among their features. The magazine did not pick an overall winner.

   Using what you have learned in this chapter, write a report on what you think was the best choice for a new car under $10,000. Include suitable plots and statistics to support your choice.

Car	Fun to Drive	Best People Mover	Best Value
Eagle Summit	72	80	76
Ford Escort	85	90	84
Ford Festiva GL	66	76	66
Geo Metro	58	68	63
Honda Civic CX	78	78	77
Hyundai Excel GS	72	84	87
Mazda 323	84	83	87
Nissan Sentra E	89	88	83
Plymouth Sundance America	66	81	74
Saturn SL	78	87	91
Subaru Justy GL	65	69	68
Toyota Tercel	80	83	89

An average of editors' ratings on a scale of 1 to 100
Source: St. Antoine, Arthur. 1992. The Econ Majors. *Car and Driver*, July, 32+

3. Recall that the Nielsen ratings provide information on the percentage of U.S. households with televisions that are tuned into various programs. The table below gives average Nielsen ratings for network televised broadcasts of individual sports for the decade from 1980–1990.

Sport	80	81	82	83	84	85	86	87	88	89	90
Auto Racing	3.1	6.5	5.4	6.1	5.6	4.2	4.7	4.3	3.8	4.4	4.1
Bowling	8.1	7.5	7.5	6.6	5.6	5.1	5.1	4.7	3.9	4.1	3.6
Golf	4.5	4.9	4.9	5.0	4.5	4.5	4.1	4.1	3.4	3.6	3.4
Boxing	9.8	9.0	5.3	5.8	3.8	4.8	3.1	3.4	2.7	3.5	3.3
Tennis	2.9	2.6	2.9	3.5	3.4	3.8	3.2	2.9	3.1	3.5	3.1
Horse Racing	8.6	13.8	8.2	8.2	6.9	4.4	6.7	6.0	4.0	3.7	2.4

Source: *Detroit Free Press*, May 12, 1992.

Use an appropriate plot to help investigate the change in ratings during this period for three sports of your choice.

a. Which of the three chosen sports showed the greatest change in ratings over the period 1980–1990?

b. Which of the three sports had the highest rating during the period? What was the rating and when did it occur? Did you use the table or the plot?

c. Were there any years in the period 1980–1990 for which two of the three sports shared the same rating? If so, what were the sports and what were the years?

d. For which of the three sports did the ratings fluctuate the most? Explain your reasoning.

e. For which of the three sports would you feel most confident estimating the Nielsen ratings in 1992? Explain why you picked that sport.

Checkpoint

Patterns in data can be seen in graphical displays of the distribution and can be summarized using measures of center and variability.

ⓐ Describe the kinds of information you can get by examining

- a stem-and-leaf plot

- a number line plot or histogram

- a box plot

- a scatterplot

- a plot over time

ⓑ Describe the kinds of situations for which each plot is most useful.

ⓒ How do you decide which measure of center to use to provide a summary of a distribution? How do you decide on which measure of variability to report?

ⓓ Which measures of center and of variability are readily found from graphical displays?

✓ *Be prepared to share your group's descriptions and thinking with the entire class.*

Chapter 2

Patterns of Change

1 *Related Variables*

Some things in life are always changing. The earth rotates on its axis and is in orbit around the sun, turning day into night and summer into winter. The prices you pay for food, clothing, and entertainment change from month to month. The cars on streets and highways change speed as traffic conditions change. Even the time you spend on homework assignments in mathematics changes.

Some changes can be observed; others can be experienced. There are changes that come and go quickly called fads. Fads occur in games, clothing, music, and even in sports.

For example, one new sport began when some young daredevils in New Zealand found a bridge over a deep river gorge. They tied one end of a strong elastic cord (called a bungee) to the bridge and the other around their waist or feet. They began jumping off the bridge and bouncing up and down at the end of the cord to entertain tourists. Soon word of this new pastime got back to the United States. It wasn't long before some Americans tried bungee jumping on their own.

As you can imagine, bungee jumping is a very risky sport, especially if the jumper doesn't plan ahead very carefully. If the apparatus isn't right, the consequences could be fatal!

Some amusement parks around the world are installing bungee jumps to attract daredevils who want a thrilling ride. Those parks have important planning to do before opening for business. First, they need to make sure their bungee apparatus is safe. Then they also want to set prices in a way that maximizes profit.

Think about this situation

Suppose the Five Star Amusement Park intends to set up a bungee jump.

ⓐ How could they design the bungee jump so that people of different weights could all have safe but exciting jumps?

ⓑ What patterns would you expect in a table or graph showing the expected stretch of a 50-foot bungee cord with different weights?

Jumper Weight in Pounds	Cord Stretch in Feet
50	?
100	
150	
200	
250	

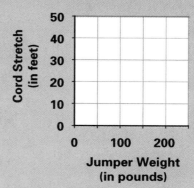

ⓒ How could they find the price to charge for each jump so the park could maximize profit?

ⓓ What other safety and business problems would Five Star have to consider to set up and operate the new bungee attraction safely and profitably?

Investigation 1.1   Modeling a Bungee Apparatus

The distance that a bungee jumper falls before bouncing back upward seems likely to depend on the jumper's weight. In designing the apparatus, it is necessary to know how far the elastic cord will stretch for different weights. It makes sense to do some testing before anyone takes a real jump.

1. a. In your group, make and test a simple model of a *bungee apparatus* using some rubber bands and small weights, such as fishing weights. Loop together several rubber bands of the same size to make an elastic rope and then attach a weight as shown.

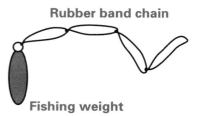

Rubber band chain

Fishing weight

b. Use your model to collect test data for at least five different weights. Record your data in a table like this:

Weight	Amount of Stretch

2. Now study the data from your experiments and write a short summary explaining, as carefully as possible, your answers to these questions:

   a. How does the weight relate to the amount of stretch of the rubber bands?

   b. How does the amount of stretch change as the weight changes?

3. Compare your results to those of other groups who might have used more, fewer, or different rubber bands; different weights; or different methods for collecting the data pairs.

The data from tests of your model bungee apparatus are ordered pairs of numbers in the form (*weight*, *stretch*). Looking for patterns in this kind of data is often easier if the data pairs are presented in a graph like the one shown here.

The sample graph shows specific information (*weight*, *stretch*) and also a pattern in the relation between the two *variables*.

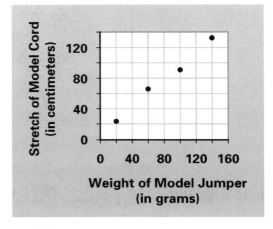

4. Make a coordinate graph of your group's experimental data. An example of such a graph is shown above. Use your graph to answer the following questions.

   a. What does the pattern of points on your graph say about the pattern of change in the amount of stretch as the weight changes?

   b. Is it reasonable to connect the points on your graph and use the resulting graph to predict the amount of stretch for weights other than those you tested? Try it and run some further tests to check your predictions.

   c. How does the pattern of your group's graph compare to those of other groups that might have used different rubber bands, different cord lengths, or different weights?

Checkpoint

ⓐ What are the important variables in the design of a bungee apparatus?

ⓑ When change in one variable is related to change in another variable, the pattern of that relation can be described in *words*, with a *table* of sample data, or with a *graph* of sample data. What are the advantages and disadvantages of describing patterns of change in related variables by each of these methods?

✓ *Be prepared to share your group's thinking with the whole class.*

In mathematical models of situations, the quantities that change are called **variables**. In many cases, we describe the relation between two variables by saying that one variable **is a function of** the other, especially if the value of one variable **depends on** the the value of the other.

On Your Own

Suppose that in designing a bungee jump, Five Star Amusement Park began by considering the weight of a typical customer. Bungee cords of different lengths were tested.

a. Assuming a fixed weight, do you think the amount of stretch in a bungee cord is a function of its length? If so, write an explanation of the change in stretch you would expect as cord length changes.

b. Make a table like the one below for data in the form (*cord length*, *amount of stretch*). Complete the table showing a pattern that you think might occur.

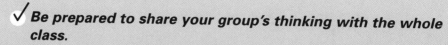

Cord Length (in meters)	5	10	15	20	25	30
Amount of Stretch (in meters)	1					

c. Sketch a graph of the (*cord length*, *amount of stretch*) data showing the pattern of change that you would expect to occur.

d. Describe an experiment, similar to the one in the investigation, to find the likely relation between *cord length* and *amount of stretch* for some fixed amount of weight.

Modeling Organizing Reflecting Extending

Modeling

Each of the following situations gives you some information about variables and relations among those variables. Then you are asked to make tables or graphs of the given information and to answer questions about the relationships. Keep an eye out for interesting patterns in the changes of related variables.

1. Before the amusement park installs the bungee jump apparatus, some business decisions must be made.

   a. Make a list of all the things you can think of that need to be done or decided before a park is ready to open a bungee attraction.

   b. In the list of business decisions for part a, which involve numbers that can be determined? Keep in mind that any good business makes a profit, and the profit is equal to the total money collected minus the expenses. What aspects of the business will be affected by the decisions?

   c. One key decision is the price to charge each jumper. That price will certainly influence the total number of customers each day. Here are some data from a survey of park customers that were used to predict the number of bungee jumpers each day:

Price Charged	$20	$30	$40	$50	$60
Daily Customers	100	70	40	20	10

   – Describe the pattern relating price and predicted number of customers.

   – Make a coordinate graph of the (*price, customers*) data and explain how the pattern of that graph matches the pattern in the number data.

      Remember to plot *price* on the horizontal axis and *customers* on the vertical axis.

   – Predict the number of customers if the price was set at $25, at $45, and at $100. Explain the reasoning that led to your predictions.

   d. The data on possible prices and the number of customers can be used to predict daily income for the bungee jump. If the price is set at $20 and the predicted 100 customers come, what would be the park's daily income from the jump?

      Use the data in part c to make a table of (*price, income*) predictions. A sample table follows.

Price Charged	$20	$30	$40	$50	$60
Daily Income					

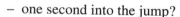

- Make a graph of the (*price, income*) data.
- Write a description of the relation between show price and daily income that is shown by your table and graph.
- What ticket price seems likely to give the greatest daily income?

2. In one test of the bungee apparatus at the amusement park, a radar gun was used to study the drop of a test jump. The radar was connected directly to a computer that produced the graph shown here.

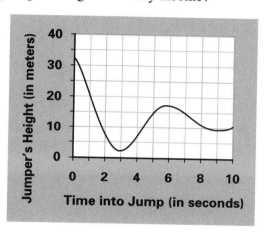

a. What does the pattern of the graph tell you about the jumper's motion?

b. According to the graph, approximately what was the jumper's height above the ground

   - one second into the jump?
   - two seconds into the jump?
   - five seconds into the jump?

c. When did the jumper come closest to the ground and how close was that?

d. How high did the jumper bounce on the first rebound? When did the jumper reach that height?

e. When and at what height was the jumper falling fastest?

f. When and at what height did the cord begin to slow the jumper's rate of fall?

3. The test team using the radar gun took the gun for a ride on the amusement park ferris wheel. They aimed it at the ground during two nonstop trips around on the wheel, giving a graph relating height above the ground to time into the trip. What is the highest the rider will be above the ground?

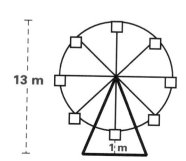

a. On a set of axes like the one at the right, sketch a graph that you believe would fit the pattern relating *height* above the ground to *time* during the ferris wheel ride. The total time for the trip was 100 seconds. Write an explanation of the pattern in your graph. **Hint:** You might experiment with a bicycle wheel as a model of a ferris wheel; as you turn the wheel, how does the height above the ground of the air valve stem change?

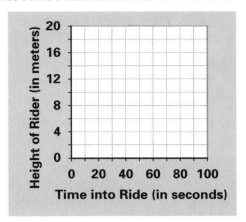

b. Given below is the graph of (*time*, *height*) data for one ferris wheel test ride. Write an explanation of what the graph tells about that test ride.

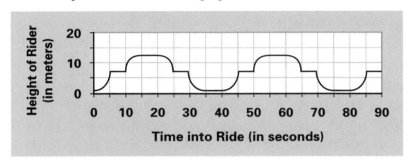

c. Given below are some (*time*, *height*) data for a second ferris wheel test ride. Write a short description of the pattern of this test ride.

Time in Seconds	0	2	5	10	15	20	22.5	25	30	35	40	42.5	45	50	55	60	62.5
Height in Meters	1	1	3	3	11	11	13	11	11	3	3	1	3	3	11	11	13

d. Sketch a graph of the relation shown in the (*time*, *height*) data in part c. Do you think the table or the graph better shows the pattern of change in height as a function of time?

4. When new motion pictures are released, they first appear in theaters all over the country. Then video cassettes are made and sold to video rental companies which rent the movies to people for home viewing. Suppose that a video rental store near you buys 30 copies of a new release and begins renting them.

a. Stores keep records of the number of times that movies rent each week. How do you think the number of rentals per week of a new release will change over time?

b. Make a table of (*week*, *rentals*) data showing what you believe is a reasonable pattern relating *time, in weeks, since the video became available* and *number of rentals of that video per week* for weeks 1 to 20.

c. Sketch a graph of the relation between *time since release* and *number of rentals per week* that matches your data in part b.

5. The Wild World Amusement Park has a huge swimming pool with a wave machine that makes you feel like you are swimming in an ocean. Unfortunately, the pool is uncovered and unheated, so the temperature forecast for a day affects the number of people who come to Wild World. On a typical summer day, when the forecast called for a high temperature of 32°C (or 90°F), about 3,000 people visited the park. On another day, when the forecast called for a high temperature of 20°C (or 68°F), only 250 people came for the ocean-wave swimming.

a. Make a table of (*temperature*, *swimmers*) data that you think shows the most likely pattern relating the two variables.

b. Sketch a graph of the sample data in part a.

c. Describe in words the patterns of your data table and your graph.

Organizing

1. As you worked on the investigations of Chapter 1, "Patterns in Data", you studied many different variables such as stride length, calories in fast foods, and production costs of movies. Examine the following data from a class survey on student time watching television, talking on the telephone, and working on homework.

Student Time in Number of Hours per Week

TV	Phone	Homework	TV	Phone	Homework	TV	Phone	Homework
10	4	10	9	10	16	10	5	9
3.5	13	25	7	8	15	8	8	18
8	4	10.5	12	4.5	8	18	4	6
5	8	15	7	5.5	13	2	10	19
14	1	5	4	9	16	13	4	9
12	4	6	6	6.5	12	1	7	15
21	5	5	10	7.5	14			

a. Prepare a box plot and a five-number summary of the survey data for each of the three variables. Explain what these graphs and statistics tell about the variables.

b. What relation would you expect between number of hours per week spent watching television and number of hours doing homework? Complete the following sentence: *As time watching television increases, time doing homework ...*

c. What relation would you expect between number of hours per week spent talking on the telephone and number of hours doing homework? Complete the following sentence: *As time talking on the telephone increases, time doing homework ...*

d. Sketch graphs showing the patterns you described in answer to parts b and c. Then make scatterplots of the data given in the table and comment on the match between your expected patterns of change and the patterns given by the survey data.

2. In Chapter 1, "Patterns in Data", you saw that changing each value of a data set by adding to it a constant number changed the mean and mean absolute deviation in a predictable way. Suppose a set of test scores has a mean $\bar{x}$.

a. If 10 points are added to each test score, write an expression for the new mean. Describe the new mean absolute deviation.

b. If a number c is added to each test score, write an expression for the new mean. Describe the new mean absolute deviation.

c. Make up a list of 10 test scores and then find the median and interquartile range. Add 5 points to each score and then find the new median and interquartile range.

d. How do the median and interquartile range of a set of data change if a constant number is added to each data point?

3. Shown at the right is a pattern of "growing" squares made from toothpicks.

a. Study the pattern and draw a picture of the next likely shape in the pattern.

b. Make a table similar to the one below. A toothpick is 1 unit long. The small square has 1 square unit of **area**.

Number of Toothpicks on One Side of the Shape	1	2	3	4	5	6
Area of the Shape in Square Units		4				

- Sketch a graph of the relation shown in the (*side length*, *area*) data.
- Describe in words the relation between the area of a shape and the number of toothpicks on a side.

c. Complete a table similar to the one below. Recall that the distance around a shape is called its **perimeter**.

Number of Toothpicks on One Side of the Shape	1	2	3	4	5	6
Perimeter of the Shape in Units	8					

- Sketch a graph of the relation shown in the (*side length*, *perimeter*) data.
- Describe in words the relation between the perimeter of a shape and the number of toothpicks on a side.

d. Describe similarities and differences in the patterns of change in parts b and c.

4. A manatee is a very large sea animal somewhat like a sea lion. The chart below gives the number of manatees killed by motor boats in the Gulf Coast of Florida every year from 1977 through 1990.

Year	Number of Manatees Killed	Year	Number of Manatees Killed	Year	Number of Manatees Killed
1977	13	1982	20	1987	39
1978	21	1983	15	1988	43
1979	24	1984	34	1989	50
1980	16	1985	33	1990	47
1981	24	1986	33		

Source: Moore, David S. *Statistics: Decisions Through Data.* Lexington, MA: CoMAP. 1992.

a. Prepare a plot over time of the number of manatees killed. Describe the pattern you see in the plot.

b. During what one-year period was there the greatest change in number of manatees killed? How can you tell this from looking at the graph? At the data table?

c. Do you think it is the calendar year or some other factor or factors that are causing the pattern of change in manatees killed by motor boats? Explain your reasoning.

Reflecting

1. Do you think that all variables are related to each other? For each of the following pairs of variables, determine whether changes in one variable are related to changes in the other and describe the pattern, if one exists.

   a. the *height* of an adult and the *cost* of a movie ticket

   b. amount of *time* spent on homework and amount of *money* spent on lunch

   c. calendar *date* and number of *daylight hours*

   d. TV *channel* setting and TV *volume* setting

   e. the *pitch* played by plucking a string and the *tension* on that string

2. Weather reports give forecasts of many important variables—temperature, humidity, rainfall, wind-chill, atmospheric pressure, and so on. Explain why it is useful to be able to predict patterns of change in those variables as time passes.

3. Notice some of the variables that are around you every day. Think about how changes in one variable seem to cause changes in others, or how changes in one variable occur as time passes in a day, week, month, or year. For example, as meal time gets closer, most people get more hungry, but after a meal the hunger decreases! Describe two variables that you notice every day that seem related. Explain how changes in one of those variables seem related to changes in the other. Sketch a graph or make up a table of possible values illustrating the pattern you notice.

4. In this investigation you used words, tables, and graphs to describe patterns of change. Do you prefer one of these forms over the others? Why?

Extending

Complex business decisions often involve patterns relating several variables. The following case studies will test your ability to think like a good businessperson.

1. At most amusement parks, the sales of food and drinks bring in a great deal of money to the park operators. A typical park might sell dozens of kinds of snacks, sandwiches, and drinks. Pick just one food item—such as popcorn, hot dogs, ice cream, or soft drinks—and consider the variables that affect *profit* from sales of that item.

   a. List several factors that will affect profit from sales of your food item.

   b. Which of the factors you listed in part a can be quantified or expressed as numerical variables, and which of those numerical variables can be changed by the park management?

c. Pick at least three variables that affect profit from your food item and sketch graphs showing the patterns relating each variable to profit. For example, you might consider the relation between the park's cost of buying hot dogs and the profit from sales of those hot dogs. What pattern would you expect in typical (*cost, profit*) data pairs?

d. Explain in words the pattern of each relation graphed in part c.

e. Make up sample tables of values showing the likely relations between the variables you identified and food sales profit.

f. Given at the right is a graph of (*hot dogs sold, hot dog profit*) data from one amusement park. Find the coordinates of each labeled point on the graph and explain what those coordinates tell about the hot dog business at the park.

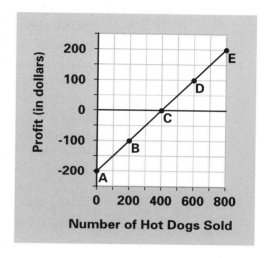

2. Suppose that for a fund-raising event, your school can rent a dunking booth. One of your teachers will sit on a platform. When a student hits a target with a ball, the platform drops the teacher into a large tub of cold water. Complete the following activities to help find the likely income from the booth.

a. Do a survey of your class to find out how many customers you might expect for various possible prices. Complete a table like the one shown here.

Price per Throw (in dollars)	0.50	1.00	1.50	2.00	2.50	3.00	3.50
Number of Customers							

b. Use your class survey to estimate the number of customers from your entire school for various possible prices. Make a table similar to the one in part a.

c. Sketch a graph of the (*price per throw, number of customers*) data. Describe the relation between those two variables. How will the number of customers change if the price is changed?

d. Use your market survey information displayed in the (*price per throw, number of customers*) table to estimate the income that would be earned by the dunking booth for various possible prices. Display that (*price per throw, income*) data in a table and in a graph and describe the pattern relating the two variables.

e. What does your work in part d suggest as the best possible price to charge?

2 *What's Next?*

The United States government—as well as local, state and other national governments around the world—does lots of counting. Government agencies make hundreds of census counts every year. They keep track of jobs and unemployment, automobiles, accidents, animals, illnesses, forests, and farmlands. Every ten years, the U.S. Census Bureau counts every American citizen.

By the mid-1990s, the world's population was estimated to be about 5.6 billion. Some projections estimate it will almost double by 2050.

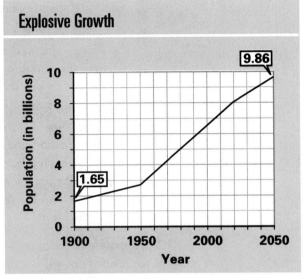

Source: *World Population Prospects*, The 1994 Revision. New York: United Nations, 1995.

Think about this situation

The population of our world changes rapidly—in ten years it is expected to grow by over one billion people.

a What are some of the major factors that might influence population change in a country?

b Why doesn't the U. S. Census Bureau make a complete count of the population every five years or every year?

c Why would it be important to know year-to-year population changes, and how you could estimate those changes without a full census survey?

Investigation 2.1 | People Watching

Brazil is the largest country in South America, with a 1990 population of about 145 million people. Census statisticians can estimate the population of Brazil from one year to the next using small surveys and the following facts about patterns of change.

Population Change in Brazil

– Based on recent trends, births every year equal about 2.6% of the total population.

– Deaths every year equal about 0.7% of the total population.

– The net change due to births and deaths is an increase of 1.9% each year.

Source: *World Population Data Sheet (1992)*, Population Reference Bureau, Washington, D.C., 1992.

Working with your group, use these facts to estimate Brazil's population after 1990.

1. What is the estimated change in Brazil's population by 1991 due to

   a. births?   **b.** deaths?

   c. both causes combined?

2. a. Explain why the net population change due to births and deaths is an increase of about 1.9% each year.

   b. What is the estimated total Brazilian population for 1991?

3. Using your group's estimation for 1991 population as a basis, calculate estimates for the change and total population in 1992; then for 1993, 1994, 1995, and 1996. Record your estimates in a table like that below.

Year	Change (millions)	New Total (millions)
1992		
1993		
1994		
1995		
1996		

The 1990 United States census report said that there were 248 million residents in the fifty states and territories at that time. Before the ink was dry on that report, the actual population had changed. So the Census Bureau makes annual estimates of the change based on current trends.

Population Change in the U.S.

- Births every year will equal about 1.6% of the total population.

- Deaths every year will equal about 0.9% of the total population.

- Immigrants from other countries will add about 0.9 million people each year.

Source: *World Population Data Sheet (1992)*, Population Reference Bureau, Washington, D.C., 1992.

Using the above statistics, work with your group on activities 4 through 7 to estimate the U.S. population after 1990.

4. If the 1990 population was 248 million, what is the estimated change in population by 1991 due to

   a. births and deaths?   **b.** immigration?   **c.** all causes combined?

5. What is the estimated total U.S. population in 1991?

6. Using your estimate for 1991 population as a basis, calculate estimates for the change and total population in 1992; then for 1993, 1994, 1995, and 1996.

7. Describe the pattern of change in the U.S. population estimates as time passes and compare that pattern to the change in Brazil's population estimates.

Checkpoint

In population studies of Brazil and the United States, you made estimates for several years, based on growth trends from the past.

a What calculations are needed to estimate population growth from one year to the next in the two different countries?

b Using the word *NOW* to stand for the population of the United States in any year, write an expression that shows how to calculate the population in the *NEXT* year.

✔ *Be prepared to compare your expression relating NOW and NEXT with those of other groups.*

On Your Own

a. Write an expression using *NOW* and *NEXT* that shows how to use the population of Brazil in one year to calculate the population in the next year.

b. If the birth rate in the United States increased to 2.6%, like Brazil, how would that change the population increase from one year to the next for the U.S.? Estimate the 1991 population using this birth rate.

Investigation 2.2 The Whale Tale

Human beings belong to a class of the animal kingdom called *mammals*. There are hundreds of different kinds of mammals, from tiny mice and flying bats to giant elephants and whales.

Commercial hunting has pushed some large mammals close to extinction. For example, in 1986 the International Whaling Commission declared a ban on commercial whale hunting to protect the small remaining stocks of different types of whales.

Scientists make census counts of whales to see if the numbers are increasing. It's not easy to count whales accurately. A 1991 research report about the bowhead whales of Alaska said that the current population of that stock is somewhere between 5,700 and 10,600. It also said that the difference between births and natural deaths gives an increase of about 3% per year. Alaskan Eskimos are allowed to take or harvest about 50 bowhead whales each year for their livelihood.

Source: Zeh, Judith, et al. 1991. Rate of increase, 1978–88, of bowhead whales, *Balaena Mysticetus*, estimated from ice-based census data. *Marine Mammal Science* 7, no. 2 (April): 105–122.

1. Assume the 1991 bowhead whale population was 5,700.

a. What one-year change in that population would be due to the difference between births and natural deaths?

b. What one-year change in that population would be due to the Alaskan Eskimo hunting?

c. What would you predict for the total 1992 population?

2. Using the word *NOW* to stand for the whale population in one year, write an expression that shows how to calculate the population in the *NEXT* year.

In studies of population increase and decrease, we often want to predict change over many years, not simply from one year to the next. Some calculators and computer software can use the answer to a calculation in the next calculation. This can be very helpful when repeating *NOW* and *NEXT* calculations. With a calculator, this often is done using a last answer function or key. In a spreadsheet, just refer to the cell that holds the calculation for the previous year.

The following calculator procedure produces estimates of the bowhead whale population up to the year 2000. (Some calculators use an EXECUTE key rather than the ENTER key.) A sample response is given, as well. Modify the procedure, if necessary, to work with your technology. The display mode is set so no digits to the right of the decimal point are displayed.

Calculator command	**Sample display**
| 5700 ENTER<br>Answer + . 03 × Answer − 50<br>ENTER | ```
5700
          5700
Ans+.03*Ans-50
          5821
■
``` |
| ENTER<br>ENTER<br>ENTER<br>ENTER<br>ENTER<br>ENTER<br>ENTER | ```
          5946
          6074
          6206
          6342
          6483
          6627
          6776
■
``` |

3. Explain the purpose of each keystroke or command in this procedure.

4. Modify the given steps to find whale population estimates starting from the high figure for 1992 of 10,600. Make a table showing the estimates for the years up to 2000.

5. Test the effects on whale populations of a larger hunt by Alaskan Eskimos. For example, suppose that they harvest 100 whales each year, instead of 50. Compare the results until the year 2000 in this case with those for an Eskimo harvest of 50.

6. How are the calculations for predicting whale populations similar to, and how are they different from, those for predicting human populations of the United States and Brazil?

Checkpoint

In this study of whale populations, you again made estimates for several years, based on growth trends from the past.

a What calculations must you do to estimate the change in number of whales from one year to the next?

b Explain how to use your technology's "last answer" function to calculate the total population in the next year.

c Explain how your calculator or computer software can be used to predict the total population many years ahead.

✓ *Be prepared to share your procedures with the entire class.*

On Your Own

Recall that the Census Bureau estimates U.S. population growth based on birth, death, and immigration data. The 1990 U.S. population was 248 million, with a birth rate of 1.6%, a death rate of 0.9% and about 0.9 million people immigrating to the U.S. each year.

a. Modify this calculator procedure to work with your technology, if necessary. Use your procedure to estimate the population in the year 2000 and the year 2010. Compare the population estimates for the years 1990, 2000, and 2010.

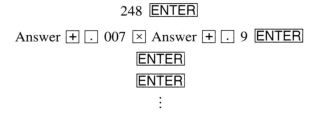

248 ENTER

Answer + . 007 × Answer + . 9 ENTER

ENTER

ENTER

⋮

b. Explain what calculations are being done at each step of the procedure.

c. Suppose the U.S. immigration rate increased to 2 million per year. Calculate the population in the years 2000 and 2010 based on this assumption.

d. How would the U.S. population change if we had 2 million people each year *leave*, rather than enter, the country? Compare the results for the years 2000 and 2010 in this case to those in part c.

Modeling Organizing Reflecting Extending

Modeling

1. Recall that data on population growth showed a U.S. population of 248 million in 1990, a growth rate of 0.7%, and 0.9 million immigrants annually. Use your calculator or computer software and this information to answer the following questions.

   a. When will the population reach 300 million?

   b. When will the population double?

2. The People's Republic of China is the country with the largest population in the world, over 1.1 billion in 1990. Despite efforts to limit families to one child, the population of China was then still growing at a rate of 1.5% per year.

   Source: *World Population Prospects*, 1994.

   a. Predict the population of China for each of the next ten years and record your predictions in a data table.

   b. When will the population of China reach the 2 billion mark?

   c. Using the word *NOW* to stand for the population in any year, write an expression that shows how to calculate the population in the *NEXT* year.

   d. Suppose that China allows 7 million people each year to leave for other countries. How would this affect the growth of the population of China over the next 10 years? (7 million = 0.007 billion)

   e. Using *NOW* to stand for the population in any year, write an expression that shows how to calculate the population in the *NEXT* year, assuming that 7 million Chinese leave annually.

   f. Experiment with different values for the growth rate and the number of people leaving China each year. Search for a balance that will lead to *zero population growth* in China.

3. The country with the second largest population in the world is India, with over 850 million people in 1990. The birth rate in India is about 3% of the total population each year, and the death rate is approximately 1% of the total population each year. About 4.5 million people leave the country each year.

   Source: *World Population Prospects*, 1994.

   a. Estimate the population of India for each of the 10 years from 1990 to 2000. Record your estimates in a table.

   b. When will the estimate of India's population reach 1 billion (1,000 million)?

c. Using *NOW* to stand for the population in any year, write an expression that shows how to calculate the population in the *NEXT* year.

d. What combinations of growth rate and number of people leaving the country could lead to *zero population growth* in India?

4. Suppose that beginning in 1992, the harvesting of bowhead whales was allowed to increase to 200 whales per year.

a. If the 1992 population was 5,700, what effect would that change have on the population over the next ten years? Record your estimates in a data table. What if the 1992 population was actually 10,600?

b. If the 1992 population was actually 8,000, what harvesting number would produce a stable population?

c. Scientists studying whales have also tried to estimate populations in earlier years, before good census data were available. For example, bowhead whale hunting was banned in 1914, because the stock was hunted to such a low figure.

– Assume the 1992 population was 8,000 (midway between low and high estimates); that growth has been 3% for some time; and that Eskimo hunting is so small that it can be ignored. You can estimate the population for earlier years using a procedure similar to the one here.

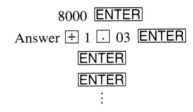

Report estimates for 1982, 1972, 1962, 1952, 1942, 1932, 1922, and 1912.

– Using *NOW* to stand for the whale population in any year and *THEN* for one year earlier, write an expression showing how to calculate *THEN* from *NOW*.

5. If money is invested in a savings account or a business or real estate, its value usually increases by some percentage each year. Suppose that when a child is born into a family the parents set aside $500 in a special savings account that earns 4% interest each year.

a. What will the value of that account be after 1 year? After 2 years? After 5 years? After 18 years when the child is ready to graduate from high school?

b. Using *NOW* to stand for the savings account value at the end of any year, write an expression for calculating the value of the account at the end of the *NEXT* year.

c. Suppose the interest rate is 8% instead of 4%. Calculate the value of the savings account after 1, 2, 5, and 18 years.

 – How do these values differ from those calculated in part a?

 – How would the *NOW-NEXT* expression for calculating the value of the savings account in this situation differ from that in part b?

d. How will your answers to parts a and b change if the account continues to earn 4% interest, but the family deposits an additional $500 each year?

Organizing

1. The studies of populations changing over time can be represented with graphs if you form ordered pairs of (*year, population*) data. Recall that the 1990 population of Brazil was 145 million people and that the growth rate each year is about 1.9%. Use your calculator to plot the (*year, population*) data for each ten-year period from 1990 to 2050.

a. Make a sketch of the plot and write a brief description summarizing the pattern of the plotted data.

Note: Sketches for parts b and c should be made on the same set of axes.

b. Sketch the pattern of (*year, population*) data you would expect in Brazil if the birth rates increased.

c. Sketch the pattern of (*year, population*) data you would expect in Brazil if the birth and death rates were equal.

d. Explain how the pattern of points on each graph shows the *NOW* to *NEXT* change in the population.

2. Calculate how a $500 bank balance would change over ten years with 4% annual interest and no withdrawals. Record your results in a data table, and then use your calculator to plot the (*year, bank balance*) data.

a. Make a sketch of the plot and write a brief description of the pattern in the plotted data.

Note: Sketches for parts b, c, and d should be made on the same set of axes.

b. Sketch the pattern of (*year, bank balance*) data you would expect if the interest rate was reduced to 3%.

c. Sketch the pattern of (*year, bank balance*) data you would expect if the interest rate was doubled to 8%.

d. Sketch the pattern of (*year, bank balance*) data you would expect if withdrawals exactly equaled interest earned each year.

e. Explain how the pattern of points on each graph shows the *NOW* to *NEXT* change in each bank account.

3. Explain what the calculator procedure here does. Predict what the result will be if this procedure is used with starting numbers different from 10. Check your ideas by modifying the procedure, if necessary, and then executing the procedure.

10 [ENTER]
Answer [+] 2 [×] Answer [−] 3 [ENTER]
[ENTER]
[ENTER]

4. **a.** Investigate the following two expressions relating *NOW* and *NEXT* using your calculator or computer. Try several different possible choices for starting values. Use the same starting values with each expression.

$$NEXT = NOW + 0.05 \times NOW \qquad NEXT = 1.05 \times NOW$$

b. What appears to be true about these two expressions? Write an explanation for your findings.

Reflecting

1. The models of population change studied in this lesson are somewhat different from those involved in the bungee modeling investigation. Look back over the examples of the investigations in this lesson and see if you can figure out the meaning of the lesson title "What's Next?" What do the prediction models have in common that involve the word *NEXT*? How does the word *NOW* get involved in describing these situations?

2. Compare the use of a "last answer" function on your calculator or computer to the equation relating *NOW* and *NEXT* for calculating the total population at a particular point in time.

3. In the population model of this lesson, you made estimations based on given assumptions about how the populations would change. Do you know anything about differences between Brazil and the United States that would help explain the differences in assumptions?

4. Invent a situation that could be modeled as follows.

Starting value = 7,000

$$NEXT = NOW - 0.12 \times NOW + 600$$

Extending

1. The kinds of models of change used in studying populations are sometimes quite different from the ones you have investigated so far. For example, many psychologists study the way people learn and remember information. Suppose that when school closes in June you know the meaning of 500 Spanish words, but you don't study or speak Spanish during the summer vacation.

a. One model of memory suggests that during each week of the summer you will forget 5% of the words you know at the beginning of that week. Make a table showing the (*weeks, words remembered*) data pairs for 10 weeks and describe the pattern of data in the table.

b. A second model suggests that you will forget 20 words each week. Make a table showing the (*weeks, words remembered*) data pairs for 10 weeks following this model and describe the pattern of data in that table.

c. Graph the data from the two models and describe the patterns of data in those graphs.

d. How would answers to parts a through c be different if you knew only 300 words at the start of summer?

e. Which model do you think best represents memory loss? Explain your reasoning.

f. Suppose 10 weeks of summer are gone and you decide to do an intensive vocabulary review for the remaining 2 weeks before school starts. If you are able to regain 20% of your vocabulary each week, how many words will you know when school begins? Which model of memory loss did you assume for the first 10 weeks?

2. The International Whaling Commission considers three factors in its population estimates that influence hunting policy: current population, percent increase by natural means, and number of kills from hunting allowed.

a. Experiment with the numbers for bowhead whales in Alaska. Try different population estimates, and then for each estimate, choose different growth rates and different numbers of hunting kills to see the long-run effects on the whale population. In a table, record your choices for the three factors and the corresponding population changes over time. What different results can you get over a period of 20 years?

b. What different graph patterns can occur in the various cases?

3. Study the calculator procedure in task 4.c of the Modeling section. Explain why the division operation (÷ key) is the proper choice for estimating populations in previous years.

3 *Variables and Rules*

Important problems often involve variables that are related by regular patterns. Those patterns make it easy to calculate the value of one variable, if the values of others are known. For example, many American teenagers have part-time jobs after school, on weekends, and in the summer. A first job might pay only the minimum wage. Even at

that rate, however, the money you earn can add up, if you are a good saver. Suppose the minimum wage is $4.25 per hour. Here is a table showing some (*time worked, money earned*) data.

Time Worked (in hours)	0	1	2	3	4	5	10	15
Money Earned (in dollars)	0	4.25	8.50	12.75	17.00	21.25	42.50	63.75

Think about this situation

The table shows money earned for a sample of hours worked. But the payroll computer for a company with many workers will have to be able to calculate pay for any number of hours.

a In this case, pay increases by $4.25 from one hour to the next. Using the words *NOW* and *NEXT*, how could you write that rule with an equation that begins *NEXT* = _____ ?

b Using the letters *H* (for number of hours worked) and *E* (for number of dollars earned) how could you write a rule that gives earnings for *any* number of hours worked with an equation that begins *E* = _____ ?

c How could you calculate the money earned for any number of hours worked such as 23 or 42 and for fractions of hours, such as 8.25 hours or 12.5 hours?

d Why might rules like those called for in parts a or b be more useful than tables or graphs of the (*time worked, pay earned*) data?

Investigation 3.1 Money Matters

Earning and spending money is an important part of daily life for most Americans. We spend a lot of time thinking about ways to earn, to save, or to shop. Unfortunately, that quite often means figuring out how to pay off bills or loans.

Installment Buying Typical American shoppers borrow money for large purchases like houses, cars, furniture, or stereo systems. Suppose your family finds a special deal for a new $1,250 home entertainment system: no interest will be charged, and the family can pay the loan back at the rate of $120 per month.

1. a. Make a table showing the relation between *number of payments* and *unpaid balance*.

Number of Payments	0	1	2	3	...	8	9	10
Unpaid Balance (in $)					...			

b. Make a plot of (*number of payments*, *unpaid balance*) data pairs. Then, in your group, discuss how the pattern in the graph matches the pattern in the data table.

2. Suppose that another store offers a different deal: A price of only $1,100 with payments of $130 per month.

a. What will the unpaid balance be after 3 payments?

b. How many payments will be required to reduce the unpaid balance to $450?

3. For the two payment plans offered in this situation, write rules showing how the unpaid balance changes from one month to the next, using the words *NOW* and *NEXT* in equations that begin *NEXT* = _____.

4. a. Complete the following sentence to give rules relating the number of payments and unpaid balance variables in the two payment plans:

To calculate the unpaid balance after any given number of payments, you...

b. Use the letters *N* for *the number of payments made* and *U* for *the number of dollars unpaid* to write rules, for both payment plans, that give the unpaid balance after any number of payments. For each plan, use an equation that begins *U* = _____.

Profits and Losses Typical businesses watch patterns of change in their costs, income, and profit from operations. For example, the Palace Theater charges a single low price of $2.50 for all shows all day. The income from ticket sales depends on the number of tickets sold.

5. a. Make a table of (*number of tickets sold, income in dollars*) data like the one below.

Number of Tickets Sold	Income in Dollars
0	
50	
100	
150	
200	
250	
300	

b. Plot these data on a graph and explain what the pattern of the plotted points tells you about the way that income changes as ticket sales increase.

c. Use the letter T to stand for the variable *number of tickets sold* and the letter I to stand for the variable *daily income in dollars*. Write a rule for calculating income from ticket sales with an equation that begins $I =$ _____.

6. a. Ignoring costs for operating the concessions stand, the operating expenses for the Palace Theater average $450 per day. Assume there are no other expenses nor sources of income. How could you determine the theater's daily profit? Use this relation to make a table of (*number of tickets sold, profit in dollars*) data like the one below.

Number of Tickets Sold	Profit in Dollars
0	
50	
100	
150	
200	
250	
300	

b. Plot these data on a graph. Explain what the pattern of the plotted points tells you about the way that profit changes as ticket sales increase.

c. Have each group member write a question about Palace Theater ticket sales and profit that can be answered using information from the data table or the graph. Share your questions with each other. Decide on the answers and discuss how the answers are revealed by the table or the graph.

d. Let *P* represent *daily profit in dollars* and *T* represent the *number of tickets sold*. Write a rule for finding profit as a function of tickets sold with an equation that begins $P =$ _____ .

7. a. Suppose the theater offers a discount ticket of $2.00 for children and senior citizens. Calculate income for these combinations of ticket sales:

Regular Tickets	Discount Tickets	Income in Dollars
100	100	
200	100	
100	200	
150	250	
250	150	

b. Use the letters *R* for the *number of regular tickets* and *D* for the *number of discount tickets*. Write a rule for calculating income *I* from ticket sales as an equation that begins $I =$ _____ .

8. a. Calculate profit for these combinations of ticket sales:

Regular Tickets	Discount Tickets	Profit
100	100	
200	100	
100	200	
150	250	
250	150	

b. Write a rule for calculating *profit* from ticket sales as a function of the *numbers of discount and regular tickets* sold: $P =$ _____ .

Checkpoint

The earnings, installment buying, and Palace Theater situations all involved variables that changed in relation to each other.

ⓐ Describe the variables involved and the patterns of change in each case.

ⓑ Explain how the patterns are similar and how they are different.

ⓒ How are the graphs similar and how are they different?

ⓓ Write at least two rules that you determined in this investigation. What is the relationship between patterns and rules?

✓ *Be prepared to share your group's descriptions and observations with the class.*

On Your Own

Rules relating variables occur in many situations. For example, here are some data about the costs of food items at a fast food restaurant.

Soft Drink	Fries	Burger	Sundae
$0.79	$0.89	$1.79	$1.25

a. What is the bill (before tax) for an order for 15 members of a school team, if each orders a soft drink, fries, burger, and sundae?

b. Write in words a rule for calculating the total cost of meals for *any number of students*, if each student gets one soft drink, one order of fries, one burger, and one sundae.

c. Use letters to write a rule that gives the total cost for any number of students if each student gets one of each item.

d. Use the words *NOW* and *NEXT* to write a rule showing how the cost changes for each additional student with an equation that begins: *NEXT* = _____.

e. Make a table and a graph of (*number of students*, *total cost*) data for any number of students from 0 to 10.

f. Write one question that can be answered by the data in your table or graph. Answer the question and explain how the table or graph provided the answer.

Investigation 3.2 Quick Tables and Graphs

Often the first step in modeling a situation is to discover patterns and then write relations among the key variables using symbolic rules. Once this is done, you can study the situation further by using your graphing calculator or computer software to calculate values, make tables, and display graphs of relationships between the variables.

Making Tables Recall that the Palace Theater took in $2.50 for each ticket sold and had daily expenses of $450 (ignoring concessions). Below are two tables of sample (*number of tickets sold, profit*) data.

Table 1		Table 2	
Number of Tickets Sold (*T*)	**Profit in Dollars (*P*)**	**Number of Tickets Sold (*T*)**	**Profit in Dollars (*P*)**
0	-450.00	0	-450.00
1	-447.50	20	-400.00
2	-445.00	40	-350.00
3	-442.50	60	-300.00
4	-440.00	80	-250.00
5	-437.50	100	-200.00
6	-435.00	120	-150.00
7	-432.50	140	-100.00
8	-430.00	160	-50.00
9	-427.50	180	0.00
10	-425.00	200	50.00

You can use computer software or a graphing calculator to produce tables like these quickly. Producing a table generally requires the following three steps.

Enter the rule.	The function rule usually must be entered in a "Y =" form. For the rule $P = 2.50T - 450$, which gives profit P as a function of the number of tickets sold T, replace T (the input variable) with X and replace P (the output variable) with Y. This gives $Y = 2.50X - 450$.
Set up the table.	Specify the beginning or minimum value for the input or *independent* variable X. Also specify the size of each step by which the variable changes. Some technological tools allow you to specify the ending or maximum value as well.
Display the table.	With most tools, displaying the table is just a matter of pressing one or two keys or giving a single command.

Examples of the screens involved are shown here. Your calculator or software may look different.

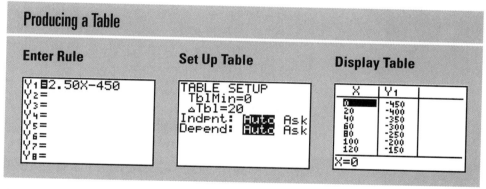

1. **a.** What is the minimum value of X for Table 1 on the previous page? For Table 2?

   b. What is the step size for Table 1? For Table 2?

   c. Produce each of these tables on your calculator or computer. The "Technology Tip" handout may be useful.

2. **a.** Use a table to find each of the following:

   – The profit if 280 tickets are sold.

   – The number of tickets that must be sold for the theater to break even.

   – The number of tickets that must be sold to make a profit of $800.

   b. How would you set up a technology-produced table to find quickly the profit if 317 tickets are sold?

3. A second way of building a table is to compare *NOW* and *NEXT* values of the output variable. In Table 1, notice that if $T = 0$ the profit in dollars is -450 (a loss). Then for each ticket sold, the profit increases by $2.50.

   a. Use the words *NOW* and *NEXT* to write a rule describing this pattern of change.

   b. Use the "last answer" function on your calculator or computer software to build a table of profit values as in Table 1. In a data table, record each profit value and the corresponding number of tickets sold.

   c. Use the method in parts a and b to build a table of profit values as in Table 2.

4. Use the table-making capabilities of your calculator or computer software to investigate the effect of changes in ticket price and operating costs at the Palace Theater.

   a. Suppose that the theater raises its price to $3.00 and cuts its operating costs to $425 per day. Write a rule giving daily profit as a function of the number of tickets sold.

   b. In your group, discuss two ways in which you can produce a table of (*number of tickets sold, profit*) data for ticket sales from 0 to 300 in steps of 25 tickets. Have each member produce the table using the method of his or her choice. Compare results.

   c. Have each group member write two questions about the relation between ticket sales and theater profit that can be answered from her or his table. Then share the questions with the group and explain how the table can be used to get the answers.

   d. Individually, make another table that would help you to answer the following questions. Compare your tables and responses with those of other group members.

   – How does profit change when ticket sales increase in steps of 15?

   – What is the theater's profit if a blockbuster movie is shown and 600 tickets are sold?

   e. What is the fewest number of tickets that can be sold in a day and still make a profit?

Making Graphs You already have used your calculator or computer software to make graphs of data and relations between data. The following graph is a plot of several of the pairs (T, P) from Table 2, entered as data points and graphed as a scatterplot.

5. Carefully compare Table 2 (reproduced below) and the scatterplot.

Table 2

Number of Tickets Sold (*T*)	Profit in Dollars (*P*)	
0	-450.00	
20	-400.00	
40	-350.00	
60	-300.00	
80	-250.00	
100	-200.00	
120	-150.00	
140	-100.00	
160	-50.00	
180	0.00	
200	50.00	

a. What do you think the minimum and maximum values are for the viewing window (Xmin, Xmax, Ymin, and Ymax)? What do you think the scales are on the *x*- and *y*-axes? Explain your answers.

b. Check your answer by producing the scatterplot using your calculator or computer software. Adjust your answer to part a if needed.

The graph shown here was made on a graphing calculator by entering the rule relating profit and ticket sales ($y = 2.50x - 450$). The viewing window is the same as the one in activity 5. You can use a trace feature to read coordinates of any point on the graph. (Be sure any plots are turned off.)

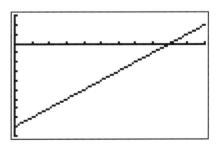

6. a. Using your calculator or computer software, produce the graph shown above. Trace along the graph and compare coordinate readouts with the data given in Table 2. Do the coordinate values look the same?

b. Re-plot the graph of this profit function using a viewing window with x values ranging from 12 to 200 with a scale of 20 and y values ranging from -475 to 60 with a scale of 50. Now trace along this new graph.

– Do the coordinate values look the same as the data given in Table 2?

– What is the change in x-coordinates from one point to the next as you trace along the graph this time?

– What is the change in y-coordinates from one point to the next as you trace along the graph?

c. Compare the graph of the original rule relating profit to number of tickets sold ($y = 2.50x - 450$) to the graph of the rule you developed in activity 4.

– Compare the break-even points of the two ticket-pricing/operating-cost plans.

– Which plan gives a better profit? How is this seen in the graphs?

7. Computer—or calculator—produced graphs of function rules often provide more information than is necessary for a problem situation. Some graphing software allows you to link graphs to tables of values. Use software with this capability to produce the graph shown in activity 5. (The calculator program AATBLPLT was written for this purpose.) Trace along the graph and compare coordinate readouts with the data given in Table 2.

The basic steps in producing a graph of a function rule follow.

– Enter the rule.

– Set the viewing window.

– Display the graph.

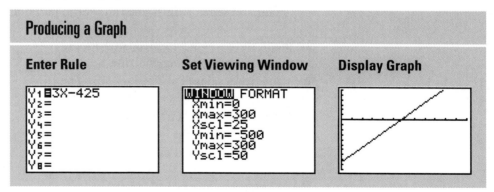

Producing a Graph

| Enter Rule | Set Viewing Window | Display Graph |

You may have to re-set the viewing window several times before getting a view of the graph that is most useful for the situation you are studying. Producing a quick table of sample data often helps.

Experiment with the graphing capabilities of your calculator or computer software, as you solve the following problem.

8. **a.** Suppose you make a deal with your parents. They buy you a $125 stereo CD-player and you promise to repay $3.50 per week. What is the rule giving what you still owe as a function of time since repayment began?

b. Use your calculator or computer software to make a graph of the rule in part a. Sketch the graph on grid paper. Then label points whose coordinates answer the questions below. Be sure your responses make sense.

– How much will you owe after 10 weeks?

– When will you owe only $55?

– When will your loan be paid in full?

c. Explain how you could produce and use a table to answer the questions in part b.

Checkpoint

Suppose a cross-country bus travels at an average speed of 50 miles per hour.

a Describe two ways to use a calculator or computer to produce a table of values showing how far that bus travels as a function of time during the trip. What are the advantages or disadvantages of each method?

b Describe two ways to use a calculator or computer to graph the relation between time and distance. What are the advantages or disadvantages of each method?

c Write and answer three different questions that can be answered using the table or the graph.

✓ *Be prepared to share your questions and methods with the class.*

On Your Own

The *Concorde* is a type of supersonic airliner that is used to carry passengers from London and Paris to distant locations around the world. It cruises at about 2,200 kilometers per hour.

a. Write a rule giving the *distance* the *Concorde* travels as a function of *flight time*.

b. Make a table of (*flight time*, *distance*) values for a trip of 8 hours and a graph showing the same data. Then use the table and graph to answer the following questions:

  – How far will the Concorde travel in 5 hours?

  – How long will it take the Concorde to make the 5,780 kilometer trip from Paris to New York?

c. What patterns do you see in the table and graph that describe the way the distance traveled changes as time passes?

Modeling Organizing Reflecting Extending

Modeling

1. The freshman class officers at Banneker High School ordered 1,200 candy bars. They paid $0.25 per bar at the time the order was placed. They plan to sell the candy bars at school football and basketball games for $0.60 per bar. No returns of unsold candy bars are possible.

a. How much money has the class already invested in this project?

b. What income will be earned if the class sells 100 bars? 400 bars?

c. What profit will be earned if the class sells 100 bars? 400 bars? 800 bars? All 1,200 bars?

d. Write two rules for calculating profit as a function of the number of candy bars sold.

  – In the first rule, use the words *NOW* and *NEXT* to show how profit changes for each additional candy bar sold.

  – In the second, use variable names *P* and *B* to show how to calculate profit for any given number of candy bars sold.

e. Use one of the rules you have written to produce a table of (*number sold, profit*) data from 0 to 1,200 bars in steps of 100 bars sold.

f. Produce a graph of the relation between *number sold* and *profit* earned.

g. Find the break-even point in sales—the number that must be sold to be sure that the class does not lose money. Show where that point appears in the table of data and on the graph.

h. Describe the overall relation of candy bar sales to class profits and explain how that pattern is shown in the table and the graph.

2. Summer thunder-and-lightning storms occur in most parts of the United States. It is very dangerous to get caught out in the open when lightning hits.

You can estimate your distance from a storm center. Count the time in seconds between a lightning flash and the clap of thunder produced by that lightning. You see the lightning flash almost instantly, but the thunder moves at the speed of sound (about 330 meters per second).

a. How far away is a lightning strike if the thunder it produced arrives

– 2 seconds after you see the lightning?

– 3 seconds after the lightning flash?

– 4.5 seconds after the lightning flash?

b. Write two rules for calculating distance of a lightning flash from you and the time it takes the sound of that flash (thunder) to reach your ears.

– In the first rule, use the words *NOW* and *NEXT* to show the change in the distance estimate for each additional second of time counted.

– In the second rule, use the variable names *T* and *D* to show how to find the distance for any given time counted.

c. Make a table of (*time*, *distance*) data and a graph for times from 0 to 10 seconds.

d. Complete each of the following sentences to describe the relation between the distance of a lightning strike from you and the time it takes the thunder of that strike to reach your ears.

– As the time increases, the distance ... .

– As the distance increases, the time ... .

e. Use your rule, table, and graph to estimate the time required for thunder to reach your ears from a lightning strike 2,500 meters away.

3. Janitorial assistants at Woodward Mall start out earning $4.50 per hour and are paid weekly. However, the $45 cost of uniforms is deducted from their first paycheck.

a. What pay would a new employee receive if she worked 5 hours in her first week? If she worked 10 hours? If she worked 20 hours?

b. Write two rules for calculating first-week's pay as a function of time worked.

- In the first rule, use the words *NOW* and *NEXT* to show the change in pay for each hour of work.

- In the second rule, use variable names *P* and *T* to show how to find the pay for any given time worked.

c. Produce tables and graphs of the relation between hours worked and pay showing the relation for 0 to 40 hours of work.

d. Write two questions about the relation between time worked and pay earned. Show how those questions can be answered with data in the table and on the graph of part c.

e. Assuming the employee worked more than 10 hours the first week, how would you change your rules in part b to calculate weekly pay after the first week?

4. Commercial jet airliners can fly at an average speed of 15 kilometers per minute. Thus the distance they travel is a function of flight time.

a. Choose letters to stand for the variables *time* in flight and *distance* covered and then write a rule for calculating distance as a function of time.

b. Write two questions about the relation between time in flight and distance covered that would be of interest to an airline or a private pilot. Then show how the answers to those questions can be found in tables of (*time*, *distance*) data and on a graph of the relation between time and distance.

c. Suppose that the speed of the airliner is increased by a strong tailwind of 2 kilometers per minute. Write a rule for calculating distance as a function of time under this condition. Write a different rule for the case when the airliner is traveling against a 2 kilometer per minute headwind.

d. The trip from New York to San Francisco is about 5,000 kilometers. Write an equation for a rule that will calculate *distance remaining to be covered* as a function of *elapsed flight time* at a speed of 15 kilometers per minute.

e. Write two questions about the relation between time in flight and distance remaining in the trip to San Francisco. Then show how the answers to those questions can be found in tables of (*time*, *distance*) data and on a graph of the relation between time and distance.

5. NASA space shuttles travel about 30,000 kilometers per hour.

a. Write two rules for calculating distance traveled as a function of time in flight.

- In the first rule, use the words *NOW* and *NEXT* to show the change in distance for each hour of flight.

- In the second rule, use variable names *T* and *D* to show how to find the distance for any given time in flight.

b. Produce tables and graphs of the relation between time in flight and distance, showing the relation for 0 to 20 hours of flight time.

c. Write two questions about the relation between time in flight and distance traveled. Show how those questions can be answered with data in the table and on the graph of part b.

d. In July, 1969, the Apollo 11 mission put a man on the moon, almost 400,000 km from the Earth. (The path taken from launch to lunar orbit was not a straight line, but we will assume the Apollo 11 traveled 400,000 km.) The speed of the vehicle varied widely, moving as fast as 39,000 km per hour. However, the average speed was only 5500 km per hour. Use the average speed to write a rule estimating *distance still to be traveled* as a function of time in flight.

e. Produce a table and a graph of the relation in part d and write two questions that can be answered from information in the table and graph.

f. Compare the patterns in the relations between time and distance traveled and time and distance still to be traveled.

Organizing

1. *Formulas* are equations which relate two or more variables according to rules. For example, you are probably familiar with formulas for area and perimeter of geometric figures. The size and shape of any rectangle can be described by two variables: *length* and *width*.

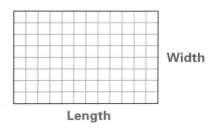

a. If the small squares in the rectangle above each represents one square meter, what are the area and perimeter of the rectangle represented by the figure?

b. Using single letter variable names, write rules for calculating the area and perimeter for any rectangle.

c. Suppose the rectangle models a grid of solar power cells, each of which produces 0.03 watts of power.

– How much power is produced by the entire grid of power cells?

– Using single letter variable names, write a rule for calculating the power produced by a rectangular solar grid of any size given in terms of the *length* and *width* in meters.

d. The area of any triangle can be calculated from the formula $A = \frac{1}{2}bh$, where *b* and *h* stand for *base* and *height* of the triangle.

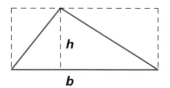

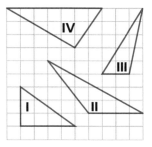

- Use the first diagram above to explain how the formula for area of a triangle is related to the one for a rectangle.

- Use the formula for the area of a triangle to find areas of the triangles at the right.

2. The diagram at the right shows a circle with one *radius* and one *diameter* drawn.

The circumference *C* and area *A* of a circle with diameter *d* and radius *r* are given by the formulas:

$$C = \pi d \qquad\qquad A = \pi r^2$$

a. Access the number π on your calculator or computer software. What number is given as the value of π?

b. Calculate the circumference of a circle with diameter 3 meters.

c. Calculate the area of a circle with radius 1.5 meters.

d. Tony's Pizza Place is advertising 2-item, 10-inch pizzas for $7.95 and 2-item, 12-inch pizzas for $9.95. Which pizza is the best buy? Explain your reasoning.

e. Write formulas giving rules for finding:

- the circumference of a circle of any given *radius*;

- the area of a circle of any given *diameter*.

3. When an object is dropped, the distance it falls is related to the time it has been falling by $d = 4.9t^2$, where *t* is time in seconds and *d* is distance in meters. Suppose a ball falls 250 meters down a mine shaft.

a. Use the table-building caability of your calculator or computer software to find, to the nearest second, how long it takes to fall this distance.

b. Find, to the nearest 0.01 second, the time the ball must have been falling.

c. Produce a graph showing distance as a function of time. Answer part b by using the trace feature and adjusting the viewing window.

d. How are the procedures you used in parts b and c similar?

4. The graph at the right shows the pattern of growth in the fish population of a lake that has been damaged by acid rain and then cleaned up and restocked with fish. Write three different questions that can be answered from the graph and explain how the answers can be found.

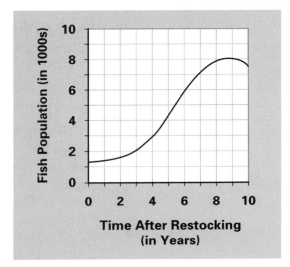

5. Write rules relating X and Y in each of the following tables of numbers.

a.

X	Y
1	2
2	4
3	6
4	8
5	10

$Y =$ _____

b.

X	Y
1	1
2	3
3	5
4	7
5	9

$Y =$ _____

c.

X	Y
1	7
2	14
3	21
4	28
5	35

$Y =$ _____

d.

X	Y
1	6
2	11
3	16
4	21
5	26

$Y =$ _____

e.

X	Y
1	2
2	5
3	10
4	17
5	26

$Y =$ _____

f.

X	Y
1	98
2	96
3	94
4	92
5	90

$Y =$ _____

Reflecting

1. When using a graphing calculator or computer software to make tables and graphs, you have to learn the special language of the tool you have. There are usually some problems in the first few attempts.

    a. What problems did you have in building tables with your calculator or computer software? How did you solve those problems?

    b. What problems did you have in making calculator or computer graphs? How did you solve those problems?

2. The relation between price P of an item in a store and the total cost C, including 5% sale tax, is given by $C = P + .05P$. Use your graphing calculator or computer software to produce a graph of the equation. Use a standard viewing window: Xmin = -10, Xmax = 10, Xscl = 1, Ymin = -10, Ymax = 10, and Yscl = 1. This ensures that you will be viewing the same screen as your classmates. Using the trace feature gives you coordinates of any point on the graph, but some of those points don't make sense! Think about the situation being modeled by the equation and graph and explain why the points don't make sense.

3. Organize your class to do a survey of teachers in all the subjects, except mathematics, taught in your school to get examples of formulas used in their fields. Science you might expect to be easy, but you should also be able to get some examples from business, art, social studies, and English.

4. Organize your class to do a survey of parents and friends who work outside of schools to get examples of formulas used in various occupations. You should be able to get examples from construction, banking, auto mechanics, and many more occupations.

Extending

1. One car rental company charges $25 per day, gives 100 free miles, and then charges 35 cents for any miles beyond the first 100.

    a. What will this company charge if the car is kept for one day and driven 130 miles?

    b. Use single-letter names for variables to write a rule for calculating rental charge as a function of the number of miles driven, if the car is kept only one day.

    c. Use single-letter names for variables to write a rule for calculating the rental charge as a function of the number of miles driven *and* the number of days.

2. At the start of a match race for two late-model stock cars, one car stalls and has to be towed to the pits for repairs. The other car roars off at an average speed of 2.5 miles per minute. After 5 minutes of repair work, the stalled car hits the track and races ahead at an average speed of 2.8 miles per minute.

   a. How far apart are the two cars 5 minutes after the start of the race? How far apart are they 10 minutes after the start of the race?

   b. Use single-letter variable names to write a rule for calculating the distance between the two cars at any time after the start of the race.

   c. On the same set of axes, sketch or produce two graphs showing the distances traveled by the two cars as time passes in the race. Discuss the patterns in the two graphs in terms of the race.

3. The price or *fare* of taxi-cab rides in many large cities is a function of the distance traveled. For example, one rule is based on distances rounded up to the nearest fifth of a mile, as follows.

   Charge 90 cents for the first one-fifth mile and 20 cents for each additional one-fifth mile or part thereof.

   a. Make a table of (*distance*, *fare*) data for 0 to 2 miles in steps of one-fifth mile.

   b. Sketch a graph of the relation between *distance* and *fare*.

   c. How far can you travel on $10 for cab fare? Explain how you found your answer.

   d. Which is the better deal for a rider, the rate rule above or a rule that charges only 30 cents for each one-fifth of a mile (including the first)? Explain your reasoning.

4. Video cassette rental stores use a variety of rules for setting the prices of their rentals. For example, one chain charges a $3.50 minimum per tape for the first two days and $1.25 for each additional day.

   a. Make a table of charges to rent a tape from 0 through 14 days.

   b. Sketch a graph showing the pattern of the (*rental days*, *rental charge*) data in part a.

   c. Compare the rental plan given above with another that simply charges $1.50 per tape per day. Which plan would you prefer and under what conditions?

5. Below is a calculator graph of the equation $y = x^2 - 4x$ for $x = -3$ to $x = 7$. Reproduce this view on your calculator or computer software.

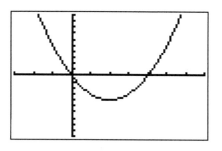

   a. Use the zoom feature to take a closer look at where the graph crosses the x-axis between $x = 3$ and $x = 5$. Make sketches and describe any patterns you see.

   b. Return to the original graph and zoom in to take a closer look at the graph at its lowest point. Make sketches and describe any patterns you see.

   c. How can you zoom in on tables of values to check the patterns you observed in parts a and b?

4 *Linear and Nonlinear Patterns*

In nearly every situation you investigated in Lesson 3, the relations between variables were fairly easy to describe with rules. The patterns in tables most often showed constant rates of change, and graphs of those data usually gave linear patterns. The table-building and graphing capabilities of calculators and computer software make it easy to study nonlinear patterns too. Consider the following situation in preparation for Investigation 4.1.

For earth-bound humans there is something especially fascinating about things that fly through the air. You follow the flight of balls in all kinds of sports, perhaps curious about how high they go or when and where they will come down. In some sports the speed at which a ball travels is also of interest. For example, baseball teams use radar guns to "clock" the speed of a pitch or the path of a long hit.

Think about this situation

Suppose you threw a ball straight up into the air at a velocity of 25 meters per second. (Major league pitches are approximately 95 miles per hour, which is about 42.5 meters per second.)

a About how high do you think the ball would go before it starts falling back to the ground?

b About how many seconds do you think it would take before the ball hits the ground?

c Which of the following graphs do you think best matches the pattern of (*time, height*) data describing the ball's flight? Explain your choice.

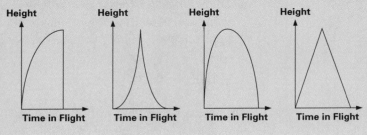

Investigation (4.1) What Goes Up ... Must Come Down

To study the flight of a baseball thrown straight up into the air, all you need to know is the velocity with which the ball leaves the hand of the thrower. Using principles of physics, you can predict the upward velocity of the ball as a function of time in flight with the following rule.

$$V = 25 - 9.8T$$

In this rule, the letter V stands for the upward velocity of the ball (in meters per second) at any time, and T stands for time since the ball was thrown (in seconds).

Use the rule relating *velocity of the ball* and *time in flight* to study the pattern of (*time, velocity*) data that could be expected. If you enter the velocity rule into your graphing calculator or computer software, the calculations will be much easier!

1. **a.** Make a table of (*time, velocity*) data for $T = 0$ to $T = 6$ in steps of 0.5 seconds.
   - What is the upward velocity of the ball 0.5 seconds after it is thrown?
   - At what time will the velocity be about 10 meters per second? About 5 meters per second?
   - What does the pair (3, -4.4) mean?
   - Describe the pattern of change in velocity for every 0.5 seconds the ball is in flight.

   b. Produce a graph of the pattern of (*time, velocity*) data obtained in part a. Use the table to help you choose an appropriate viewing window.

   c. Write an explanation of what the table and graph say about the pattern of the ball's velocity. Be sure to explain any points or trends in the graph that are surprising or important.

2. Looking at the rule $V = 25 - 9.8T$, can you see how the numbers and operations in the rule relate to flight of the ball? For example, does the 25 look familiar? What is the effect of the "$- 9.8T$" part of the rule?

3. Use your calculator table or graph tools to **solve these equations**. That is, find values for T and V that will make the statements true. Explain what the solutions tell about flight of the ball. Find times to the nearest 0.1 seconds.

   a. $10 = 25 - 9.8T$ **c.** $V = 25 - (9.8 \times 2)$

   b. $0 = 25 - 9.8T$ **d.** $-5 = 25 - 9.8T$

The rule relating time in flight and upward velocity of the baseball gives some information about the path of the ball, but it also leaves some interesting questions unanswered. More can be learned from a second rule that estimates the height of the ball H in meters as a function of its time in flight. Again, scientific principles suggest that this relation will be given by the following rule.

$$H = 1 + 25T - 4.9T^2$$

4. Make a table of (*time*, *height*) data for $T = 0$ to $T = 6$ seconds in steps of 0.5 seconds. Remember to use your table to help set your viewing window. Then plot a graph of the same data. Adjust your table or graph as necessary to estimate:

   a. The height of the ball after 3 seconds. After 5 seconds.

   b. The time or times, to the nearest 0.1 seconds, when the ball is 20 meters above the ground.

   c. The maximum height of the ball and the time when the ball reaches that height.

   d. The time when the ball hits the ground.

   e. The upward velocity of the ball when it hits the ground.

5. **a.** Look at the patterns in the tables and graphs for your (*time*, *height*) and (*time*, *velocity*) data and try to explain how those patterns relate to each other. Look at both graphs on the same axes using a viewing window of x from 0 to 7 and y from -40 to 35.

   b. What does the shape of the graph relating *time* and *height* tell about the velocity of the ball during its flight? How is that shape illustrated by the trend of numbers in the data tables for (*time*, *height*) and (*time*, *velocity*)?

6. Compare the shape of your graph relating *time* and *height* with the choice you made in answering part c of "Think about this situation" on page 141.

Checkpoint

> As you worked on questions about the baseball's flight, how did you use your calculator or computer to find:
>
> **a** the maximum height and the time it took the ball to reach that height?
>
> **b** the time the ball returned to the ground and the speed it was traveling when it hit?
>
> ✔ *Be prepared to share your group's methods with the whole class.*

On Your Own

If a tennis ball is lobbed into the air with upward velocity 12 meters per second, its velocity and height will be functions of time in flight described by the following rules.

$$V = 12 - 9.8T \quad \text{and} \quad H = 1 + 12T - 4.9T^2$$

a. Find the maximum height of that tennis ball and the time it takes to reach the height.

b. What is the velocity of the ball at its maximum height?

c. Find when the ball will hit the ground. Round your answer to the nearest tenth of a second.

d. What is the velocity of the ball when it hits the ground?

Investigation  4.2 The Shape of Rules

Finding symbolic rules for relations between variables is a big part of mathematical model building. It is common to start the search with some data in a table or graph. But to find a rule fitting patterns in that data, it helps to know about the match between types of rules and shapes of graphs and patterns in tables. You can discover useful connections between rules and graphs by some experimentation with your graphing calculator or computer software.

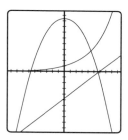

Experiment 1

1. For each rule listed below:

– Produce a table of values and a graph. Use the standard viewing window: Xmin = -10, Ymin = -10, Xmax = 10, Ymax = 10, Xscl = 1, and Yscl = 1.

– On a separate sheet of paper, write the rule and make a sketch of the graph. How does the pattern of values in the table match the pattern in the graph?

– Have each member of your group examine how the graph appears using a different viewing window. Compare your graphs and viewing windows.

a. $y = 2x - 4$ **b.** $y = 2x + 4$ **c.** $y = 0.5x + 2$

d. $y = -0.5x + 2$ **e.** $y = 10 - 1.5x$ **f.** $y = x^2 - 4$

2. As a group, discuss similarities and differences in the graphs you produced.

3. As a group, make some conjectures about the shapes of graphs for certain types of rules. Have individual members test various conjectures and report back to the group.

Experiment 2

1. For each rule listed below:
   - Produce a table of values and a graph. Use the standard viewing window (x and y values from -10 to 10, with a scale of 1).
   - On a separate sheet of paper, write the rule and make a sketch of the graph. How does the pattern of values in the table match the pattern in the graph?
   - Have each member of your group examine how the graph appears using a different viewing window. Compare your graphs and viewing windows.

   a. $y = x^2$ **b.** $y = x^2 - 3$ **c.** $y = -x^2$

   d. $y = -x^2 + 5$ **e.** $y = (x + 3)^2$ **f.** $y = \dfrac{2}{x}$

2. As a group, look for patterns in the rules that seem connected to special patterns in the graphs. Make and test some conjectures about the shapes of graphs for certain types of rules.

Experiment 3

1. For each rule listed below:
   - Produce a table of values and a graph. Modify the standard viewing window so that the x-axis only shows values from -5 to 5.
   - On a separate sheet of paper, write the rule and make a sketch of the graph. How does the pattern of values in the table match the pattern in the graph?
   - Have each member of your group examine how the graph appears using a different viewing window. Compare your graphs and viewing windows.

   a. $y = \dfrac{1}{x}$ **b.** $y = \dfrac{3}{x}$ **c.** $y = \dfrac{5}{x}$

   d. $y = \dfrac{-5}{x}$ **e.** $y = \dfrac{5}{x+1}$ **f.** $y = \dfrac{x}{3}$

2. As a group, look for patterns in the rules that seem connected to special patterns in the graphs. Make and test some conjectures about the shapes of graphs for certain types of rules.

Experiment 4

1. For each rule listed below:

- Produce a table of values and a graph. Decide as a group on a common viewing window to use.

- On a separate sheet of paper, write the rule and make a sketch of the graph. How does the pattern of values in the table match the pattern in the graph?

- Have each member of your group examine how the graph appears using a different viewing window. Compare your graphs and viewing windows.

a. $y = 2^x$ **b.** $y = (1.5)^x$ **c.** $y = 3^x$

d. $y = x^3$ **e.** $y = (0.5)^x$ **f.** $y = x^{0.5}$

2. As a group, look for patterns in the rules that seem connected to special patterns in the graphs. Make and test some conjectures about the shapes of graphs for certain types of rules.

Checkpoint

As a result of the experiments, your group probably has some hunches about matches between the form of a symbolic rule and the pattern of data in tables and the shape of graphs. Summarize your ideas in statements like this:

If we see a rule like ... , we expect to get a table like ... .

If we see a rule like ... , we expect to get a graph like ... .

✓ **Be prepared to compare your summary statements with those of other groups.**

On Your Own

Without using your calculator, match as best you can each table or graph with one of the given rules. In each case, explain the reason for your choice.

I   II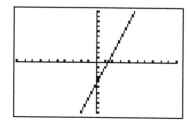

III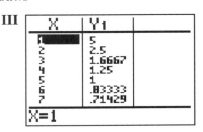

IV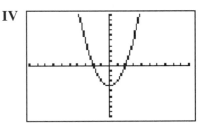

a. $y = x^2 - 4$ **c.** $y = -4x - 3$ **e.** $y = 4^x$

b. $y = \dfrac{5}{x}$ **d.** $y = -x^2 + 4$ **f.** $y = 3x - 4$

In this investigation you have explored only a few of many possible types of equations that can be used to model relations between variables. Your study of the match between rule types and patterns in tables and graphs of sample data from relations continues in the "MORE" section and will be an important task in chapters ahead.

Modeling **O**rganizing **R**eflecting **E**xtending

Modeling

1. On a clear summer day, the temperature of the air around you might be warm, like 25°C. But if you flew up into the atmosphere in an airplane, a balloon, or a glider, the temperature would decrease. A scatterplot of some sample data obtained by a weather balloon is shown here.

   a. Write a sentence describing the way temperature changes as altitude changes.

   b. Which of the following rules seem to fit the data in the graph?

   $T = 25 - 2A$

   $T = 25 + A^2$

   $T = \dfrac{25}{A}$

   $T = 25(0.8^A)$

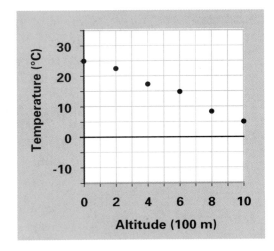

c. Use what you believe is the best modeling rule to find the temperature at 300 meters. At 700 meters. At 2,000 meters.

d. To the nearest ten meters, what altitude would correspond with a temperature of 0°C?

2. The cost of a long-distance phone call depends on the time of day and the length of the call. To save money, one family always makes calls to their relatives and friends in the evening. The following table shows (*call length*, *cost*) data for a sample of their calls to one city.

Call Length L (in minutes)	1	2	3	4	5	10	15	20
Cost C (in dollars)	3.00	3.50	4.00	4.50	5.00	7.50	10.00	12.50

a. Plot the data on a graph.

b. Write a sentence describing the way cost changes as call length changes.

c. Which of the following rules seem to fit the data in the table?

$C = 3L$ $C = 3L + 0.50$

$C = L + 0.50$ $C = 2.50 + 0.50L$

d. Use what you believe is the correct rule to find the cost of calls of these lengths: 8 minutes; 17 minutes; 30 minutes.

e. If you have $15 to make an evening call to a friend in the same city, how long would you be able to talk?

3. Suppose a golf ball is hit high into the air with an initial upward velocity of 18 meters per second. The upward velocity and height of the ball will vary as time passes. Those changes can be modeled by the rules $V = 18 - 9.8T$ and $H = 18T - 4.9T^2$.

a. Use the rules to calculate these values. For each T, explain what the values of V and H tell you about the flight of the golf ball:

V when $T = 0$	and	H when $T = 0$
V when $T = 1$	and	H when $T = 1$
V when $T = 2$	and	H when $T = 2$
V when $T = 3$	and	H when $T = 3$

b. Use your calculator or computer software to make tables and graphs of the (*time, velocity*) and (*time, height*) data.

c. Use the graphs or tables of upward velocity and height data to estimate, to the nearest tenth unit, answers for these questions.

- When will the ball reach its maximum height and what is that height?

- What is the velocity of the ball when it reaches its maximum height?

- When will the ball return to earth?

- How fast will the ball be falling when it hits the ground?

d. Describe the change in velocity of the ball for each 1 second change in time. Describe the change in height of the ball for each 1 second change in time.

4. When businesses do market research for new products, they are interested in the relation between the prices they charge and the income they will receive from sales. For example, suppose that the owners of Video City are trying to set the best rental price for video game cartridges. Using information on operation costs and survey data from potential customers, their market research staff might produce a recommendation that says *Profit (in dollars per week) depends on charge per rental (in dollars) according to the rule*

$$P = -750 + 900C - 150C^2.$$

a. Calculate these values and explain what each tells you about prices and profits for Video City rentals.

P when *C* = 1	*P* when *C* = 7
P when *C* = 4	*P* when *C* = 2.50

b. Make a table and a graph of (*price charged*, *profits earned*) data for charges varying from $0 to $8.

c. Use the table and graph from part b to answer the following questions:

- For what prices charged will Video City make a positive profit?

- For what prices charged will they lose money?

- Is there a price that will give maximum profit? If so, what is it?

d. What is the weekly cost of operating the store? How can you tell by looking at the rule? By looking at the graph?

e. Explain what the shape of the graph relating *price charged* and *profits earned* tells about the relation between those two variables. Why is that relation reasonable?

f. What other tables and graphs have you already worked with that have the same shape as the graph relating *price charged* and *profits earned*? How are those rules similar to and how are they different from the rule in this problem?

5. The stopping distance D of a car depends on reaction distance R and braking distance B. Each of these variables is a function of the speed s of the car. You can calculate reaction distance and braking distance in *feet* by using the rules

$$R = 1.1s \quad \text{and} \quad B = 0.05s^2$$

where s is the speed of the car in miles per hour.

a. Write a rule that gives stopping distance as a function of the speed of a car.

b. Make a table and a graph of the relation between *speed* and *stopping distance* for speeds from 0 to 80 miles per hour in steps of 5 miles per hour.

c. What is the stopping distance for a car traveling at 20 miles per hour? At 40 miles per hour?

d. Would 200 feet be a safe distance to follow a car on the highway traveling at 60 miles per hour? Explain your reasoning.

e. Produce graphs of (*speed, reaction distance*) and (*speed, braking distance*) on the same set of coordinate axes. Compare the patterns of change in distances as speed increases. How could these patterns of change be predicted by looking at the rules for reaction distance and for braking distance?

f. Suppose that an investigating officer at the scene of a car accident in front of school finds skid marks 100 feet in length. What, if anything, can you conclude about the speed of the associated car?

Organizing

1. Look back over the various problem situations in earlier investigations. Find several examples where two variables were related in a pattern similar to that of task 1 in the Modeling section. Explain what those examples have in common.

2. Look back over the various problem situations in earlier investigations. Find several examples where two variables were related in a pattern similar to that of task 4 in the Modeling section. Explain what those examples have in common.

3. For each rule below, use your calculator or computer software to produce a table and then write an equation relating *NOW* and *NEXT* values of the y variable.

a. $y = 5x + 2$ b. $y = -10x - 3$ c. $y = 2^x$ d. $y = 4^x$

4. Use your calculator or computer software to produce side-by-side tables for each of the following rules in steps of 1 unit starting at $x = 0$.

a. $y = 2x$ b. $y = x^2$ c. $y = 2^x$

Write a short paragraph summarizing similarities in overall patterns of change and differences in *rates* of change of the three relations.

5. A cube is a three-dimensional shape whose faces are squares.

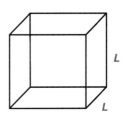

   a. If the length of an edge of a cube is L, write an expression for the area of one of its faces.

   b. Write a rule that gives the total surface area A of a cube as a function of the length L of an edge.

   c. Suppose you wished to design a cube whose surface area is 1,000 square centimeters. To the nearest 0.1 centimeter, what should be the length of the edge of the cube?

   d. Did you use a graph or a table in answering part c? Why?

   e. Could you answer part c without using a graph or a table? If so, describe your method.

Reflecting

1. Graphing calculators and computer software can be useful tools in modeling real situations with mathematics. What features of your calculator or computer software have you found to be most useful for the activities in this lesson? What calculator or computer skills do you think you need to develop further?

2. If you enter the rule $Y = 5X + 100$ in your calculator or computer software and press the GRAPH key or enter the graph command, you might at first find no part of the graph on your screen. The plotted points will not appear in your graphing window. Compare notes with others in your class to get some ideas about making good window choices. Write your advice as a reminder to yourself and help to others.

3. When you model a relation between variables by a rule written symbolically, which approach do you find most useful in finding answers to related questions—making tables, making graphs, or some other method? Explain your reasoning and give some examples from the problems you have done in this chapter.

4. Drivers' education classes often give a rule-of-thumb for the space to leave between you and a car in front for every 10 miles per hour you are traveling. Find out what this rule is by talking with a drivers' education instructor or reading a manual. Judge how good the rule is in light of task 4 in the Modeling section.

Extending

1. Consider the relation between variables given by $y = 2x + 1$. Make a table of (x, y) data for this relation from $x = -10$ to $x = 10$ in steps of 1. Using the same window settings for x, produce a graph of the rule. Use your table to help you decide on appropriate window settings for y.

   a. Explore the changes in the table and graph that result when the number 2 in the rule is changed to other values, including some decimals and some negative numbers. What stays the same and what changes in the table? In the graph?

   b. Next explore the changes in the table and graph that result when the number 1 is changed in the rule to other values, including some decimals and some negative numbers. What stays the same and what changes in the table? In the graph?

   c. Can you find a clue in the rule that explains why the tables and graphs fit the observed patterns and why changing the 2 and the 1 cause the observed changes in the tables and graphs?

2. Each of the following graphs is in a viewing window with x and y settings from -5 to 5. Write a rule for each graph and test your prediction using your calculator or computer software. Explain whether or not you think your rule is the only possible one.

   a.   **b.**

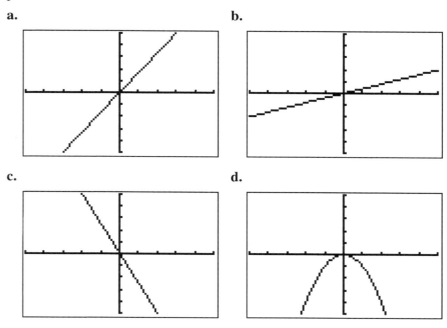

   c.   **d.**

3. When a baseball is hit, you can consider its velocity toward the outfield wall and its velocity into the air.

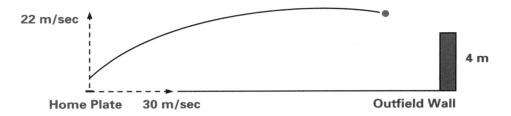

Suppose a long hit toward the outfield wall has initial upward velocity of 22 meters per second and velocity toward the outfield wall of 30 meters per second. The outfield wall is 4 meters high and 120 meters from home plate. Will the ball go over the wall? Answer the following questions to help you analyze this problem.

a. The distance of the ball from home plate is a function of time since it was hit with rule $D = 30T$. When will the ball reach the outfield wall?

b. The height of the ball at any time T seconds into its flight is given by the rule $H = 1.5 + 22T - 4.9T^2$. How high will the ball be when it reaches the outfield wall? Will it be an automatic home run?

4. For task 5 of the Modeling section you were given the rule relating reaction distance in feet to speed of a car in miles per hour: $R = 1.1s$. The reaction time for a typical driver has been found to be about 0.75 seconds. Explain how this experimental finding can be used to create the rule for reaction distance.

5. On some graphing calculators and with some computer software, you can display at the same time both a graph and a table, or a graph and the rule for a function entered in the "Y=" menu.

a. Examine the split-screen capability of a graphing calculator or computer software to which you have access.

b. Consider the relation between variables given by $y = 2^x$. Make a table of data for this relation and a graph. Use the split-screen capability to explore changes in the table and graph when the number 2 is changed in the rule to other values, including some numbers greater than 1 and some positive numbers less than 1.

5 *Looking Back*

In your work of this chapter you
have studied many kinds of relations between variables. You have
been asked to describe the patterns
relating changes in those variables
in graphs, tables of values, words,
and symbolic rules. The activities
in this final lesson of the chapter
ask you to put it all together.

1. In some public transportation systems of U. S. cities, the fare is related to distance traveled, time of day (higher in morning and evening rush hours), or both.
       The fare pattern for one city's subway system is illustrated in the following
   table.

Distance (in miles)	1	2	3	4	5	6	7	8	9
Fare (in $)	1.10	1.20	1.30	1.40	1.50	1.60	1.70	1.80	1.90

   a. Write a brief description of the pattern relating distance traveled to fare charged
      on this subway system. How does the fare change as distance increases?

   b. Write two rules for calculating fare from distance.
      – In the first rule, write an equation showing how each additional mile in-
        creases the subway fare.
      – In the second rule, use the variable names F (for fare) and D (for distance)
        to show how to calculate the fare for any given distance.

   c. Make a graph of the rule relating distance and fare for distances from 0 to 15
      miles.

   d. Does the fare pattern used seem fair to your group? Discuss your ideas with
      other groups.

   e. How would the table, graph, and rules change if during rush hour each fare is
      increased by $0.05?

   f. How would the table, graph, and rules change if during rush hour each fare is
      doubled?

2. When private pilots make flight plans for their trips, they must estimate the amount of fuel required to reach their destination airport. When the plane is in flight, the pilots watch to see how much fuel they have left in their tanks. The graph below shows fuel that would remain in the tanks as a function of time in flight (assuming an average air speed) for one type of small plane.

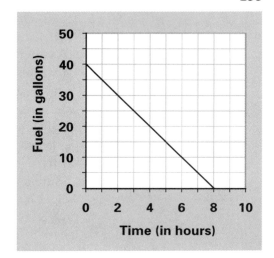

a. Make a table showing gallons of fuel left from 0 to 10 hours in steps of 1.0 hours.

b. Describe the pattern of change in fuel remaining as time in flight passes.

c. Write two rules relating time in flight to fuel left in the tanks.

- In the first rule, show how fuel changes from one hour to the next.

- In the second rule, show how to calculate fuel left at any given time in the flight.

d. Assume that the plane's tanks are full at the start of a flight.

- How much fuel would be left after 1.5 hours? After 3.75 hours?

- How much fuel would be used in a trip of 5.8 hours?

e. If the plane flies at an average speed of 125 miles per hour, how much fuel would be required for a trip of 525 miles? How is the answer shown in the graph?

f. What conditions can you imagine that would make the amount of actual fuel used different from the predictions of the graph, the table, and the rule you found?

g. Suppose two hours into the flight, the pilot discovers that the fuel attendant neglected to fill both tanks. Only 24.5 gallons of fuel remain. Assuming the same rate of fuel consumption as shown in the graph, sketch a graph representing this situation. How much flight time does the pilot have left?

3. Metal springs of various lengths and strengths are used for many important tasks—for example, absorbing shocks in car wheels and bumpers, pulling garage doors closed, weighing people and products on scales, and testing the strength of weight lifters. When a spring is stretched, the length of the spring is a function of the force pulling on it.

Suppose that for a spring used in weight training equipment, its length L (in feet) is related to the force pulling on it F (in pounds) by the rule $L = 2 + 0.01F$.

a. Make a table of sample data, (F, L), for $F = 0$ to 200 in steps of 20.

b. Make a graph of the relation between force and length for $F = 0$ to 200.

c. Describe the pattern that you see in the table and the graph relating change in force to change in length.

d. To what length will that spring be stretched by forces of 50 pounds? Of 200 pounds?

e. What is the length of the spring when the equipment is not in use? Describe two different ways in which you could answer this question.

f. If the spring stretches to a length of 3.5 feet, what force is pulling on it?

g. What do the two numbers, 2 and 0.01, in the rule tell about the pattern of change in the spring length as force is applied?

Checkpoint

When two variables change in relation to each other, the pattern of change often fits one of several common forms.

ⓐ Make sketches of at least five different graphs showing different patterns relating change in two variables.

ⓑ For each graph, write a brief explanation of the pattern of change shown in the graph and describe a real-life situation that fits the pattern.

✓ *Be prepared to share your sketches and descriptions with the whole class.*

Chapter **3**   *Linear Models*

1 *Predicting from Data*

On Tuesday, May 10, 1994, millions of people across the United States witnessed a very rare event—a near total eclipse of the sun. Did you see the moon pass between our earth and the sun, dimming the sky in mid-day? If not, you'll have to wait until the year 2012 for the next chance!

Rare and spectacular events like eclipses get everyone's attention focused on the skies. Astronomers have been watching the movement of the sun, moon, earth, and stars for thousands of years. They've found patterns that are used to design yearly calendars and our latitude/longitude system for locating places on the earth.

The sun and its shadows have been used in clever ways to find directions and take measurements. One use of sunlight and shadows gives a method of finding heights of very tall objects.

The method is based on the fact that the taller any object is, the longer its shadow will be. To make use of this relation to get actual measurements, you need to know the numerical pattern of the relation between *height* and *shadow*. You can collect that sort of data easily on a sunny day.

The graph on the next page shows data from several measurements as a flag was raised up its pole. A line has been drawn on the plot to highlight the pattern relating *length L* of the shadow and *height H* of the flag causing that shadow. That graph is called a **linear model** of the relation between the two variables.

The graph itself can be described by the equation $H = 1.5L$, giving another form of the linear model. As you know from your work in the "Patterns of Change" chapter, both the graph and the equation can be used to answer important questions.

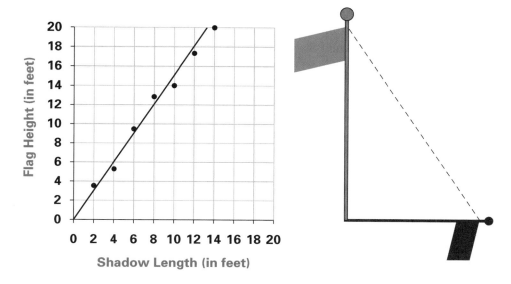

Think about this situation

As in many experiments, the shadow data do not fall exactly on a line. No simple equation will relate all of the data pairs (*shadow length, flag height*).

a How would you decide where to draw a line fitting the pattern in a plot like the one above?

b What predictions could you make from the given linear model?

c What kinds of equations do you expect for linear graphs?

Linear models occur in many other situations. To use linear models in solving problems, it is helpful to know the connections between the graphs, the rules that produce those graphs, and the tables of values related to the graphs and rules. Finding and using linear models is the focus of this unit.

Investigation **1.1** Where Should the Projector Go?

The search for a useful linear model relating variables often starts with a plot of data about those variables. That data often comes from an experiment. For example, consider this question about the many kinds of film projectors that show pictures in homes, theaters, classrooms, and auditoriums:

How can the projector be positioned so that its images will fit the screen ?

Whenever such a projector is pointed directly at the screen, it enlarges images on the film into similar images on the screen. The enlargement factor depends on the distance from the projector to the screen (and special lens features of the projector). You can discover more about that relation with some simple experiments using an overhead projector.

As a class, make a test-pattern figure on an overhead transparency. Include line segments of many different lengths from 5 to 30 cm. In the experiment you will be checking to see how those segments are lengthened when projected on a screen from various distances.

1. The first step is to collect some (*projector distance*, *enlargement factor*) data.

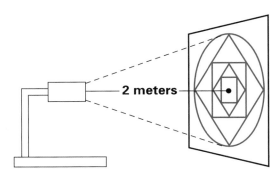

    a. Place the overhead projector so that its lens is 2 meters from a screen. Focus the test pattern with the projector aimed directly at the screen. Then collect data comparing lengths on your overhead transparency to lengths on the screen. Estimate the enlargement factor of projection at that distance.

(Hint: If a 5 cm segment projects as 15 cm, 10 cm projects as 30 cm, and 15 cm projects as 45 cm, *what enlargement factor would you record?*)

    b. Move the projector to a distance of 3 meters from the screen and focus the test pattern. Collect data for estimating the enlargement factor from that distance.

    c. Repeat the process to find enlargement factors called for in this table:

Projector Distance (m)	1	2	3	4	5	6
Enlargement Factor						

2. Plot the (*projector distance*, *enlargement factor*) data on a coordinate graph. Draw a linear model that you believe fits the trend in that data well.

3. Describe the pattern of change in enlargement E as the distance D changes. Explain how that pattern is shown in the data table and in the modeling line.

4. Now look for symbolic rules of the relation between distance and enlargement.

    a. Find an equation using *NOW* and *NEXT* to show how the enlargement factors increase as projector distance increases in steps of 1 meter at a time.

    b. Find an equation relating D and E that matches both the linear model and the data trend.

5. Algebraic models often are used to summarize patterns in data. They are also useful in making predictions about untested values of the variables.

   a. Use your linear model or equation to predict the enlargement factor when the projector is placed 2.5 meters from the screen. Also predict the enlargement factor for a distance of 4.25 meters from the screen.

   b. Carefully make actual measurements to test both predictions. Then make a report assessing the accuracy of your predictions. If they were inaccurate, revise your model and equation.

Checkpoint

a Suppose you were to draw one line segment on an overhead transparency. The relation between the length of the screen image of that segment and the distance the projector lens is from the screen can be represented by a data table, a graph model, or an equation. Which representation do you think is easiest to use and most accurate for making predictions? Give reasons for your choice.

b What could cause inaccurate predictions from a linear model of (*projector distance, enlargement factor*) data?

✓ *Be prepared to share your group's responses with the entire class.*

On Your Own

Suppose that two line segments are drawn on an overhead transparency. One segment is 4 cm long and the other is 10 cm long. An overhead projector is positioned so that the shorter segment shows up as a 12 cm segment on the screen. The longer segment shows up as a 30 cm segment on the screen.

a. Complete this table in a pattern that you would expect for other data pairs.

Sketch Length	0	2	4	6	8	10	12	14	16	18
Screen Image Length			12			30				

b. Draw a graph of the relation you would expect between *sketch length* and *screen image length*.

c. Write an equation relating *sketch length S* and *screen image length I*.

Investigation 1.2 The Ratings Game

Linear models can be used to summarize data patterns and make predictions in different kinds of situations. For example, consider the relation between rankings and audience size for television shows on the major networks. Those variables are important because they set advertising rates and the survival of the shows themselves.

The table below shows a sample from the complete list of ratings for regular television programs during the 1992–93 season.

Rank	Show	Average Weekly Audience*
10	Full House, ABC	14.7
20	Unsolved Mysteries, NBC	13.2
30	The Simpsons, Fox	12.1
40	L. A. Law, NBC	10.8
50	Day One, ABC	10.0
60	Beverly Hills 90210, Fox	9.4

*In millions of households

Source: USA TODAY, April 21, 1993.

A scatterplot of the table data looks like this:

1. Study the data and then answer these questions as a group.

   a. What do the table and graph show about the relation between average weekly audience and ranking for television programs?

   b. How can you predict the ranking of a show from the average weekly audience using the graph? Using the table?

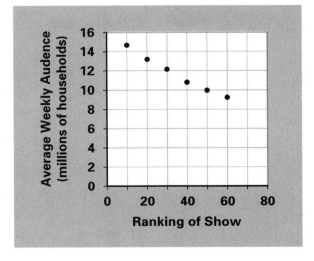

   c. How can you predict the average weekly audience from the rankings of a show using the graph? Using the table?

d. Which display do you find easier to use in making ranking or audience estimates?

e. Which display would be more effective in a report to another group?

f. What are the differences in average weekly audience between the shows ranked 20, 40, and 60? If you worked for a company choosing a show to sponsor, how would those differences affect your decision? What other factors would you consider?

The table and graph of television program rankings and audiences do not include data for every 1992–93 show. They do give enough information to make some predictions. Those predictions would be done more easily and accurately if the data were modeled by a smooth graph. It looks like a straight line is a reasonable model in this case.

2. For the following, use a copy of the scatterplot showing ranking and audience size. Your teacher may have copies made for you.

   a. Draw a linear model that you believe fits the trend in that data well.

   b. Explain why you drew your modeling line where you did. Consider the number of points on the line and points above or below the line.

   c. Use your linear model to answer the following questions.

   – *The Simpsons* was the 30th ranked show for the year. What audience does your model estimate for that show?

   – *L.A. Law* had an average weekly audience of 10.8 million households. What ranking does your model predict for that show?

   d. The actual average weekly audience for *The Simpsons* was 12.1 million households. *L.A. Law* was ranked 40. Compare these values to your estimates in part c. Explain any differences between predicted and actual numbers.

3. Refer back to the sample ratings on page 162.

   a. Use your graphing calculator or computer software to make a scatterplot of the sample (*ranking*, *average weekly audience*) data.

   b. One equation proposed as a model of the data pattern was $y = -0.1x + 16$. Enter that equation in your calculator or software's function list. Test the equation's accuracy as a model. Then experiment to find another equation whose graph seems to model the data better.

   c. Use your modeling equation from part b to estimate audience size for the shows ranked 30 and 60. Then compare those estimates to the actual data. Explain why there are differences.

Checkpoint

In Investigations 1.1 and 1.2 you used tables and graphs of sample (x, y) data pairs to find a line that would fit all data in a collection reasonably well.

ⓐ How do you use a modeling line to estimate y values related to any chosen x values?

ⓑ How do you use a modeling line to estimate the x values that will predict any chosen y value?

✓ *Be prepared to share your group's procedures with the whole class.*

On Your Own

In 1975 a new Ford Mustang car had a base price of $4,906. In 1981 a comparable car had a base price of $7,900. In 1987 the base price was $9,750, and in 1993 it was $13,245.

a. On graph paper, make a plot of the sample (*year, base price*) data. Use a time scale where 1975 is year 0. Then draw a line that fits the pattern of the data well.

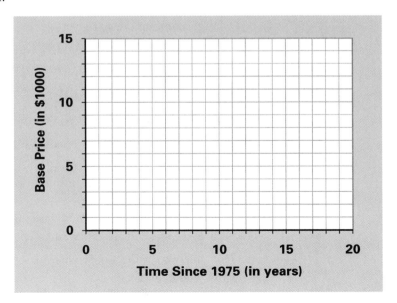

b. Use your linear model from part a to estimate base price for Ford Mustangs in 1978, 1984, 1990, 1994, and the current year.

c. Produce a scatterplot of the data with your calculator or computer software. Test the equation $y = 500x + 5000$ to see if it seems a good model of the relation between years since 1975 and base price y. Then experiment with variations on that equation to find what you think might be a better model.

d. Use the trace or table feature of your calculator or computer software to compare prices predicted by your revised model from part c to the original data for 1975, 1981, 1987, and 1993. Try to explain differences between predicted and actual base prices.

Investigation  **Choosing a Good Linear Model**

When you are looking for a pattern relating two variables, it often helps to make a scatterplot of sample (x, y) data pairs. In many cases that plot will show points that lie in a roughly linear pattern. Then you can draw a single straight line that seems to summarize the overall trend in that pattern. The challenge is finding the right place to draw that modeling line.

The table below and scatterplot on the next page give information about tuition costs at fourteen major American state universities in 1994. Public universities charge different tuition fees for in-state and out-of-state students. This is because taxes paid by state residents help support these universities. The given data show the relation between those two fees at some universities. How would you describe the relation between in-state and out-of-state tuition at these universities?

University	In-State Tuition ($)	Out-of-State Tuition ($)	University	In-State Tuition ($)	Out-of-State Tuition ($)
Delaware	4100	10,630	Ohio State	3087	9315
Florida	1798	6700	Penn State	4878	7470
Georgia	2154	6744	Texas	1813	6193
Illinois	3544	8926	Utah	2013	6138
Kansas	2085	7429	Washington	2907	8199
Maryland	3168	8720	West Virginia	2128	6370
Oklahoma	1892	5096	Wisconsin	2735	9094

Source: *The College Handbook 1996.* New York: College Entrance Examination Board, 1995.

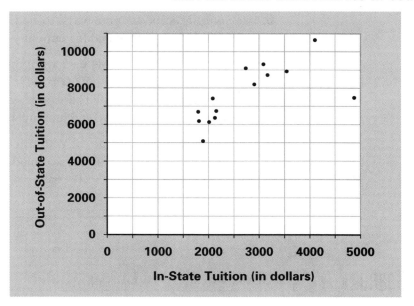

Think about drawing a straight line to model the trend in tuition data pairs. It might seem reasonable to send that line through points that are typical of the trend. In the case of the tuition scatterplot, one such point would be (*mean in-state tuition, mean out-of-state tuition*) or ($\bar{x}$, $\bar{y}$). That point is shown with a square on the scatterplot below.

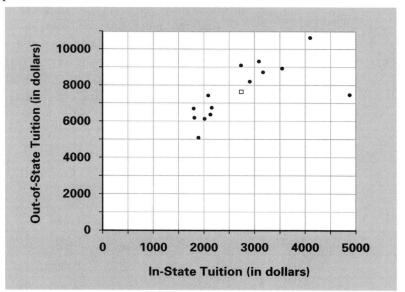

1. Calculate the mean in-state and out-of-state tuition prices for data in the table. Check your answers by comparing them to approximate coordinates of the square on the plot.

2. On a copy of the scatterplot, experiment with different positions for a straight-line model through the $(\bar{x}, \bar{y})$ point. Use a clear ruler or a long narrow object such as uncooked spaghetti. Draw the line that you believe best fits the overall trend in the data. Use that linear model to answer the questions below.

    a. What would the out-of-state tuition be for a typical university that set in-state tuition at $2500?

    b. What would the out-of-state tuition be for a typical university that set in-state tuition at $4000?

    c. At the University of Hawaii in Manoa, in-state tuition is $1631. Out-of-state tuition is $3194. How does that combination compare to the pattern described by your linear model?

Even if it makes sense that a good modeling line should pass through the point $(\bar{x}, \bar{y})$, there are still many choices for a line. You might wonder if there is a way to choose the "best" among those options. Here's a simple example to explore. It uses ten data points on the scatterplot and two possible modeling lines. The point $(\bar{x}, \bar{y})$ is marked by a square. Which of the two lines shown would you choose as the better linear model for the data pattern?

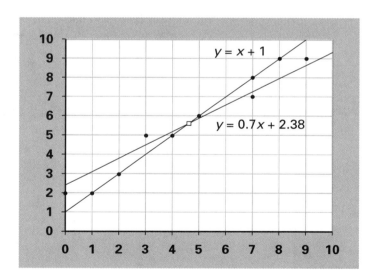

3. One way to choose between the two modeling lines is to compare their **mean error of prediction**. The mean error of prediction is the average difference (ignoring signs) between actual and predicted y values for the various x values.

    a. How does an error of prediction show up on the previous diagram?

    b. Calculate the missing entries in a copy of the following table. Then calculate the mean error of prediction for the modeling line $y = x + 1$.

x	Actual y	Predicted from y = x + 1	Error Actual – Predicted	Absolute Error
0	2	1	1	1
1	2	2	0	0
2	3			
3	5			
4	5			
5	6			
7	7			
7	8			
8	9			
9	9	10	-1	1

Mean error of prediction = _____

c. Finding the mean error of prediction requires many calculations. You can simplify the work by using your calculator or computer software. The "Technology Tip" on using data lists and calculating y values can be helpful. Complete a copy of this table for the modeling line $y = 0.7x + 2.38$. Then calculate the mean error of prediction.

x	Actual y	Predicted from y = 0.7x + 2.38	Error Actual – Predicted	Absolute Error
0	2	2.38	-0.38	0.38
1	2	3.08	-1.08	1.08
2	3			
3	5			
4	5			
5	6			
7	7			
7	8			
8	9			
9	9			

Mean error of prediction = _____

d. Which line would you choose as the better model? Why?

e. What are the coordinates of the point $(\bar{x}, \bar{y})$ for this scatterplot? Verify that it is on both modeling lines.

Checkpoint

In this investigation you considered the problem of choosing the best linear models for given data patterns.

a What strategies seem sensible in finding a good linear model?

b If two different linear models are proposed, how could you compare them to see which is the better fit to the data pattern?

✓ **Be prepared to share your strategies and reasoning with the class.**

The mean error of prediction is the average (vertical) distance of data points from a modeling line. It provides a measure of how close a modeling line is to the data points themselves.

On Your Own

The student government at Banneker Middle School was planning a fund-raising carnival. They considered renting a "moon walk." First they wanted to see how much students would pay for 5-minute walks. They collected the following data.

Price for 5-minute Walk (in cents)	25	50	75	100	125	150
Number of Customers	100	80	55	35	20	5

a. Make a scatterplot of these data and locate the point $(\bar{x}, \bar{y})$ on the plot.

b. Draw what you believe is a good modeling line for the pattern in the data. Use that model to estimate the number of customers if the price is set at $0.35 and at $1.15.

c. Two possible equation models are given below. In each model, x stands for price and y stands for number of customers. Calculate the mean error of prediction for these two models.

  i. $y = -0.7x + 100$

  ii. $y = -0.8x + 110$

d. Use your calculator or computer to produce a scatterplot of the (*price*, *number of customers*) data. Then experiment to see if you can find a better fitting model than either proposed in part c.

Modeling Organizing Reflecting Extending

Modeling

1. To find the enlargement factor of a film or slide projector at some given distance from the screen, you really only need to look at the size of one object. Use this fact to complete the table of data describing a slide projector. Then use that information to complete the items that follow.

Projector Distance	Size on Film	Size on Screen	Enlargement
1 meter	10 mm	25 mm	
2 meters	10 mm	50 mm	
3 meters	10 mm	75 mm	
4 meters	10 mm	100 mm	

   a. Make a scatterplot of the (*projector distance, enlargement factor*) data. Draw a linear model that fits the pattern of that data well.

   b. Use the model or the pattern of the table to estimate the enlargement factor when the projector is:

   – 2.5 meters from the screen

   – 5 meters from the screen

   c. How would you describe the pattern of change in enlargement factor as projector distance from the screen increases? How is the pattern illustrated by the graph and the table?

2. The *Sun and Surf Company* rents boogie boards, beach chairs, and umbrellas at the Atlantic Ocean in Bethany Beach, Delaware. Naturally, their business is affected by the weather. Following are some boogie board rental data from sixteen weekend days during July and August of 1992. Study the data to answer the following questions.

Rentals

High Temperature (°F)	Boogie Board Rentals	High Temperature (°F)	Boogie Board Rentals
72	4	92	37
78	14	94	41
87	29	85	26
89	33	87	30
87	28	71	6
94	40	79	12
78	15	95	41
83	22	94	42

a. Obtain a copy of the scatterplot of the (*temperature, boogie board rentals*) data. Plot the point ($\bar{x}$, $\bar{y}$) on the scatterplot. What does ($\bar{x}$, $\bar{y}$) represent?

b. Draw a linear model which contains the point ($\bar{x}$, $\bar{y}$) and represents the trend in the data.

c. Use your linear model to predict the number of boogie board rentals on a 60° day. Do the same for a 75° day and a 100° day.

d. On a day when the temperature reached 100° at Bethany Beach, the manager of the *Sun and Surf Company* reported rentals of 38 boogie boards. The owner was suspicious that some rentals were not being reported. What do you think?

3. The graph shows data from a market research survey of potential customers for a helicopter ride over some mountains. People were asked how much they would pay for a ten-minute ride. Based on those results, the survey company predicted likely numbers of customers each day at several typical prices.

a. Describe the trend of the relation between price per ride and customers per day as shown in the data plot. How will number of customers probably change as price is raised higher and higher?

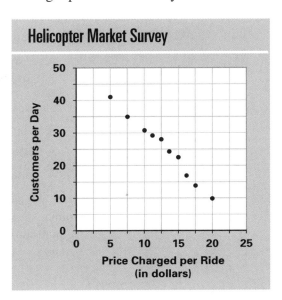

b. Draw a linear model that you believe fits the pattern in the data well. Explain how you arrived at your model choice.

c. Use your model to estimate the number of customers when the price is set at $7.50, $12.50, and $17.50.

d. Suppose you found that the helicopter ride averaged 32 customers per day in one month. What guess would you make about the price that had been set?

4. The following shadow data was collected at 10:00 a.m. on a sunny spring day in Washington, DC. Use it to investigate the connection between heights of objects and lengths of their shadows.

Object Height (m)	Shadow Length (m)
1.0	3.1
1.5	4.5
2.0	5.9
2.5	7.4
3.0	9.2
3.5	10.6

a. Plot the (*object height, shadow length*) data on a graph. Draw a line that fits the pattern of this data well.

b. Use your linear model to estimate shadow lengths for:
  - A flagpole that is 4 meters tall.
  - A person who is 1.75 meters tall.
  - The Washington Monument, which is 169 meters tall.

c. Use your linear model to estimate heights for:
  - A light pole that casts a shadow 8 meters long.
  - A tree whose shadow is 15 meters long.
  - A water tower that casts a shadow 50 meters long.

d. Use your calculator or computer to produce a scatterplot of the data in the table. Experiment with different expressions in the function list to find an equation whose graph models the data well. Compare shadow lengths predicted by the rule with those in the table.

5. Each March, many people in the United States are caught in "March Madness"— the national college basketball championship. Below are statistics from the final game for the 1996 women's champion.

Tennessee Lady Vols

Player	Minutes	Points	Rebounds
Holdsclaw	34	16	14
Conklin	23	14	4
Johnson	28	16	5
Marciniak	37	10	4
Davis	32	8	7
Smallwood	1	1	1
Milligan	1	0	0
Greene	1	0	0
Jolly	10	2	0
Laxton	12	4	3
Thompson	21	12	11
Team Totals	200	83	49

Georgia Lady Bulldogs

Player	Minutes	Points	Rebounds
Frett	37	25	16
Holland	33	11	1
Henderson	36	16	7
Roundtree	37	8	5
Powell	12	0	0
Irwin	16	3	2
Antvorskov	3	0	0
Thompson	1	0	1
Taylor	1	0	1
Bush	16	2	2
Walker	1	0	2
Decker	6	0	2
Walls	1	0	0
Team Totals	200	65	39

Source: University of Tennessee Sports Info, University of Georgia Sports Info

a. Combine the data for the two teams to study the relation between minutes played and points scored. Use your graphing calculator or computer software to produce a scatterplot of the (*minutes played, points scored*) combined data.

 – Describe the overall relation between those variables and any interesting deviations from that pattern.

 – Would a linear graph be a good model of the pattern in this data? Explain your reasoning.

b. Repeat the analysis of part a to study the relation between *minutes played* and *rebounds*.

c. Repeat the analysis of part a to study the relation between *points scored* and *rebounds*.

6. The next set of data gives information about the skills of professional football quarterbacks. The table shows the relation between number of touchdown passes and number of interceptions thrown in the careers of the top 15 rated quarterbacks in the history of the National Football League (at the end of the 1992 season).

National Football League Quarterbacks

Name	Touchdowns	Interceptions	Name	Touchdowns	Interceptions
Joe Montana	244	123	Sonny Jurgensen	255	189
Steve Young	76	42	Len Dawson	239	183
Dan Marino	290	165	Dave Krieg	210	160
Jim Kelly	161	108	Ken Anderson	197	160
Warren Moon	175	145	Bernie Kosar	111	78
Mark Rypien	97	65	Boomer Esiason	174	129
Roger Staubach	153	109	Danny White	155	132
Neil Lomax	136	90			

Source: *Official 1993 National Football League Record Fact Book.* New York: Workman Publishing Co. 1993.

a. Use your calculator or computer to produce a scatterplot of the (*touchdowns, interceptions*) data.

b. Rona and Aaron each found an equation for modeling lines relating touchdown passes x to interceptions y.

Rona's equation was $y = 0.5x + 25$.

Aaron's equation was $y = 0.8x + 10$.

Do these lines contain the point $(\bar{x}, \bar{y})$?

c. Visually compare the graphs of these lines on the scatterplot. Does one appear to fit the pattern in the data better than the other? Explain why or why not.

d. Decide which of the lines is the better model by comparing their mean errors of prediction.

e. Use the better model to predict the number of career interceptions to be expected from a top-rated quarterback who threw 120 touchdowns.

Organizing

1. When using coordinate graphs, mathematicians usually refer to the horizontal axis as the *x*-axis and the vertical axis as the *y*-axis. Each point on the graph has a pair of coordinates (*x*, *y*).

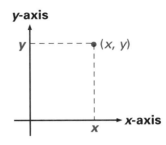

To make a scatterplot of data or a graph of an equation relating two variables, some decisions must be made. One is which variable should have its values listed first in the ordered pair to be plotted. The values of that variable are represented on the *x*-axis. The values that are listed second in the data pairs are represented on the *y*-axis.

There are two general rules for guiding this decision. First, if you are studying the way some variable changes as time passes, the time variable is usually listed first in the ordered pair. Second, in many cases one variable depends on the other. That means you can control or choose the values of one variable. The other variable responds to those changes or choices. In such a situation, the variable you can control or choose directly is called the **independent variable**. It is usually listed first in the coordinate pairs. The other variable, the **dependent variable**, is listed second in the coordinate pairs. In some cases there is no natural order to the variables involved.

The following list gives eight situations involving variables. In each case, name the two variables involved. Explain which you would list first and represent by the *x*-axis. Which would you list second and represent by the *y*-axis?

a. Whale population in the Arctic changing over the years

b. Profit from a concert and tickets sold for the concert

c. Height and weight of players on a soccer team

d. Shoe size and length of the wearer's foot

e. Money earned and hours worked at a job

f. Age and height of young people from ages 1–20

g. Size of world population from 1900 to 2000

h. Driving speed and time required for a trip

2. The graph on the next page shows data from a market research survey of potential audience for a local "battle of the bands." People were asked how much they would pay to attend the concert. Based on those results, the survey company predicted likely audience sizes at several typical prices.

a. Suppose you were asked to experiment with different expressions to find an equation whose graph models the data well. What equation would you try first?

b. Explain why you chose that equation.

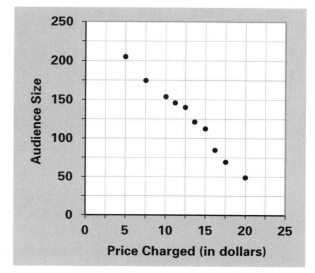

3. The enlargement factors of film projectors and overhead projectors can be studied using the arithmetic of *ratios* and *proportions*. Study the following table which gives some sample data from an experiment on projection of overhead transparencies.

Transparency Image Length (in cm)	1	3	5	7	9
Screen Image Length (in cm)	4	12	20	28	36

a. Write the ratio

$$\frac{\text{transparency image length}}{\text{screen image length}}$$

for each data pair. How are the ratios related?

b. If a transparency image length was 6 cm and its screen image had length x, complete the proportion:

$$\frac{6}{x} = \frac{?}{?}.$$

c. Solve the proportion in part b.

d. Write and solve proportions corresponding to each of the following questions.

– What screen image length will correspond to a transparency image length of 8 cm?

– What transparency image length will correspond to a screen image length of 16 cm?

4. Refer back to the data about shadows in Modeling task 4.

    a. Write and compare the ratios of *object height* to *shadow length* for each of the data pairs.

    b. Write and solve proportions to answer each of the following questions.

        – What shadow length will be produced by an object of height 3 meters?

        – What object height will produce a shadow of length 8 meters?

5. The graph at the right shows a scatterplot of data and two different possible modeling lines.

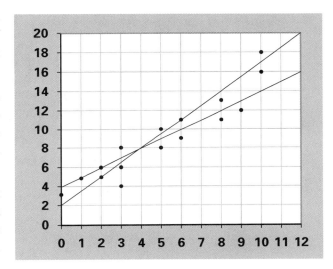

    a. Which of the two modeling lines do you believe is the best fit to the data pattern?

    b. How can you support your choice with a numerical measure of accuracy of model fit? Use these facts:

    i. The equations of the modeling lines are $y = 1.5x + 2$ and $y = x + 4$.

    ii. The data points all have whole number coordinates, beginning with $(0, 3)$, $(1, 5)$, $(2, 5)$, and so on.

Reflecting

1. The sketches that follow show five ways of drawing a linear model on the same scatterplot. See if you can figure out the reasoning used to make each drawing. Then decide which linear model seems best. Explain why the others are not based on sensible strategies.

    a.   **b.**   **c.**

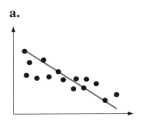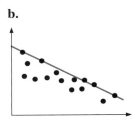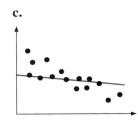

d.   **e.**

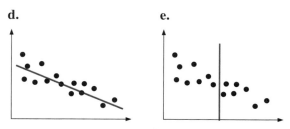

2. How are the two statistics *mean absolute deviation* and *mean error of prediction* similar? How are they different?

3. Think about the variety of theaters in which you have seen movies. How do the size and shape of those theaters affect the size of the screen images you see and the effect that those images have on you as a viewer? What kind of theater do you like best? How does theater viewing of a movie compare to watching it on home TV?

4. Organize your class to make a survey of television viewing patterns.

   a. Check the weekly television rankings in a newspaper or on TV. Ask students to report which of the top 20 shows they watch regularly themselves. Then rank the shows from most to least popular. Compare your class results to the national survey.

   b. Make a scatterplot of (*number of students*, *show rank*) data for your class.

   c. Are the variables *number of students* and *show rank* linearly related? Explain your reasoning.

5. Agricultural and medical scientists conduct experiments to uncover possible relationships between pairs of variables. They often speak about *explanatory variables* and *response variables*.

   a. Many scientists have studied how drug dosage relates to blood pressure. Which of these factors would you consider as the response variable? Which is the explanatory variable? Give reasons for your choice.

   b. How do you think the ideas of response and explanatory variables are related to the ideas of independent and dependent variables as described in Organizing task 1?

Extending

1. Refer to your group's data on the bungee apparatus from Investigation 1.1 in Chapter 2. See if you can find a linear model, including a rule, that predicts stretch length from weight.

a. Describe two ways in which you can use the rule and your graphing calculator or computer software to predict stretch length for given weights.

b. Apply the method of your choice to the weight data in your group's table. Compare your predictions with experimental results from Chapter 2. Write a short report describing similarities and differences in the theoretical and experimental results. Be sure to provide explanations for any differences.

2. A common contest at carnivals or school game nights is to guess the number of beans or coins in a large jar. One way to arrive at good estimates for this amount, without actually counting every bean or coin, is to take some samples and look for a pattern. Test this strategy by performing the following experiment.

   a. Weigh a large jar and then fill it with beans.

   b. Take and then weigh some samples from the jar. Organize your data in a table like that below.

Number in Sample	Weight of Sample
5	
10	
15	
20	
25	
50	
100	

   c. Draw a graph modeling the pattern in your data.

   d. Find a rule relating *number in sample* and *weight of sample*.

   e. Weigh the entire jar. Use the table, graph, and rule to calculate a good estimate of the number of beans in the jar.

3. Design and carry out an experiment to study the pattern relating the shadow length of an object as a function of the time of day. Make a table and a graph to display your data. Try to find an equation for *shadow length* as a function of *time of day*. Use your equation to predict the shadow lengths for various times of day. Then test your predictions with actual measurements. Would your equation model shadow length as a function of time of day for next month? Explain your response.

4. The ratio of height to width of many movies shown in a theater is typically about 1 to 2. For example, a picture 25 feet high is about 50 feet wide. Height and width of television screens have a ratio of about 4 to 5.

  a. Usually, made-for-theater movies shown on TV are broadcast so that the image fills the entire height of the screen. This means that the whole width of the movie cannot be shown. What percentage of the movie image is cut off on a typical TV screen?

  b. Some video cassettes and some television broadcasts use a "letterbox" format to show the full width. This means that the height of the image does not fill the full TV screen. What percentage of the TV screen is not used?

  c. Which broadcast form do or would you prefer, and why?

2 *Linear Graphs, Tables, and Rules*

When two variables are related in a pattern that is roughly linear, it is helpful to model the pattern with a straight line graph. The scatterplot below shows data from a test of a single rubber band cord in a bungee-apparatus experiment. A linear graph has been drawn to model the pattern of change in length for increasing weight.

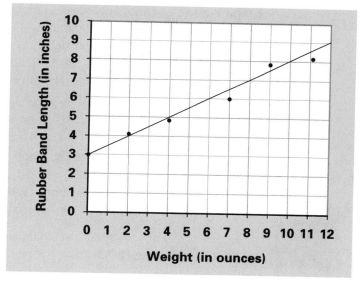

Think about this situation

The graph shows the overall pattern relating *weight* and rubber band *length*.

a Based on the linear model (not the data points themselves), what pattern would you expect in a table of (*weight, length*) pairs for weights from 0 to 10 ounces?

b How long is this rubber band with no weight attached, and how is that fact shown on the graph?

c How much does the rubber band stretch for each ounce of weight added, and how is that shown on the graph?

Investigation **2.1** Stretching Things Out

One of the most common examples of linear models is the way that forces stretch things such as rubber bands or coil springs. The more weight on the rubber band, the longer it stretches. The same is true about coil springs.

An equation for a linear model gives the simplest and most useful summary of the relation between the variables. In the following activities you will explore the variety of patterns that can occur in linear equations as they model rubber bands being stretched by increasing forces. As you complete the activities in this investigation, look for clues that will help you answer this basic question:

How are patterns in linear graphs, tables, and equations related to each other?

1. One key to the connection between graphs, tables, and equations for linear models can be found by comparing patterns of change in the two related variables. In mathematics, the Greek letter *delta* (Δ) is used to represent "change." For example, the change in weight can be written Δ **weight** (read "delta weight"). The matching change in rubber band length would be Δ **length** (read "delta length"). The **rate of change** in length as a function of weight is given by

$$\frac{\Delta \textbf{length}}{\Delta \textbf{weight}} .$$

For example, look back at the graph model on page 181. The linear model passes through the points (0, 3) and (10, 8). The change in length between these points is $(8 - 3) = 5$; the change in weight is $(10 - 0) = 10$. The rate of change is $\frac{5}{10} = \frac{1}{2}$. Notice that the subtracted numbers came from the same point (0, 3).

   a. Use the graph to estimate the change in rubber band length when the attached weight increases from

   0 to 1 ounce
   1 ounce to 3 ounces
   5 ounces to 9 ounces

   In each case find the rate of change in length as attached weight changes. Explain the units that should be used to describe that rate of change.

   b. How is the rate of change pattern in part a illustrated by the shape of the graph?

   c. The length of the rubber band with no weight attached is 3 inches. Use that fact and the rate of change pattern discovered in part a to find the length of the stretched rubber band when the weight is

   2 ounces
   4 ounces
   10 ounces
   W ounces

d. Write an equation using the words *NOW* and *NEXT* showing how the length of the stretched rubber band changes for each ounce of weight added.

e. Using the letters *L* (for *length in inches*) and *W* (for *weight in ounces*), write an equation that shows how the two variables are related: $L =$ _____.

f. How is the rate of change shown in the equations of parts d and e?

g. How is the length of the rubber band with no weight attached shown in the equation for part e?

h. Use your equations to predict stretch lengths for each of these weights:

   4.5 ounces

   17 ounces

   0.25 ounces

2. The diagram at the right shows linear models based on experiments with three coil springs. The models are all plotted on the same grid. What do the patterns of these graphs suggest about ways the springs are alike and different?

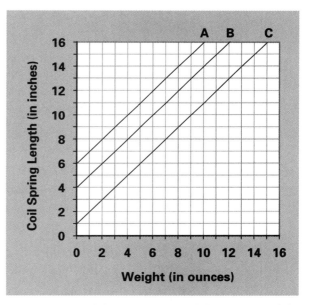

a. Sharing the work among your group members, make three tables of (*weight, length*) pairs. Make one table for each linear model. Include weights from 0 to 10 ounces.

b. According to the tables, how long were the different springs without any weight attached? How is that information shown on the graphs?

c. Looking at data in the tables, estimate the rates of change in length as weight is added to the three springs. How are those patterns shown on the graphs?

d. Write an equation using *NOW* and *NEXT* showing how the spring length changes with each added ounce of weight in each case.

e. Using the letters *L* (for *length in inches*) and *W* (for *weight in ounces*), write equations that show how the two variables are related in each case.

f. How can you use the equations from part e to find the lengths of each spring with no weight attached?

g. How are the rates of change in length of the various springs related? How is this fact shown in the equations?

3. The diagram at the right shows graphs of linear models from another set of coil springs experiments. What do the patterns of these graphs suggest about ways the springs are alike and different?

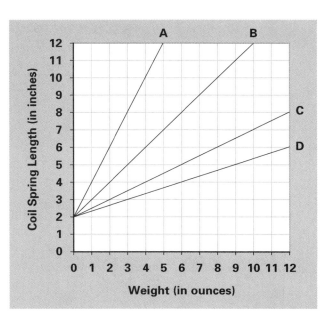

a. Sharing the work among your group members, make tables of (*weight, length*) pairs. Make one table for each linear model shown. Include weights from 0 to 10 ounces.

b. According to the tables, how long were the springs without any weight attached? How is that information shown on the graphs?

c. Looking at the data in the tables or the graphs, estimate the rates of change in length as weight is added. How can the rates be determined from the graph? From the table?

d. For each linear model, write an equation using *NOW* and *NEXT* showing how the length changes as each ounce of weight is added.

e. Using the letters *L* (for *length in inches*) and *W* (for *weight in ounces*), write equations that show how the two variables are related in each case.

f. What do the numbers in your equations tell you about the graphs?

g. What differences in the springs could cause the differences in graphs, tables, and equations that modeled the data from the experiments?

4. In some places where springs are used, the springs are made shorter by pressure from force or weights. For example, the springs in a bed or chair are pressed shorter when you sit on them. The springs in a scale are pressed shorter when you stand on the scale.

The following diagram shows graphs of four different linear relations. Those graphs model data from an experiment which tested bed springs. What do the patterns of these graphs suggest about the similarities and differences in the springs?

a. Sharing the work with members of your group, make four tables of (*weight*, *length*) pairs. Make one table for each linear model. Include weights starting at 0 kg.

b. How long are the springs with no weight applied?

c. What are the rates of change in spring length with increasing weight? (Remember, the subtracted numbers for both length and weight must come from the same point.) How can you calculate these rates using points on the lines? Using pairs of values in the tables?

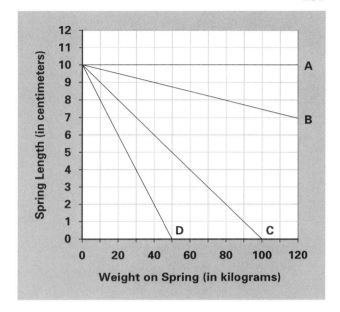

d. Write equations using *NOW* and *NEXT* showing how the springs change length as each kilogram of weight is added.

e. For each linear model, write an equation expressing *L* (*length in centimeters*) as a function of *W* (*weight in kilograms*).

f. Which linear model might correspond to springs in an extra firm bed? In a medium firm bed? Explain your choices.

g. For each of the tested springs, estimate the length of the spring with a weight of 30 kg. Which do you prefer to use in making estimates: a graph, table, or equation?

5. Each linear equation below models a spring stretching or compressing experiment. Identify the following:

   – The initial length of the spring

   – The rate of change of the length

   – Whether the experiment was designed to measure spring stretch or compression

   a. $L = 5 + 4W$

   b. $L = 1 + 2.3W$

   c. $L = 3 + (-1.5W)$

   d. $L = 8 + (-0.1W)$

When studying a linear graph, it helps to think about weights and lengths of rubber bands or springs. But the connections between graphs, tables, and equations are the same for linear models relating *any* two variables x and y. By now you've probably noticed the following key features of linear models and their graphs.

– Linear models always have a **constant rate of change**. That is, $\frac{\Delta y}{\Delta x}$ is a constant.

– The constant rate of change can be seen in the **slope** of the linear graph. The **slope** is the direction and steepness of a walk along the graph from left to right.

– The **y-intercept** of the linear graph is the point where the graph intersects the *y*-axis.

How could the connections between tables, graphs, and equations of linear models be used to locate the y-intercept and to measure the slope of a graph?

6. Study the two linear models on this graph.

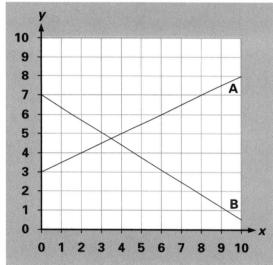

   a. Find the *y*-intercept of each graph. Then explain how those *y*-intercepts relate to the following:

   – Tables of (x, y) values for each graph

   – Equations relating *NOW* and *NEXT* for each graph

   – Equations relating x and y for each graph

   b. Find the slope of each graph. Then explain how the slopes relate to the following:

   – Tables of (x, y) values for each graph

   – Equations relating *NOW* and *NEXT* for each graph

   – Equations relating x and y for each graph

7. Look back over the examples of linear models for (*weight*, *length*) data from experiments with rubber bands and springs.

   a. How are linear graphs related when they have the same slope?

   b. How are linear graphs with the same *y*-intercept, but different slopes, related to each other?

Checkpoint

Linear models relating any two variables *x* and *y* can be represented using tables, graphs, or equations. Important features of a linear model can be seen in each representation.

ⓐ How can the rate of change in two variables be seen:
- in a table of (*x, y*) values?
- in a linear graph?
- in an equation relating *NOW* and *NEXT* for the model?
- in an equation relating *x* and *y*?

ⓑ How can the *y*-intercept be seen:
- in a table of (*x, y*) values?
- in a linear graph?
- in an equation relating *NOW* and *NEXT* for the model?
- in an equation relating *x* and *y*?

✓ *Be prepared to share your group's descriptions with the whole class.*

On Your Own

Every business has to deal with two important patterns of change, *depreciation* and *inflation*. When they buy new equipment, the value of that equipment declines as it is used. The cost of buying new replacement equipment increases from inflation as time passes.

The owners of *Laser Games Unlimited* operate a series of video game arcades in malls across the midwest. They keep a close eye on costs for new and used arcade games. One set of predictions is shown in the graph at the right.

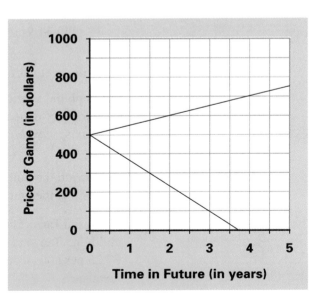

a. Which of the two graph models represents the price of a new game? The price of a used game?

b. For each linear graph, do the following.
  - Find the slope and *y*-intercept
  - Make a table of (*time*, *game value*) data and find the rate of change.
  - Write an equation relating *NOW* and *NEXT* showing how game price changes each year.
  - Write an equation relating game price *P* and time *T*.

c. Compare:
  - Slopes and *y*-intercept of the two graphs
  - Rates of change in the tables
  - Equations relating *NOW* and *NEXT*
  - The equations relating *P* and *T*

Modeling **O**rganizing **R**eflecting **E**xtending

Modeling

1. Mary and Jeff Jordan both have jobs at their local baseball park selling programs. They get paid $10 per game plus $0.25 for each program they sell.

  a. Make a table showing the pay they can expect for any game as a function of the number of programs they sell. Include values for 0 to 100 programs in steps of 5.

  b. Write an equation relating *programs sold S* and *pay P* for a game.

  c. Graph the relation between *programs sold* and *pay* (for 0 to 100 programs). Since pay depends on the number of programs sold, pay is the *dependent* (*y*-axis) *variable*. The number of programs sold is the *independent variable* (*x*-axis).

  d. How do the numbers from the pay rule of $10 plus $0.25 per program sold relate to the patterns in the table, the graph, and the equation?

2. Jamal and Tanya Guinier work at city recreation department day camps for young children. Tanya is a coordinator with several years of experience, so she earns $7.25 per hour. This is Jamal's first year on the job, so he earns only $4.50 per hour.

a. Make a table showing how Tanya's and Jamal's earnings will grow over the summer as a function of hours worked.

b. Write equations relating *hours worked H* and pay earned for each worker. Use *T* for *Tanya's earnings* and *J* for *Jamal's earnings.*

c. Sketch graphs of the two pay rules on the same coordinate system.

d. How do the pay rates of $4.50 per hour and $7.25 per hour relate to the table, the graphs, and the equations?

3. Jose Alvarez got a job with a lawn service. He earned $400 during the summer and saved quite a bit of that money. When school started again in the fall, he needed to use some of his savings. The following table shows his bank balance over a 9-week period in the fall.

Week Number	1	2	3	4	5	6	7	8	9
Money Left	210	198	190	175	155	142	128	110	95

a. Make a scatterplot of Jose's bank balance data. Draw a line that models the trend in that plot.

b. Write an equation for the linear model. Use *W* for *weeks* and *M* for *money left*. Remember that money left depends on the week number.

c. Predict Jose's bank balance after 10, 15, and 20 weeks.

d. Explain how the patterns in the table, graph, and equation are related to each other. What do they say about Jose's spending habits?

4. Victoria DeStefano got a job at her school as scorekeeper for a summer basketball league. The job pays $450 for the summer and the league plays on 25 nights. Some nights Victoria will have to get a substitute for her job and give her pay for that night to the substitute.

a. What should Victoria pay a substitute for one night?

b. Use the letters *N* for *nights a substitute works*, *S* for *pay to the substitute*, and *E* for *Victoria's total summer earnings*,

   – Write an equation relating *N* and *S*, beginning *S* = ...

   – Write an equation relating *N* and *E*, beginning *E* = ...

c. Produce graphs of the equations in part b.

d. How do the equations and the patterns of the graphs show Victoria's earning prospects from two views?

Organizing

1. On the diagram shown here, there are five graphs of relations between variables. Following are five tables of sample (x, y) data. Match each graph with the table that best describes its pattern. In each case, explain the clues that you used to make the matches. Are there any other clues that could have been used?

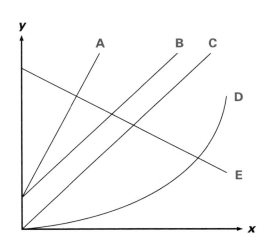

a.

x	1	2	3	4	5	6	7	8	9
y	1	2	3	4	5	6	7	8	9

b.

x	1	2	3	4	5	6	7	8	9
y	9.5	9.0	8.5	8.0	7.5	7.0	6.5	6.0	5.5

c.

x	1	2	3	4	5	6	7	8	9
y	3	4	5	6	7	8	9	10	11

d.

x	1	2	3	4	5	6	7	8	9
y	0.04	0.17	0.38	0.69	1.09	1.61	2.25	3.06	4.06

e.

x	1	2	3	4	5	6	7	8	9
y	4	6	8	10	12	14	16	18	20

2. The diagram here shows four linear graphs. For each graph, do the following.

   a. Find the rate at which y changes as x changes.

   b. Write an equation using *NOW* and *NEXT* that describes the pattern of change shown by the graph.

   c. Write an equation relating x and y beginning $y = \ldots$.

   d. How do your answers to parts a through c relate to each other for each graph?

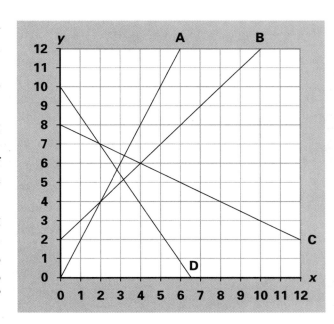

3. When the pattern relating two variables x and y can be described by a linear model, the rate of change in the variables tells the slope of the graph. The reverse is also true: the slope tells the rate of change.

   a. Suppose $(7, 2)$ and $(9, 5)$ are two points on the graph of a linear model. What is the slope of the line containing the points?

   b. Use the ordered pairs (r, s) and (t, u) to stand for coordinates of any two points on a graph or entries in a table of values for some linear model.

   – Write an expression for calculating the slope of the linear graph.

   – Write an expression for calculating the rate of change in y as x changes.

   c. Explain the meaning of the numerator and denominator of the expressions you wrote for part b.

   d. What is the connection between slope or rate of change of a linear model and the equation for the model?

4. Linear models often are described by equations of the form $y = a + bx$. For each of the equations below, describe what the numbers corresponding to a and b tell you about the tables and graphs of that model.

   a. $y = 4 + 2x$

   b. $y = 12.5 + 7.3x$

   c. $y = 200 - 25x$

5. Linear models also can be described using equations relating *NOW* and *NEXT*.

   a. Consider the equation $y = 4 + 2x$. Use the equation to complete a table like the one shown here. Then use the table to help answer the following questions.

x	y
0	
1	
2	
3	
4	

   – If *NOW* = 4, what is *NEXT* when x increases by 1?

   – Write an equation relating *NEXT* to *NOW* for an increase of 1 in x.

   – How does your equation relating *NOW* and *NEXT* show constant rate of change?

   b. If *NOW* $- 6 = $ *NEXT*, what is the slope of the linear model? Why?

Reflecting

1. Describe a situation with which you are familiar in which one variable is:

   a. increasing at a constant rate.

   b. decreasing at a constant rate.

   c. increasing, but not at a constant rate.

2. Measuring the slope of a linear graph is very similar to measuring the pitch of the roof line on a house.

   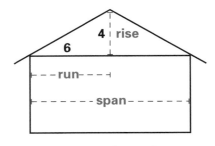

   $$\text{slope} = \frac{\text{rise}}{\text{run}} = \frac{4}{6}$$

   $$\text{pitch} = \frac{\text{rise}}{\text{span}} = \frac{4}{12}$$

   a. Describe at least 5 different roof slopes that you see around school, near home, or around your city or town. Estimate each slope using the $\frac{\text{rise}}{\text{run}}$ relation shown in the diagram. Estimate the pitch of the same roofs.

   b. Which roofs have the steepest slope? Which have the most gradual slope?

   c. What are some reasons for having steep or gradual slopes in buildings?

3. Sloping lines show up many other places in the world around us. Make sketches illustrating at least 5 examples other than roofs.

4. On hilly roads you sometimes see signs warning of steep grades ahead. What do you think a sign like the one at the left tells you about the slope of the road ahead?

Extending

1. If a linear model is represented by an equation of the form $y = a + bx$, what do a and b tell you about the table of values and graph of that model?

2. The table at the right gives the amount of money spent on national health care for selected years 1960 to 1990.

   a. Make a scatterplot of this data.

Annual U.S. Health Care Expenditures, 1960-1990 (in billions of dollars)			
1960	**1970**	**1980**	**1990**
27.1	74.4	250.1	675.0

Source: *The World Almanac and Book of Facts 1995*. Mahwah, NJ: World Almanac, 1994.

b. What is the rate of change in health care expenditures from 1960 to 1970? From 1970 to 1980? From 1980 to 1990? From 1960 to 1990?

c. Do you think the scatterplot data could be modeled well by a line? Explain.

d. How could you estimate health care costs for the year 2000?

3. The graph at the right illustrates the relationship between time in flight and height of a soccer ball kicked straight up in the air. The equation for that relation is $H = -5T^2 + 20T$ where T is in seconds and H is in meters.

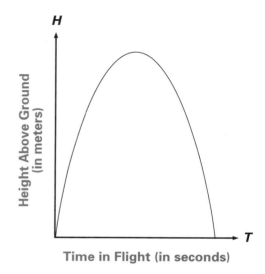

   a. What could it mean to talk about the slope of this curved graph?

   b. How would you measure the rate of change in height of the ball?

   c. How would rate of change and slope relate to each other?

   d. What would rate of change and slope tell about the flight of the ball?

4. The table below gives data on mass and volume for various measures of olive oil and diamonds.

Volume (cm³)	Oil (grams)	Diamonds (grams)
1	0.91	3.49
2	1.84	7.02
3	2.70	10.65
4	3.64	13.92
5	4.65	17.35
6	5.40	21.00
7	6.37	24.64
8	7.44	27.92

   a. Make scatterplots of the relations between volume and mass of olive oil and between volume and mass of diamonds. On each plot draw a graph that seems to fit the pattern of the data well.

b. Write *NOW-NEXT* equations showing how the mass of oil or diamonds increases as the volume increases.

c. Use the models drawn in part a to find rules for predicting mass M from volume V for the two substances:

$-\ M_{oil} =$ _____

$-\ M_{diamonds} =$ _____

What connections do you see between the two types of equations for each relationship?

d. The ratio $\dfrac{mass}{volume}$ is called the *density* of a substance. It often is measured in grams per cubic centimeter.

    – How can the density of oil and of diamonds be seen in the modeling equations?

    – What is the density of these two substances?

e. What differences in the table data and the equations show differences in the densities of the two substances?

f. Mary Jo inherited a 5.5 carat clear gem stone from her rich great-aunt. The volume of the stone is 0.4 cm^3.

    – If one carat is equal to 0.2 grams, what is the mass of the stone?

    – How could Mary Jo have figured out the volume of the stone?

    – Is the stone a diamond?

Investigation (2.2) Finding Linear Equations

A symbolic rule showing how the variables x and y are related is a concise and simple way to record a linear model. The most common way to write rules for linear models is using equations of the form

$$y = a + bx$$

where a and b are specific numbers that set the relation between x and y. In earlier investigations, you've probably found several ways to determine the values of a and b in particular cases.

1. In many problems you can discover the right equation simply by thinking about given facts relating the variables. For example:

     The music department at Kennedy High School operates a soft drink machine for students. Profits go to the band, orchestra, and chorus. The department pays $100 per month to rent the machine and $7.50 per case for soft drinks in cans.

a. What equation relates monthly sales *S* in cases of soda to monthly costs *C* paid to the distributor?

b. In your equation $C = a + bS$, what are the values of *a* and *b*? What do they tell about the situation?

c. If you made a graph of the (*sales*, *cost*) relation, what would the *y*-intercept and slope of the graph be?

d. Suppose you made a table of sample (*sales*, *cost*) values. What rate of change in cost, as a function of sales, would appear in that table?

e. What *NOW-NEXT* equation shows how monthly costs increase for each case of soft drinks sold? How does that equation relate to the following:

    – The equation in $C = a + bS$ form?

    – The slope of a graph for the model?

    – The rate of change in cost as a function of sales?

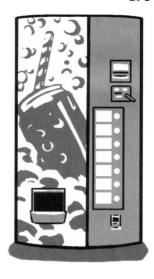

2. In some cases you can draw a straight line model for the pattern in a scatterplot and find the equation relating *x* and *y* from the *y*-intercept and slope of that graph. For example:

The music department experimented with several different prices on soft drinks. The (*price*, *sales*) data are shown on the graph at the right. A linear model has been drawn in to match the trend in that data.

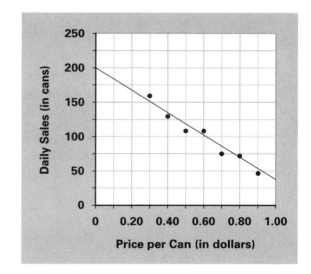

a. What overall pattern relates price and daily sales in this graph?

b. What are the slope and *y*-intercept of the linear model?

c. Using your answers to part b, write an equation that fits the model.

3. In some cases the modeling line does not show a clear choice for slope or
y-intercept.

   For example, the pattern of growth for one bean plant grown under special
lighting is shown in the table and graph below.

Day	Height
3	4.2
4	4.7
5	5.1
6	6.3
7	7.4

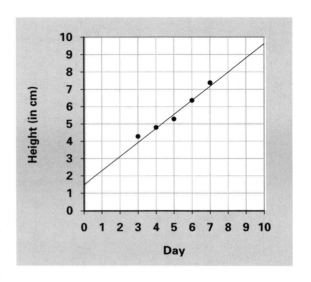

Unfortunately, neither the
slope nor the y-intercept is
easy to see accurately from
the graph. In such a case you
can try the following steps to
find a and b in an equation of
the form $y = a + bx$.

– To find the slope b, pick any two points on the line for which you know
  coordinates. In this example, you could try $(4, 4.7)$ and $(6, 6.3)$. Using those
  two points to estimate the slope, $b = \frac{6.3-4.7}{6-4} = \frac{1.6}{2} = 0.8$. So the equation becomes $y = a + 0.8x$.

– To find the y-intercept a, pick the x and y values for any point on the line. For
  example, try $(7, 7.1)$. These values of x and y must satisfy the model relation,
  $y = a + 0.8x$. So, it must be true that

$$7.1 = a + 0.8(7)$$
$$7.1 = a + 5.6$$

   This means that, in this case, a must be 1.5. So the model equation is
$y = 1.5 + 0.8x$.

a. Try the method just outlined using these three points on the line: $(5, 5.5)$,
   $(7, 7.1)$, and $(3, 3.9)$.

   – What slope do you get by using $(5, 5.5)$ and $(7, 7.1)$?

   – What value of a do you get by using the point $(3, 3.9)$ and substituting 3
     for x and 3.9 for y?

b. Try the method for finding a and b using a combination of just *two* points.

4. In many cases you will need to fit a linear model to a scatterplot pattern that is more complicated. For example, it may include many data points, numbers that are not simple whole numbers, and a trend for which it is not clear what modeling line will be best. For example, the following table gives list prices for new Toyota Celicas and Mercury Cougars.

Year	Base Price Toyota Celica	Base Price Mercury Cougar	Year	Base Price Toyota Celica	Base Price Mercury Cougar
1979	5899	5524	1989	11,808	15,448
1981	6699	7009	1991	12,698	16,094
1983	7299	9809	1993	14,198	14,855
1985	8449	10,650	1995	15,775	14,900
1987	10,598	13,595			

Source: *N.A.D.A. Official Used Car Guide*. McLean, VA: N.A.D.A. Official Used Car Guide Company. 1996.

a. Working in pairs, make a scatterplot of the Toyota Celica (*year*, *price*) data. Draw what you believe will be a good linear model for that pattern. It will simplify your work if you treat 1979 as year 1 on the time axis and scale the price axis in $1000 units.

b. Find an equation for the linear model you've drawn.

c. Compare the graph and equation models you found to those of other members of your group. Try to explain any differences.

5. Most graphing calculators and computers offer efficient and systematic ways to find good equation models for linear data patterns. One way, called **linear regression**, finds the equation of the line that minimizes the mean of the *squared* errors of prediction. Like the linear models you sketched in Investigation 1.3, the **linear regression model** passes through the point $(\bar{x}, \bar{y})$.

a. Use your calculator or computer software to enter the data for *year* and *Celica price* into the first and second data lists.

b. Produce a scatterplot of the (*year*, *Celica price*) data.

c. Compute the slope and *y*-intercept of the linear regression model. The "Technology Tip" handout may be helpful.

d. Write the equation of the linear regression line.

e. What is the estimated rate at which Celicas increased in cost per year?

6. If you display the graph of the linear regression line on the scatterplot, you can use the equation model for estimating Celica prices in other years. Enter the appropriate equation in your calculator or software's function list.

   a. What price for a new Celica is predicted for 1980? 1984? 1994?

   b. In what year is the new Celica price predicted to exceed $16,800?

   c. For how many years is the price of a new Celica predicted to stay under $20,000?

7. Enter the data for *Cougar price* into a new list. Practice use of the calculator modeling procedure by finding the linear regression model for the (*year, Cougar price*) data. Then use your model to answer the questions below.

   a. What new Cougar price is predicted for 1984? 1994?

   b. In what year is the new Cougar price predicted to reach $20,000?

Checkpoint

There are several different methods of finding an equation for a linear model.

ⓐ To find an equation in the form $y = a + bx$, how can you use information about:
  - Slope and y-intercept of the graph of that model?
  - Rate of change and other values in a table of (x, y) data?

ⓑ How can you find the equation if slope and y-intercept are not given?

ⓒ In what cases does it make sense to use a graphing calculator or computer software to find the modeling line and equation? What steps are involved?

✓ *Be prepared to share descriptions of your methods with the class.*

On Your Own

The athletic department at Kennedy High School operates a soft drink machine near the gymnasium. The distributor regularly collects the money from the machine. The school is paid $50 per month plus $3 per case of soft drinks sold.

a. What equation gives the rule showing monthly profit P to the athletic department as a function of number of cases sold S?

b. Using the graph alone, estimate monthly profit figures for the following table entries. (Do not use the rule you wrote in part a.) Then use your graphing calculator or computer software to find the *linear regression line* that fits those estimates. Compare the result to your equation in part a.

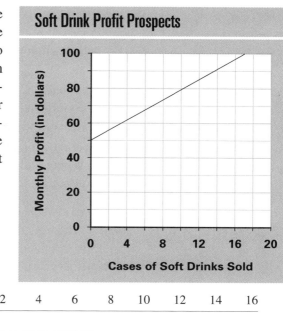

Soft Drink Profit Prospects

Cases Sold	1	2	4	6	8	10	12	14	16
Profit in Dollars	53								

c. What might explain any difference between your two equations?

Investigation 2.3 Lines All Over the Plane

The investigations in this unit and in Chapter 2, "Patterns of Change," have shown many places where linear models help you to describe and reason about relations between variables. But the range of linear models is even broader than what you have studied so far.

For example, you might recall that in Chapter 2, profits for operation of the Palace Theater were related to daily ticket sales with an equation $P = -450 + 2.50T$. If you graph this equation with a window like the one shown, some important parts of the Palace Theater business story will not appear.

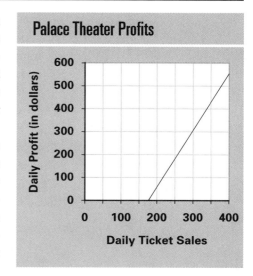

Palace Theater Profits

1. If you use your graphing calculator or computer to reproduce the graph of $P = -450 + 2.50T$ in the window shown on the previous page, what would the out-of-window points tell you about the business?

   a. Modify your window settings to show the entire linear graph from the case of no audience to a full house of 400 viewers. Use the trace function to find coordinates of some of the new points shown. Explain what they tell about theater business prospects.

   b. What values of P come from this model for negative values of T, like -100? Where will those values appear on the graph of the model? What do they say about the theater profit situation?

The Palace Theater profit questions show again why it is important to know how to work with equations $y = a + bx$. To solve problems involving linear models it is helpful to understand the connections between the equations and their tables and graphs, even for points outside the first coordinate quadrant. To sort out the possibilities, organize your group for the following exploration of cases.

2. Assign each member to explore two of the cases for the equation $y = a + bx$ which are listed below. Use the following guidelines for the exploration. Each member should report and explain his or her conclusions to the group.

   Each explorer should do the following, using the graphing calculator or computer as a tool.

   – Choose 4 different sets of values for a and b.
   – Make tables and graphs for Xmin = -10 to Xmax = 10.
   – Identify properties common to all graphs and common to all tables.
   – Identify ways the graphs differ and ways the tables differ.
   – Identify ways that patterns in tables can be predicted from the values of a and b.
   – Identify ways that patterns in graphs can be predicted from the values of a and b.
   – Think about the reasons that the predictions work.

   Case 1: a and b are both positive numbers.
   Case 2: a is negative and b is positive.
   Case 3: a and b are both negative numbers.
   Case 4: a is positive and b is negative.
   Case 5: $a = 0$ and b is positive or negative.
   Case 6: a is positive or negative and $b = 0$.

3. As a result of your group work, each group member should be able to make a quick and accurate sketch of any linear equation. To test your skill, divide your group into pairs. Each pair should complete the following challenge.

The Brain–Machine Challenge

For each equation in list A, one partner should sketch a graph by hand while the other partner produces the graph using a calculator or computer. Compare results. For equations in list B, partners should change roles and repeat the process.

List A	List B
$y = 5 + 3x$	$y = -3 - 5x$
$y = -5 + 3x$	$y = 8 + 2x$
$y = 5 - 3x$	$y = -10 + 0.2x$
$y = -2x + 8$	$y = -4 - 3x$
$y = 6 + 0x$	$y = 2 - 0x$

After completing the challenge, make a list of things you look for in an equation to help make a quick sketch.

Checkpoint

How can the equation of a linear model be used to predict:

a the slope and location of its graph?

b the rate of change in a table of the equation's values?

✓ **Be prepared to share your group's thinking with the entire class.**

On Your Own

For equations in the form $y = a + bx$, find values of a and b that have graphs that pass through the following quadrants of the plane.

a. I, II, and III

b. I, II, and IV

c. I, III, and IV

d. II, III, and IV

e. I and III

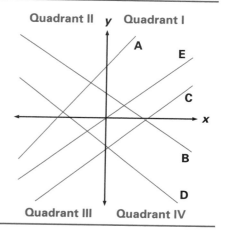

Modeling Organizing Reflecting Extending

Modeling

1. A phone call to two plumbing repair shops gave the following quotations for repair work.

   Pride Plumbing: $35 for the service call, plus $32 per hour for repair time.

   Kovach: $25 for the service call, plus $40 per hour for repair time.

   a. For each shop, write an equation that shows the relation between total repair cost in dollars and the number of hours to complete the repair.

   b. If the repair took less than an 8-hour working day, what would be the possible values for the input variable and the output variable for your model of Pride Plumbing's cost? For your model of Kovach's cost?

   c. Without actually graphing, describe how the graphs of your equations in part a would be related in terms of location and slope.

   d. If the graphs of the equations in part a intersect, what would the point of intersection tell you?

   e. Will the graphs of the equations in part a intersect? Explain.

2. Many Americans love to eat fast food. But we also are concerned about weight gain and the cholesterol that is generated by eating saturated fat. Many fast-food restaurants now advertise special "lite" menus. They give information about the fat and calorie content of those foods, like the data in the following table.

Item	Grams Fat	Total Calories	Calories from Fat
McDonald's			
McLean Deluxe Sandwich	12	350	110
Filet O'Fish Sandwich	16	360	150
McLean Deluxe & Small Fries	22	560	200
KFC			
Skinfree Crispy Breast	17	293	153
Chicken Sandwich	27	482	243

Item	Grams Fat	Total Calories	Calories from Fat
Wendy's			
Chicken Sandwich	20	450	180
Baked Potato with Broccoli & Cheese	14	460	120
Taco Salad	30	580	270
Hardee's			
Fisherman's Fillet	20	450	180
Grilled Chicken Sandwich	9	290	80

Sources: *McDonald's Nutrition Facts*, McDonald's Corporation, 1995; *KFC Nutrition Facts*, KFC, 1995; *Good Nutrition News From Wendy's*, Wendy's International, Inc., 1994; Hardee's Nutritional Information, 1996.

a. Make a scatterplot of data relating grams of fat F to total calories T in the menu items shown.

b. Draw a linear model joining the points (12, 350) and (30, 580). Find its equation in the form $T = a + bF$. Explain what the values of a and b tell about the model graph and about the relation between grams of fat and total calories in the food items.

c. Use your graphing calculator or computer to find the linear regression model for the data (F, T) in the table. Compare this result to what you found in part b.

3. Use the table from Modeling task 2 to analyze the relation between grams of fat F and calories from fat C in the menu items.

a. Make a scatterplot of data relating F and C.

b. Draw a linear model joining the points (12, 110) and (30, 270). Find its equation in the form $C = a + bF$. Explain what the values of a and b tell about the model graph and about the relation between grams of fat and calories from fat in the food items.

c. If a food item contained 13 grams of fat, how many calories of the item would you expect to be from the fat content?

d. Use your graphing calculator or computer to find the linear regression model for the (*grams of fat*, *calories from fat*) data. Compare with the model you found in part b. Explain your findings.

4. Over the past 40 years, more and more women have taken full-time jobs outside the home. As women have entered the work force, there has been a great deal of controversy about whether they are being paid fairly. The table below shows patterns of change from 1970 to 1990 in median incomes for men and women employed full-time outside the home. This data does not show pay for comparable jobs, but average pay for all jobs.

Median Income (in dollars)

Year	Men	Women	Year	Men	Women	Year	Men	Women
1970	8,966	5,323	1978	15,730	9,350	1986	25,256	16,232
1972	10,202	5,903	1980	18,612	11,197	1988	26,656	17,606
1974	11,889	6,970	1982	21,077	13,014	1990	27,678	19,822
1976	13,455	8,099	1984	23,218	14,780			

Sources: *The 1993 Information Please Almanac*. Boston: Houghton Mifflin. 1992. *The 1982 Information Please Almanac*. Boston: Houghton Mifflin. 1981.

a. What do you believe are the most interesting and important patterns in this data?

b. Did women's incomes improve in relation to men's incomes between 1970 and 1990?

c. The next diagram shows a scatterplot of the (*year, median income*) data for women, using 0 for the year 1970. A linear model for the pattern in those data is drawn on the coordinate grid. Use two points on the line to find the slope of the line. Estimate the *y*-intercept. Then write an equation for the line.

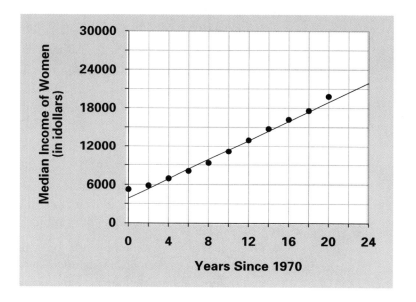

d. Using the linear median-income model, estimate the income of women in 1963, 1973, 1983, 1993, and 2003.

e. Use a linear regression procedure on your calculator or computer to find another equation for a linear model of the (*year, median income*) data. Compare the predictions of that model with your results from part d.

5. Use a linear regression procedure to find an equation modeling the pattern of (*year, median income*) data for men.

a. Compare the slope and *y*-intercept of the model for men's income to those for women's income found in Modeling task 4. Explain what each tells about the situation.

b. Use the equation to estimate median income for men in 1963, 1973, 1983, 1993, and 2003. Compare the results to what you found for women.

Organizing

1. Find equations for each of the linear models graphed on the diagram at the right.

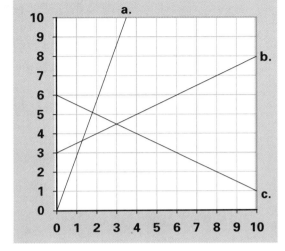

2. For each of the following ordered pairs of numbers:

   – Plot the points on a coordinate grid and draw a line through the points.

   – Find the equation of the line through the points.

   a. (0, 3) and (6, 6)

   b. (0, -4) and (5, 6)

   c. (-4, -3) and (2, 3)

   d. (-6, 4) and (3, -8)

3. Draw sketches of possible graphs of equations $y = a + bx$ in each of the following cases:

   a. $a < 0$ and $b > 0$

   b. $a > 0$ and $b < 0$

   c. $a < 0$ and $b < 0$

   d. $a > 0$ and $b > 0$

4. Plot the two points A (2, 4) and B (8, 8) on graph paper. Label the points with the coordinates and the letters A and B. Then draw the line containing points A and B.

   a. What is the slope of the line containing points A and B?

   b. Sketch the line $y = \frac{2}{3} x$ on the same coordinate grid. Describe how this line compares to the line which cotains points A and B.

   – Find the y-coordinates for the two points on the line $y = \frac{2}{3} x$ whose x-coordinates are 2 and 8. Label these points with their coordinates.

   – How far vertically (up or down) must you move each point of the line $y = \frac{2}{3} x$ to get corresponding points on the line containing the points (2, 4) and (8, 8)? Explain your answer.

   c. Explain how you can find the value of the y-intercept for the line containing points A and B.

   d. Write the equation for the line through points (2, 4) and (8, 8).

   e. Use a similar method to find the equation of the line through the points (4, 5) and (14, 30).

Reflecting

1. What can you tell about the signs of the coordinates (positive or negative) for points:

   a. in quadrant I?

   b. in quadrant II?

   c. in quadrant III?

   d. in quadrant IV?

2. **a.** Describe the effect of increasing or decreasing the value of b on the graph of $y = 4 + bx$.

   b. Describe the effect of increasing or decreasing the value of a on the graph of $y = a + 2x$.

3. To use linear models wisely it helps to be in the habit of asking, "What sorts of numbers would make sense in this situation?" For example, in the relation between ticket sales T and profits P of the Palace Theater, it would not make much sense to substitute negative values for T in the equation $P = -450 + 2.50T$. In each of the following situations, decide what range of values for the variables would make sense.

   a. Temperature can be expressed in many different scales. You probably are familiar with two, Celsius and Fahrenheit. The linear model to convert from one scale to another is $F = \frac{9}{5}C + 32$, where F is degrees Fahrenheit and C is degrees Celsius. What range of values for F and C make sense for temperatures that you might encounter?

   b. Suppose a ball is tossed into the air with an upward velocity of 40 feet per second. Its upward velocity is a function of time in flight, modeled by the equation $V = 40 - 32T$. *Velocity V* is in feet per second and *time T* is in seconds. What range of values for T and V make sense in this context?

   c. The cost of buying a used Ford Mustang automobile can be modeled by $C = 10,000 - 560Y$, where C is the cost in dollars and Y is the age of the car in years. What range of values for Y and C make sense?

   d. In one apartment building, new renters are offered $150 off their first month's rent. They pay a normal rate of $450 per month. The total rent paid for an apartment in that building is modeled by $R = 450T - 150$, where T is the number of months. What range of values for R and T make sense?

4. Discuss the pros and cons of each method described below for finding equation models of linear patterns in data.

a. Draw a line that seems to fit the data pattern. Estimate the slope of the line. Estimate the *y*-intercept of the line. Write the equation.

b. Draw a line through two data points that seem typical of the pattern. Calculate the slope of that line from the data points. Estimate the *y*-intercept. Write the equation.

c. Draw a line that seems to fit the data pattern. Estimate coordinates of several points on that line. Use the coordinates to calculate the slope. Then substitute values from one of the points to get an equation for finding the *y*-intercept.

d. Enter the data in a calculator or computer. Then use the linear regression procedure for finding an equation to fit the data.

Extending

1. Investigate the linear regression procedure for finding a linear model to fit data patterns.

   a. For each of the following data sets, use your graphing calculator or computer to make a scatterplot. Then find the modeling equation calculated by the linear regression procedure.

   i.

x	0	1	2	3	4	5	6	7	8
y	3	5	7	9	11	13	15	17	19

   ii.

x	0	1	2	3	4	5	6	7	8
y	1	5	7	9	11	13	15	17	29

   iii.

x	0	1	2	3	4	5	6	7	8
y	4	6	8	10	12	14	16	18	20

   iv.

x	0	1	2	3	4	5	6	7	8
y	1	2	5	10	17	26	37	50	65

   v.

x	0	1	2	3	4	5	6	7	8
y	3	8	11	12	12	11	8	3	-4

   b. Compare the graph produced by the linear regression equation to the actual data in each case of part a. Comment on the fit in each case and explain places where the fit is not good.

   c. What limitations of using the linear regression procedure are suggested by the results in parts a and b?

2. Graph the line $y = 5 + 3x$.

   a. Find the equations of all lines that cross the vertical axis 2 units from $y = 5 + 3x$ and are parallel to that line.

   b. Imagine jumping from $y = 5 + 3x$ to any of the lines found in part a. How long is that jump in these cases:
   - Jumping vertically
   - Jumping horizontally
   - Jumping the direction that gives the shortest jump

   c. Describe the form of the equation of all lines that cross the vertical axis exactly 2 units away from the given line.

3. The 100-meter run for men has been run in the Olympics since 1896. The winning times for each of the years through 1992 are given in the following table.

Winning Times for Men: Olympic 100 Meters			
Year	**Time (Sec)**	**Year**	**Time (Sec)**
1896	12.0	1952	10.4
1900	10.8	1956	10.5
1904	11.0	1960	10.2
1908	10.8	1964	10.0
1912	10.8	1968	9.95
1920	10.8	1972	10.14
1924	10.6	1976	10.06
1928	10.8	1980	10.25
1932	10.3	1984	9.99
1936	10.3	1988	9.92
1948	10.3	1992	9.96

Source: *The World Almanac and Book of Facts 1995*, Mahwah, NJ: World Almanac, 1994.

   a. Study the data. Notice the pattern in the years. Are there gaps that don't fit the pattern? Why were races not run those years?

b. Make a scatterplot of the (*year*, *time*) data using 1880 as year 0. Then decide whether you think a linear model is reasonable for the pattern in your plot.

c. Find the ($\bar{x}$, $\bar{y}$) point for the data. Locate it on your scatterplot. Then draw a linear model that goes through ($\bar{x}$, $\bar{y}$) and fits the trend in the data as well as you think is possible.

d. Compare your line with those of other students. Are they nearly the same? If not, how do they differ?

e. Find the linear regression equation for the data pattern using your calculator or computer. Compare its graph to the linear model you drew in part c. If the hand-drawn and technological models differ, why do you think that happens?

f. Use the linear regression line model to predict the 100-meter winning time for the 1940, 1996, and 2000 Olympics. Find the actual winning time for 1996 and compare it to your prediction.

g. Use your linear model to predict the approximate year in which the winning time for the 100-meter dash will be 9.8 seconds.

h. According to your model, in which Olympics should the race have been won in 10.4 seconds or less?

4. Women began running 100-meter Olympic races in 1928. The winning times for women are shown in the table below.

Winning Times for Women: Olympic 100 Meters			
Year	**Time (Sec)**	**Year**	**Time (Sec)**
1928	12.2	1964	11.4
1932	11.9	1968	11.0
1936	11.5	1972	11.07
1948	11.9	1976	11.08
1952	11.5	1984	10.97
1956	11.5	1988	10.54
1960	11.0	1992	10.82

Source: *The World Almanac and Book of Facts 1995*, Mahwah, NJ: World Almanac, 1994.

a. Study the data. What patterns do you see?

b. Make a scatterplot and then find a linear regression model.

c. Use your linear model to answer each of the following questions.

  – What winning time would you predict for 1944?

  – What winning time would you predict for 1996? Find the actual winning time for 1996 and compare it to your prediction.

  – What Olympic year does the model suggest for a winning time of 10.7 seconds?

  – According to the model, when should a winning time of 11.2 seconds have occurred?

d. According to the model, by about how much does the women's winning time change from one Olympic year to the next?

e. According to the model in Extending task 3, by about how much does the men's winning time change from one Olympic year to the next? Compare this to your answer for part d.

3 *Linear Equations and Inequalities*

How many different television stations do you watch in a typical day or week? With the spread of local cable systems, American television watchers now have access to dozens of different special-focus stations—from music videos to home shopping. As a result, the audience for shows on the major networks has declined rather steadily. The graph at the right shows the trend from 1982 to 1990.

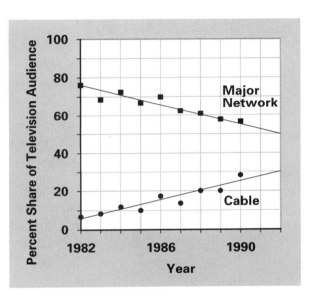

Think about this situation

The graph shows trends in American television viewing habits for a period of 9 years from 1982 to 1990.

a What significant patterns do you see in the data?

b Would you expect the trends in the data from 1982 to 1990 to continue until the year 2000? Explain your reasoning.

c How would you go about finding linear models for these data on TV audience share?

d Suppose you were asked to make a report on future prospects of cable and major network television audiences. What kinds of questions would you be able to answer using the linear models?

Investigation 3.1 Using Tables and Graphs

There are several kinds of questions that occur naturally in thinking about the television audience trends. For example, people planning to invest in a television business might wonder:

– When might the cable audience share reach 30 percent?

– When might the cable and network audience shares be equal?

– How long will the network audience share remain above 40 percent?

Trends in network and cable television audience shares can be modeled by the following linear equations.

Major Networks: $Y_1 = 75 - 2.5X$

Cable: $Y_2 = 5 + 2.5X$

Here, X stands for years since 1982. Y_1 and Y_2 stand for percentage of audience share. Using symbolic models, the three prediction questions above can be written as algebraic equations and inequalities:

$30 = 5 + 2.5X$

$5 + 2.5X = 75 - 2.5X$

$75 - 2.5X > 40$

The problem is finding values of X (years since 1982) when various audience share conditions hold.

1. Write symbolic equations and inequalities that can be used to answer each of the following questions about the relation between cable and network audience shares:

   a. When will the network share fall to only 25%?

   b. How long will the cable share remain below 50%?

   c. When was the network share double the cable share?

2. Write questions corresponding to each of the following symbolic equations and inequalities:

   a. $75 - 2.5X = 40$

   b. $5 + 2.5X \geq 20$

   c. $75 - 2.5X = 3(5 + 2.5X)$

Of course, writing equations and inequalities related to important questions is only the first task in solving the problems they represent. The essential next step is to **solve the equations and inequalities**. That is, find values of the variables that satisfy the conditions.

One way to solve the equations or inequality is to make tables and graphs of (*years since 1982*, *audience share*) data for the two models.

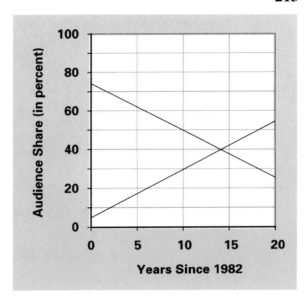

X	Y_1	Y_2
0	75	5
1	72.5	7.5
2	70	10
3	67.5	12.5
4	65	15
5	62.5	17.5
6	60	20

X	Y_1	Y_2
7	57.5	22.5
8	55	25
9	52.5	27.5
10	50	30
11	47.5	32.5
12	45	35
13	42.5	37.5

X	Y_1	Y_2
14	40	40
15	37.5	42.5
16	35	45
17	32.5	47.5
18	30	50
19	27.5	52.5
20	25	55

3. When you solve an equation or inequality using a table or graph, what do you think would be important points to find?

4. Solve each of the following equations and inequalities by finding the point or range of points that satisfy the conditions. Then explain what each solution tells about prospects for network and cable television audience shares. Describe how the solutions can be found (or at least estimated) in tables and graphs of Y_1 and Y_2. Recall that $Y_1 = 75 - 2.5X$ and $Y_2 = 5 + 2.5X$ giving audience share over time.

   a. $30 = 5 + 2.5X$

   b. $50 = 75 - 2.5X$

   c. $75 - 2.5X > 40$

   d. $75 - 2.5X = 25$

e. $5 + 2.5X < 50$

f. $5 + 2.5X = 75 - 2.5X$

g. $5 + 2.5X \leq 75 - 2.5X$

h. $75 - 2.5X = 2(5 + 2.5X)$ [Hint: Consider $Y_3 = 2 \times Y_2$]

i. $75 - 2.5X = 3(5 + 2.5X)$ [Hint: Consider $Y_4 = 3 \times Y_2$]

5. Write and solve equations and inequalities to answer each of the following questions about network and cable television audience shares. In each case, explain how you can use tables and graphs of the linear models to find solutions.

   a. When will the major network audience share decline to 30 percent?

   b. When will the cable audience share reach 40 percent?

   c. When will the major network audience share be below 50 percent?

   d. When will the major network audience share be less than the cable audience share?

6. When you solve an equation or inequality, it is always a good idea to check the solution you find. If someone told you that the solution to $45 = 75 - 2.5X$ is $X = 10$, would you believe them? How could you check their suggestion, without using either the table or the graph?

7. If someone told you that the solution to $5 + 2.5X \leq 30$ is $X \leq 11$, how could you check their suggestion:

   a. in the table?

   b. on the graph?

   c. without using either table or graph?

8. What cable and network shares do the models predict for 2012 (30 years from 1982)? How confident would you be of such a prediction?

Checkpoint

Many important questions about linear models lead to solution of equations and inequalities like $40 = 75 - 2.5x$ or $5 + 2.5x \geq 50$.

ⓐ What does it mean to solve an equation or inequality?

ⓑ How do you check a solution?

ⓒ How can tables and graphs of linear models be used to find solutions of equations and inequalities?

✓ *Be prepared to share your group's responses with the class.*

On Your Own

Bronco Electronics is a regional distributor for graphing calculators. When an order is received, the shipping department packs the calculators in a box. They place the box on a scale which automatically finds the shipping cost. The cost C is a function of the number N of calculators in the box, with rule $C = 4.95 + 1.25N$.

Use your graphing calculator or computer to make a table and a graph showing the relation between number of calculators and shipping cost. Include information for 0 to 20 calculators. Use the table and graph to answer the following questions:

a. How much would it cost to ship an empty box? How is that information shown in the table, the graph, and the cost rule?

b. How much does a single calculator add to the cost of shipping a box? How is that information shown in the table, the graph, and the cost rule?

c. Write and solve equations and inequalities to answer the following questions about Bronco Electronics shipping costs.

– If the shipping cost is $17.45, how many calculators are in the box?

– How many calculators can be shipped if the cost is to be held below $25?

– What is the cost of shipping 8 calculators?

d. What questions about shipping costs could be answered using the following equation and inequality?

$$27.45 = 4.95 + 1.25N$$

$$4.95 + 1.25N \le 10$$

e. Bronco Electronics got an offer from a different shipping company. The new company would charge based on the rule $C = 7.45 + 1.00N$. Write and solve equations or inequalities to answer the following questions:

– For what number of calculators in a box will the two shippers make the same charge?

– For what number of calculators in a box will the new shipping company's offer be better?

Modeling **O**rganizing **R**eflecting **E**xtending

Modeling

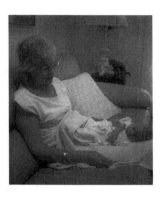

1. Parents often weigh their child at regular intervals during the first several months after birth. The data usually can be modeled well with a line. For example, the rule $y = 96 + 2.1x$ gives the relationship between *weight in ounces* and *age in days* for Rachel.

   a. How much did Rachel weigh at birth?

   b. Make a table and a graph of this equation (for Xmin = 0 to Xmax = 90).

   c. For each equation or inequality below:

   – Write a question about the infant's age and weight that the equation or inequality could help answer.

   – Use the table or graph to solve the equation or inequality and then answer your question.

   i. $y = 96 + 2.1(10)$

   ii. $159 = 96 + 2.1x$

   iii. $264 = 96 + 2.1x$

   iv. $96 + 2.1x \leq 201$

2. A concession stand at the Ann Arbor Art Fair sells soft drinks in paper cups that are filled by a dispensing machine. There is a gauge on the machine that shows the amount of each drink left in the supply tank. Wendy collected the following data one day.

Number of Drinks Sold	0	50	100	150	200	250
Ounces of Soft Drink Left	2500	2030	1525	1000	540	20

   a. Plot this data and draw a line that fits the pattern relating *number of drinks N* and *ounces of soft drink left L*.

   b. Find the slope of the linear model. Explain what it tells about the soft drink business.

   c. Find the coordinates of the point where the linear model crosses the vertical axis. What do the coordinates tell about the soft drink business?

   d. Find an equation for the linear model relating N and L.

   e. Write calculations, equations, or inequalities that can be used to answer each of the following questions. Answer the questions. Show how the answers can be found on the graph.

    – About how many drinks should have been sold when the machine had 1200 ounces left in the tank?

    – How many ounces were left in the tank when 125 drinks had been sold?

    – How many drinks were sold before the amount left fell below 1750 ounces?

3. Mary and Jeff Jordan each sell programs at the local baseball park. They are paid $10 per game and $0.25 per program sold.

  a. Write a rule relating number of programs sold X and pay earned Y.

  b. Write equations, inequalities, or calculations that can be used to answer each of the following questions:

    – How many programs does Jeff need to sell to earn $25 per game?

    – How much will Mary earn if she sells 75 programs?

    – How many programs does Jeff need to sell to earn at least $35 per game?

  c. Produce a table and a graph of the relation between sales and pay from which the questions in part b can be answered. Show on the graph and in the table how the answers can be found. Find the answers.

4. Emily works as a waitress at Pietro's Restaurant. The restaurant owners have a policy of automatically adding a 15% tip on all customers' bills as a courtesy to their waitresses and waiters. Emily works the 4 pm to 10 pm shift. She is paid $15 per shift plus tips.

  a. Write an equation to model Emily's evening wage W based on the total of her customers' bills B. Use your calculator or computer software to produce a table and a graph of this relation.

  b. If the customers' bills total $110, what calculation will give Emily's wage for the evening?

  c. If Emily's wage last night was $47, write an equation showing the total for her customers' bills. Solve the equation.

  d. What is the minimum wage that Emily could make in an evening? Which point on the graph represents her minimum wage? How is her minimum wage reflected in the equation?

  e. After six months at Pietro's, Emily will receive a raise to $17 per shift. She will continue to receive 15% tips.

    – Write an equation to model her new wage. Graph it along with her previous wage equation in the same viewing window.

    – Compare the minimum wages of the two wage scales and the rate of change in the wages. Describe the similarities and differences in the equations and graphs.

Organizing

1. Suppose two variables x and y are related by the rule $y = 4 - 0.5x$. Make a table and a graph of this relation (for Xmin = -20 to Xmax = 20). Use the table and graph to solve each equation or inequality below.

   a. $y = 4 - 0.5(12)$ **b.** $-1 = 4 - 0.5x$

   c. $-5 = 4 - 0.5x$ **d.** $4 - 0.5x \geq 0$

2. Graph the two equations $y = 2 + 0.25x$ and $y = -8 + 1.5x$ (for Xmin = -5 to Xmax = 10). Use those graphs to solve these equations and inequalities.

   a. $2 + 0.25x = -8 + 1.5x$ **b.** $2 + 0.25x \geq -8 + 1.5x$

   c. $2 + 0.25x \leq -8 + 1.5x$ **d.** $-8 + 1.5x \geq 0$

3. For any linear relation with rule of the form $y = a + bx$:

   a. Explain, with sketches, how to solve equations of the form $c = a + bx$ using the graph of the linear model.

   b. Explain, with sketches, how to solve inequalities of the form $c \leq a + bx$ using the graph of the linear model.

   c. Explain, with sketches, how to solve equations of the form $a + bx = c + dx$ using graphs of linear models.

   d. Explain, with sketches, how to solve inequalities of the form $a + bx \leq c + dx$ using graphs of linear models.

4. The linear equations you have solved in this investigation have been of two forms.

   a. How many different values of x can be found that satisfy any specific equation of the form $c = a + bx$? Explain your answer with sketches of linear models.

   b. How many different values of x can be found that satisfy any specific equation of the form $a + bx = c + dx$? Explain your answer with sketches of linear models.

5. The linear inequalities you have solved in this investigation have been of two forms.

   a. How many different values of x can be found that satisfy any specific inequality of the form $c \leq a + bx$? Explain your answer with sketches of linear models.

   b. How many different values of x can be found that satisfy any specific inequality of the form $a + bx \leq c + dx$? Explain your answer with sketches of linear models.

Reflecting

1. If you have a graphing calculator to study a linear model like $y = 125 + 35x$, would you prefer to use a graph or a table of this relation? Give reasons for your preference.

2. a. Describe a problem situation which could be modeled by the equation $y = 10 + 4.35x$.

    b. What would solving $109 \geq 10 + 4.35x$ mean in your situation?

    c. Solve $109 \geq 10 + 4.35x$.

3. Describe a strategy for solving inequalities of the form $c \leq a + bx$ using the table-building capability of your graphing calculator or computer software. How would you modify your strategy in order to solve inequalities of the form $c > a + bx$?

4. When solving equations or inequalities that model real situations, why is it important not only to check the solution, but also to check if the solution makes sense? Show your reasoning with an example.

Extending

1. The diagram at the right shows graphs of two relations between variables: $y = x + 3$ and $y = x^2 - 3$. Reproduce that diagram on your graphing calculator or computer. Use the trace function to solve the equation $x + 3 = x^2 - 3$.

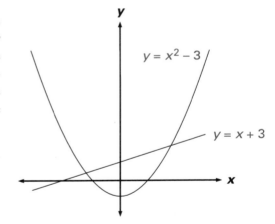

2. Use the graph from Extending task 1 to solve each inequality.

    a. $x + 3 \geq x^2 - 3$

    b. $x + 3 < x^2 - 3$

3. Refer to task 4 of the Modeling section. A new policy at the restaurant requires wait staff to share their tips with bussers. Wait staff will receive $20 per shift plus 10% in tips. Bussers will receive $25 per shift plus 5% in tips.

    a. Write one equation to model the bussers' wages and another equation to model the wait staffs' wages. Graph these two equations on the same coordinate axes.

    b. Write and answer three questions about the wages for bussers and wait staff. Based on your analysis of the graphs, write equations or inequalities corresponding to your questions.

Investigation **3.2** Quick Solutions

Linear models are common. They are easy to find with or without a calculator or computer. They are also easy to use. In fact, it is often possible to solve problems that involve linear equations without the use of tables or graphs. For example, to solve $3x + 12 = 45$ you might reason like one of these students:

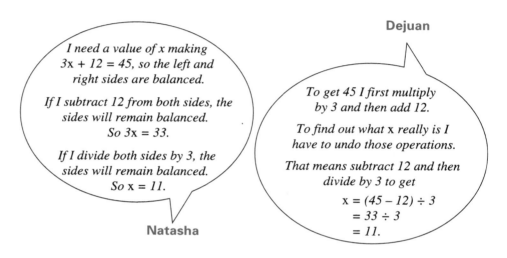

Dejuan

I need a value of x making 3x + 12 = 45, so the left and right sides are balanced.

If I subtract 12 from both sides, the sides will remain balanced. So 3x = 33.

If I divide both sides by 3, the sides will remain balanced. So x = 11.

Natasha

To get 45 I first multiply by 3 and then add 12.

To find out what x really is I have to undo those operations.

That means subtract 12 and then divide by 3 to get
$$x = (45 - 12) \div 3$$
$$= 33 \div 3$$
$$= 11.$$

1. In your group, try to figure out the reasoning used above.

    a. Natasha and Dejuan both found that $x = 11$. How can you be sure the answer is correct?

    b. Analyze Natasha's thinking.

    – Why did she subtract 12 from both sides? Why didn't she add 12 to both sides? What if she subtracted 10 from both sides?

    – Why did she divide both sides by 3?

    c. Analyze Dejuan's thinking.

    – What did he mean by *undoing* the operations?

    – Why did he subtract 12 and then divide by 3? Why not divide by 3 and then subtract 12?

2. Solve the equation $8x + 20 = 116$ in a way that makes sense to you. Check your answer.

3. A calculator can help with the arithmetic involved in solving equations.

   a. What would appear on your screen if you used a calculator to solve the equation $30x + 50 = 120$ by the "undoing" method?

   b. When one student used her calculator to solve an equation by undoing, her screen showed this:

   What equation could she have been solving?

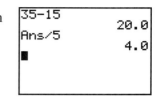

```
35-15
                20.0
Ans/5
                 4.0
■
```

4. When people shop for cars or trucks, they usually look closely at data on fuel economy. This data is given as miles per gallon in city and in highway driving. Let *C* stand for *miles per gallon in city driving* and *H* stand for *miles per gallon in highway driving*. Data from tests of the 20 most popular American cars and trucks show that the equation $H = 1.4 + 1.25C$ is a good model for the relation between the variables. Solve the following equations without making a calculator table or graph. Explain what the results tell about the relation between city and highway mileage. Be prepared to explain the reasoning you used to find each solution.

   a. $35 = 1.4 + 1.25C$ **b.** $10 = 1.4 + 1.25C$ **c.** $H = 1.4 + 1.25(20)$

5. Profit at the Palace Theater is a function of number of tickets sold according to the rule $P = -450 + 2.5T$. Without making a table or graph, solve the following equations and explain what the results tell about ticket sales and theater profit. Again, be prepared to explain your reasoning in each case.

   a. $-200 = -450 + 2.5T$ **b.** $0 = -450 + 2.5T$ **c.** $500 = -450 + 2.5T$

6. Martina and Ann experimented with the strengths of different springs. They found that the length of one spring was a function of the weight attached with rule $L = 4.8 + 1.2W$. The length was measured in inches and the weight in ounces. To find the weight that could be attached to produce a stretched spring length of 15 inches, they reasoned as follows:

   – We need to solve $15 = 4.8 + 1.2W$.

   – This is the same as $10.2 = 1.2W$.

   – This is the same as $10.2 \div 1.2 = W$.

   – This means $8.5 = W$.

   a. Is each step of their reasoning correct? If so, how would you justify each step? If not, which steps contain errors and what are those errors?

   b. What does the answer tell about the spring?

7. The Yummy Yogurt Shop makes several different flavors of frozen yogurt. Each new batch is 650 ounces, and a typical cone uses 8 ounces. As sales take place, the amount A of each flavor remaining from a fresh batch is a function of the number N of cones of that flavor that have been sold. The rule relating number of cones sold to amount of yogurt left is $A = 650 - 8N$.

   a. Solve each equation. Show all your work.

   $$570 = 650 - 8N$$

   $$250 = 650 - 8N$$

   $$A = 650 - 8(42)$$

   b. Use the rule to write and solve equations to answer the following questions:

   – How many cones have been sold if 390 ounces remain?

   – How much yogurt will be left when 75 cones have been sold?

   – If the machine shows 370 ounces left, how many cones have been sold?

8. Bronco Electronics received bids from two shipping companies that wanted the business of shipping all calculator orders. For shipping N calculators, Speedy Package Express would charge $3 + 2.25N$. Fly-By-Night Express would charge $4 + 2N$. Solve the equation $3 + 2.25N = 4 + 2N$. Explain what the solution tells about the shipping bids.

Checkpoint

a Suppose you are going to tell someone how to solve an equation like $43 = 7 - 4x$ without the use of a table or graph. What steps would you recommend? Why?

b When would you recommend solving an equation like the ones you've seen so far without a table or graph? When would you advise use of the calculator methods?

✔ *Be prepared to explain and defend your procedures.*

On Your Own

When a soccer ball, a volleyball, or a tennis ball is hit into the air, its upward velocity changes as time passes. The ball slows down as it reaches its maximum height and then speeds up in its return flight toward the ground. Suppose the upward velocity of a high volleyball serve is given by the rule $V = 64 - 32T$. (T is *time* in seconds and V is *velocity* in feet per second.)

a. Solve each of the following equations and explain what each tells about the flight of the ball. In your report, show your reasoning in finding the solutions.

$$16 = 64 - 32T \qquad\qquad 0 = 64 - 32T$$

$$-24 = 64 - 32T \qquad\qquad 96 = 64 - 32T$$

b. Use your graphing calculator or computer software to make a table and a graph of the relation between time and velocity of the ball for $0 \leq T \leq 5$. Show how to find the solution for each equation in part a in the table and on the graph.

Modeling **O**rganizing **R**eflecting **E**xtending

Modeling

1. Victoria DeStefano can earn as much as \$450 as scorekeeper for a summer basketball league. But she must pay \$18 per game for substitutes when she misses a day of work. Her *summer earnings E* will depend on the *number of days D* she misses according to the rule $E = 450 - 18D$. Solve each of the following equations and explain what they tell about Victoria's summer earnings.

   a. $306 = 450 - 18D$ **b.** $360 = 450 - 18D$

   c. $0 = 450 - 18D$ **d.** $E = 450 - 18(2)$

   e. $315 = 450 - 18D$ **f.** $486 = 450 - 18D$

2. Mary and Jeff Jordan work at a baseball park selling programs. Their pay P per game is given by $P = 10 + 0.25S$ where S is number of programs sold. Solve each of the following equations. Explain what the answers tell about Mary's and Jeff's summer earnings.

   a. $10 + 0.25S = 17.50$ **b.** $10 + 0.25S = 20$

   c. $10 + 0.25S = 7.50$ **d.** $10 + 0.25(38) = P$

3. The ball park manager offered Mary and Jeff a different pay plan, $P_2 = 5 + 0.4S$.

   a. What do the 5 and 0.4 each tell you about this new pay plan?

   b. Solve the equation below. Explain the meaning of the solution.

   $$10 + 0.25S = 5 + 0.4S$$

   c. Use your graphing calculator or computer to produce a graph of the two possible pay plans. Explain how the graph shows which is better for different numbers of sales.

d. Suppose the manager offered yet another pay plan P_3, \$0.75 per program sold and no minimum pay. What equation relating S and P_3 would fit this rule? When would this rule give the same earnings as each of the other two plans?

4. Garrett and Luis conducted a bouncing ball experiment. They dropped a tennis ball from various heights x and measured the height y of the rebound. They modeled their data with the rule $y = 5 + 0.4x$. Write three questions involving this model that can be answered by solving corresponding equations. Write and then solve the equations without using tables or graphs.

Organizing

1. Solve each of the following equations. Show the steps in your reasoning and the check of your answers.

   a. $25 = 13 + 3x$ **b.** $74 = 8.5x - 62$

   c. $34 + 12x = 76$ **d.** $76 = 34 - 12x$

   e. $3141 = 2718 + 42x$

2. If a, b, and c are any numbers, what operations are required to solve these equations?

   a. $c = a + bx$

   b. $c = a - bx$

   c. $c = -a + bx$

3. If a, b, c, and d are any numbers, what operations are required to solve equations of this type: $a + bx = c + dx$?

4. Below are two properties of arithmetic operations. The first relates addition and subtraction. The second relates multiplication and division.

   - *For any numbers* a, b, *and* c, a + b = c *is true if and only if* a = c − b.
   - *For any numbers* a, b, *and* c, a × b = c *is true if and only if* a = c ÷ b *and* b ≠ 0.

   Erik solved the equation $3x + 12 = 45$ given at the beginning of this investigation as follows:

   If $3x + 12 = 45$, then $3x = 45 - 12$ or 33.

   If $3x = 33$, then $x = 33 \div 3$ or 11.

   So $x = 11$.

a. Explain how the above properties of operations can be used to support each step in Erik's reasoning.

b. Solve the equation $130 + 30x = 250$ using the properties of operations. Check your answer.

Reflecting

1. Why is it a good idea to check solutions to equations?

2. If a question about two related variables involves solving an equation in the form $c = a + bx$, how do you decide which of the following methods to use to search for a solution?

a. Guessing and testing the guesses

b. Looking at a graph of the equation $y = a + bx$

c. Looking at a table of values for $y = a + bx$

d. Reasoning with the symbolic form itself as follows:

$$c = a + bx$$
$$c - a = bx$$
$$(c - a) \div b = x$$

3. Consider Mary and Jeff Jordan's pay possibilities for selling programs at the ball park. Let S represent the number of programs sold and P represent their pay.

a. Using the rule $P = 10 + 0.25S$, what operations are needed to find the pay for selling 36 programs on a night?

b. What operations are needed to solve the equation $19 = 10 + 0.25S$?

c. In what sense do the operations in part b "undo" the operations in part a?

d. How does the order in which you do the operations in part a compare with the order in part b? Why does this make sense?

4. a. What are two different, but reasonable, first steps in solving $2x + 8 = 5x - 4$?

b. What does the solution to the equation in part a tell you about the graphs of $y = 2x + 8$ and $y = 5x - 4$?

c. What does the solution to the equation in part a tell you about tables of values for $y = 2x + 8$ and $y = 5x - 4$?

Extending

1. How is $y = a + bx$ related to $c = a + bx$ where x and y are variables and a, b, and c are fixed numbers?

2. One linear model relating *grams of fat F* and *calories C* in popular "lite" menu items of fast food restaurants is given by the equation $C = 300 + 13(F - 10)$. Solve each of the following equations in three different ways:

- Use a graph of the equation.
- Use a table for the equation.
- Use symbolic reasoning as in the examples of this investigation.

    a. $430 = 300 + 13(F - 10)$

    b. $685 = 300 + 13(F - 10)$

    c. $170 = 300 + 13(F - 10)$

    d. $685 \leq 300 + 13(F - 10)$

Investigation 3.3   Making Comparisons

In many problems where linear equations occur, the key question asks for comparison of two or more different models. For example, in Investigation 3.1 you used linear models to compare the patterns of change in audience share of cable and major television networks. In this investigation you will examine methods for making sense of situations modeled by *systems of linear equations*.

You probably have noticed from ads on television and in newspapers that the market for long-distance telephone service has become very competitive. Deregulation of the communication industry in 1996 promised that similar competition would come to local telephone services as well. Suppose that two telephone companies, Regional Exchange and General Telephone, advertise their services for rural areas as shown below. Installation charges are the same for both companies. Which telephone company offers the better deal for local service?

Regional Exchange

You can have reliable and efficient telephone service for only $8.00 per month plus $0.15 per call.

General Telephone

We offer top quality phone service for only $14.00 per month plus $0.10 per call.

1. For both companies, the monthly charge is a function of the number of calls made.

   a. Write linear equations giving the relations between number of calls and monthly charge for each company.

   b. Compare the monthly charges by each company for 80 calls.

   c. How many calls could you make in a month for $30 under the pricing plans of the two companies?

   d. For what number of calls does Regional Exchange offer the better deal? For what number of calls does General Telephone offer the better deal?

   e. Which plan would be more sensible for the way your family uses the telephone?

2. To compare the price of service from the two telephone companies, the key problem is finding the number of calls for which these two rules give the same monthly charge. That means finding a value of x for which each rule gives the same y.

   a. How could you use tables and graphs to find the number of calls for which the two telephone companies have the same monthly charge?

   b. When one class discussed their methods for comparing the price of service from the two companies, they concluded, "All we have to do is solve the equation $8 + 0.15x = 14 + 0.10x$." Is this correct?

   c. How could you solve the equation in part b by using reasoning like that applied by Natasha or Dejuan (see page 220) to solve $3x + 12 = 45$?

The questions about monthly telephone charges from two different companies involve comparisons of two linear models. The models can be expressed with equations.

Regional Exchange: $y = 8 + 0.15x$
General Telephone: $y = 14 + 0.10x$

The pair of linear models is called a **system of linear equations**. Finding the single pair of numbers x and y that satisfy both equations is called **solving the system**. In this case the solution was $x = 120$ and $y = 26$ because

$$26 = 8 + 0.15(120) \quad \text{and} \quad 26 = 14 + 0.10(120).$$

3. How is the solution to a system of equations seen in the graphs of the equations? In tables of values?

4. Each of the following systems of linear equations could represent the cost y of a service that is used x times. Use tables, graphs, or other reasoning with the symbolic forms themselves to solve each system. Check each answer by substituting the solution values of x and y back in the original equations. If a system does not have a solution, explain why.

a. $y = 2x + 5$
$\quad\; y = 3x + 1$

b. $y = 0.5x + 8$
$\quad\; y = x + 1$

c. $y = 1.5x + 2$
$\quad\; y = 1.5x + 5$

d. $y = -1.6x + 10$
$\quad\; y = 0.4x + 2$

Checkpoint

In solving a system of linear equations like $y = 5x + 8$ and $y = -3x + 14$:

a What is the objective?

b How could the solution be found on a graph of the two equations?

c How could the solution be found in a table of (x, y) values for both equations?

d How could the solution be found using reasoning with the symbolic forms themselves?

e What patterns in the tables, graphs, and equations of a system will indicate that there is no pair of values for x and y that satisfies both equations?

✓ *Be prepared to explain your solution methods and reasoning.*

On Your Own

Charter boat fishing for walleyes is popular on Lake Erie. The charge for an eight-hour charter trip is as follows.

Charter Company	Boat Rental	Charge per Person
Wally's	$200	$29
Pike's	$50	$60

Each boat can carry a maximum of 10 people in addition to the crew.

a. Model the cost for charter service by Wally's and by Pike's with equations.

b. Determine which service is the better buy for a party of 4 and for a party of 8.

c. Assuming you want to minimize your costs, under what circumstances would you choose Wally's charter service?

Modeling Organizing Reflecting Extending

Modeling

1. Competition between telephone companies is intense. General Telephone Company wanted to become more competitive for customers who make fewer calls per month. They decided to change the monthly base charge from $14 to $12, but maintained the $0.10 per call charge.

   a. Write an equation that models the monthly charges under the new program.

   b. How are the graphs of the new and old service charges related?

   c. What would be the monthly bill for 30 calls using the new program?

   d. How many calls would you need to make in order for the new program to be more economical than Regional Exchange?

   e. If your bill is $16.30 under the new program, how many calls did you make? What is Regional Exchange's bill for the same number of calls?

2. General Telephone did not notice any large increase in subscriptions when they changed their base monthly charge from $14 to $12. They decided to change it back to $14 and reduce the per call charge from $0.10 to $0.08.

   a. Write an equation that models their new service charge.

   b. How are the graphs of the new and original service charges related?

   c. What is the cost of 30 calls under this new plan?

   d. How many calls would need to be made for the General Telephone monthly bill to be competitive with Regional Exchange?

   e. Compare the cost of service under this plan with that proposed in Modeling task 1. Which plan do you think will attract more customers? Explain your reasoning.

3. Suppose General Telephone decides to lower its base monthly charge to $10 but is unsure what to charge per call. They do want to advertise monthly bills that are lower than Regional Exchange if one makes more than 40 calls per month. Regional Exchange has an $8 base monthly charge plus $0.15 per call.

   a. To meet their goal, at what point will the General Telephone charge graph need to cross the Regional Exchange graph?

   b. What charge per call by General Telephone will meet that condition?

   c. Suppose a customer makes 60 calls per month. By how much is the new General Telephone plan lower than the Regional Exchange plan for this many calls?

   d. If a customer makes only 20 calls per month, how much less will they spend by using Regional Exchange rather than the new General Telephone plan?

4. From the situations described below, choose two situations that most interest you. Identify the variables involved and write equations showing how those variables are related. Graph the equations. Then explain how the graphs show the costs of different decisions in each case.

   a. A school club decides to have customized T-shirts made. For their design, the Clothing Shack will charge $15 each for the first ten shirts and $12 for each additional one. The cost of having them made at Clever Creations is a $50 initial fee for the setup and $8 for each T-shirt.

   b. The Evening News charges $4 for the first 3 lines and $1.75 for each additional line of a listing placed in the Classified Section. The Morning Journal charges $8 for the first five lines and $1.25 for every additional line.

   c. Speedy telegram service charges a $30 base fee and $0.75 for letter or symbol. Quick Delivery charges a $25 base fee and $0.90 for each character.

   d. Cheezy's charges $5 for a 12-inch pepperoni pizza and $5 for delivery. Pizza Palace delivers for free, but charges $7 for a 12-inch pizza.

Organizing

1. The table on the following page shows the winning times for women and men in the Olympic 100-meter swim.

Year	Women (Time in Seconds)	Men (Time in Seconds)	Year	Women (Time in Seconds)	Men (Time in Seconds)
1912	82	63	1960	61	55.2
1920	74	61	1964	59.5	53.4
1924	72	59	1968	60	52.2
1928	71	58.6	1972	58.6	51.2
1932	67	58.2	1976	55.6	50
1936	66	57.6	1980	54.8	50.4
1948	66	57.3	1984	55.9	49.8
1952	67	57.4	1988	54.9	48.6
1956	62	55.4	1992	54.6	49

Source: *The World Almanac and Book of Facts 1995*, Mahwah, NJ: World Almanac, 1994.

a. Make scatterplots for the (*year, winning time*) data for both genders.

b. Find the linear regression model for each scatterplot. Write the equations.

c. Which gender has shown the greater improvement in time? Explain.

d. Use your calculator or computer to graph the regression lines. Where do they intersect?

e. What is the significance of the point of intersection of the two lines in part b? How much confidence do you have that the lines accurately predict the future? Explain.

2. Solve each of the following systems of linear equations using at least two different methods (tables, graphs, or other reasoning with the symbolic forms themselves). Check each solution.

a. $y = x + 4$
$y = 2x - 9$

b. $y = -2x + 18$
$y = -x + 10$

c. $y = 3x - 12$
$y = 1.5x + 3$

d. $y = x$
$y = -0.4x + 7$

3. Write a system of equations for which there is no pair of values for x and y that satisfies both equations. Explain how one can predict this result from the equations, without using tables or graphs.

Reflecting

1. Describe a situation for which a graph of a system of linear equations would help you make a good decision.

2. Comparing various consumer service plans often involves analyzing and solving a system of equations of the form:

$$y = a + bx$$
$$y = c + dx$$

   How do you decide which method to use in solving the system of equations?

3. What seems to be the best way to use the information from tables and graphs to solve a system of linear equations?

4. When asked to solve the system of linear equations $y = 2x + 9$ and $y = 5x - 18$, Sabrina reasoned as follows:

   a. I want x so that $2x + 9 = 5x - 18$.

   b. Adding 18 to each side of that equation must give an equivalent equation $2x + 27 = 5x$.

   c. Subtracting $2x$ from each side of the new equation must give an equivalent equation $27 = 3x$.

   d. Dividing each side of that equation by 3 must give an equivalent equation, so $x = 9$.

   e. If $x = 9$, then $y = 2(9) + 9$ and $y = 5(9) - 18$. That means $y = 27$.

   f. The solution of the system must be $x = 9$ and $y = 27$.

   Do you believe each step of her reasoning? Why or why not?

Extending

1. Refer back to "On Your Own" on page 228. Suppose it was noticed that most fishing parties coming to the dock were four or fewer persons.

   a. How should Wally revise his boat rental fee so that his rates are lower than the competition's (Pike's) for parties of three or more? Write an equation that models the new rate system.

   b. How much less would a party of four pay by hiring Wally's charter service instead of Pike's?

   c. Which service should you hire for a party of two? How much more would you spend on the other service?

   d. Suppose Pike's charter service lowers the per-person rate from $60 to $40. For what size parties is Pike's the best buy?

e. If Wally wants to change his per-person rate so that both services charge the same for parties of four, what per-person rate should Wally charge? Write an equation that models the new rate structure.

2. A discount card at a local movie theater costs $10.00. It is valid for 3 months. With this card it costs only $3.00 to attend a movie, instead of the usual $5.00.

   a. How many movies would you need to attend in order to spend the same amount with and without the discount card?

   b. Movie theaters view discount card plans as a way to increase attendance, and ultimately profits. Devise a data-gathering plan that would help a theater set the price of a discount plan in your community. Write a summary outlining your recommendation.

3. Make up a linear system relating cost to number of uses of a service for which Company A's rate per service is 1.5 times that of Company B's, but Company B's is not more economical until 15 services have been performed.

Investigation **3.4**   Equivalent Rules and Equations

From network television, movies, and concert tours to local school plays and musical shows, entertainment is a big business in the United States. Each live or recorded performance is prepared with weeks, months, or even years of creative work and business planning.

For example, a reasonable cost for production of a CD by a popular recording artist is $100,000. Depending on various things, each copy of the CD could cost about $1.50 for materials and reproduction. Royalties to the composers, producers, and performers could be about $2.25 for each CD. The producer might charge about $5 per copy to the stores that will sell the CD. Using these numbers, how does the *producer's gross profit P* relate to the *number of copies N* that are made and sold?

1. Here are four possible rules relating P and N.

$$P = 5.00N - 1.50N - 2.25N - 100,000$$

$$P = 5.00N - 3.75N - 100,000$$

$$P = 1.25N - 100,000$$

$$P = -100,000 + 1.25N$$

a. How was each rule constructed from the information given?

b. Which of the four equations seems the best way to express the relation between copies sold and profits? Explain your reasoning in making a choice.

c. Compare tables of (*sales, profit*) data to see the pattern defined by each of the four equations. (Consider CD sales of 0 to 500,000 in steps of about 10,000.)

d. Create graphs of the four rules with your calculator or computer. Compare the graphs to see the pattern each gives relating sales and profits. Use the trace function to examine each graph.

Your tables, graphs, and thinking about possible profit rules for a new CD release show an important fact about linear models:

Several different equations can each model the same linear pattern.

Since tables and graphs require some effort to construct (even with a graphing calculator), it is helpful to be able to tell quickly when two equations are **equivalent**—that is, when they describe the *same* linear model. As you explore the following situations, look for patterns in linear expressions that help in predicting equivalence of different forms.

2. Companies that make motion pictures deal with many of the same kinds of cost and income questions as music producers. Contracts sometimes designate parts of the income from a movie to the writers, directors, and actors. Suppose that for one film those payments are:

    4% to the writer of the screenplay

    6% to the director

    15% to the leading actors

a. Suppose the company receives income of $50 million dollars from the film. What payments will go to the writer, the director, the actors, and to all these people combined?

b. Let I represent film income and E represent producer expenses for the writer, director, and actors. Write two equivalent equations showing how E is a function of I. Make one of those equations in a form that shows the breakdown to each person or group. Make the other the shortest form that shows the combined payments.

c. The movie producer might have other expenses, before any income occurs. For example, there will be costs for shooting and editing the film. Suppose those pre-release expenses are $20 million. Assuming there are no other expenses, what will the producer's **profit** be if income is $50 million? (Remember, the profit is income minus expenses.)

d. Here is one expression for profit P as a function of income I for that movie:

$$P = I - (20 + 0.25I).$$

- In your group, discuss how this rule was constructed from the given information.

- Write two other equivalent expressions for profit as a function of income. Make one of those equations as short as possible. Make the other a longer expression that shows how the separate payments to the writer, the director, and the actors affect profit.

3. For theaters, there are two main sources of income. Money is collected from ticket sales and concession stand sales. Suppose that for a major new film the theater is charging $6 for each admission ticket and that concession stand income averages $2 per person.

a. Write two equivalent equations showing how theater income I depends on number of people N who come to the show. Make one equation as short as possible. Make the other a longer expression that shows the two components of income.

b. Suppose that the theater has to send 35% of its ticket sale income to the Hollywood producer of the film. The cost of stocking the concession stand averages about 15% of its income from those items. Suppose also that the theater has to pay rent, electricity, and staff salaries of about $15,000 per month. Combine these facts with the information from part a to write two different but equivalent equations showing how theater profit P depends on the number N of ticket buyers in a month.

4. The movie theater described in activity 3 charges $6 per admission ticket sold and receives an average of $2 per person from the concession stand. The theater has to pay taxes on its receipts. Often the taxes are included in the admission and concession prices. Suppose the theater has to pay taxes equal to 9% of its receipts.

a. Calculate the tax due if 1000 tickets are sold. Report the results in two ways—first showing the tax on ticket sales and concession stand sales separately and second showing the combination of those two tax sources.

b. Write two different, but equivalent, equations giving tax due T as a function of the number N of tickets sold. First, show how taxes can be calculated on each income source separately and then combined to give total tax due. Second, show how these sources can be combined before calculating tax due.

c. After paying the 35% rental fee for the film, the theater's income from ticket sales is $3.90 per ticket sold. The concession stand income is about $1.70 per person, after paying its stocking costs. In addition to rental and stocking costs, the theater has operating expenses of $15,000 per month. A new proposal will tax profits, receipts minus expenses, at 5%. The tax due can be given by

$$T = 0.05(5.60N - 15000)$$

– Explain how this rule was constructed from the given information.

– Write an equivalent equation without use of parentheses.

In activities 1–4 you translated information about variables and relations into equations and then into different, but equivalent, equations. You used facts about the numbers and variables involved to guide and check writing of new equivalent symbolic expressions.

For example, if it costs $1.50 per copy to make a music CD and $2.25 per copy to pay royalties for the performers, it makes sense to combine $1.50x$ and $2.25x$ to get $3.75x$ expressing the cost for x copies. If the producer gets income of $5.00 per copy from retail stores, it makes sense to simplify the expression for the profit on x copies from $5.00x - 3.75x$ to $1.25x$.

Do the examples in activities 1–4 suggest some ways to rewrite symbolic expressions that will produce equivalent forms regardless of the situation being modeled? Can you rewrite expressions and equations involving variables x and y in equivalent forms even if you do not know what the variables represent?

5. For each of the following symbolic expressions, write three different forms that you believe are equivalent to the original. In each case,

– Write one equivalent form that is as short as possible.

– Write one equivalent form that is longer than the original.

– Test the equivalence of each new expression by comparing its tables and graph to those of the original.

a. $7x + 11x$	**b.** $7x - 11x$
c. $8x + 5 - 3x$	**d.** $5 + 3x + 12 + 7x$
e. $2 + 3x - 5 - 7x$	**f.** $10 - (5x + 3)$
g. $10 - (5x - 3)$	**h.** $5(x + 3)$
i. $7(2x - 12)$	**j.** $2 - 3x + 5x^2 + 7x$

Symbolic expressions like $2 - 3x + 5x^2 + 7x$ are built by combining numbers and variables through operations like $+$, $-$, $\times$, $\div$, and using exponents. Each part of the expression that involves only multiplication, division, or exponents is called a **term**. So the terms of this expression are 2, $3x$, $5x^2$, and $7x$.

6. Writing symbolic expressions in equivalent forms involves rearranging, combining, and expanding terms of the original. Based on your experience in activities 1–4, answer the following questions. Give specific examples to illustrate your ideas. Be prepared to explain why you think the rewriting procedures you recommend seem likely to work consistently.

   a. In what ways can terms in an expression be rearranged to produce equivalent forms?

   b. In what ways can terms of an expression be combined into shorter or longer equivalent forms?

   c. How can expressions be rewritten in equivalent forms without parentheses?

Checkpoint

In many situations two people can suggest rules for linear models that are equivalent, but look quite different. For example, these two symbolic expressions for linear models are equivalent:

$$y = 15x - (12 + 7x) \quad \text{and} \quad y = 8x - 12$$

ⓐ How could you test the equivalence using tables of (x, y) values?

ⓑ How could you test the equivalence using graphs of the relations?

ⓒ What reasoning with the symbolic forms alone would confirm the equivalence of the relations?

✓ *Be prepared to explain your responses to the entire class.*

On Your Own

Many college basketball teams play in winter tournaments that are sponsored by businesses who want the advertising opportunity. For one such tournament the projected income and expenses are as follows:

– Income is $60 per ticket sold, $75,000 from television and radio broadcast rights, and $5 per person from concession stand sales.

– Expenses are $200,000 for the teams, $50,000 for rent of the arena and its staff, and a tax of $2.50 per ticket sold.

a. Find the projected income, expenses, and profit if 15,000 tickets are sold for the tournament.

b. Write two equivalent expressions giving tournament income I as a function of the number N of tickets sold. In one expression, use terms that show each source of income. In the other, combine and rearrange terms to give the shortest possible expression.

c. Write two equivalent expressions giving tournament expenses E as a function of the number N of tickets sold. In one expression, use terms that show each source of expense. In the other, combine and rearrange terms to give the shortest possible expression.

d. Write two equivalent expressions giving tournament profit P as a function of the number N of tickets sold. In one expression, use terms that show each source of income. In the other, combine and rearrange terms to give the shortest possible expression.

Modeling **O**rganizing **R**eflecting **E**xtending

Modeling

1. To advertise a concert tour, the concert promoter paid an artist $2500 to design a special poster. The posters cost $2.50 apiece to print and package in a cardboard cylinder. They are to be sold for $7.95 apiece.

   a. Write equations giving *production cost C, income I*, and *gross profit P* as functions of the *number of posters N* printed and sold.

   b. Write two equations that are different from, but equivalent to, the profit equation you wrote in part a. Explain how you are sure they are equivalent.

2. One equation modeling the growth of median salary for working women since 1970 is $S = 4000 + 750(Y - 1970)$.

   a. Write an equivalent equation in the form $S = A + By$. Explain how you know the new equation is equivalent to the original.

   b. What do the numbers 4000, 750, and 1970 tell about the salary pattern?

   c. What do the numbers A and B you found in the simpler rule of part a tell about the salary pattern?

3. The video game industry is a big business around the world. Development of a new game might cost millions of dollars. Then to make and package each game cartridge will cost several more dollars per copy. Suppose the development costs for one game are $5,000,000; each cartridge costs $4.75 to make and package. The wholesale price is set at $53.50 per cartridge.

  a. Write equations giving the *total cost C* of designing and making *N* cartridges and the *income I* that would be earned from selling those *N* cartridges.

  b. Write two different equivalent equations relating *number of copies sold N* and *gross profit P* from those sales.

  c. Use evidence in tables, graphs, and properties of the operations involved in the equations to prove the equivalence of the equations.

4. Pick any number. Multiply it by 2 and subtract 10. Multiply the result by 3 and add 30. Finally, divide by your original number. Repeat the process several times with different starting numbers.

  a. What are your answers in each case?

  b. Let *x* represent the starting number and *y* represent the ending number. Write an equation showing how *y* is calculated from any value of *x*.

  c. Write the equation from part b in simplest equivalent form. Explain how it makes the results in part a reasonable.

Organizing

1. The reordering and combining of terms to produce equivalent expressions illustrates some basic properties of numbers and operations. Here are two of the most useful properties.

   For any numbers *a*, *b*, and *c*,

   Commutative Property of Addition: $a + b = b + a$

   Distributive Property of Multiplication Over Addition: $a(b + c) = ab + ac$

Show how the commutative and distributive properties are involved in writing simple equivalent forms for the following expressions.

  a. $3x + 5 + 8x$

  b. $7 + 3x + 12 + 9x$

  c. $8(5 + 2x)$

  d. $2(5x + 6) + 3 + 4x$

2. Invent and test a distributive property that would apply to expressions involving multiplication and subtraction. Use your ideas to find simple equivalent forms for the following expressions, recording each step of your reasoning.

   a. $5(2x - 8)$

   b. $5x + 7 - 3x + 12$

   c. $3x - 7 + 4(3x - 6)$

   d. $-7x + 13 + 12x - 10$

3. In Unit 2 you revisited the formula for the area of a triangle: $A = \frac{1}{2}bh$ where b is the length of the base and h is the height of the triangle. Shown here is a *trapezoid* with bases of lengths b_1 and b_2 and height h.

   a. Make a copy of the diagram at the right.

   b. Draw $\triangle ACD$ and write an expression for its area.

   c. Write an expression for the area of $\triangle ABC$.

   d. Write an expression for the area of trapezoid $ABCD$.

   e. Write an equivalent expression for the area of the trapezoid.

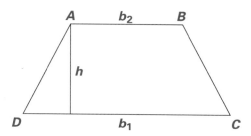

4. In transforming algebraic expressions to equivalent forms, it's easy to make some slips and use "illegal" moves. Given below are 6 pairs of algebraic expressions. Some are equivalent and some are not.

   – Use tables, graphs, and reasoning with algebraic properties to decide which pairs are actually equivalent and which involve slips in reasoning.

   – In each case of equivalent expressions, identify the use of commutative and distributive properties that justify the equivalence.

   – In each case of an algebra "slip," spot the reasoning error. Write an explanation that you would use to help clear up the problem for the student who made the error.

   a. Is $3(2x + 8)$ equivalent to $6x + 8$?

   b. Is $4x - 6x$ equivalent to $2x$?

   c. Is $8x(2 - 6x)$ equivalent to $16x - 48x^2$?

   d. Is $10 + 3x - 12$ equivalent to $3x + 2$?

   e. Is $10x + 5$ equivalent to $10(x + 5)$?

   f. Is $-4(x - 3)$ equivalent to $-4x - 12$?

Reflecting

1. In Modeling task 3 about a video game cartridge, any one of the following equations would show the relation of gross profit to number sold:

$$P = 53.50N - 4.75N - 5,000,000$$

$$P = 48.75N - 5,000,000$$

$$P = 53.50N - (5,000,000 + 4.75N)$$

   a. Which equation do you believe shows the factors involved in the best way? Explain the reasons for your choice.

   b. Explain how you can be sure that all three equations are equivalent.

2. Describe a real situation which could be modeled by at least two different, but equivalent, symbolic rules.

3. How do you prefer to check whether one form of an equation is equivalent to another form: tables of values, graphs, or rewriting one of the equations using commutative and distributive properties? Why?

4. In Chapter 1, "Patterns in Data," you encountered the rule

$$C = \tfrac{5}{9}(F - 32)$$

   for transforming temperature in degrees Fahrenheit F to temperature in degrees Celsius C.

   a. Use the number properties to rewrite this equation in the standard form of a linear model $y = a + bx$.

   b. Write a question that is more easily answered using the original form of the rule. Explain why you think the original form is better.

   c. Write a question that is more easily answered using the standard form in part a. Explain why you think the standard form is better.

Extending

1. Are the following pairs of equations equivalent?

   a. $y = 7 - 5(x + 4 - 3x)$ and $y = 7 - 5x + 20 - 15x$

   b. $y = 7x - 12 + 3x - 8 + 9x - 5$ and $y = 7x - 4 + 2x + 8 + 10x - 13$

2. If you graph the equations in Extending task 1, all will be lines, though none look exactly like the familiar form of equations for linear models: $y = a + bx$.

   a. What features of the equations like those in task 1 give a clue that the graph will be a line?

   b. What might appear in an equation that would give a clue that the graph would not be a line? Give some examples and sketch the graphs of those examples.

3. The real value of linear models for data patterns, relating two variables, occurs when you can recognize a problem to which those ideas apply. Then you can build a good model and use it to solve the problem. Using the examples of this unit as a guide:

a. Identify a situation from your experiences in which two related variables change in a pattern that seems linear.

b. Collect data on the two variables. Make a scatterplot of that data and fit a linear model to the data. Find an equation that matches that model.

c. Write five different questions about the relation between the variables that you are studying. Use your model to answer your questions.

d. Prepare a brief report describing the situation you investigated and your findings.

4 *Looking Back*

The lessons of this unit have shown that variables in many situations are related in patterns which can be modeled by linear graphs. You have learned how to find equations that describe those graphs and the corresponding tables of values. You also have learned to use the equations to answer questions about the variables and relations. This final lesson of the unit has problems which will help you review, pull together, and apply your new knowledge.

1. Athletic shoes are made by dozens of international companies and worn by young people and adults all over the world. To help buyers in different countries pick shoes that will fit, most shoes show sizes on little tabs sewn inside the shoe.

   The sizes are given in three systems—US (for United States), UK (for United Kingdom), and EUR (for European). Do you know the relation between shoe size and shoe length? Do you know the relation between US, UK, and EUR sizes?

   You can figure out the pattern relating shoe size and shoe length and the patterns relating shoe sizes in different systems by collecting and analyzing data from your classmates.

   a. To get started, ask everyone in your class who is wearing some sort of athletic shoe to look for the size tab inside his or her shoe. Then measure the length of the shoes using an agreed-upon unit. Record the data in a table with headings like those below. Make separate tables for data from females and males.

US	11
UK	10
EUR	46

Shoe Length	US Size	UK Size	EUR Size

b. Next have various groups in the class make different scatterplots of these combinations of data for females and for males.

(Length of shoe, US Size)

(US Size, UK Size)

(US Size, EUR Size)

- Find linear models and equations that fit the patterns of data points well.

- When you have an equation of the form $y = a + bx$ relating the shoe length and US size, use the information from that model to write an equation using *NOW* and *NEXT* to show how US size increases as shoe length increases.

c. When groups report the models they have found, do the following:

- Identify the slope of each linear graph from its modeling equation. Explain what the slope tells about patterns of change in shoe size and length.

- Compare the patterns for women's and men's sizes in each case.

d. Use the appropriate linear model of size and length to answer these questions. In each case, write an appropriate equation or inequality.

- What EUR size matches a women's US size 6?

- What is the approximate length of a women's US size 10 shoe?

- If a man's shoe is 14 inches long, what US size do you think it would have?

- One professional basketball player's shoes are US size 22. About how long is his shoe?

2. Most Americans can afford nutritious and varied diets, even if we do not always eat what is best for us. In many countries of the world, life is a constant struggle to find enough food. This struggle causes health problems such as reduced life expectancy and infant mortality.

a. The following data show how daily food supply (in calories) is related to life expectancy (in years) and infant mortality rates (in deaths per 1000 births) in a sample of countries in the western hemisphere. Working in pairs, make scatterplots of the *(calories, life expectancy)* and *(calories, infant mortality)* data.

Country	Daily Calories	Life Expectancy	Infant Mortality
Argentina	3113	71	29
Bolivia	1916	60	82
Canada	3482	78	7
Dominican Republic	2359	68	53
Haiti	2013	55	93
Mexico	3052	70	35
United States	3671	76	9
Venezuela	2582	70	33

Source: *The Universal Almanac 1996.* Kansas City, MO: Andrews and McMeel, 1995.

Study the patterns in the table and the scatterplots. Then answer these questions as a group.
- What seems to be the general relation between average daily calorie supply and length of life in the sample countries?
- What seems to be the general relation between average daily calorie supply and infant mortality in the sample countries?
- What factors other than daily calorie supply might affect the two variables of life expectancy and infant mortality?

b. Increasing the food supply in a country usually takes money. Economists try to predict the likely increase of life expectancy or decrease of infant mortality for various increases in food supply. Continuing to work in pairs, find equations for linear models of the (*calories*, *life expectancy*) and (*calories*, *infant mortality*) data patterns.

c. What do the slopes of your linear models say about the pattern relating daily calorie supply and life expectancy in the sample countries? How about the relation between calorie supply and infant mortality?

d. Average daily calorie supply in Chile is 2581. What life expectancy and infant mortality would you predict from the calorie data?

e. Brazil has a life expectancy of 66 years.
- What daily calorie supply would you predict in Brazil?
- The actual data for Brazil is 2751 calories. What does the difference between your predicted value and the actual value tell about the usefulness of the model you have found?

f. What life expectancy does your model predict for a daily calorie supply of 5000? How close to that prediction would you expect the life expectancy to be in a country with calorie supply of 5000?

3. Many people who go to movies like to have popcorn to munch on during the show. But movie theater popcorn is often very expensive. The manager of the Cineplex Odeon Theater wondered how much more she might sell if the price was lower. She also wondered whether such a reduced price would actually bring in more popcorn profit.

One week she set the price for popcorn at $1.00 and sold an average of 120 cups per night. The next week she set the price at $1.50 and sold an average of 90 cups per night. She graphed a linear model to predict number of cups sold at other possible prices.

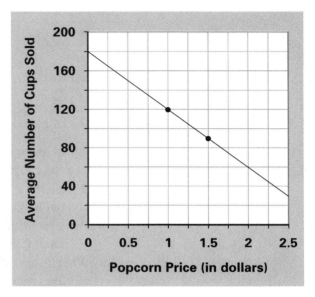

a. Find the equation of the linear model. Explain what the slope and intercept of the model tell about the prospective number of popcorn cups sold at various prices.

b. Write and solve equations or inequalities to answer the following questions.

  – What price results in average daily number sold of about 150 cups?

  – What price results in average daily number sold of less than 60 cups?

  – What number sold is predicted for a price of $1.80?

c. Use the graph or rule relating price to average daily number of cups sold to make another table relating price to revenue from popcorn. Explain what the pattern in that table tells about the relation between price, number of cups sold, and revenue.

d. Solve this equation and inequality, which are similar to those about popcorn price and number of cups sold. Use at least three different methods to solve them: table, graph, and reasoning with the symbolic form itself. Show how each answer could be checked.

$$9 + 6x = 24$$

$$1.5x + 8 \leq 3 + 2x$$

4. The ninth grade class at Frederick Douglas High School has a tradition of closing the school year with a big party. The class officers researched costs for the dance they have in mind and came up with these items to consider:

Item	Cost
DJ for the dance	$250
Food	$3.75 per student
Drinks	$1.50 per student
Custodians and Security	$175

The question is whether tne class treasury has enough money to pay for the dance or whether a special charge will be needed.

a. Which of the following equations correctly models dance cost C as a function of the number of students N who plan to come to the dance?

$C = 250 + 3.75N + 1.50N + 175$

$C = 425 + 5.25N$

$C = 5.25N + 425$

$C = 430.25N$

b. Write equations or inequalities whose solutions would answer these questions:

- How many students could come to the dance without extra charge if the class treasury has $950?
- How many students could come to the dance with a charge of only $2 if the class treasury has $950?

5. Using algebraic expressions to help make sense out of problem situations is an important part of mathematics. Writing modeling expressions and equations is often a first step. Developing an understanding of equivalent algebraic expressions and how to obtain them is another important aspect of mathematics.

a. Find equations for the linear models passing through these pairs of points:

$(0, 0)$ and $(5, 8)$

$(0, 3)$ and $(6, 0)$

$(0, -3)$ and $(4, 1)$

$(2, -6)$ and $(8, 12)$

b. Compare the following pairs of linear models. Are they equivalent?

$y = 4.2x + 6$	and	$y = (1 - 0.7x)6$
$N = 4C - 3(C + 2)$	and	$C = N + 6$
$P = 0.3S - 0.4S + 2$	and	$S = 10(P - 2)$

c. Solve each equation.

$$34 = 6 - 4x$$

$$-25 = 8 + 1.1x$$

$$14 + 3k = 27 - 10k$$

$$286 = 7p + 69$$

$$17y - 34 = 8y - 16$$

d. Solve the following system of equations using calculator or computer-based methods and by reasoning with the symbolic forms.

$$y = 35 + 0.2x$$
$$y = 85 + 0.7x$$

Checkpoint

Linear patterns in data and linear relationships between quantities can be recognized in graphs, tables, symbolic rules, or conditions in applied problems.

a Describe how you can tell whether a situation can be (or is) represented by a linear model by looking at:

- a scatterplot

- a table of values

- the form of the modeling equation

- a description of the conditions of the setting

b Linear models often describe relationships between an input variable x and an output variable y.

- Write a general form for the rule of a linear model. What do the parts of the equation tell you about the relation being modeled?

- Explain how to find a value of y corresponding to a given value of x:

  i. using a graph   **ii.** using a table   **iii.** using a symbolic rule

- Explain how you can solve a linear equation:

  i. using a graph   **ii.** using a table   **iii.** using symbolic reasoning

- Explain how you can solve a system of linear equations:

  i. using a graph   **ii.** using a table   **iii.** using symbolic reasoning

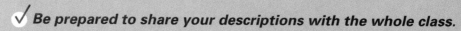 ✓ *Be prepared to share your descriptions with the whole class.*

Chapter  *Graph Models*

1 *Careful Planning*

Planning is something that people do every day. You might be planning a party or a vacation. You and your classmates might be planning a school play or the latest issue of the school newspaper. Businesses plan everything from advertising campaigns to new construction projects. City planners plan for the growth of their cities. Concert promoters must plan ahead to avoid scheduling conflicts, arrange for ticket sales, and ensure crowd control. With almost any project, careful planning is essential for success.

But it's not always easy to plan carefully. That's where mathematics can be helpful. Many mathematical models have been developed to help make planning more systematic and efficient. In this chapter you will use graph models to plan efficient routes, to schedule events and projects, and to plan ahead to avoid conflicts. This chapter will give you another example of the power of mathematics. You can plan on it!

Think about this situation

Suppose you have a job with a local school district for the summer. Your first assignment is to paint all the lockers in the high school.

a What are some tasks that would need to be completed before you could begin the actual painting?

b Would some tasks need to be completed before others? If so, in what order should the tasks be completed?

c Sketch a diagram of the arrangement of the lockers on one floor of your school.

d In what order would you paint the lockers? Do you think your plan involves the most efficient procedure? Why or why not?

Investigation 1.1   Planning Efficient Routes

You can save time, energy, and expense by studying a complex project before you begin your work. The order in which to complete the parts of the project may be important. There may be many ways to do this. However, one way may be judged to be the "best" or *optimal*, in some sense.

Suppose you are expected to paint all the lockers around eight classrooms on the first floor of a high school. The lockers are located along the walls of the halls as shown here. Letters are placed at points where you would stop painting one row of lockers and start painting another. Five-gallon buckets of paint, a spray paint compressor, and other equipment are located in the first-floor equipment room E. You must move this bulky equipment with you as you paint the lockers. You also must

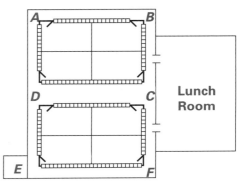

First-floor Lockers

return it to the equipment room when you are finished painting. (The lockers in the center hall must be painted one row at a time.)

1. Since you are being paid for the job, not by the hour, you would like to paint the lockers as quickly and efficiently as possible.

   a. Which row would you paint first? Is there more than one choice for the first row to paint?

   b. Which row would you paint last? Why?

2. Here are three plans that have been suggested for painting the first-floor lockers.

   Plan I: Paint from E to F, F to C, C to D (one side), D to E, D to A, A to B, B to C, C to D (the other side).

   Plan II: Paint from A to B, B to C, C to D (one side), D to A, D to C (other side), C to F, F to E, E to D.

   Plan III: Paint from E to D, D to A, A to B, B to C, C to F, F to E, D to C (one side), C to D (other side).

   a. Do you think any of these plans are optimal; that is, the "best" way to do the painting? Explain your reasoning.

b. Without help from others in your group, find a plan you think is optimal for painting the lockers.

c. Compare your plan with those of others in your group. How are they alike? How are they different?

d. Write a list of criteria to decide whether a plan is optimal.

3. Suppose the lockers on the second floor of a high school are located as shown here. Suppose the equipment room located at *G* is at the bottom of a stairway leading to the second floor. Find two optimal plans for painting the lockers that satisfy the criteria you listed in part d of the previous activity.

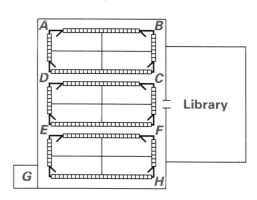

4. A **mathematical model** is a symbolic or pictorial representation including only the important features of a problem situation. The floor-plan maps of the first and second floors of the school show the rows of lockers, classrooms, equipment room, hallways, outer walls, and other rooms. There are some features of these maps that you do not need in order to solve the locker-painting problems.

a. Which of the features of the maps did you use as you tried to solve the locker-painting problems? Which features were not needed?

b. Refer to the first-floor map of the school on page 251. Draw a simplified diagram (a mathematical model) that includes only the important features of the locker-painting problem. For example, the lettered points on the map are important because *E* is the beginning and ending point. The other letters mark where one row of lockers ends and another begins. Complete the diagram.

$$\begin{array}{ll} A \bullet & \bullet\ B \\ D \bullet & \bullet\ C \\ E \bullet & \bullet\ F \end{array}$$

5. Now examine mathematical models drawn by some other students.

a. Michael drew the diagram at the right. Does his diagram show all the essential features of the locker-painting problem? If so, explain. If not, describe what is needed.

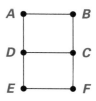

Michael's Model

b. Deonna drew the diagram at the right. Is it an appropriate model for the locker-painting problem? Explain.

c. Why do you think Deonna joined points *C* and *D* with two segments or arcs?

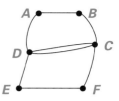

Deonna's Model

6. In activity 2, you were asked to find an optimal plan for painting the first-floor lockers.

  a. Use that plan to trace an optimal painting route on the diagram you drew in activity 4. If you cannot trace your optimal route on your diagram, carefully check both your optimal plan and your diagram.

  b. Trace the same painting route on Deonna's model. Does it matter if the points are connected by straight line segments or curved arcs? Does it matter how long the segments or arcs are?

7. To the right is a diagram that models one arrangement of lockers.

  a. Draw a school floor-plan map that corresponds to this diagram. Assume that the equipment room is at *V*.

  b. Find, if possible, an optimal route for painting these lockers.

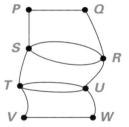

Checkpoint

ⓐ What is the difference between a floor-plan map of a school showing the lockers to be painted and a mathematical model of the locker-painting problem?

ⓑ Refer back to Deonna's model. What do the points and the connecting segments and arcs represent in terms of the locker-painting problem?

ⓒ Can two diagrams that have different shapes and sizes represent the same problem situation? Explain.

ⓓ In activity 2 you wrote a list of criteria for an optimal locker-painting plan. Restate those criteria in terms of tracing around a diagram that models the situation.

✓ *Be prepared to share your group's thinking with the entire class.*

A diagram consisting of a set of points along with segments or arcs joining some of the points is called a **graph.** The points are called **vertices**, and each point is called a **vertex**. The segments or arcs joining the vertices are called **edges**. A key step in modeling a problem situation with a graph is to decide what the vertices and edges will represent.

The word "graph" is used to mean different things at different times. In this chapter, the word "graph" refers to a diagram consisting of vertices and edges.

On Your Own

Suppose the lockers and an equipment room on the west wing of a high school are located as shown below.

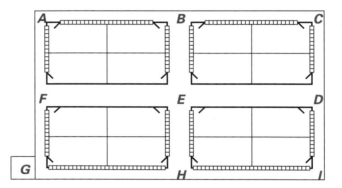

a. If you were to model the problem of painting these lockers with a vertex-edge graph, what would the vertices represent? The edges?

b. Draw a graph model for this problem.

c. Determine an optimal plan for painting the lockers. Use the criteria for tracing the edges and vertices of a graph that you arrived at in "Checkpoint" on page 253.

Investigation 1.2 Making the Circuit

Your criteria for the optimal sequence for painting the lockers are the defining characteristics of an important property of a graph. An **Euler** (pronounced *oy'lur*) **circuit** is a route through a connected graph such that (1) each edge of the graph is traced exactly once, and (2) the route starts and ends at the same vertex. Given a connected graph, it often is helpful to know if it has an Euler circuit. (The name "Euler" is in recognition of the eighteenth-century Swiss mathematician Leonhard Euler. He was the first to study and write about these circuits.)

1. Shown below are graph models of the sidewalks in two sections of a town. Parking meters are placed along these sidewalks.

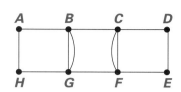

East Town Model   **West Town Model**

    a. Why would it be helpful for a parking control officer to know if these graphs had Euler circuits?

    b. Does the graph model of the east section of town have an Euler circuit? Explain your reasoning.

    c. Does the graph model of the west section of town have an Euler circuit? Explain.

2. Graphs a, b, and c below are similar to puzzles enjoyed by people all over the world. In each case, the challenge is to trace the figure. You must trace every edge exactly once without lifting your pencil and return to where you started. That is, the challenge is to trace an Euler circuit through the figure or graph. Place a sheet of paper over each graph and try to trace an Euler circuit. If the graph has an Euler circuit, write down the vertices in order as you trace the circuit.

a.   **b.**   **c.**

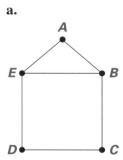
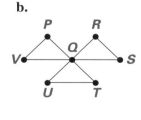
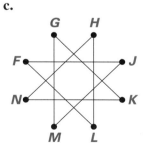

3. By looking at the form of an equation you often can predict the shape of the graph of the equation without plotting any points. Similarly, it would be helpful to be able to examine a vertex-edge graph and predict if it has an Euler circuit without trying to trace it.

a. Have each member of your group draw a graph with five or more edges that has an Euler circuit. On a separate sheet of paper, draw a graph with five or more edges that does *not* have an Euler circuit.

b. Sort your group's graphs into two piles, those that have an Euler circuit and those that do not.

c. Carefully examine the graphs in the two piles. Describe key ways that graphs with Euler circuits differ from those with no Euler circuit.

d. Try to figure out a way to predict if a graph has an Euler circuit simply by examining its vertices. Check your method of prediction using the graphs on page 255.

e. Make a conjecture about the properties of a graph that has an Euler circuit. Explain why you think your conjecture is true for *any* graph with an Euler circuit.

4. Once you can predict whether a graph has an Euler circuit, it is often still necessary to find the circuit. Consider the graphs below.

i.    **ii.**

a. For each graph, predict whether it has an Euler circuit.

b. Find an Euler circuit in the graph that has one.

c. Describe the method you used to find your Euler circuit. Describe other possible methods for finding Euler circuits.

5. One systematic method for finding an Euler circuit is to trace the circuit in stages. For example, suppose you and your classmates want to find an Euler circuit that begins and ends at *A* in the graph below. You can trace the circuit in three stages.

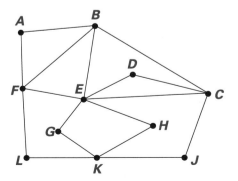   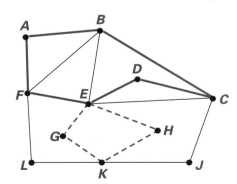

Stage I: Alicia began by drawing a circuit that begins and ends at *A*. The circuit she drew, shown in the diagram by the heavy edges, was *A-B-C-D-E-F-A*. But this does not trace all edges.

Stage II: George added another circuit shown by the dashed edges starting at *E*: *E-G-K-H-E*.

a. Alicia's and George's circuits can be combined to form a single circuit beginning and ending at *A*. List the order of vertices for that combined circuit.

Stage III: Since this circuit still does not trace each edge, a third stage is required.

b. Trace a third circuit which covers the rest of the edges.

c. Combine all the circuits to form an Euler circuit that begins and ends at *A*. List the vertices of your Euler circuit in order.

6. Choose your preferred method for finding Euler circuits from activities 4 and 5. Write specific step-by-step instructions that describe the method you chose. Your instructions should be written so that they apply to *any* graph, not just the one that you may be working on at the moment. Such a list of step-by-step instructions is called an **algorithm**.

Checkpoint

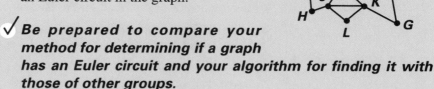

a How can you tell if a graph like the one at the right has an Euler circuit without actually trying to trace the graph?

b Use your algorithm from activity 6 to find an Euler circuit in the graph.

✓ *Be prepared to compare your method for determining if a graph has an Euler circuit and your algorithm for finding it with those of other groups.*

Creating algorithms is an important aspect of mathematics. Two questions you should ask about any algorithm are *Does it work?* and *Is it efficient?* You will consider these questions in more detail later.

In devising a way to predict whether a graph has an Euler circuit, you probably counted the number of edges at each vertex of the graph. The number of edges touching a vertex is called the **degree of the vertex**. (If an edge loops back to the same vertex, that counts as two edge touchings. For an example, see Extending task 4 on page 264.)

On Your Own

For each of the graphs below, check the degree of each vertex and then decide if an Euler circuit exists. If an Euler circuit exists, use your algorithm to find one.

a.   **b.**

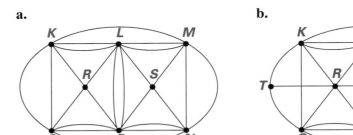

Modeling **O**rganizing **R**eflecting **E**xtending

Modeling

1. Some popular puzzles involve trying to trace a figure without lifting your pencil or tracing an edge more than once. That is, you try to find an Euler circuit.

   a. Identify those graphs below and on the next page which you believe do not have an Euler circuit. Explain why you believe that.

   b. For each of the graphs which has an Euler circuit, use the algorithm you developed to find a circuit.

   i.   **ii.**

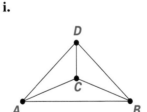   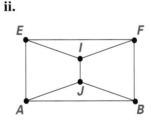

iii.

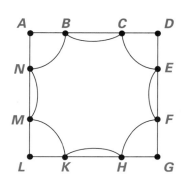

iv.

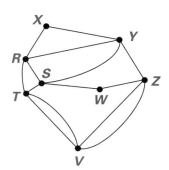

c. Draw two graphs that would be difficult to trace without lifting your pencil from the page or tracing an edge more than once. Draw one so that it has an Euler circuit and the other so that it does not. Challenge someone outside of class to trace your graphs, starting and ending at the same point. Then ask them to challenge you in the same way with any graph they draw. See if you can amaze them with how quickly you can tell whether or not it is possible to trace the graph without lifting your pencil or tracing any edge more than once.

2. The city of Kaliningrad in Russia is located on the banks and on two islands of the Pregel River. In the eighteenth century, the city was named Königsberg. Various parts of the city were connected by seven bridges as illustrated here. Citizens often would take walking tours of the city by crossing over the bridges.

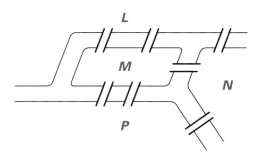

Some people wondered whether it was possible to tour the city by beginning at a point on land, walking across each bridge exactly once, and returning to the same point. The problem intrigued the mathematician Leonhard Euler, who lived at that time. Euler used a graph model to solve the problem.

a. Draw a graph in which the vertices represent the four land areas (lettered in the figure) and the edges represent bridges.

b. What do you think Euler's solution was? Explain your response.

c. In the time since Euler solved the problem, two more bridges were built. One bridge was added at the left to connect areas labeled *L* and *P*. A second bridge was added to connect areas labeled *N* and *P*.

    – Draw a graph model for this new situation of land areas and bridges.

    – Use your graph to determine if it is possible to take a tour of the city that crosses each of the nine bridges exactly once and allows you to return to the point where you started.

3. a. Compare the graph below to the school floor-plan showing locker placement. If *E* represents the equipment room and *C* and *D* are the endpoints of the center hallway, identify the row(s) of lockers represented by each edge of the graph.

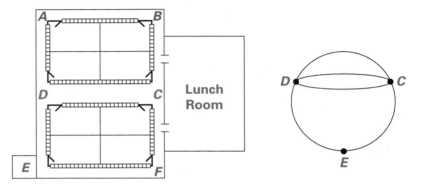

b. Trace a path around the graph that begins and ends at *E* and that traces each edge exactly once. Describe the order of painting the lockers that your path suggests. Is that order optimal?

c. Why is the graph still an accurate representation of the locker-painting problem when locations *A*, *B*, and *F* are not represented by vertices?

d. Are there any other points which could be deleted while maintaining an accurate graph model? Explain why or why not.

4. Suppose the lockers on the third floor of the high school in the locker-painting problem are located as shown here.

a. Draw a graph that represents this situation. Be sure to describe what the vertices and edges of your graph represent.

b. Is there a way to paint the lockers by starting and ending at the equipment room and never moving equipment down a hall without painting lockers on one side?

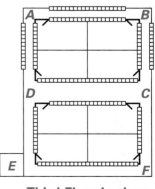

Third-Floor Lockers

5. A newspaper carrier wants to complete a delivery route without retracing steps. Some streets on the route have houses facing each other. Whenever there are houses on both sides of a street, papers must be delivered to both sides by going along one side and then along the other side.

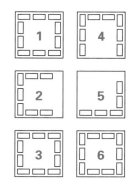

a. Suppose the paper carrier only delivers to the houses on blocks 1, 2, and 3. Construct a vertex-edge graph model for this situation. What do the edges and vertices represent? Find an optimal delivery route.

b. Suppose the paper carrier delivers to the houses on all six blocks. Construct a vertex-edge graph model for this situation. Find an optimal delivery route.

c. Now assume that *all* blocks have houses on all four sides. Add three more blocks that are adjacent to the given blocks on the street map. Find an optimal delivery route.

d. Can you find an Euler circuit no matter where the three new blocks are placed on the route? Explain your response.

e. Is it possible to place any number of new blocks on the route and still have an Euler circuit? Explain your reasoning.

Organizing

1. Graphs have interesting properties that can be discovered by collecting data and looking for patterns.

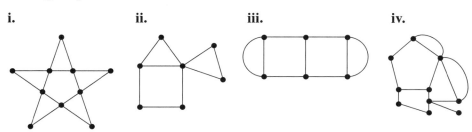

i.   **ii.**   **iii.**   **iv.**

a. Complete a table like the one on the following page using the graphs above.

Graph	Sum of the Degrees of All Vertices	Number of Vertices of Odd Degree
i	30	
ii		2
iii		
iv		

b. Write down any patterns you see in the table.

c. Explain why the sum of the degrees of all the vertices in *any* graph is an even number.

d. Explain why *every* graph has an even number of vertices with odd degree.

2. The following graphs divide the plane into several *regions*. The exterior of the graph is an infinite region. The interior regions are enclosed by the edges. For example, graph i divides the plane into four regions.

i.   **ii.**   **iii.**   **iv.**

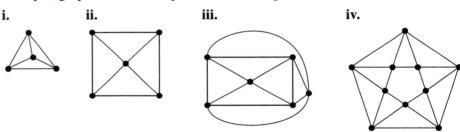

a. Complete the following table for each graph above. Be sure to count the exterior of the graph as one region.

Graph	Number of Vertices (V)	Number of Regions (R)	Number of Edges (E)
i			
ii			
iii			
iv			

b. Find a rule relating the numbers of vertices V, regions R, and edges E by using addition and subtraction to combine V, R, and E.

c. Draw several more graphs, and count V, R, and E. Does your rule also work for these graphs?

d. How many regions would be formed by a graph with 5 vertices and 12 edges? Draw such a graph to verify your answer.

3. Decide whether each of the following statements is true or false. If a statement is true, explain why it is true. If a statement is false, draw a graph that illustrates why it is false. (An example that shows why a statement is false is called a **counterexample**.)

   a. Every vertex of a graph with an Euler circuit has degree greater than 1.

   b. If every vertex of a graph has the same degree, the graph has an Euler circuit.

4. The word "graph" in this chapter means a diagram consisting of vertices and edges. List and draw sketches of the other types of graphs that you have used in this course.

Reflecting

1. What did you find most challenging in this investigation? Why was it difficult for you?

2. Make a list of businesses or professions in which knowledge of Euler circuits might play an important role in lowering operating costs. Explain specifically how Euler circuits might be used in each case.

3. Write a question that you think would test whether your classmates understood the difference between graphs that have an Euler circuit and those that do not.

4. Explain Euler circuits to a friend or family member. Ask them to work a few problems like the ones you have worked. Write a summary of how well that person understood the ideas.

5. An Euler circuit is described as a certain kind of route through a connected graph. A **connected graph** is a graph that is all in one piece. That is, from each vertex there is at least one path to every other vertex. Draw a graph that is connected and one that is not. Why do you think Euler circuits are only considered for connected graphs?

Extending

1. Find information in the library or on the Internet about the life of Leonhard Euler. Write a report of what you find with particular attention to the contributions he made to graph theory.

2. Write an argument to support each of the following statements.

   a. If a graph has an Euler circuit, then all of its vertices are of even degree.

   b. If the vertices of a connected graph are all of even degree, then the graph has an Euler circuit.

3. Decide whether you agree with the following statement, and then write an argument to support your position: If a graph has an Euler circuit that begins and ends at a particular vertex, then it will have an Euler circuit that begins and ends at any vertex of the graph.

4. Many new housing developments have houses built on streets that are shaped into a "cul-de-sac" so that traffic past the houses is minimized.

   a. Suppose a cul-de-sac is located at the end of the street between blocks 5 and 6 as shown here. Draw a vertex-edge graph that represents this housing development.

   b. Find an optimal path for delivering papers to houses in this development.

   c. You know from this lesson that the degree of a vertex is the number of edges that touch it, except that loops count as two edge touchings. Find the degree of each vertex in your graph model.

   d. Repeat parts a, b, and c with a second cul-de-sac constructed at the end of blocks 1 and 4.

   e. How does adding a cul-de-sac affect the graph model?

   f. Does the condition about degrees of vertices for graphs with Euler circuits still hold for graphs with loops?

5. Euler circuits are also useful in manufacturing processes where a piece of metal is cut with a mechanical torch. To reduce the number of times the torch is turned on and off, it is desirable to make the cut continuous. However, the metal piece must be clamped in air so that the torch does not burn a surface. Thus, there is an added condition; namely, any piece that falls off should not require additional cutting. Otherwise, it would have to be picked up and re-clamped, a time-consuming process. Find a way to make all the cuts indicated on the pictured piece of metal, so that you begin and end at S and the above conditions are satisfied.

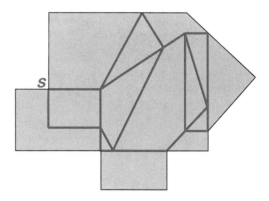

Investigation 1.3 Tracing Figures from One Point to Another

Graph-like figures have a rich and long history in many cultures, as illustrated in the following activities.

1. The Bushoong are a subgroup of the Kuba chiefdom in Zaire, Africa. Bushoong children have a long tradition of playing games that involve tracing figures in the sand using a stick. The challenge is to trace each line once and only once without lifting the stick from the sand. Two such figures are given below.

   Place a sheet of paper over the figures. Try to trace each figure without lifting your pencil and without any retracing.

   a.   **b.**

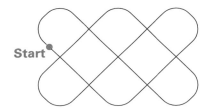

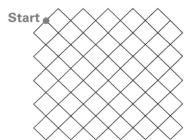

2. The Tshokwe (pronounced $sh\bar{o}$ - $kw\bar{a}'$) people, located near the Bushoong in Africa, made games of trying to trace pictures of objects. The two figures below represent intertwined rushes (tall flexible plants). Starting at S, is it possible to trace each figure without lifting your pencil? If so, where do you end your tracing?

   a.   **b.**

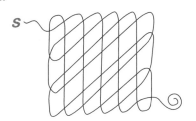

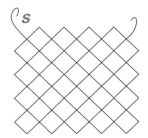

3. In the last investigation, you discovered that some graphs do not have an Euler circuit.

a. If you do not have to start and end at the same vertex, do you think the edges of every graph can be traced exactly once without lifting your pencil? Why or why not?

b. Place a sheet of paper over the graphs below. Try to copy the graphs by tracing each edge exactly once.

c. For those graphs which can be traced in this manner, how do the starting and ending vertices differ from the other vertices?

i.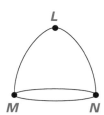

ii.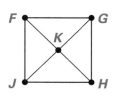

iii.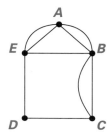

Checkpoint

You know that a graph has an Euler circuit whenever all vertices of the graph have even degree.

ⓐ Find a similar criterion for determining whether a graph *has* a traceable path when it does *not* have an Euler circuit.

ⓑ Test your criterion on the graphs in activity 3 and on a graph that you create.

ⓒ Write an explanation for why your criterion is correct.

✓ *Be prepared to share your group's criterion and explanation with the entire class.*

An **Euler path** is a path which traces each edge of the graph exactly once. Thus, an Euler circuit is a special type of Euler path—one which starts and ends at the same vertex.

On Your Own

Draw three graphs, each with at least five vertices, that meet the following criteria:

– One has an Euler circuit.

– One has an Euler path but no Euler circuit.

– One has neither an Euler circuit nor an Euler path.

Explain to a classmate or to someone at home which is which and why.

For the remainder of this investigation, work with your group to explore how to revise a graph so that it has an Euler circuit.

4. The graph shown here is a model of the arrangement of lockers along hallways of the second floor of a high school.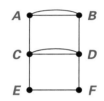

   a. Explain why these lockers *cannot* be painted by starting and ending at the equipment room *E* and never moving down a hall without painting lockers on one side.

   b. Find a way to paint the lockers so that the process starts and ends at *E*, and the number of already-painted rows along which the equipment must be moved is as small as possible. Write down the route that you would walk.

   c. Revise the graph to represent your route. What do the vertices and edges of the revised graph represent?

   d. How many additional edges did you add? Can you use fewer additional edges?

The process of revising a graph by adding edges so that the revised graph has an Euler circuit is called **Eulerizing** the graph. When Eulerizing a graph, you should only add edges that are duplicates of existing edges.

5. The graph at the right represents a network of streets.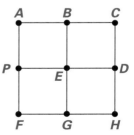

   a. Is it possible for a police car to patrol the streets beginning and ending at *P* (a police station) and traveling each street exactly once? Explain your reasoning.

b. Albert proposed the solution route at the right in response to the problem. Is this an acceptable solution? Why or why not?

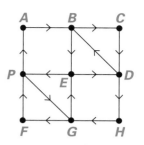

c. Design a route for a police car so that (i) it begins and ends at *P*; (ii) it only uses the existing streets shown in the graph in part a; (iii) it travels each street at least once; and (iv) the number of streets it travels more than once is as small as possible.

d. Provide an argument for why the number of streets your route travels more than once is as small as possible.

Checkpoint

ⓐ As a group, write an algorithm to Eulerize a graph.

ⓑ Test your algorithm by Eulerizing the graph shown here.

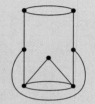

✓ *Be prepared to compare your algorithm with those of other groups.*

On Your Own

Eulerize each of the following graphs.

a.

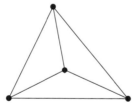

b.

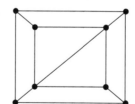

Investigation 1.4 — Graphs and Matrices

Information often is organized and displayed in tables. The use of tables to summarize information can be seen in almost every section of most newspapers. In this investigation you will explore how table-like arrays also can be used to represent information contained in vertex-edge graphs.

1. As a group, examine this information on medals awarded at the 1994 Winter Olympics.

Medal Count

Country	G	S	B	Total
Norway	10	11	5	26
Germany	9	7	8	24
Russia	11	8	4	23
Italy	7	5	8	20
United States	6	5	2	13
Canada	3	6	4	13

Source: *USA Today*, February 28, 1994

   a. What do each of the numbers in the first row represent?

   b. What is the meaning of the number in the fifth row and second column? In the third row and third column?

   c. France did not win any gold medals. However, the French team did take home one silver medal and four bronze medals. How could you modify this chart to include this additional information?

2. Arrays of numbers, like the one above, are sometimes called **matrices**. Matrices can be used to represent graphs.

   One way in which a graph can be represented by a **matrix** is shown here.

   a. Study the first and fourth rows of the matrix. Explain what each entry means in terms of the graph.

   b. Copy the matrix and then fill in the missing entries.

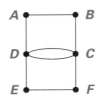

$$
\begin{array}{c c c c c c c}
 & A & B & C & D & E & F \\
A & 0 & 1 & 0 & 1 & 0 & 0 \\
B & - & - & - & - & - & - \\
C & - & - & - & - & - & - \\
D & 1 & 0 & 2 & 0 & 1 & 0 \\
E & - & - & - & - & - & - \\
F & - & - & - & - & - & - \\
\end{array}
$$

c. Construct a similar matrix for each of the three graphs below.

i. 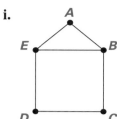   **ii.** 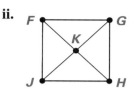   **iii.**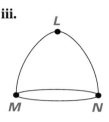

3. a. The sums of the numbers in each row of a matrix are called the **row sums** of the matrix. Find the row sums of each of the matrices in part c of activity 2.

   b. What do these row sums represent in the graphs?

   c. Is it possible to tell by looking at the matrix for a graph whether the graph has an Euler path or an Euler circuit? Explain your response.

Checkpoint

> **ⓐ** A matrix corresponding to a graph that has five vertices, A, B, C, D, and E, in that order, has a 2 in the third row, fifth column. What does the 2 represent? What does a 1 in the first row, second column mean?
>
> **ⓑ** Explain the differences you see between the row sums of matrices for graphs with and without Euler circuits. Explain the differences between the row sums for graphs with and without Euler paths.
>
> ✓ *Be prepared to share your group's thinking with the entire class.*

Matrices like those you have been constructing are called **adjacency matrices**. Each entry in an adjacency matrix for a graph is the number of direct connections (edges) between the corresponding pair of vertices.

On Your Own

a. Does each of the graphs whose adjacency matrix is given below have an Euler circuit? An Euler path? How can you tell without drawing the graphs?

i.

$$\begin{array}{c} \\ A \\ B \\ C \end{array} \begin{array}{c} \begin{array}{ccc} A & B & C \end{array} \\ \begin{pmatrix} 0 & 2 & 0 \\ 2 & 0 & 1 \\ 0 & 1 & 0 \end{pmatrix} \end{array}$$

ii.

$$\begin{array}{c} \\ P \\ Q \\ R \\ S \end{array} \begin{array}{c} \begin{array}{cccc} P & Q & R & S \end{array} \\ \begin{pmatrix} 0 & 1 & 2 & 1 \\ 1 & 0 & 1 & 2 \\ 2 & 1 & 0 & 2 \\ 1 & 2 & 2 & 0 \end{pmatrix} \end{array}$$

b. Draw and label a graph corresponding to each adjacency matrix in part a. Find an Euler circuit or Euler path if there is one.

c. If a graph has an Euler path, can you tell from the adjacency matrix at what vertex the path begins or ends? Explain.

Modeling Organizing Reflecting Extending

Modeling

1. The diagram shown here represents the streets of downtown Springfield. The ovals represent parking meters. A city employee, Dianna, must regularly check these meters for expiration.

   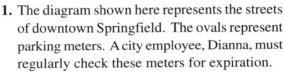

   a. Model the situation of checking the meters with a graph. Use the vertices to represent where one block ends and another block begins. Use the edges to represent the presence of meters.

   b. What is the most efficient route for Dianna to use when checking the meters?

   c. Is this route an Euler path? Explain.

   d. Eulerize the graph.

2. An auditorium floor is arranged for an art show as diagrammed in the floor plan at the right. Artwork will be exhibited on all four sides of the display boards (shown as gray rectangles). The art show organizers plan to mark off a route for customers to follow so that they can view each piece of art exactly one time. Assume customers can view the art displayed on only one side of an aisle on each walk down the aisle.

   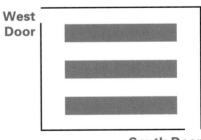

   a. Model this situation with a graph. What do the vertices represent? What do the edges represent?

   b. Suppose customers hang up their coats outside the West door and pick them up there on their way out. How would you route customers to allow for viewing each piece of art exactly one time?

c. Is it possible to route people from the West Door to the South Door so that they can view all of the artwork while not going past a row of exhibits more than once? How does the graph model show this?

d. As an exhibit coordinator, how would you add, delete, or rearrange the display boards so that a route exists that satisfies the conditions in part c?

e. Is the route that you have designed an Euler path? Explain.

3. The map below shows the trails in Tongass State Park. The labeled dots represent rest areas scattered throughout the park.

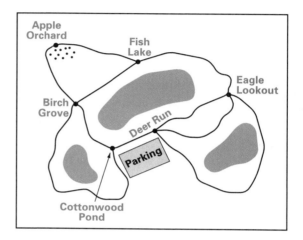

a. How would a graph model of this situation differ from the map? Is it necessary or useful to draw a graph model in this situation? Why or why not?

b. Construct an adjacency matrix related to the park map.

c. Is it possible to hike each of the trails in the park once and return to your car in the parking lot? Explain your answer by using the adjacency matrix from part b and your knowledge of Euler paths and Euler circuits.

d. The Park Department has received money to build additional trails. Between which rest stops should they build a new trail (or trails) so that people can hike each trail once and return to their cars?

e. Does your solution to part d Eulerize the graph? Why or why not?

f. Find two ways to Eulerize the graph. For each way, which paths would be repeated?

4. Certain towns in southern Alaska are on islands or isolated by mountain ranges. When traveling between these communities, you must take a boat or a plane. Listed below are the routes provided by a local airline.

Routes between:

Anchorage and Cordova
Anchorage and Juneau
Cordova and Yakutat
Juneau and Ketchikan
Juneau and Petersburg
Juneau and Sitka
Petersburg and Wrangell
Sitka and Ketchikan
Wrangell and Ketchikan
Yakutat and Juneau

a. Make a graph model of the airline routes.

b. In what ways is your graph model like the map? In what ways is it different?

c. An airline inspector wants to evaluate the airline's operations by flying each route. It is sufficient to fly each route one-way. Can the inspector start in Juneau, fly all the routes exactly once, and return to Juneau?

d. How would an adjacency matrix for the graph show whether or not there is a route as described in part c?

Organizing

1. In this task, you will examine further the tradition of tracing continuous figures exhibited in cultures around the world.

a. The Malekula live on an island in the South Pacific chain of some eighty islands that comprise the Republic of Vanuatu. As with the Bushoong and Tshokwe in Africa, the Malekula also have figures that represent objects or symbols of the culture. For example, figure i represents a yam. Figure ii is called "the stone of Ambat."

– Can you trace each of these figures without lifting your pencil or repeating any edges?

– Describe any *symmetry* you see in each figure. Be as complete with your descriptions as possible.

i.

ii.

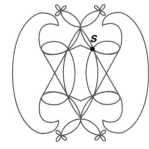

b. The ancient inhabitants of Pre-Inca Peru built ground-cover figures (some hundreds of yards in length). For each of the two figures below:

  – Discuss its traceability.

  – Discuss its symmetry.

  – Discuss how it seems to be related to similar figures you examined from other cultures.

i.    ii.

2. Explain why the row sum of an adjacency matrix of a graph is the degree of the vertex corresponding to that row.

3. Consider the regular pentagon at the right as a graph.

  a. Write the adjacency matrix for this graph.

  b. Modify a copy of this graph by adding all the *diagonals* (segments connecting pairs of vertices). Write the adjacency matrix for this modified graph.

  c. Write a description of the adjacency matrix for a graph in the shape of a regular polygon with n sides. How would you modify the description of the adjacency matrix if the graph consisted of the polygon *and* its diagonals?

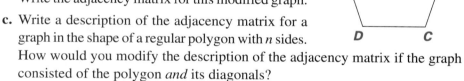

4. Eulerize the graph at the right using a minimum of repeated edges. Write an argument for why your solution involves the minimum number of repeated edge-tracings.

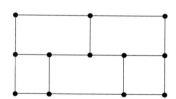

Reflecting

1. In a world atlas, find the countries mentioned earlier in this chapter: Zaire in Africa, Peru in South America, and the Republic of Vanuatu in the South Pacific. Why do you think the concept of tracing a continuous line to create a pattern is evident in so many cultures?

2. Obtain a map of your town or city or of a nearby town or city (perhaps from a telephone book). Select one section of the town or city (approximately 6 blocks by 6 blocks) and design an efficient street-sweeping route for that area. Then design an efficient postal-carrier walking route for that area. Discuss some of the reasons why these two routes may be different.

3. Answer the following, based on your experiences in the investigations of this lesson.

   a. Is it possible for a vertex-edge graph to be a mathematical model for two different situations? Explain your reasoning.

   b. Is it possible for a matrix to be the adjacency matrix for two different vertex-edge graphs? Explain.

4. In what real-world situations would it be important to have an Euler circuit rather than a non-circuit Euler path?

Extending

1. Identify a real-world application of Euler paths or circuits, different from those in this lesson. Prepare a class presentation about how Euler paths or circuits are used in that application.

2. The stone of Ambat (figure ii in Organizing task 1.a) can be traced in three stages, each beginning and ending at S. Two of the stages are given at the right. Find the third stage and then put them all together to produce a complete tracing.

Stage 1   **Stage 2**

3. A **loop** is an edge connecting a vertex to itself. When constructing an adjacency matrix for a graph with loops, a 1 is placed in the position in the matrix that corresponds with an edge joining a vertex to itself. An example of such a graph and its adjacency matrix is shown at the right. (Extending task 4 on page 264 presents a practical situation that can be modeled by a graph with a loop.)

$$\begin{array}{c} \\ \\ \end{array} \begin{array}{cc} A & B \end{array}$$
$$\begin{array}{c} A \\ B \end{array} \begin{pmatrix} 1 & 1 \\ 1 & 0 \end{pmatrix}$$

   a. You have learned in this chapter that the degree of a vertex is the number of edges touching the vertex, except that a loop counts for two edge touchings. What is the degree of vertex A?

b. What is the row sum of the first row of the adjacency matrix? In Investigation 1.4, you found a connection between row sums of an adjacency matrix and the degree of the corresponding vertex. Does this connection still hold for graphs with loops like the one on the previous page?

c. Try to draw graphs with the following adjacency matrices.

i.

$$\begin{pmatrix} 2 & 3 \\ 3 & 0 \end{pmatrix}$$

ii.

$$\begin{pmatrix} 0 & 1 & 2 \\ 1 & 1 & 1 \\ 2 & 1 & 0 \end{pmatrix}$$

iii.

$$\begin{pmatrix} 0 & 2 & 1 \\ 2 & 0 & 2 \\ 1 & 1 & 0 \end{pmatrix}$$

d. Some matrices cannot be adjacency matrices for graphs. Write a description of the characteristics of a matrix that could be the adjacency matrix for a graph.

4. a. What is the minimum number of edges needed to Eulerize a graph in the shape of a pentagon with all the diagonals from one vertex as shown here? In the shape of a hexagon (6 sides) with all diagonals from one vertex? A heptagon (7 sides)? An octagon (8 sides)?

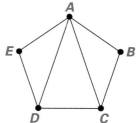

b. Organize your data from part a in a table. Do you see any pattern relating the number of vertices and minimum number of edges needed to Eulerize these graphs? If so, write a rule. If not, collect additional data until you see a pattern and can write a rule.

c. Suppose you know the minimum number of edges needed to Eulerize a polygon with n vertices with all diagonals from one vertex. Is it possible to write an equation using *NOW* and *NEXT* to describe the minimum number of edges needed to Eulerize a polygonal graph of this sort with $n + 1$ vertices? Explain your response.

2 *Managing Conflicts*

Have you ever noticed how many different radio channels there are? Each radio station has its own transmitter which broadcasts on a particular channel, or frequency.

The Federal Communications Commission (FCC) makes sure that the broadcast from one radio station does not interfere with the broadcast from any other radio station. This is done by assigning an appropriate frequency to each station. The FCC requires that stations within transmitting range of each other must use different frequencies. Otherwise, you might tune into "ROCK 101.7" and get Mozart instead!

Think about this situation

Seven new radio stations are planning to start broadcasting in the same region of the country. The FCC wants to assign a frequency to each station so that no two stations interfere with each other. The FCC also wants to assign the fewest possible number of new frequencies.

a What factors need to be considered before the frequencies can be assigned?

b What method can the FCC use to assign the frequencies?

Investigation (2.1) Building a Model

Suppose that because of geographic conditions and the strength of each station's transmitter, the FCC determines that stations within 500 miles of each other must be assigned different frequencies. Otherwise their broadcasts will interfere with each other. The location of the seven stations is shown on the grid at the right. A side of each small square on the grid represents 100 miles.

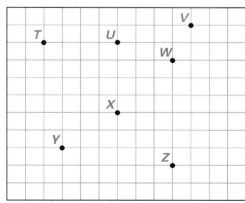

Scale: ⊢—⊣ **= 100 miles**

1. Working on your own, figure out how many different frequencies are needed for the seven radio stations. Remember that stations 500 miles or *less* apart must have different frequencies. Stations more than 500 miles apart can use the same frequency. *Try to use as few frequencies as possible.*

2. Compare your answer with others in your group.

   a. Did everyone use the same number of frequencies? Reach agreement in your group about the minimum number of frequencies needed for the seven radio stations.

   b. Suppose one person assigns two stations the same frequency and another person assigns them different frequencies. Is it possible that both assignments are acceptable? Explain.

In this case, it is possible to find the minimum number of frequencies by trial and error. What would you do when there are many more radio stations? A more systematic method is needed for more complicated situations. You could begin by modeling the problem with a graph similar to the graphs in the previous lesson. Remember, *to model a problem with a graph, you must first decide what the vertices and edges represent.*

3. Working on your own, begin modeling this problem with a graph.

   a. What should the vertices represent?

   b. How will you decide whether or not to connect two vertices with an edge? Complete this statement:

   Two vertices are connected by an edge if ...

   c. Now that you have specified the vertices and edges, draw a graph for this problem.

4. Compare your graph with others in your group.

   a. Did everyone in your group define the vertices and edges in the same way? Discuss any differences.

   b. For a given situation, suppose two people define the vertices and edges in two different ways. Is it possible that both ways accurately represent the situation? Explain your reasoning.

   c. For a given situation, suppose two people define the vertices and edges in the same way. Is it possible that their graphs could look different but both be correct? Explain your reasoning.

5. A common choice for the vertices is to let them represent the radio stations. Edges might be thought of in two ways as described in parts a and b below.

   a. You might connect two vertices by an edge whenever the stations they represent are 500 miles or *less* apart. Did anyone in your group do this? If not, draw a graph where two vertices are connected by an edge whenever the stations they represent are 500 miles or *less* apart.

   b. You might connect two vertices by an edge whenever the stations they represent are *more* than 500 miles apart. Did anyone in your group do this? If not, draw a graph where two vertices are connected by an edge whenever the stations they represent are *more* than 500 miles apart.

   c. Compare the graphs from parts a and b.

   – Are both graphs accurate ways of representing the situation?

   – Which graph do you think will be more useful and easier to use as a mathematical model for this situation? Why?

6. For the rest of this investigation, you will use the graph where edges connect vertices that are 500 miles or less apart. Make sure you have a neat copy of this graph.

   a. Are vertices (stations) *X* and *W* connected by an edge? Are they 500 miles or less apart? Will their broadcasts interfere with each other?

   b. Are vertices (stations) *Y* and *Z* connected by an edge? Will their broadcasts interfere with each other?

   c. Compare your graph to the graph at the right.

   – Does this graph also represent the radio-station problem?

   – What criteria can you use to decide if two graphs both represent the same situation?

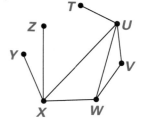

7. So far you have a model that shows all the radio stations and which stations are within 500 miles of each other. The goal is to assign frequencies so that there will be no interference between stations. You still need to build the frequencies into the model. So, as the last step in building the graph model, represent the frequencies as **colors**. To **color a graph** means to assign colors to the vertices so that two vertices connected by an edge have different colors.

   You can now think about the problem in terms of *coloring the vertices of a graph*. The following table contains statements about stations and frequencies in the left-hand column. Corresponding statements about vertices and colors are in the right-hand column. Write statements to complete the right-hand column of the table.

Statements about stations and frequencies	Statements about vertices and colors
Two stations have different frequencies.	Two vertices have different colors.
Find a way to assign frequencies so that stations within 500 miles of each other get different frequencies.	
Use the fewest number of frequencies.	

8. Now use as few colors as possible to color your graph for the radio station problem. That is, assign a color to each vertex so that any two vertices that are connected by an edge have different colors. You can use colored pencils or just the names of some colors to do the coloring. Color or write a color name next to each vertex. Try to use the smallest number of colors possible.

9. Compare your coloring with that of another group.

   a. Do both colorings satisfy the condition that vertices connected by an edge must have different colors?

   b. Do both colorings use the same number of colors to color the vertices of the graph?

   c. Reach agreement about the minimum number of colors needed. Explain, in writing, why the graph cannot be colored with fewer colors.

   d. Suppose one group assigns two vertices the same color and another group assigns them different colors. Is it possible that both assignments are acceptable? Why or why not?

   e. What is the connection between graph coloring and assigning frequencies to radio stations? As you answer this question, compare the results of this activity to those in activity 2.

10. Think about the strategy you used in activity 8 to color the radio station graph with as few colors as possible.

   a. Write down a step-by-step description of your coloring strategy. Write the description so that your strategy can be applied to graphs other than just the radio station graph.

   b. Use the description of your strategy to color a copy of the graph at the right.

   c. Refine the directions for your coloring strategy so that any one of your classmates could follow the directions.

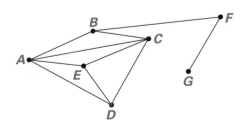

11. Exchange your written coloring directions with another group. Then do the following:

   a. Use the other group's directions to color a second copy of the graph in part b of activity 10. The other group will be doing the same thing with your directions.

   b. Compare your colorings with the other group's colorings.
- Are they the same?
- Are they each legitimate colorings?
- Do they each use the least number of colors possible? Reach agreement with the other group about the minimum number of colors needed to color the graph.

   c. Discuss any problems that came up with either group's coloring directions. If necessary, rewrite your directions so that they work better and are easier to follow.

As you saw in the previous lesson, a careful list of directions for carrying out a procedure is called an *algorithm*. Designing and applying algorithms is an important method for solving problems. There are lots of possible algorithms for coloring the vertices of any graph, including the ones you developed.

Checkpoint

   (a) What do the vertices, edges, and colors represent in the graph model that you have been using for the radio station problem?

   (b) How does "coloring a graph" help solve the radio station problem?

   (c) In what ways can two graph models differ and yet still both accurately represent a given situation?

   (d) What are some strengths and weaknesses of the graph-coloring algorithm created by your group?

   ✓ *Be prepared to share your group's thinking and coloring algorithm with the entire class. Decide as a class on algorithms that seem most efficient and are easily understood.*

Graph-coloring algorithms continue to be an active area of mathematical research with many applications. It has proven quite difficult to find an algorithm that colors the vertices of any graph using as few colors as possible. You often can figure out how to do this for a given small graph, as you have done in this investigation. However, no one knows an efficient algorithm that will color *any* graph with the *fewest* number of colors. This is a famous unsolved problem in mathematics. At the time this book was written, at least, the problem was still unsolved....

On Your Own

Copy the grid with the seven radio stations on page 277. (Your teacher may have a copy ready for you.) Add three more stations to the grid so that at least two of them are within 500 miles of one of the existing seven stations. Use graph coloring to assign frequencies optimally to all ten stations so that their broadcasts do not interfere with each other.

Investigation 2.2 Coloring, Map Making, and Scheduling

Now that you know how to color a graph, you can use graph coloring to solve many other types of problems.

For example, there are six clubs at King High School that all want to meet once a week for one hour, right after school lets out. The problem is that several students belong to more than one of the clubs, so not all the clubs can meet on the same day. Also, the school wants to schedule as few days per week for after-school club meetings as possible. Below is the list of the clubs and the students who belong to more than one club.

Club	Students belonging to more than one club
Varsity Club	Christina, Shanda, Carlos
Math Club	Christina, Carlos, Wendy
French Club	Shanda
Drama Club	Carlos, Vikas, Wendy
Computer Club	Vikas, Shanda
Art Club	Shanda

Your goal is to assign a meeting day (Monday–Friday) to each club in such a way that no two clubs that share a member meet on the same day. Also, you want to use as few days as possible.

1. Consider this problem as a graph-coloring problem.

   a. Working on your own, decide what you think the vertices, edges, and colors should represent in the club-scheduling problem.

b. Compare representations with the other members of your group. Decide as a group which representations are best. Complete these three statements:

The vertices represent ...

Two vertices are connected by an edge if ...

The colors represent ...

c. Draw a graph that models the problem.

d. Color the club-scheduling graph using as few colors as possible.

e. Use your coloring to answer these questions:

    – Is it possible for every club to meet once per week?

    – What is the fewest number of days needed to schedule all the club meetings?

    – On what day should each club meeting be scheduled?

    – Explain how your coloring of the graph helps you answer each of these questions.

Another class of problems in which graph coloring is useful involves coloring maps. You may have noticed in your geography or social studies course that maps are always colored so that neighboring countries do not have the same color. This is done so that the countries are easily distinguished and don't blend into each other. In the following activities you will explore the number of different colors necessary to color *any* map in such a way that no two countries that share a border have the same color. This is a question that mathematicians worked on for many years, resulting in a lot of new and useful mathematics.

2. Shown here is an uncolored map of a portion of southern Africa in 1980. Using a copy of this map, color the map so that no two countries that share a border have the same color.

a. How many colors did you use? Try to color the map with fewer colors.

b. Compare your map coloring with that of other classmates.

    – Are the colorings different?

    – Are the colorings legitimate; that is, do neighboring countries have different colors? If a coloring is not legitimate, fix it.

c. What was the fewest number of colors that were needed to color this map?

3. In activity 2 you found the fewest number of colors needed to color the Africa map. Now think about the fewest number of colors needed to color *any* map.

   a. Do you think you can color *any* map with, say, 5 different colors? Can the map of Africa be colored with 5 colors?

   b. The map here has been colored with 5 colors. Is it possible to color the map with fewer than five colors? If so, copy it onto your own paper and color it with as few colors as possible.

   c. What do you think is the *fewest* number of colors needed to color *any* map? Make a conjecture now. Then, over the next few days, check your conjecture on other maps outside of class. Revise your conjecture as necessary. Compare it to the conjectures of your classmates. Conclude your outside-of-class investigation of map coloring by examining Extending task 3 on page 293.

Maps can be colored by working directly with the maps, as you have been doing. But it is also possible to turn a map-coloring problem into a graph-coloring problem. This can be helpful since it allows you to use all the properties and techniques for graphs to help you understand and solve the map-coloring problems.

4. To build a graph model for a map-coloring problem, first think about what you did with the radio station and club-scheduling problems. In both of those problems, the edges were used to indicate some kind of *conflict* between the vertices. The vertices in conflict were connected by an edge and colored different colors. A crucial step in building a graph-coloring model is to decide what the conflict is. Once you know the conflict, you can figure out what the vertices, edges, and colors should represent.

   a. What was the conflict in the club-scheduling problem? What was the conflict in the radio station problem?

   b. Make and complete a table like the one at the top of the following page.

	Conflict	Vertices	Connect with an Edge if:	Colors
Radio station problem	*Two radio stations are in conflict if _____ .*	*Radio Stations*	*Stations 500 miles apart or less*	*Frequencies*
Club-scheduling problem	*Two clubs are in conflict if _____ .*			
Map-coloring problem	*Two countries are in conflict if _____ .*			

5. a. Draw a graph that represents the map shown on page 283. Use the vertices and edges to represent aspects of the map as you determined in activity 4.

b. Color the vertices of the graph. Remember that coloring always means that vertices connected by an edge must have different colors. Also, as usual, use as few colors as possible.

c. Compare your coloring with that of other classmates.

 – Are all the colorings legitimate?

 – Reach agreement on the fewest number of colors needed to color the graph.

 – Is the minimum number of colors for this *graph*-coloring problem the same as the minimum number of colors for the *map*-coloring problem in part c of activity 2? Explain.

Checkpoint

In this lesson, you have seen three different problems that can be modeled by graph coloring:

 – assigning frequencies to radio stations

 – scheduling club meetings

 – coloring maps

The title of this lesson is "Managing Conflicts". Explain how graph coloring allows you to "manage conflicts" in each of the three problems.

✓ *Be prepared to share your explanations with the entire class.*

On Your Own

Hospitals must have comprehensive and up-to-date evacuation plans in case of an emergency. A combination of buses and ambulances can be used to evacuate most patients. Of particular concern are patients under quarantine in the contagious disease wards. These patients cannot ride in buses with non-quarantine patients. However, some quarantine patients can be transported together. The records of who can be bused together and who cannot are updated daily.

Suppose that on a given day there are six patients in the contagious disease wards. The patients are identified by letters. Here is the list of who cannot ride with whom:

A cannot ride with *B, C,* or *D*	*B* cannot ride with *A, C,* or *E*
C cannot ride with *A, B,* or *D*	*D* cannot ride with *A* or *C*
E cannot ride with *F* or *B*	*F* cannot ride with *E*

The problem is to determine how many vehicles are needed to evacuate these six patients. Use a graph-coloring model to solve this problem. Describe the conflict and state what the vertices, edges, and colors represent.

Modeling **O**rganizing **R**eflecting **E**xtending

Modeling

1. A nursery and garden center plants a certain number of "mix-and-match" flower beds. Each bed contains several different varieties and colors. This allows customers to see possible arrangements of flowers that they might plant.

   However, the beds are planted so that no bed contains two colors of the same variety. For example, no bed contains both red roses and gold roses. Also, no bed contains two varieties of the same color. For example, no bed contains both yellow tulips and yellow marigolds. This is done so that the customer can distinguish among and appreciate the different colors and varieties. A list of the varieties and colors that will be planted follows.

Varieties	Colors
Roses	Red, Gold, White
Tulips	Yellow, Purple, Red
Marigolds	Yellow, Orange

The nursery wants to plant as few of the mix-and-match beds as possible. In this problem you will determine the minimum number of mix-and-match flower beds.

a. The varieties and colors listed above yield eight different types of flowers, such as red roses, red tulips, and yellow tulips. List all the other types of flowers that are possible.

b. It is the types of flowers from part a that will be planted in the mix-and-match beds. The problem is to figure out the minimum number of beds needed to plant these types of flowers so that no bed contains flowers that are the same variety or the same color. First, you need to build a graph-coloring model.

　　－ What should the vertices represent?

　　－ What should the edges represent?

　　－ What should the colors of the graph represent?

c. Draw the graph model and color it with as few colors as possible.

d. What is the minimum number of mix-and-match beds needed?

e. Using your graph coloring, recommend to the nursery which types of flowers should go in each of the mix-and-match beds.

f. When using a graph-coloring model, you connect vertices by an edge whenever there is some kind of conflict between the vertices. What was the conflict in this problem?

2. A local zoo wants to take visitors on animal feeding tours. They propose the following tours:

Tour 1 Visit lions, elephants, buffaloes

Tour 2 Visit monkeys, hippos, deer

Tour 3 Visit elephants, zebras, giraffes

Tour 4 Visit hippos, reptiles, bears

Tour 5 Visit kangaroos, monkeys, seals

The animals should not be fed more than once a day. Also, there is only room for one tour group at a time at any one site. Can these tours be scheduled using only Monday, Wednesday, and Friday? Explain your answer in terms of graph coloring.

3. You often can color small maps directly from the map, without translating to a graph model. However, using a graph model is essential when the maps are more complicated. The map of South America shown here can be colored either directly or by using a graph-coloring model.

a. Color a copy of the map of South America directly. Use as few colors as possible and make sure that no two bordering countries have the same color.

b. Represent the map as a graph. Then color the vertices of the graph with as few colors as possible.

c. Did you use the same number of colors in parts a and b?

4. The figure shown here is part of what is called a *Sierpinski triangle*. (The complete figure is actually drawn by an infinite process described in Extending task 2.)

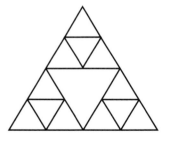

a. Think of this figure as a map in which each triangle not containing another triangle is a country. Make and color a copy of the map with as few colors as possible.

b. Construct a graph model for this map. Color the vertices of the graph with as few colors as possible. Compare the number of colors used with that in part a.

c. Think of this figure as a map as Sierpinski did: the triangles with points upwards are countries and the triangles with points downwards are water. Using this interpretation of countries, color a copy of the map with as few colors as possible.

d. Construct a graph model for this second map. Color this graph with as few colors as possible. Did you use the same number of colors as in part c?

Organizing

1. Shown here is Shanda's graph model for the radio-station problem from page 277.

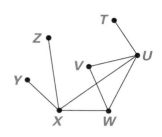

a. Is this a legitimate model for the radio-station problem? Explain your reasoning.

b. In Shanda's graph model, some edges cross at places that are not vertices. Can Shanda's graph be re-drawn without edge-crossings? Explain.

c. Graphs that *can* be drawn in the plane with edges crossing only at the vertices are called **planar graphs**. Which of the graphs below are planar graphs?

i.   **ii.** 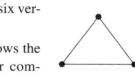   **iii.**

2. This task explores some properties of *complete graphs*. A **complete graph** is a graph that has an edge between every pair of vertices. Complete graphs with three and five vertices are shown below.

a. Draw the complete graph with four vertices. Draw the complete graph with six vertices.

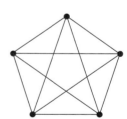

b. Make a table that shows the number of edges for complete graphs with three, four, five, and six vertices.

c. Look for a pattern in your table. How many edges does the complete graph with seven vertices have? The complete graph with *n* vertices?

d. Recall the *NOW-NEXT* notation that you have used in previous chapters. Let *NOW* represent the number of edges for the given complete graph. Let *NEXT* represent the number of edges for the complete graph with one more vertex. Write an expression that shows how to calculate *NEXT* using *NOW*.

3. Refer to the definition of a complete graph given in Organizing task 2.

   a. What is the minimum number of colors needed to color the vertices of the complete graph with three vertices? The complete graph with four vertices? The complete graph with five vertices?

   b. Make a table showing the number of vertices and the corresponding minimum number of colors needed to color a complete graph with that many vertices. Enter your answers from part a into the table. Find several more entries for the table.

   c. Describe any patterns you see in the table.

   d. What is the minimum number of colors needed to color a complete graph with 100 vertices? With n vertices?

4. Besides coloring graphs, it is also possible to color polyhedra. Shown below are three of the five **regular polyhedra**.

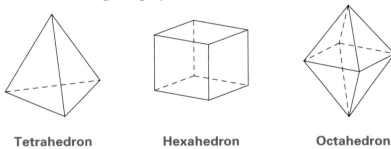

Tetrahedron   **Hexahedron**   **Octahedron**

Complete each coloring scheme below for each of the above polyhedra. Record your answers for each of these coloring schemes in a table like the one below. You may use the "Coloring Polyhedra" worksheet, if available.

   a. Color the vertices. Use the minimum number of colors. (No two vertices connected by an edge can have the same color.)

   b. Color the edges. Use the minimum number of colors. (No two edges that share a vertex can have the same color.)

   c. Color the faces. Use the minimum number of colors. (Faces that are adjacent must have different colors.)

| | **Minimum Number of Colors** | | |
Regular Polyhedron	for Vertices	for Edges	for Faces
Tetrahedron			
Hexahedron			
Octahedron			

5. A **circuit** is a path that goes from vertex to vertex and ends where it started.

   a. Color the vertices of each of the circuits below using as few colors as possible.

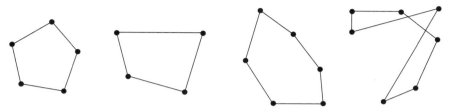

   b. Make a conjecture about the minimum number of colors needed to color circuits. Write an argument supporting your conjecture.

Reflecting

1. Throughout this course, and in this chapter in particular, you have been doing **mathematical modeling**. Below is a diagram that summarizes the process of mathematical modeling.

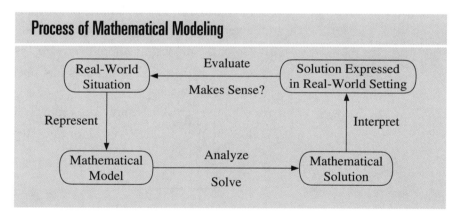

Choose one example of mathematical modeling from this lesson. Use the example to illustrate each part of the diagram.

2. Think of a problem situation, different from those in this investigation, where you think graph coloring would be useful. Review the applications in this lesson to get started. Describe the problem situation, and then describe how you would solve it using graph coloring.

3. Think back over your work in Lessons 1 and 2. What did you find to be the most difficult part of modeling a problem with a graph? How did you resolve the difficulty?

4. Compare a current map of the southern part of Africa with the 1980 map on page 283.

   a. Are there differences between the old map and the current one? If so, what are they?

   b. Draw a graph model for the current map. Color the vertices of the graph with the fewest number of colors possible.

   c. How many colors are used to color the map as it appears in a social studies book or atlas?

5. Research to find mathematicians who have worked on map coloring. Write a one-page report on one mathematician's contribution to the field.

Extending

1. Graph coloring is such an important application that several algorithms have been developed that are used on computers around the world. One commonly used algorithm is called the *Welsh and Powell algorithm*. Here's how it works:

   i. Begin by making a list of all the vertices starting with the ones of highest degree and ending with those of lowest degree. (Recall that the *degree* of a vertex is the number of edges touching the vertex.)

   ii. Color the highest uncolored vertex on your list with an unused color.

   iii. Go down the list coloring as many uncolored vertices with the current color as you can.

   iv. If all the vertices are now colored, you're done. If not, go to ii.

   a. Follow the Welsh and Powell algorithm, step by step, to color the two graphs below.

   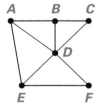 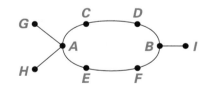

   b. Does the Welsh and Powell algorithm always yield a coloring that uses the fewest number of colors possible? Explain your reasoning.

   c. Use the Welsh and Powell algorithm to color the radio station graph and the club-scheduling graph from this lesson.

   d. Compare the algorithm you wrote in this lesson to the Welsh and Powell algorithm. Are they similar? Which one do you like better? Why?

2. The Sierpinski Triangle is a very interesting geometric figure. If you try to draw it, you will never finish! That's because it is defined by a repetitive set of instructions. Here are the instructions:

 i. Draw an equilateral triangle.

 ii. Find the midpoint of each side.

 iii. Connect the midpoints. This will subdivide the triangle into four smaller triangles.

 iv. Remove the center triangle. (Don't actually cut it out, just think about it as being removed. If you wish, you can shade it with a pencil to remind yourself it has been "removed".) Now there are three smaller triangles left.

 v. Repeat steps ii–iv with each of the remaining triangles.

You never get finished with these instructions because there always will be smaller and smaller triangles to subdivide. The first few passes through the instructions are illustrated here.

Sierpinski's Triangle by Diana Venters. From *Mathematical Quilts*, Janson Publications, 1997.

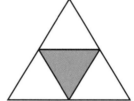 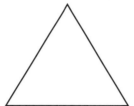 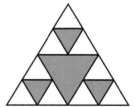

a. On an enlarged copy of the third stage, draw the next few steps of the process. Your teacher may provide you with a copy for your work.

b. If you think of the Sierpinski Triangle as a map (a very strange map with an infinite number of countries), what is the minimum number of colors needed to color the map?

3. In the 19th century, mathematicians made a conjecture about the minimum number of colors needed to color any map so that regions with a common boundary have different colors. This conjecture became one of the most famous unsolved problems in mathematics—until 1976 when the problem was solved. Based on your work in this investigation, how many colors do you think are needed to color any map? For this problem, you should only consider maps where the regions are connected. So, for example, do not consider a country that is split into two separate parts.

a. Try to draw a map that requires 3 colors and cannot be colored with less.

b. Try to draw a map that requires 4 colors and cannot be colored with less.

c. Try to draw a map that requires 5 colors and cannot be colored with less.

d. How many colors do you think are necessary to color any map? After you have worked on this problem for a while, search the Internet or a library for some recent information on graph theory. Find the answer and compare it to your answer. Write a brief report on your findings.

4. In this lesson, coloring a graph has always meant coloring the *vertices* of the graph. It also can be useful to think about **coloring the edges** of a graph. For example, suppose there are 6 teams in a basketball tournament and each team plays every other team exactly once. Games involving different pairs of teams can be played during the same round, that is, at the same time. The problem is to figure out the fewest number of rounds that must be played. One way to solve this problem is to represent it as a graph and then color the *edges*.

   a. Represent the teams as vertices. Connect two vertices with an edge if the two teams will play each other in the tournament. Draw the graph model.

   b. Color the edges of the graph so that *no two edges that share a vertex have the same color*. Use as few colors as possible.

   c. Think about what the colors mean in terms of the tournament and the number of rounds that must be played. Use the edge coloring to answer these questions:

   – What is the fewest number of rounds needed for the tournament?

   – Which teams play in which rounds?

   d. Describe another problem situation that could be solved by edge coloring.

5. Described below is an interesting game involving a type of edge coloring which you can play with a friend.

   – Place six points on a sheet of paper to mark the vertices of a regular hexagon, as shown here.

   – Each player selects a color different from the other.

   – Take turns connecting two vertices with an edge. Each player should use his or her color when adding an edge.

   – The first player who is forced to form a triangle of his or her own color loses! (Only triangles whose vertices are among the six starting vertices count.)

   a. Play this game several times and then answer the questions below.

   – Is there always a winner? Explain.

   – Which player has the better chance of winning? Explain.

   b. Use the results of part a to help you solve the following problem.

   Of any six students in a room, must there be at least three mutual acquaintances or at least three mutual strangers?

3 *Scheduling Large Projects*

Careful planning is important to ensure the success of any project. This is particularly true in the case of planning large projects such as a party or a house remodeling job.

Suppose, for example, that you and some of your classmates are helping to plan a formal Spring Dance. You decide that a poster advertising the dance should be posted around the school four weeks before the dance. But there are many other tasks that must be done before the poster can be posted.

Think about this situation

ⓐ What are some tasks related to putting on a spring dance that should be completed before advertising posters are printed and posted? As a class, brainstorm as many tasks as possible.

ⓑ How can you make sure everything gets done on time?

Investigation (3.1) Building a Model

1. As you have seen before, as a first step in modeling a situation such as planning a dance, it is often helpful to make a diagram.

   a. Working together in your group, draw a diagram that illustrates the schedule of tasks to be completed before posters for the spring dance can be displayed.

   b. List two tasks that can be worked on at the same time by different teams.

   c. Do some tasks need to be done before others? Tasks that need to be done before a particular task are called **prerequisites** for that task. Give one example of a task and a prerequisite for that task.

d. A prerequisite task might be done a long time before, or just before, a particular task. Construct a table that shows each task and the tasks that need to be done *just* before that task.

e. Does your diagram clearly show which tasks are prerequisites to others and which can be worked on at the same time? If not, make changes in your diagram to make it more accurate.

2. Exchange diagrams and tables with another group.

a. What are some similarities and differences between your group's table and diagram and the other group's table and diagram?

b. If necessary, modify your diagram and table so that they better show which tasks are prerequisites to other tasks.

Listed here are some of the tasks you may have found necessary in planning a spring dance. *These are the tasks that will be used for the rest of this investigation.* The order in which these tasks would need to be completed may vary from school to school.

Tasks
_____

Book a Band or D.J. (*B*)

Design the Poster (*D*)

Choose and Reserve the Location (*L*)

Post the Posters (*P*)

Choose a Theme (*T*)

Arrange for Decorations (*DC*)

At Marshall High School, the prerequisites for the various tasks are as follows:

– The tasks that need to be done just before booking the band are choosing and reserving the location *and* choosing a theme.

– The tasks that need to be done just before designing the poster are booking the band *and* arranging for decorations.

– There are *no* tasks that need to be done just before choosing and reserving the location.

– The task that needs to be done just before posting the posters is designing the posters.

– There are no tasks that need to be done just before choosing a theme.

– The task that needs to be done just before arranging for decorations is choosing a theme.

Tasks to be done *just* before a particular task are called **immediate prerequisites.**

3. Using the prerequisite information for Marshall High School, complete a table like the one below showing which tasks are immediate prerequisites for others. Such a table is called an **immediate prerequisite table**.

Task	Immediate Prerequisites
Book a Band (*B*)	*L, T*
Design the Poster (*D*)	
Choose and Reserve the Location (*L*)	
Post the Posters (*P*)	
Choose a Theme (*T*)	
Arrange for Decorations (*DC*)	

4. Working on your own, complete a diagram like the one here showing how all the tasks are related to each other.

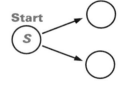

   a. Copy the diagram onto your own paper. Place the circle labeled *S* at the far left of your paper. Put a new circle at the far right of your paper, where the diagram will end. Label it *F* for "finish." The circles labeled *S* and *F* do not represent actual tasks. They simply indicate the start and finish of the project.

   b. To the right of *S* are drawn two empty circles representing tasks that do not have any immediate prerequisites. Which tasks in the immediate prerequisite table from activity 3 should be represented by the two empty circles? Label the two circles with those tasks.

   c. Moving to the right again, draw a circle for each remaining task. Draw an arrow between two circles if one task (at the tail of the arrow) is an immediate prerequisite for the other task (at the tip of the arrow).

   d. Finish the diagram by drawing connecting arrows from the final task or tasks to the circle marked *F*.

   e. Your diagram may look a bit messy. Redraw your diagram so that it looks orderly.

5. Compare your diagram with the diagrams of other members of your group.

   a. Do the diagrams look different? Explain the differences.

   b. Does everyone's diagram accurately represent the information in the immediate prerequisite table?

   c. Decide as a group on one organized, orderly diagram.

6. Use your diagram and the immediate prerequisite table to help you answer the following questions.

   a. Which of the following pairs of tasks can be worked on at the same time by different teams? Explain your reasoning.

   – Can tasks *L* and *B* be worked on at the same time by different teams?

   – Tasks *L* and *T*?

   – Tasks *L* and *DC*?

   – Tasks *L* and *D*?

   b. How do tasks that can be worked on at the same time appear in the diagram?

   c. Find one other pair of tasks that can be worked on at the same time.

   d. Explain, in terms of the school dance poster project and the individual tasks involved, why it is reasonable for the tasks you identified in part c to be worked on at the same time.

7. How do tasks that are prerequisites appear in the diagram?

The diagram you have drawn is called a *directed* graph, or **digraph**. Digraphs are graphs that have *directed* edges. That is, the edges are arrows.

Checkpoint

The digraph showing how tasks involved in the dance poster project are related to each other is a mathematical model of the situation.

ⓐ What do the vertices of the project digraph represent?

ⓑ How are tasks that can be worked on at the same time represented in the project digraph?

ⓒ How are prerequisite tasks represented in the project digraph?

✓ *Be prepared to compare and discuss your digraph with other groups.*

On Your Own

"Turning around" a commercial airplane at an airport is a complex project that happens many times every day.

Suppose that the tasks involved are unloading arriving passengers, cleaning the cabin, unloading arriving luggage, boarding departing passengers, and loading departing luggage. The relationships among these tasks are as follows:

- Unloading the arriving passengers must be done just before cleaning the cabin.
- Cleaning the cabin must be done just before boarding the departing passengers.
- Unloading the arriving luggage must be done just before loading the departing luggage.
- All activities in the cabin of the airplane (unloading and boarding passengers and cleaning the cabin) can be done at the same time as loading and unloading luggage.

Construct the immediate prerequisite table and the project digraph for this situation.

Investigation 3.2 — Finding the Earliest Finish Time

You have seen that a large project, like a school dance or "turning around" a commercial airplane, consists of many individual tasks that are related to each other. Some tasks must be done before others can be started. Other tasks can be worked on at the same time. A graph is a good way to show how all the tasks are related to each other.

The real concern in a large project is to get all the tasks done most efficiently. In particular, it is important to know the least amount of time required to complete the entire project. This minimum completion time is called the **earliest finish time (EFT).**

1. There are many reasonable estimates that you and your classmates might make for how long it will take to complete each task of the school dance poster project. Experience at one school suggested the task times and prerequisites displayed in the following table. These task times will be used for the rest of this lesson.

Task	Task Time	Immediate Prerequisites
Choose & Reserve Location (*L*)	2 days	none
Choose a Theme (*T*)	3 days	none
Book the Band or D.J. (*B*)	7 days	*L, T*
Arrange for Decorations (*DC*)	5 days	*T*
Design the Poster (*D*)	5 days	*B, DC*
Post the Poster (*P*)	2 days	*D*

Put these task times into the project digraph you constructed in the last investigation by entering the task times into the circles (vertices) of the digraph.

2. Now use the immediate prerequisite table and the project digraph to help you figure out how to complete the project most efficiently.

    a. Using all the individual task times, what is the least amount of time required to complete the whole project (that is, what is the EFT for the project)? Each group member should write down a response *and* an explanation.

    b. Compare responses and explanations with others in your group.

    c. Is the earliest finish time for the whole project equal to the sum of all the individual task times? Explain.

    d. How many paths are there through the project digraph, from *S* to *F*? List in order the vertices of all the different paths. For each path, compute the total time of all tasks on the path.

    e. Which path through the graph corresponds to the earliest finish time for all the tasks? Write down your response *and* an explanation.

    f. A path through the poster project graph that corresponds to the earliest finish time is called a **critical path**. Mark the edges of the critical path so that it is easily visible.

        – What is the connection between the critical path and the EFT?

        – What is the connection between the EFT and the path with the greatest total task time?

        – What is the connection between the critical path and the path with the greatest total task time?

    g. Compare your critical path from part f to another group's critical path. If the paths are different, discuss the differences and decide on the correct critical path.

    h. If all the posters are to be posted 30 days before the dance, how many days before the dance should work on the project begin?

3. Now explore what happens to the EFT and critical path if certain tasks take longer to complete than expected.

    a. What happens to the earliest finish time if it takes 6 days, instead of 5 days, to design the poster (task D)?

    b. What happens to the earliest finish time if it takes 9 days, instead of 7 days, to book the band (task B)?

    c. What happens to the earliest finish time if one of the tasks *on the critical path* takes longer than expected to complete? A task on a critical path is called a **critical task**.

    d. What happens to the earliest finish time if it takes 6 days, instead of 5 days, to arrange for the decorations (task DC)?

    e. Suppose it takes 3 days, instead of 2 days, to choose and reserve a location (task L).

        – What happens to the EFT?

        – What happens to the critical path?

    f. Suppose it takes 6 days, instead of 2 days, to choose and reserve a location (task L).

        – What happens to the critical path?

        – What happens to the EFT?

    g. What happens to the earliest finish time and the critical path if one of the tasks that is *not on the critical path* takes longer than expected to complete?

Checkpoint

    ⓐ How can you find the EFT by examining a digraph for a project?

    ⓑ Why is a critical path for a project "critical?"

    ✓ *Be prepared to share your group's thinking with the entire class.*

On Your Own

Examine the digraph below.

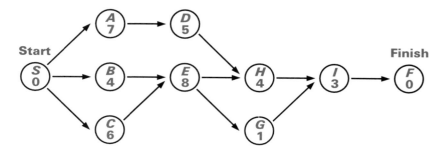

a. How many paths are there through this digraph, from *S* to *F*? List all the different paths, and compute the length of each path.

b. Find the critical path and the EFT. What are the critical tasks?

c. Are there any tasks that can have their task times increased by 3 units and yet not cause a change in the EFT for the whole project? If so, which tasks? If not, why not?

Modeling **O**rganizing **R**eflecting **E**xtending

Modeling

1. Refer back to the beginning of the lesson and the entire list of tasks that your class came up with for the school dance poster project.

   a. Assign reasonable task times to the various tasks.

   b. Construct the immediate prerequisite table for the tasks.

   c. Construct the project digraph.

   d. Find a critical path and the EFT.

   e. How do the critical tasks and EFT compare with those found in activity 2 of this investigation?

2. Suppose that your school is planning to organize an Earth Day. You will have booths, speakers, and activities related to planet Earth and its environment. Such a project will require careful planning and coordination among many different teams that will be working on it.

   Here are six tasks that will need to be done as part of the Earth Day project and estimates for the time to complete each task.

Task	Task Time
Decide on Topics for the Speakers, Booths, and Activities	6 days
Get Speakers	5 days
Choose Date and Location	3 days
Design Booths	2 weeks
Build Booths	1 week
Make Posters	6 days

a. Decide on immediate prerequisites for each of the tasks and construct the immediate prerequisite table.

b. Draw the project digraph.

c. Find the critical tasks and EFT.

3. Suppose that you and some friends are preparing a big dinner for 20 friends and family members.

a. List 4–8 tasks that must be done as part of this project.

b. Decide how long each task will reasonably take to complete.

c. Decide on the immediate prerequisites for each task and construct the immediate prerequisite table.

d. Draw the project digraph.

e. Find the critical tasks and EFT.

4. Shown below is the immediate prerequisite table for preparing a baseball field for play.

Task	Task Time	Immediate Prerequisites
Pick up Litter (L)	4 hours	none
Clean Dugouts (D)	2 hours	L
Drag the Infield (I)	2 hours	L
Mow the Grass (G)	3 hours	L
Paint the Foul Lines (P)	2 hours	I, G
Install the Bases (B)	1 hour	P

a. Find at least two tasks that can be worked on at the same time.

b. Draw the digraph for this project.

c. What is the EFT for the whole project?

  d. Mark the critical path.

  e. Do you think that the task times given in the table are reasonable? Change any times that you think are unreasonable. Use your new times to find the critical tasks and EFT.

5. Shown below is the immediate prerequisite table for building a house.

Task	Task Time	Immediate Prerequisites
Clear Land (*C*)	2 days	none
Build Foundation (*F*)	3 days	*C*
Build Upper Structure (*U*)	15 days	*F*
Electrical Work (*EL*)	9 days	*U*
Plumbing Work (*P*)	5 days	*U*
Complete Exterior Work (*EX*)	12 days	*U*
Complete Interior Work (*IN*)	10 days	*EL, P*
Landscaping (*L*)	6 days	*EX*

  a. Find at least two tasks that can be worked on at the same time.

  b. Draw the digraph for this project.

  c. Mark the critical path.

  d. What is the EFT for the whole project?

  e. Suppose three people are working on each task, and they are paid an average of $20 per hour. What will the total labor costs be if each person works 8 hours per day?

  f. Suppose some plumbing supplies will be late in arriving, so it will take 10 days to install the plumbing. How does this affect the EFT and critical path?

Organizing

1. Reproduced below is the digraph from "On Your Own" on page 302. The critical path is shown by the dashed arrows. Verify that the EFT is 21.

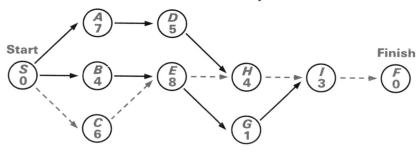

    a. How do the critical path and EFT change if:

       – the time for task C decreases by 5?

       – the time for task C increases by 5?

       – the time for task D increases by 2?

       – the time for task D increases by 3?

       – the time for task D decreases by 5?

    b. Write a summary describing how changes in times for tasks on and off the critical path affect the EFT and the critical path.

    c. Construct the immediate prerequisite table for the project digraph.

2. What are some similarities and differences between Euler paths and critical paths?

3. a. How might you modify the concept of an adjacency matrix to make it useful with digraphs?

    b. Make an adjacency matrix for the digraph at the right.

    c. How are adjacency matrices for digraphs different from adjacency matrices for graphs that do not have directed edges?

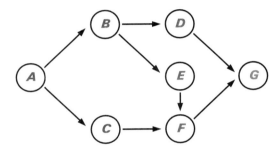

4. It is possible for a project digraph to have more than one critical path. That is, there can be more than one path through the project digraph that has maximum length.

    a. Consider a modified version of the school dance poster project digraph, below.

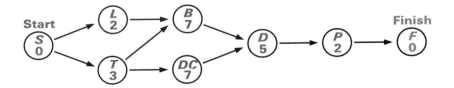

      – Find the EFT for the project.

      – How many critical paths are there? That is, how many paths are there with maximum length?

      – List all the critical tasks.

b. Consider a modified version of the project digraph from "On Your Own" on page 302, shown below.

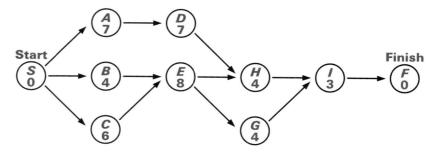

- Find the EFT for the project.
- How many critical paths are there? That is, how many paths are there with maximum length?
- List all the critical tasks.

Reflecting

1. Did you find anything particularly difficult in finding EFTs and critical paths for projects? If so, what did you do to overcome your difficulties?

2. Refer back to the project digraph in "On Your Own" on page 302. As a manager of the project, which tasks might require less management attention or supervision? Why?

3. Do you think the method of immediate prerequisite tables and critical paths is useful? Why or why not?

4. Write a brief description of a project you or someone you know is working on, or of a project you read about in the paper or heard about on TV. Explain how this critical path method might be used to help organize and manage the project.

Extending

1. Write an algorithm for finding a critical path in a digraph.

2. Explain why the digraphs below could *not* be used to model a simple project.

a.   **b.**

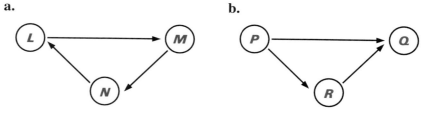

c. Are there any four-vertex configurations that can never occur in a project digraph? Explain and illustrate.

3. Refer to the immediate prerequisite table for the project of preparing a baseball field for play in task 4 of the Modeling section.

    a. What is the EFT for the project?

    b. Suppose that there are only two people available for preparing the field. Does this change the EFT? Explain. If it does change the EFT, what is the new EFT?

    c. Suppose that there are plenty of people to help prepare the field. However, mowing the grass in the time allotted (3 hours) can be done only if two people are mowing at the same time and, unfortunately, there is only one mower that is working. Propose a plan for how to deal with this problem. Will your plan change the EFT? Explain. If it does change the EFT, what is the new EFT?

4. Think of a project that could be modeled by this project digraph. Describe the project and each task.

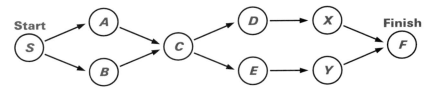

5. Read the newspaper article about airline turnarounds entitled "Beat the Clock" from the *Chicago Tribune*, August 29, 1993 (Travel section, page 1).

    a. List all the tasks described in the article that are involved in turning around an international flight. Estimate task times.

    b. Based on the information in the article and your own judgment, construct a prerequisite table and project digraph.

    c. Write a proposal for the airlines which suggests ways that they might reduce turnaround time.

Investigation 3.3 Scheduling a Project

So far in this lesson you have found a useful model for representing the school dance poster project—a digraph. Also, you know how to use the model to find the earliest finish time for the project—just find a critical (longest) path in the digraph. In this investigation, you will find out how to schedule the project.

Before working further on the poster project digraph, consider the simpler digraph below, which represents a simpler project. Tasks in the project are represented by letters, and the numbers represent the number of days needed to complete the tasks.

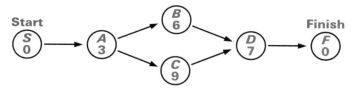

1. Working together as a group, find the EFT and record the critical path for this project.

2. Now you will find the **earliest finish time (EFT)** for *each* task.

   a. The earliest finish time (EFT) for a given task is the least amount of time required to finish that task. Keep in mind that in order to finish the task, all of its prerequisites must be finished as well.

   – What is the least amount of time needed to finish task *A*?

   – What is the least amount of time needed to finish task *C*?

   – Find the EFT for the rest of the tasks in this project.

   b. Make a large copy of the project digraph on your own paper. Write the EFT for each task just above and to the right of the vertex representing the task in the digraph. Label it as "EFT".

   c. How does the EFT for the last task compare to the EFT for the whole project?

   d. Describe the method you used to figure out the EFTs.

3. **a.** Now you will figure out the **earliest start time (EST)** for each task.

   – The EST for task *B* is 3. Does this mean that the earliest start time for task *B* is "at the beginning of day 3" or "after 3 days"? Explain.

   – Find the EST for each task.

   – Write the earliest start time for each task just above the EFT number on the digraph. Label it "EST".

   b. Write down the method you used to find the earliest start time (EST) for each task.

   c. How can you use the EFT for a particular task to compute the EST for that task?

4. The **latest start time (LST)** for a task is the *latest* time that you can start work on that task and still stay on schedule to finish the whole project by the EFT for the entire project.

a. Figure out the LST for each task *on* the critical path. Explain how you did it.

b. Figure out the LST for each task *off* the critical path. Explain how you did it.

c. Enter the LST numbers just to the left of the EST numbers on the digraph. Label them "LST".

5. Another important piece of information that is used to help manage a project is called **slack time**.

    a. The slack time for a given task is the difference between the latest start time (LST) and the earliest start time (EST). That is, slack time = LST − EST. Why do you think this is called "slack time"?

    b. Figure out the slack time for each task.

    c. What does it mean for a task to have a slack time of 3 days? 0 days?

    d. What can you say about the slack time for critical tasks?

    e. Are there other ways to determine the slack time, besides calculating LST − EST? Explain.

6. Now you are ready to schedule the project.

    a. When should you schedule work to begin on each task?

    b. Which of the numbers EFT, EST, or LST did you choose as the scheduled time to begin? Explain your reasoning.

    c. Put an asterisk (*) next to the number on the digraph that is the scheduled time to begin each task.

    d. Do some tasks have some flexibility concerning their scheduled time to begin? Which ones? Why?

    e. Which tasks have no flexibility with respect to their scheduled time to begin? Why?

7. Create a table like the one shown here, or use the "Scheduling a Project" handout. For each task, enter the EST, LST, EFT, and slack time. Also put "yes" or "no" for each task depending on whether or not it is a critical task.

Task	EST	LST	EFT	Slack Time	Critical Task?
A					
B					
C					
D					

Checkpoint

> **a** In this investigation, you determined these numbers: EFT, EST, LST, slack time, and scheduled time to begin. Summarize what these numbers mean and how they are related to each other.
>
> **b** How can you use the digraph for a given project and the numbers EFT, EST, LST, slack time, and scheduled time to begin, to make sure that the project gets done on time?
>
> ✓ *Be prepared to share your management ideas with the entire class.*

The method you have been using to model and manage the poster project is called the Critical Path Method (**CPM**) or the Program Evaluation and Review Technique (**PERT**). It was developed in the late 1950s to aid in the development of defense systems. This method is used extensively in business and industry. In fact, it is one of the most frequently used mathematical management techniques. And now you know how to do it!

On Your Own

Consider the project digraph below.

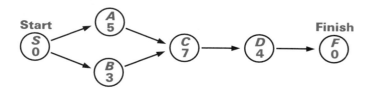

a. Determine the critical path and the earliest finish time for the whole project.

b. Find the EFT, EST, LST, and slack time for each task in the project.

c. Which tasks should a manager watch particularly closely? Explain your reasoning.

d. Are there some tasks that have some flexibility in terms of when they begin and end? Which ones? How much flexibility in scheduling the tasks would a manager have? Explain.

Investigation 3.4 Uncertain Task Times

In many applications of PERT, the projects are so complex that computer processing of the digraphs is required. Also, it is unlikely that you would know the exact time required to complete each of the many project tasks. In this investigation, you will modify the critical path technique you have learned so far to take into account uncertain task times. You will also use software to help reduce the time and effort required for your analysis.

Suppose a car manufacturer is considering a new fuel-efficient car. Since this new car will cost a lot of money to produce, the company wants to be sure that it is a good idea before they begin production. To help them decide if it is a good idea, they do a feasibility study. (In a feasibility study, you look at things like estimated cost and consumer demand to see if the idea is practical.) The feasibility study itself is a big project that involves many different tasks. As is often the case, the exact time needed to finish each of the tasks in the feasibility study is not known. However, for each task they have an estimate of the *best time* (the shortest amount of time to finish the task), the *worst time* (the longest amount of time needed to finish the task), and the *most likely time* needed to finish the task. All of these estimates, and the prerequisite information, are summarized in the following table.

Tasks, Times, and Prerequisites for the Feasibility Study

Task	Best Task Time	Most Likely Task Time	Worst Task Time	Immediate Prerequisites
Design the Car (A)	5 weeks	7 weeks	10 weeks	none
Plan Market Research (B)	1 week	2 weeks	4 weeks	none
Build Prototype Car (C)	8 weeks	10 weeks	16 weeks	A
Prepare Advertising (D)	2.5 weeks	4 weeks	7 weeks	A
Prepare Initial Cost Estimates (E)	1.5 weeks	2 weeks	4 weeks	C
Test the Car (F)	3.5 weeks	5 weeks	8 weeks	C
Finish the Market Research (G)	2 weeks	3.5 weeks	6 weeks	B, D
Prepare Final Cost Estimates (H)	1 week	2.5 weeks	5 weeks	E
Prepare Final Report (I)	0.5 week	1 week	2 weeks	F, G, H

1. Think about how to analyze this information to arrive at a schedule for the feasibility study project.

   a. Draw a digraph for this project. Just show the tasks, not the task times.

   b. How can you use all the information about best, worst, and most likely task times to figure out the critical tasks and schedule for this project? Write down as many methods and ideas as you can.

   c. Which method do you think is the best? Why?

For the remainder of this lesson you should use critical path software to find critical tasks and EFTs.

2. This activity illustrates how one PERT software program called AAPERT can be used. Your software may work differently.

   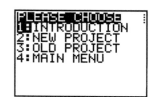

   On a graphing calculator, run the program AAPERT. Continue pressing ENTER until you see a screen similar to the one displayed here.

   a. Press 2 in order to enter the data for the project. Enter the data for *best task times* into your calculator. Follow the screen prompts. When the screen prompt asks for the number of prerequisites, it is asking for the *immediate* prerequisites. Check your data entries by choosing SHOW DATA from the *main* menu.

   b. Find the critical tasks and the EFT for the whole project, based on the best task times, by choosing SCHEDULE from the main menu. Mark the critical path on your digraph.

   c. Using EDIT from the main menu, enter the project a second time using the *most likely task times.* Then find the EFT for the whole project and the critical tasks. Using a different color pen or pencil, mark the corresponding critical path on your digraph.

   d. Using the *worst task times,* enter the data into your calculator. Then find the EFT and critical tasks. Draw the critical path on your digraph using a different color pen or pencil.

3. Compare the project EFTs and critical paths that you found in activity 2.

   a. Do you get a different critical path and EFT depending on the times you use?

   b. Is there some way to combine the three EFTs you calculated in activity 2? Explain.

   c. If just one EFT must be reported to the president of the company, what should be reported? Explain your reasoning.

4. Now consider one way to combine the best, worst, and most likely task times.

a. For each task, describe some way to compute an "average" time for completing the task.

b. In a later chapter, you will learn more about how to analyze mathematically "most likely" and "average" time. For now, one way to estimate an "average" time is to multiply the most likely time by 4, add the best time and the worst time, and divide by 6.

– Explain why this is a reasonable computation of average time.

– Sometimes an average like this is called a *weighted average*. Why do you think it is called a *weighted* average?

– Compute the average time for each task in the feasibility study project using the formula:

$$\text{Average time} = \frac{\text{best time} + 4(\text{most likely time}) + \text{worst time}}{6}$$

c. Use the average times from part b and the PERT software to compute the EFT for the whole project and the critical tasks.

d. How do the EFT and critical tasks compare with your answers to activity 2?

Checkpoint

ⓐ What are some possible methods for planning a project when the exact times for finishing certain tasks are not known?

ⓑ Which method do you think is the best? Why?

✓ *Be prepared to share your thinking with the entire class.*

On Your Own

Suppose all the worst task times doubled in the new car feasibility study project.

a. Find the EFT and critical tasks, using the average task time method used in activity 4.

b. Draw the project digraph and highlight the critical tasks.

Modeling Organizing Reflecting Extending

Modeling

1. Refer back to task 2 of the Modeling section on page 302. In that task, you constructed an immediate prerequisite table and drew a project digraph for the Earth Day project. Now schedule that project. Include EFT, EST, LST, and slack time for each task.

2. On a large construction project, there usually is a general contractor (the company that coordinates and supervises the whole project) and smaller contractors (the companies that carry out specific parts of the project, like plumbing or framing).

   Suppose that on a housing project, the company responsible for putting in the foundation for the next building estimates the times shown in the following prerequisite table. The general contractor wants the foundation done in 13 days. Can the foundation crew meet this schedule? If so, explain. If not, propose a plan for what they should do in order to shorten task times and finish on schedule.

Task	Task Time	Immediate Prerequisites
Measure the Foundation (*A*)	1 day	none
Dig Foundation (*B*)	4 days	*A*
Erect Forms (*C*)	6 days	*B*
Obtain Reinforcing Steel (*D*)	2 days	*A*
Assemble Steel (*E*)	3 days	*D*
Place Steel in Forms (*F*)	2 days	*C, E*
Order Concrete (*G*)	1 days	*A*
Pour Concrete (*H*)	3 days	*F, G*

3. A task-times-prerequisite table for putting on a school play is shown at the top of the following page.

Task	Best Task Time (days)	Most Likely Task Time (days)	Worst Task Time (days)	Immediate Prerequisites
Choose a Play (*A*)	7	9	14	none
Tryouts (*B*)	5	8	12	*A*
Select Cast (*C*)	3	5	10	*B*
Rehearsals (*D*)	25	35	40	*C*
Build Sets and Props (*E*)	20	22	25	*A*
Create Advertising (*F*)	4	5	6	*C*
Sell Tickets (*G*)	10	12	15	*F*
Make/Get Costumes (*H*)	20	25	30	*C*
Lighting (*I*)	7	10	14	*E, H*
Sound and Music (*J*)	9	10	12	*E*
Dress Rehearsals (*K*)	5	6	9	*D, I, J*
Opening Night (*L*)	1	1	1	*G, K*

a. You must report to the principal how long it will take before the play is ready to open. Based on EFTs, what will you report? Explain your method and reasoning. (Remember that you may use critical path software, if it is helpful.)

For parts b through d, consider only the best task times.

b. Suppose that because of a conflict with another special event, you find out that you must complete the project in 6 days less than the "best task time" EFT. In order to meet this new timetable, you recruit some more helpers and put them to work. This will allow you to cut the time on some of the tasks. For which task or tasks should you cut time in order to meet the new deadline? Show which tasks you will shorten and how this will result in a new EFT that is 6 days shorter than the "best task time" EFT. (Shortening task times like this is sometimes called **crashing** the task times.)

c. Another way to attempt to shorten the EFT is to figure out a way to change some of the prerequisites. Suppose you decide to change the prerequisites for setting up the lighting by doing that task whether or not the set and props are built. Thus, "*E*" is no longer an immediate prerequisite for "*I*". How much time will this save for the "best task time" EFT?

d. Describe at least one other reasonable rearrangement of prerequisites. By how many days does your rearrangement increase or decrease the "best task time" EFT?

4. The music department of City High School is doing a production of *A Christmas Carol*. One scene has many villagers singing carols. The costume committee needs to schedule sewing dresses for this scene. From previous productions, times for various tasks in making a dress have been recorded. The times are listed below.

Task	Best Task Time (minutes)	Worst Task Time (minutes)	Immediate Prerequisites
Interface Collar (*A*)	5	10	none
Put Gathers in the Sleeves (*B*)	30	45	none
Interface the Cuffs (*C*)	5	10	none
Put Gathers in the Skirt (*D*)	30	45	none
Sew the Bodice (*E*)	30	60	none
Sew the Collar (*F*)	15	30	*A*
Attach the Cuffs to the Sleeves (*G*)	15	30	*B, C*
Sew Buttonhole and Attach the Buttons (*H*)	30	60	*G*
Attach the Skirt and Bodice (*I*)	30	45	*D, E*
Insert the Zipper (*J*)	30	60	*I*
Attach the Sleeves to the Dress (*K*)	30	60	*H, J*
Attach the Collar to the Dress (*L*)	30	60	*F, K*
Hem the Dress (*M*)	30	60	*J*

a. Using the best task time, find the EFT and critical tasks for this project.

b. Using the worst task time, find the EFT and critical tasks for this project.

c. In the investigation, you used "average" task times to compute an EFT for the project. Use a similar idea here to find a better estimate for this project's EFT.

5. Recall the school dance poster project that you investigated at the beginning of this lesson. The immediate prerequisite table and project digraph for that project are reproduced below.

Task	Task Time	Immediate Prerequisites
Choose & Reserve Location (*L*)	2 days	none
Choose a Theme (*T*)	3 days	none
Book the Band or D.J. (*B*)	7 days	*L, T*
Arrange for Decorations (*DC*)	5 days	*T*
Design the Poster (*D*)	5 days	*B, DC*
Post the Poster (*P*)	2 days	*D*

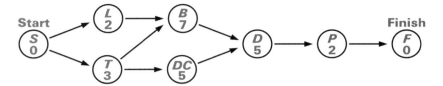

Schedule this project by finding the EFT, EST, LST, slack time, and scheduled time to begin for each task. (Note: If you use the AAPERT software you will first need to relabel the tasks alphabetically.)

Organizing

1. The adjacency matrix for a graph can be used to enter the graph into a computer. You also can get information about the graph and the project just by looking at the adjacency matrix.

   a. Write the adjacency matrix for this digraph, ignoring S and F.

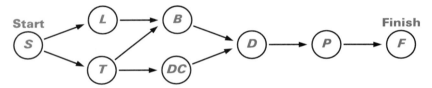

   - Add up all the numbers in row B. What does this sum mean in terms of B as an immediate prerequisite?
   - Add up all the numbers in column B. What does this sum mean in terms of how many immediate prerequisites B has?
   - What does a row of all zeroes mean in terms of prerequisites?
   - What does a column of all zeroes mean in terms of prerequisites?

   b. The **indegree** of a vertex is the number of arrows coming into it. The **outdegree** is the number of arrows going out of it.
   - What are the indegree and outdegree of B?
   - What is the outdegree of T?
   - Ignoring S and F, what is the indegree of T? The outdegree of P?
   - What do indegree and outdegree mean in terms of prerequisites?
   - How can you compute indegree and outdegree by looking at the rows and columns of the adjacency matrix for a digraph?

2. Describe one of the methods you suggested for determining the critical tasks and EFT for the feasibility study project. (See activity 1 of Investigation 3.4 on page 312.) Then, use that method to actually find the critical tasks and EFT.

3. Write an algorithm for finding the LST for a task.

Reflecting

1. Interview some adults in business who use ideas from PERT to schedule projects, or do some library or Internet research. Find out how EFTs and critical paths are used. Write a brief report on what you discover.

2. Consider the project digraph for some project.

    a. If a task has many immediate prerequisites, will it have many arrows coming into it or many going out?

    b. If a task is an immediate prerequisite to many other tasks, will it have many arrows coming into it or many going out?

3. Suppose you are using critical path software like AAPERT for scheduling a project. What additional advantages would you gain if you use a digraph as well?

4. In this chapter, you have seen how vertex-edge graphs can be used to represent and analyze relationships in many different contexts. Some examples are prerequisite relationships among tasks in a large project, conflicts between club meetings or radio stations, or connections between locations in a street network. You even can use graphs to represent and analyze relationships among the new concepts that you are learning in this course. This is done using a type of graph called a **concept map**. In a concept map, the vertices represent ideas or concepts and edges join concepts which are connected. The start of a concept map for this chapter is shown here.

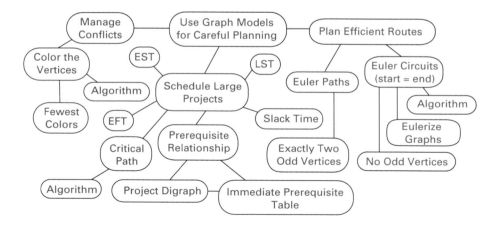

a. Explain why there is an edge between the vertices "Color the Vertices" and "Manage Conflicts."

b. Explain why there are edges connecting the vertices "Prerequisite Relationship," "Immediate Prerequisite Table," and "Project Digraph."

c. Obtain a copy of this concept map. Add other concepts and draw other edges that show concepts which are related.

d. Study the completed concept map. Should any of the edges be directed? Explain your reasoning.

Extending

1. Another interesting number for a project task is the latest finish time (LFT) for the task.

   a. Find the LFT for each task in this project digraph:

   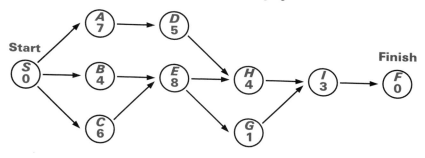

   b. In terms of managing a project, why do you think it would be useful to know the LFT?

2. Write a software program that will find and report:
   a. EFT
   b. EST
   c. LST
   d. slack time

3. In an immediate prerequisite table, the task times given are the times needed to complete each task using the available resources. For example, the table on the following page shows the task times for preparing the school softball field for a game. Several people are available to work on the project. However, each task time assumes that only one person is working on that particular task.

Task	Task Time	Immediate Prerequisites
Pick up Litter (*L*)	4 hours	none
Clean Dugouts (*D*)	2 hours	*L*
Drag the Infield (*I*)	2 hours	*L*
Mow the Grass (*G*)	3 hours	*L*
Paint the Foul Lines (*P*)	2 hours	*I, G*
Install the Bases (*B*)	1 hour	*P*

a. What is the EFT for preparing the softball field?

b. In order to finish by this EFT, what is the fewest number of people needed to work on the project? Explain.

c. Suppose you have to complete the project by yourself. That is, you must do every task. How long will it take you to complete the project?

d. Suppose that you and two friends are hired to prepare the field. You and your friends decide that you might work together or separately to complete any task. If you work together on a task, then you can finish that task in less time than is shown in the prerequisite table above. The only task that must be done by someone working alone is mowing the grass, since there is only one mower. How would you assign duties in order to complete the project in the least amount of time?

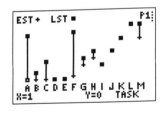

4. Refer to the immediate prerequisite table for making a dress on page 316. Using the AAPERT software you used in Investigation 3.4, enter the *best task times* into your calculator. Choose the menu item ST GRAPH under SCHEDULE. A graph similar to the one at the left should be displayed. ESTs are indicated by a "+" and LSTs by a "■". Use the trace key to explore the graph.

a. What do the down arrows represent?

b. Tasks *A* and *F* have the largest slack times. What are the slack times for *A* and *F*? Does this mean that each of tasks *A* and *F* can be delayed by an amount of time equal to their slack times? Explain your reasoning.

5. So far in this lesson you have scheduled a project by finding the EFT, EST, LST, slack time, and scheduled time to begin. For a specific project you would go even further and assign days to each task. Reconsider the school dance poster project. Assume that the first day of work on this project will be Tuesday, March 15. Make a timeline chart showing which days will be allocated for each of the tasks. Such a timeline chart is called a **Gantt chart**. (Optional: Construct a Gantt chart for the school dance poster project using scheduling software such as *Microsoft Project*.)

4 *Looking Back*

In this chapter you have used graph models to solve problems related to careful planning. The problems you have explored include finding efficient routes, managing conflicts, and scheduling projects and events. The models you have used include Euler circuits and paths, graph coloring, and critical paths. In this final lesson of the chapter you will put it all together to solve problems that might involve any of the graph models.

For each of the problems below, decide which graph model will be the most useful representation. Use that model to solve the problem. Be prepared to explain your solution.

1. One city's Department of Sanitation organizes garbage collection by setting up precise garbage truck routes. Each route takes one day. Some sites that need garbage collection more often are on more than one route. However, if a site is on more than one route, the routes should not visit that site on the same day. Here is a list of routes and the sites that are on more than one route.

   Route 1: Site A, Site C
   Route 2: Site D, Site A, Site F
   Route 3: Site C, Site D, Site G
   Route 4: Site G
   Route 5: Site B, Site F
   Route 6: Site D
   Route 7: Site C, Site F

   a. Can all seven routes be scheduled in one week (Monday–Friday)?

   b. Set up a schedule for the garbage truck routes, showing which routes run on which day of the week.

2. Suppose that you are the editor for a school newspaper. Study the following background information about the publishing process.

   It takes 10 days for the reporters to research all the news stories. It takes 12 days for other students, working at the same time as the reporters, to arrange for the advertising. The photographers need 8 days to get all the photos. However, they can't start working until the research and the advertising arrangements are complete. The reporters need 15 days to write the stories after they have done the research. They can write while the photographers are getting photos. It takes 5 days to edit everything after the stories and the photos are done. Then it takes another 4 days to lay out the newspaper and 2 more days to get it back from the printer.

Write a report to your teacher-advisor explaining how long it will take to turn out the next edition of the paper. State which steps of the publishing process will need to be monitored most closely. Include diagrams and complete explanations in your report.

3. The security guard for an office building must check the building several times throughout the night. The figures below are the floor plans for office complexes on two floors of the building. An outer corridor surrounds each office complex. In order to check the electronic security system completely, the guard must pass through each door at least once.

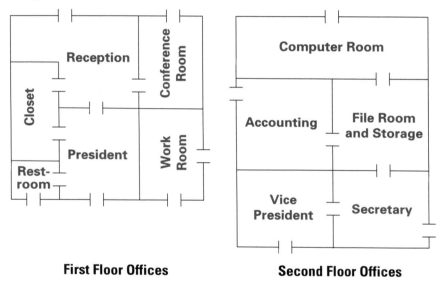

First Floor Offices   **Second Floor Offices**

a. For each office complex, can the guard walk through each door exactly once, starting and ending in the outer corridor? If so, show a route the guard could take. If not, explain why not.

b. If it is not possible to walk through each door exactly once starting and ending in the outer corridor, what is the fewest number of doors that need to be passed through more than once? Show a route the guard could take. Indicate the doors that are passed through more than once.

4. Traffic lights are essential for controlling the flow of traffic on city streets, but nobody wants to wait at a light any longer than necessary. Consider the intersection diagrammed below. The arrows show the streams of traffic. There is a set of traffic lights in the center of the intersection.

 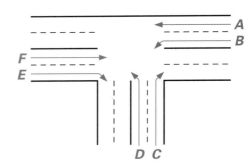

a. Can traffic streams *B* and *D* have a green light at the same time? How about *B* and *C*? List all the traffic streams that conflict with *B*.

b. Streams of traffic that have a green light at the same time are said to be on the same green-light cycle. What is the fewest number of green-light cycles necessary to safely accommodate all six streams of traffic?

c. For each of the green-light cycles you found in part b, list the streams of traffic that can be on that cycle.

Checkpoint

a For each of the problems in this lesson:

- Which graph model did you use?

- What did the vertices and edges represent?

- Explain why you chose the graph model you used.

b For each of the graph models you have studied—Euler circuits and paths, graph coloring, and critical paths—describe the types of problems that can be solved using the model.

✓ *Be prepared to share your descriptions and explanations with the entire class.*

Chapter **5**

Patterns in Space
and Visualization

1 *The Shape of Things*

The world, the space in which you live, is three-dimensional. Buildings, plants, animals, toys, tools, even molecules are three-dimensional; they are **space-shapes**. Space-shapes develop in nature and are built, observed, and used in all countries and cultures. They can be beautiful, unusual, large, or small. If a space-shape is to serve a purpose, it may need to have special characteristics. For example, it may need to bounce or resist strong wind forces. It also may need to support great weight, use space efficiently, or be hollow or filled.

Think about this situation

Look at the photo of Biosphere 2 shown here and at objects around your classroom. Identify two or three space-shapes.

a List some characteristics of the space-shapes you see.

b How are two-dimensional shapes (*plane-shapes*) used to make these space-shapes?

c Choose one of the space-shapes in your classroom.

– Draw a sketch of it.

– Explain how you might use numbers to describe its size.

Investigation 1.1 Designing and Testing Columns

Space-shapes come in all shapes and sizes and have many uses. For example, many ancient cultures used filled or solid space-shapes to make columns in their buildings. The Greek Parthenon shown here is made of marble. Thus, the columns had to be designed to support great weights.

The columns the Greeks used were solid marble. You can model the Greek columns with *shells* rather than solids. That is, your columns will be hollow like tin cans (with no top or bottom) rather than filled like hockey pucks. In this investigation, you will seek an answer to the question:

"What type of column supports the most weight?"

1. As a group, brainstorm about a possible answer to this question. What column characteristics do you think support your choice?

2. Now, work in pairs to complete the experiment described below.

   a. Select four sheets of 8.5×11 inch paper such as typing paper, copy machine paper, or computer printer paper.

   b. Make four columns, each 8.5 inches high. The bases of the columns should have the following shapes:
   - triangular with all equal sides
   - square
   - eight-sided with all equal sides
   - circular

   For consistency, leave a half-inch overlap and tape the columns closed. Be sure to tape near each end.

   8.5"

   c. Set up the following weight-supporting situation to collect data.
   - Choose a level surface.
   - Place a small rectangle of cardboard (about 6×8 inches) on top of a column.
   - Choose a sequence of objects to be placed on the cardboard platform. (*Note:* Be sure to use the same sequence for each test.)
   - Carefully add objects until the column crumbles. Measure and record the maximum weight supported.
   - Organize and display your data in a table.

3. a. Make a graph of your data with *number of sides* on the horizontal axis and *maximum weight supported* on the vertical axis.

   b. Where along the horizontal axis did you put "circular column"? Why?

   c. What appears to happen to the maximum weight supported as the number of sides of the column increases?

   d. Use your table or graph to estimate the weight-supporting capacity of a 6-sided column. To check your estimate, make a 6-sided column and find the maximum weight it supports.

Checkpoint

ⓐ Why do you think the ancient Greeks chose to use cylindrical columns?

ⓑ What are some other questions about column design that seem important and which you could answer by experimentation?

✓ *Be prepared to share your group's questions and thinking with the class.*

On Your Own

Latoya investigated what happened to the amount of weight supported when she increased the number of columns underneath the cardboard platform. She kept the shape and area of the base the same for all columns in each experiment. Her data for the three experiments are summarized in the table below.

Triangular Columns		Square Columns		Circular Columns	
Number of Columns	Weight (kg) Supported	Number of Columns	Weight (kg) Supported	Number of Columns	Weight (kg) Supported
1	1.7	1	2.1	1	3.3
2	3.5	2	4.1	2	6.4
3	5.1	3	6.4	3	10.0
4	7.0	4	8.5	4	13.2
5	8.3	5	10.4	5	16.6

a. Make a scatterplot of Latoya's data. Use a different symbol for the data from each of the three experiments.

b. What do you think is true about the relationship between *number of columns* and *weight supported*?

c. How are the patterns of change in *weight supported* as the *number of columns* increases similar for the different types of columns? How are they different?

d. For each type of column, estimate the number of columns needed to support a weight of 20 kg. Explain your method.

Investigation **1.2**

Recognizing and Constructing Space-Shapes

The columns studied in Investigation 1.1 are examples of space-shapes. Most everyday space-shapes are designed with special characteristics in mind. As a class, examine the space-shapes depicted below.

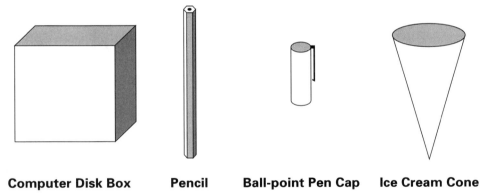

Computer Disk Box   **Pencil**   **Ball-point Pen Cap**   **Ice Cream Cone**

1. a. Which shapes above have common characteristics? What are those characteristics?

   b. In what ways might the word "parallel" be used to describe characteristics of some of the space-shapes?

2. On the following page are pictures of structures built through the centuries by various cultures. Describe the different space-shapes you see in these photographs. Name those that you can. Are some forms of space-shapes more common in some cultures than in others?

a.

Igloo in the Arctic

b.

Pyramid at Chichen Itza, Mexico

c.

Native American Teepees

d.

Stave church, Norway

e.

Himeji Castle, Japan

f.

Taj Mahal, India

3. Two important classifications of space-shapes are **prisms** and **pyramids**. In your group, study the examples and non-examples below.

Examples	Non-examples

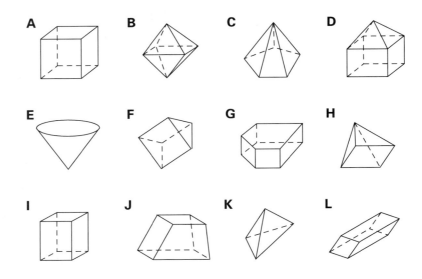

a. Which of the space-shapes below are prisms? Explain your reasoning.

b. Which of the space-shapes below are pyramids? Explain your reasoning.

c. Explain why the remaining space-shapes are neither pyramids nor prisms.

4. a. What are the characteristics of a space-shape that make it a pyramid?

   b. What are the characteristics of a space-shape that make it a prism?

5. **Cones** and **cylinders** are two other common space-shapes. How are they similar to pyramids and prisms? How are they different?

6. **a.** Develop a method for naming types of prisms and types of pyramids. Could you use the shape of the base in your naming procedure? Try it.

   b. Use your method to name a cube as a type of prism.

   c. Cardboard boxes are usually prisms. What would you name such a prism?

Checkpoint

> **ⓐ** Sketch a prism in which the bases are five-sided. Name the prism.
>
> **ⓑ** What space-shape best describes a Native American teepee?
>
> ✓ *Be prepared to share your sketch and descriptions with the class.*

On Your Own

An "A-Frame" is a style of architecture sometimes used in building houses. What space-shape is basic to the "A-Frame" construction?

Space-shapes can be modeled in three different ways. One way is as a *solid object* such as a brick, a cake, or a die. Another is as a *shell* such as a paper bag, a house, or a water pipe. The third way is as a *skeleton*, which includes only the edges like a jungle gym. The solid model can be made of material such as clay, wood, or styrofoam. The shell model can be made of paper or cardboard and tape, for example. The skeleton model can be made with things like toothpicks and clay or straws and pipe cleaners.

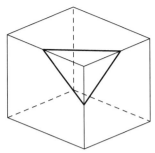

7. Use a piece of modeling clay or Play-Doh to make a cube.

    a. How many flat surfaces or *faces* does it have?

    b. Imagine slicing a corner off. Now how many faces are there? What would you see as the shape of the new face on the cube? This is a **plane slice** since the new face is flat. Slice your cube to check your prediction.

    c. Imagine slicing your cube through a line joining two opposite corners of a face. Make a plane slice all the way through to the corresponding line on the opposite face. What is the shape of the new face formed? Check by slicing your cube. What do you notice about the two pieces of the cube?

    d. Think of two other ways of slicing your cube (remade of course). Predict and sketch the shape of the new face. Do the slicing to check your predictions.

8. Get a collection of straws and pipe cleaners from your teacher. Cut the pipe cleaners into 5 or 6 centimeter pieces and bend them in half. These pieces will be used to connect two straw edges at a vertex, as shown here. Carefully cut the straws into the lengths shown in part a. Your group will need about 75 of the 10 cm straws, 27 of the 12 cm straws, and 6 of the 16 cm straws.

    a. Make the following models from straws and pipe cleaners. Divide the work among the group members. Each student should build at least one prism and one pyramid.

        – Cube: 10 cm edges

        – Triangular prism: 10 cm edges on bases, 12 cm height

        – Square prism: 10 cm edges on bases, 12 cm height

        – Pentagonal prism: 10 cm edges on bases, 12 cm height

        – Hexagonal prism: 10 cm edges on bases, 12 cm height

        – Triangular pyramid: 10 cm edges on bases, other edges 10 cm

        – Square pyramid: 10 cm edges on bases, other edges 12 cm

        – Pentagonal pyramid: 10 cm edges on bases, other edges 12 cm

        – Hexagonal pyramid: 10 cm edges on bases, other edges 16 cm

b. Imagine slicing your triangular prism with a single plane slice. What is the shape of the new face produced by a single plane slice? Check by slicing a clay model if you have any doubts.

c. Think about the shapes of faces that are created when the triangular prism is sliced. Identify as many *different* shapes of these faces as you can. Sketch the shape of each new face. Check each with clay models if it is helpful.

d. Now imagine slicing each of the other prisms with planes. What new face shapes do you get with a single plane slice? Sketch each, and check with clay models if group members are not all in agreement.

e. Do any of your plane slices produce two identical space-shapes for halves? If so, describe the slice location(s).

Some planes may slice a space-shape into two identical mirror-image halves. When this is possible, the space-shape is said to have **reflection symmetry**. The plane is called a **symmetry plane** for the space-shape. For example, when you want to share a piece of cake fairly, you cut it into two identical mirror-image halves.

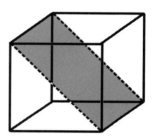

9. Which of the space-shapes constructed in activity 8 have reflection symmetry? Find and describe all the symmetry planes for each shape. Compare your results with those of other groups.

Checkpoint

ⓐ Imagine a prism and a plane. Describe several ways the plane could slice the prism without intersecting either base.

ⓑ Think about how the symmetry planes for prisms and pyramids are related to the bases. Explain how the symmetry planes differ for the two kinds of space-shapes.

✓ *Be prepared to share your ideas with the entire class.*

On Your Own

Imagine or construct a rectangular prism. Determine the number of symmetry planes for the shape. Describe their locations.

Modeling Organizing Reflecting Extending

Modeling

1. What do you think is true about the relationship between the height of a square column and the weight it can support?

    a. With a partner, investigate the weight-bearing capability of square columns of different heights. Vary the column heights, but keep the shape and area of the base the same.

    b. Organize your data in a table and display it in a graph.

    c. What appears to be true about the relationship between the height of a column and the weight it can support?

2. Make a conjecture about the relationship between the circumference of a circular column and the weight it can support.

    a. With a partner, conduct an experiment to test your conjecture about the weight-bearing capability of circular columns from this new perspective. Use columns of the same height, but with different circumferences.

    b. Organize your data in a table and display it in a graph.

    c. What appears to be true about the relationship between the circumference of a column and the weight it can support? Why do you think this happens?

3. Space-shapes form the basis of atomic structures as well as of common structures for work, living, and play. Often a single space-shape is not used, but rather a combination.

    a. Study this photograph of a tower in Europe. What space-shapes appear to be used in this tower?

    b. Scientists use space-shapes to model molecules of compounds. Shown at the left is a model of a methane molecule. Describe the space-shape whose skeleton would be formed by joining the four hydrogen atoms that are equally-spaced around the central carbon atom. Describe all possible planes of symmetry.

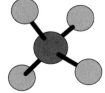

c. The square pyramids at Giza are pictured here. Describe them so that some-one who had never seen one could visualize it in his or her mind. Describe all possible planes of symmetry of one of the pyramids.

4. a. Examine a die (one of several dice). How are the dots (called *pips*) on opposite faces related?

b. Use cubes made of wood or clay to help you determine how many different ways the pips can be put on the faces so that opposite faces add to seven.

c. Place your models on your desk so that the face with one pip is on the top and the face with two pips is toward you. How are the models related to each other?

Organizing

1. Refer to the model of a cube in activity 7 of Investigation 1.2.

a. How many faces, edges, and vertices does it have?

b. Slice a corner off (as shown), making a small triangular face. Repeat at each corner so that the slices do not overlap. Make a table showing the number of faces, edges, and vertices of the modified cube after each "corner slice."

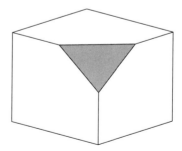

c. Using *NOW* and *NEXT*, write a rule describing the pattern of change in the number of faces after a slice. Write similar *NOW-NEXT* rules for the number of edges and for the number of vertices after each slice.

d. How many faces, edges, and vertices does the new solid have when all the corners are sliced off?

2. A mirror acts like a symmetry plane for you and your "mirror" image.

   a. If you walk toward a mirror, what appears to happen to your image?

   b. If your nose is one meter from a mirror, how far does your "image" nose appear to be from the mirror?

   c. Imagine tying your index finger to its mirror image with a taut rubberband. How would the rubberband (a segment) be related to the mirror (a plane)? Would this relationship change as you moved your finger? Why or why not?

3. The figure here shows a space-shape and one of its symmetry planes. Points A and B are on the space-shape and are symmetrically placed with respect to the plane.

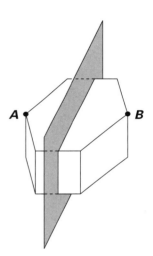

   a. If you connected A and B with a segment, would it intersect the symmetry plane?

   b. How is segment AB related to the symmetry plane?

   c. Compare the distances from A and from B to the symmetry plane.

   d. How can the word "perpendicular" be used in discussing a symmetry plane and any two symmetrically placed points such as A and B?

4. The first three elements of a sequence of staircases made from cubes glued together are shown here.

 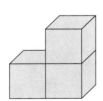 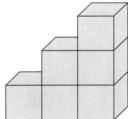

   a. Sketch the 4th and 5th staircases.

   b. If the 4th staircase has 10 blocks, how can you determine the number of blocks in the 5th staircase without counting?

   c. If the staircase in the nth position has B blocks in it, how many blocks are in the next staircase?

   d. Describe any symmetry planes for the staircases.

e. Imagine taking a staircase and fitting a copy of it on top to form a rectangular prism.

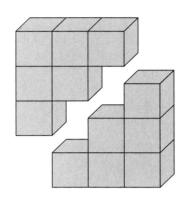

In this way, form rectangular prisms from the first, second, fourth, and fifth staircases. Answer the following questions.

- How many blocks are in each prism?

- How are the number of blocks in each prism related to the number of blocks in the original staircase?

- How can you use the number of blocks on the bottom row of a staircase to predict the number of blocks in the prism?

- How can you use the number of blocks on the bottom row of a staircase to predict the total number of blocks in the staircase?

f. Write a formula for predicting the number of blocks in a staircase with n blocks on the bottom row.

- Use your formula to predict the total number of blocks in a staircase with 10 blocks on the bottom row.

- Use your result in part c to help check your answer.

- How many blocks are on the bottom row of a staircase made up of 276 blocks?

g. What happens when you fit a staircase to the one immediately following it in the sequence of staircases?

Reflecting

1. Pyramids were built by the Egyptians as tombs for their rulers. What other cultures built structures shaped as pyramids? What purposes did they serve?

2. a. Every prism has at least one symmetry plane that can be described using the idea of *parallel*. Draw a prism, then sketch in a symmetry plane whose description could involve the idea of parallel.

b. The symmetry plane you drew for part a could also be described using the idea of *perpendicular*. To what is the symmetry plane perpendicular?

3. Cedar posts are circular columns often used for building fences.

   a. How could you pack cedar posts for shipment? Sketch your arrangement (the end view).

   b. Are other post-packing arrangements possible? Illustrate those you find with sketches.

   c. In your experience, what consumer goods have you seen packaged in the manner of part a? In the manner of part b?

4. Reflection symmetry (sometimes called *bilateral symmetry*) is often found in nature. What examples of bilateral symmetry in nature have you learned about in your science classes?

Extending

1. A cube is a square prism with all faces and bases congruent. For each figure below, describe how a plane and a cube could intersect so that the intersection is the figure given. If the figure is not possible, explain your reasoning.

   a. a point   **b.** a segment

   c. a triangle   **d.** an equilateral triangle

   e. a square   **f.** a rectangle

   g. a five-sided shape   **h.** a six-sided shape

2. Recall your column-building experiment in Investigation 1.1. Can you improve the weight-bearing capability of the poorest-performing column to equal the capability of the best-performing column? Choose one of the two methods below. Describe a procedure you could use to see if the method will improve the column performance. Conduct the experiment and write a summary of your findings.

   a. Increase the thickness of the walls of a column.

   b. Increase the number of columns used to support weight.

3. The prisms you examined in Investigation 1.2 are right prisms because the edges connecting the bases are perpendicular to the edges of the bases. Use your skeleton models to help you visualize prisms where these edges are *not perpendicular* to the edges of the bases. These prisms are called **oblique**.

   a. What shape are the faces of an oblique prism?

   b. Look up the definition of a prism in the dictionary. Is a particular kind of prism defined? If so, what kind?

   c. Do oblique prisms have symmetry planes?

   d. Given an oblique prism with five or fewer faces, imagine its intersection with a plane. What is the shape of the intersection? Find as many such shapes as you can. Name each of them.

4. Suppose each face of a cube is painted one of six different colors. How many cubes with different coloring patterns are possible?

5. Make six cubes with different coloring patterns, as described in Extending task 4. Is it possible to join them together in a row so that all faces along the row are the same color, the colors of the touching faces match, and the colors of the two end faces match? If so, display your solution.

Investigation (1.3) Visualizing and Sketching Space-Shapes

Models of space-shapes are valuable for several reasons. For an architect, a scale model of a building gives the client a visual impression of the finished product. When the characteristics of a space-shape need to be understood, models allow those characteristics to be more easily visualized and verified.

However, it is not always practical to construct models of space-shapes. For example, you cannot fax a scale model of an off-shore oil rig to a Saudi engineer. Rather, the space-shape needs to be represented in two dimensions and still convey the important information about the shape. In this investigation, you will explore various ways of drawing and sketching space-shapes.

Model of Biosphere 2

One way to depict space-shapes is to sketch the shape from various views. A method commonly used by architects is to draw **face-views**. For the house at the right, a *top view*, a *front view*, and a *right-side view* are shown below. Together these views display the width, depth, and height of the building. (You'll notice the top view is different from the other two. Frequently, floor plans such as this are used instead of an exterior top view.)

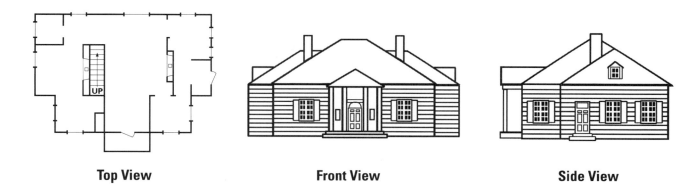

| Top View | Front View | Side View |

1. Below are three face-views of a simple model of a hotel made from cubes.

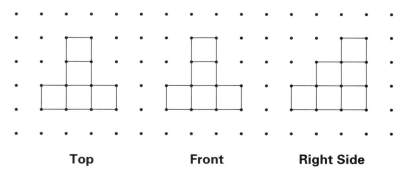

Top   Front   Right Side

a. How many cubes are in the model?

b. Use blocks or sugar cubes to make a model of this hotel. Build your model on a sheet of paper or poster board that can be rotated.

c. Could you make the model using information from only two of these views? Explain your reasoning.

2. Shown here is a corner view of a model hotel drawn on *isometric* dot paper.

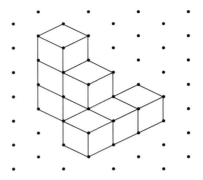

  a. Try to rotate your model from activity 1 so that it appears as in this *isometric drawing*.

  b. Describe as completely as possible the vantage point from which the model is being viewed in this drawing.

  c. On your own, use isometric dot paper to draw a *top-front-right corner view* of your model. Compare your drawing with those of others in your group.

  d. Use dot paper to draw an isometric view of a model hotel that has top, front, and right-side views as shown below.

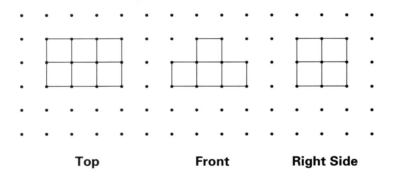

  Top   **Front**   **Right Side**

  e. Compare your drawing with those of other group members.

  – Does each drawing accurately depict the hotel? If not, work together to modify any inaccurate drawings.

  – Describe as well as you can the vantage point from which the hotel is viewed in each drawing.

  f. Draw top, front, and right-side views for the model hotel at the right.

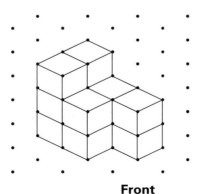

Front

3. Shown below are similar ways to depict a space-shape such as a box of computer disks without the aid of dot paper.

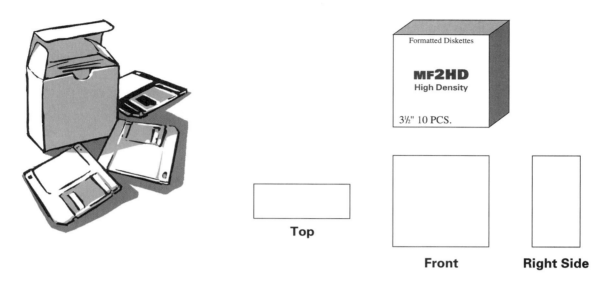

Formatted Diskettes

MF2HD
High Density

3½" 10 PCS.

Top

Front　　**Right Side**

a. What space-shape is a box of computer disks?

b. How are the shapes shown in the three face-views related to the actual faces of the box?

c. Examine the sketch showing the box from the top-front-right corner view.
   – What appear to be the shapes of the three faces as shown in the sketch? What are the true shapes of the three faces on the box itself?
   – In this type of sketch, how do you know how long to draw each edge?
   – What edges are parallel in the real object? Should they be drawn parallel? Explain your reasoning.

d. Draw top, front, and right-side views of the straw prisms you constructed for activity 8 on page 333.

e. Now sketch each of your prism models from a top-front-right corner view.

f. Each member of your group should select a different prism. Sketch your prism from a top-front-left corner view. Check the other sketches and suggest modifications as necessary.

g. Compare representations of space-shapes by sketching face-views and by making isometric drawings. What are the advantages and drawbacks of each method?

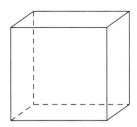

4. When sketching a space-shape, sometimes edges of the shape are *hidden* by your viewing angle. In these situations, it is helpful to imagine that the space-shape is transparent and to represent the hidden edges with *dotted lines*. For example, the box of disks in activity 3 would appear like this from a top-front-right corner view.

   a. Which faces in the drawing have true shape? That is, which faces have the same shape as their shape on the box itself?

   b. In this type of sketch, how do you know how long to make the dotted edges?

   c. Modify the sketches you made in parts e and f of activity 3 to show the hidden edges.

5. For this activity, refer to your pyramid models made in activity 8, page 333.

   a. Sketch each of these pyramid models from a view in front and above the base. Show all hidden edges.

   b. How does drawing hidden edges help you visualize the entire space-shape?

Checkpoint

> **ⓐ** Make a model of a space-shape that is two square pyramids sharing a common base. Sketch the two-piece shape using the method you think is best.
>
> **ⓑ** Explain your reasons for using the sketching method you did.
>
> ✓ *Be prepared to share your sketch and discuss reasons for your choice of sketching method.*

On Your Own

Sketch the space-shape formed when a pentagonal pyramid is placed on top of a pentagonal prism. Describe a possible real-world application of a shape with this design.

Investigation  1.4   Rigidity of Space-Shapes

Buildings, bridges, and other outdoor structures must withstand great forces from the environment. While there are many types of space-shapes, only certain kinds of shapes are used to make structures which do not collapse under pressure.

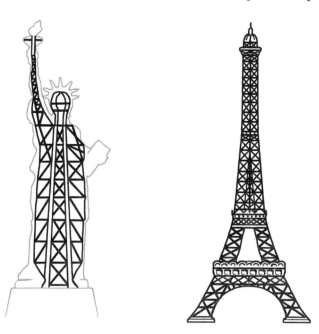

1. As a class, examine the frameworks used to design the Statue of Liberty and the Eiffel Tower, as shown.

   a. What simple plane shape is fundamental to these frames?

   b. Why do you think Gustave Eiffel used this shape as the basis for his design of both structures?

2. **a.** Working in groups, examine your models from activity 8 of Investigation 1.2 (page 333). Which of these are **rigid**? That is, which of the space-shapes will not change form when a force is applied to any part of it? Consider cases where a base of the shape rests on a plane surface and where the shape does not rest on a surface.

   b. Do the rigid space-shapes have anything in common? Explain.

3. a. Add reinforcing straws to your model of a triangular prism to make it rigid. How many reinforcements did you use? Describe where you placed them and why you placed them there.

   b. Could you have placed the reinforcements in different positions and still made the triangular prism rigid? Explain and illustrate.

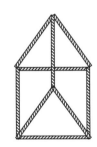

4. a. Add reinforcements to your model of a cube so that it becomes a rigid structure. Note the number of reinforcing straws which you used and describe the position of each straw.

   b. Find a different way to reinforce the cube so that it becomes a rigid structure. Describe the pattern of reinforcement straws.

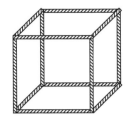

   c. Of the methods you used to reinforce the cube, which could be used to make a rectangular building stand rigidly?

5. a. For a pentagonal prism, predict the minimum number of reinforcing straws needed to make it rigid.

   b. Make the prism rigid and compare the number of reinforcing straws needed with your prediction. Can you find a way to make the prism rigid with fewer reinforcements?

Checkpoint

> **ⓐ** What is the simplest rigid space-shape?
>
> **ⓑ** What reinforcement patterns are used to make a space-shape rigid?
>
> ✓ *Be prepared to share your group's findings with the class.*

On Your Own

How many reinforcing straws would be needed to make a hexagonal prism rigid? Where would you place the reinforcements? Draw a sketch of the prism with reinforcements.

Modeling **O**rganizing **R**eflecting **E**xtending

Modeling

1. Designers of structures like motels can test their designs by using identical cubes to represent the rooms. They can use the cubes to try various arrangements of rooms. Suppose you have a three-room motel and that cubes must join face-to-face. A sample model is shown at the right.

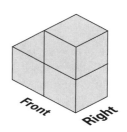

   a. How many different three-room motels can you construct?

   b. Make top, front, and right-side view sketches of each possible motel.

   c. Make isometric drawings of the same motels. What vantage point did you use for the drawings?

   d. Which motel would be the least costly to construct? Why?

2. Increase the number of rooms in your motel from three to four.

   a. Find all the four-room motels you can build if they must connect face-to-face. How many did you find?

   b. Make face-view sketches or isometric drawings of each motel.

   c. How many of your motels form an L-shape?

   d. Land in and around cities is very expensive. Which of your motels would require that the least amount of land be purchased? The greatest amount? Explain your reasoning.

3. Study this sketch of a cube motel.

   a. How many cubes are there in the model?

   b. Draw the top, front, and right-side views of this shape.

   c. Suppose this model is half of a twin towers structure. The towers are symmetrically built about the plane of the right side. Make an isometric drawing of the complete structure.

   d. Provide top, front, and right-side view sketches of the completed building.

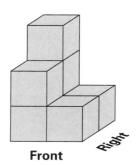

Front

4. Below are three views of a cube model of a hotel.

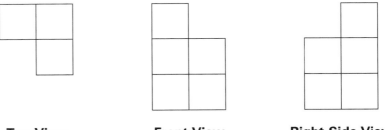

Top View   **Front View**   **Right-Side View**

    a. Construct cube models which match these views.

    b. Can you construct more than one model? If so, explain how they differ.

    c. Make a three-dimensional drawing of your model. Choose a vantage point that shows clearly all the characteristics of your model.

5. a. How are the legs of a folding "director's chair" positioned? Why do you think the chair is designed this way?

    b. Identify at least two other items which must remain rigid when "unfolded" and analyze their designs.

Organizing

1. In Investigation 1.3, you learned how to represent three-dimensional space-shapes in two dimensions. Another way to do this with a rectangular prism is illustrated below.

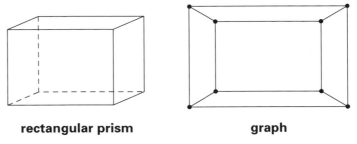

rectangular prism   **graph**

    a. The figure on the right is a representation of a rectangular prism as a vertex-edge graph with no edge crossings. You can think of this graph resulting from "compressing" a rectangular prism with elastic edges down into two dimensions. The graph does not look much like the three-dimensional prism, but it shares many of the prism's properties. Name as many shared properties as you can.

b. Use the idea of *compressing* illustrated in part a to draw vertex-edge graphs representing the following polyhedra. After compressing the octahedron, non-intersecting edges in the octahedron should not intersect in the graph. You will need to stretch the edges that go to one vertex to be sure this does not happen.

i. **ii.** **iii.**

2. In this task you will re-examine the straw space-shapes you constructed. Count the edges, vertices (points where two or more edges meet), and faces of each space-shape. Organize your data in a table.

a. Look for a pattern relating the number of faces, vertices, and edges for each shape. Describe any patterns you see.

b. In Chapter 4, "Graph Models," you discovered that the vertices V and regions R formed by edges E of certain graphs are related by the formula $V + R - E = 2$. Compare this pattern to your pattern for the shapes in part a. Write a similar equation relating the number of vertices V, faces F, and edges E of each of your space-shapes.

c. Write two equations that are equivalent to the equation $V + R - E = 2$. Which form of the equation would be easiest to remember? Why?

3. a. Examine the triangular pyramid constructed from six equal-length straws. It is called a **tetrahedron**. Imagine the centers of each face.

– How many such centers are there?

– Imagine connecting the centers with segments. How many such segments are there?

– Visualize the space-skeleton formed by the segments. What are the shapes of its faces?

– What space-shape would be formed?

b. Examine visually the straw model of a cube. Imagine the centers of each face.

- How many such centers are there?

- Imagine connecting, with segments, each center to the centers on **adjacent faces**. Adjacent faces are faces that have a common edge. How many such segments are there?

- Visualize the space-skeleton formed by the segments. What are the shapes of its faces? How many faces are there?

c. Make a straw model of the space-skeleton in part b. This shape is called an **octahedron**.

4. Bridge trusses are examples of rigid space-shapes. Shown here is a Warren truss in Del Rio, Texas.

In addition to the Warren truss, there are several other types of trusses that vary in cost, strength, and other factors. Three of them are illustrated below.

i.   **ii.**   **iii.**

Pratt Truss   **Parker Truss**   **Howe Truss**

a. Determine if it is possible to make a model of each using a single piece of wire. If possible, draw sketches showing the manner in which you would bend the wire.

b. Explain your results in terms of vertex-edge graphs and Euler paths.

5. a. Here is a quick way to make a tetrahedron from a sealed letter envelope.

- Find point C so that segments AB, AC and BC are the same length. (Hint: Try folding, measuring, or using a compass.)

- Cut along segment DE parallel to segment AB.

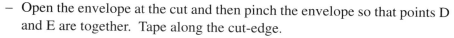

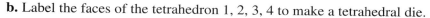

- Fold back and forth along segments AC and BC.

- Open the envelope at the cut and then pinch the envelope so that points D and E are together. Tape along the cut-edge.

b. Label the faces of the tetrahedron 1, 2, 3, 4 to make a tetrahedral die.

- Toss the die 100 times. Record the number of times each face lands down.

- Make a histogram of your data.

- Describe the shape of the histogram.

6. Obtain or make a tetrahedral die as described in Organizing task 5. Gather data on the following experiment. Use a table to organize your work.

- Toss the die 10 times; record the number of times the face labeled 3 lands down. Determine the ratio: Number of 3s ÷ Total tosses (10).

- Toss 10 more times and determine the ratio: Number of 3s (in both sets of tosses) ÷ Total tosses (20).

- Repeat until you have 100 tosses.

a. Create a graph with "number of tosses" on the horizontal axis and "ratio of 3s to tosses" on the vertical axis.

b. What does the graph tell you?

Reflecting

1. In this lesson, as well as in previous chapters, you have engaged in important kinds of mathematical thinking. From time to time, it is helpful to step back and think about the kinds of thinking that are broadly useful in doing mathematics. Look back over the four investigations in this lesson and consider some of the mathematical thinking you have done. Describe an example where you did each of the following:

a. Experiment

b. Search for patterns

   c. Formulate or find a mathematical model such as a function rule

   d. Visualize

   e. Make and check conjectures

   f. Make connections

      – between mathematics and the real world

      – between mathematical strands (between geometry and algebra, geometry and statistics, or geometry and graph theory)

2. Which of the methods of sketching space-shapes is most difficult for you? Why?

3. Which sketching method provides the most complete information regarding a space-shape? Explain your reasoning.

4. A particular space-shape is symmetrical about a plane cutting the front of the shape. What can you conclude about the front view of the shape? Why?

5. Buildings in areas that are subject to the stresses of earthquakes must have "flex" built into them. How can a space-shape have both rigidity and flex?

Extending

1. Models of solids can be made by folding a pattern drawn on paper and taping or gluing the edges. Here is such a pattern for a square pyramid. Find and sketch two other patterns that would fold into a square pyramid. How many straight cuts are needed in order to cut out your patterns?

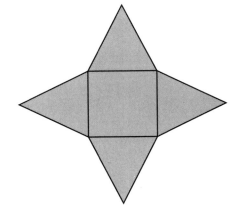

2. Try to imagine a space-shape that has a rectangle as its front view, a triangle as its side view, and a circular top view. Is such a space-shape possible? If so, sketch it. If not, explain why it is impossible.

3. Use your results from Modeling tasks 1 and 2 to identify all the three- and four-room motels with right-angle bends in them. If possible, make models of each using cubes taped or glued together. For some of the motels, there is another that is actually the same space-shape. Only include one of these motels.

a. How many motels with right-angle bends are there?

b. How many individual cubes are needed to make the whole collection of these shapes?

c. Which of the shapes have reflection symmetry? For shapes that are symmetric, write the number of planes of symmetry.

d. Are any two of your shapes related by symmetry? If so, identify them.

4. One of the strongest types of structures is a dome. However, it is very difficult to build a dome without the weight of the building material being too great. To lighten the weight, dome-like space frames are used to approximate the shape of a true dome. These dome-like space frames are generally referred to as *geodesic domes*. The work of R. Buckminster Fuller greatly influenced the popularity of the dome. A picture of Fuller's dome at the Montreal Expo in 1968 is shown below.

a. Look up the meaning of the roots of the word "geodesic." Explain why you think Fuller used this term to describe the dome.

b. What are the fundamental units of the Expo dome? What other polygons do you notice in this dome?

c. Conduct research on other geodesic domes such as the Epcot Center at Disney World in Orlando, Florida. What are the fundamental units of those domes? What other polygons do you notice in the domes?

5. a. Some space-shapes can be made by weaving strips of paper together. Obtain a copy of the following patterns. Cut along segment *ST*, making two strips of 5 equilateral triangles. Letter the corners as shown. Fold along the sides of the triangles. Try to weave these strips into a tetrahedron. If you need assistance, use the instructions below the figures. "$A_2 \rightarrow A_1$" means face A_2 goes under face A_1 with the letters on top of each other.

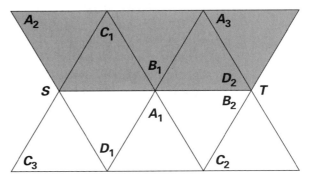

Weaving Procedure: $A_2 \rightarrow A_1$; $C_2 \rightarrow C_1$; $B_2 \rightarrow B_1$; $A_3 \rightarrow A_1$ and A_2;
slide C_3 through the open slot so $C_3 \rightarrow C_1$ and C_2, and $D_2 \rightarrow D_1$.

b. You can also weave a cube. Cut out the 3 strips from your copy of this pattern and follow the weaving procedure below the figure. "$A_2 \rightarrow A_1$" means face A_2 goes under face A_1 with the letters on top of each other. "D_2 (D_3)" means face D_2 with face D_3 under it.

	D_1	A_2	B_1	
F_2				F_3
E_3			A_1	E_2
	F_1	C_2		
	C_1	B_2		
D_2			E_1	D_3

Weaving Procedure: $A_2 \rightarrow A_1$; $B_2 \rightarrow B_1$; $C_2 \rightarrow C_1$; $E_2 \rightarrow E_1$; $D_3 \rightarrow D_2$;
D_2 (D_3) $\rightarrow D_1$; $F_3 \rightarrow F_2$; slide E_3 in the slot so that $E_3 \rightarrow E_1$ (E_2) and F_2 (F_3) $\rightarrow F_1$.

2 *The Size of Things*

If you were asked to identify the largest building in the area where you live, how would you respond? Deciding which of the buildings in your area is largest might be easy. If all the buildings in the United States were included, it may be difficult to decide. The Sears Tower in Chicago might be a candidate since it has a height (without antenna) of 1454 feet. The World Trade Center in New York City has a height of 1377 feet, but it could be considered since it has 4,370,000 square feet of rentable space.

Sears Tower

World Trade Center

The Boeing Company 747 aircraft assembly plant in Everett, Washington could be considered since it contains 200 million cubic feet of space. However, its maximum height is only 115 feet. *Length*, *area*, and *volume* are three measures often used to describe size. You will extend your understanding of these and other measures in the following investigations.

Think about this situation

a What measure was used to describe the size of the Sears Tower? The World Trade Center? The Boeing assembly plant?

b When describing the size of a space-shape, how do you know what measure to use?

c How is the unit of measure determined by this choice?

Investigation 2.1 Describing Size

Length, perimeter, area, and volume are ideas used to describe the size of geometric shapes. These measures commonly are used in daily life as well as in manufacturing and technical trades. This investigation will help you review and deepen your understanding of these basic ideas.

1. Obtain measuring equipment from your teacher and individually select a box such as a cereal or laundry detergent box.

   a. Make a sketch of your box. What technique did you choose? Why?

   b. Working with a partner, compare your boxes. Which do you think is the largest?

   c. What characteristics of the boxes did you use to predict which was the largest?

2. Working individually, measure your box in as many different ways as you can. Use your measurements to answer each of the following questions.

   a. What is the total length of all the edges? Describe the procedure you used to determine this total. Is there a shortcut? If so, describe it.

   b. Suppose the box could be formed by simply attaching the faces along their edges. How much material would be needed to make it? Describe how you found your answer and note any shortcuts taken.

   c. About how many sugar cubes could your box hold? How did you find your answer?

   d. With your partner, review the prediction you made in part b of activity 1. Do all your measures in this activity support your choice? Explain why or why not.

3. **a.** On the sketch of your chosen box, write only the lengths that are *absolutely* necessary to answer parts a through c of activity 2.

   b. Explain how the lengths you wrote are used to obtain the measures asked for in activity 2.

   c. If you used any formulas in completing activity 2, write them down. Explain how each works.

The number you were asked to find in part b of activity 2 is the *surface area* of your box. The **surface area** of a space-shape is the sum of the areas of each face—top, bottom, and *lateral* faces. In activity 2, part c, you were asked to find the *volume* of your box.

4. The perimeter and area of some plane-shapes are not as easy to find as those for the faces of the boxes. Shown below are several plane-shapes drawn on a background of a square grid. The grid squares have a side length of 0.5 cm.

   a. Find the perimeter of each plane-shape to the nearest 0.5 centimeters. Divide up the work among your group. Which shape has the greatest perimeter?

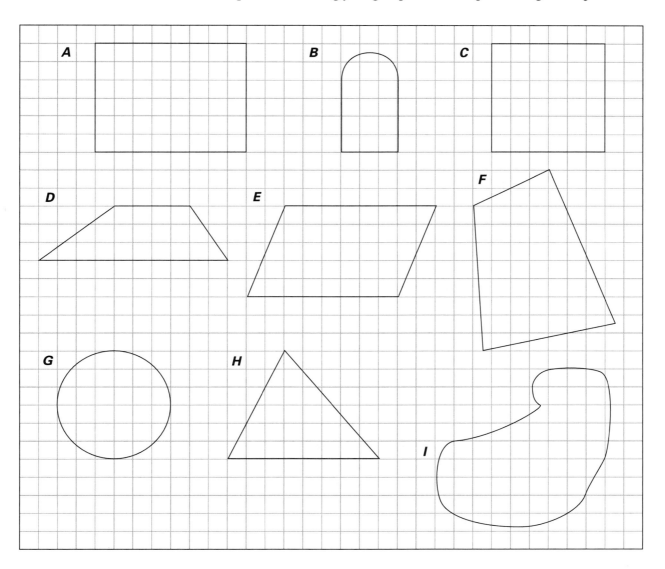

b. Describe the procedure you used to determine each perimeter. If you used any formulas to help you, include them and describe how they were used.

c. Of the procedures you identified in part b, could any be used for all the plane-shapes? If so, which ones? Why don't the other procedures work for all shapes?

Area of a plane-shape can be measured in different ways. One way is to find the number of same-sized square regions needed to completely cover the enclosed region.

5. Refer back to the plane-shapes in activity 4.

a. Explain why the area of each grid square is 0.25 square centimeters.

b. For each of the plane-shapes, estimate its area to the nearest 0.25 square centimeters. Again, divide up the work among the members of your group. Describe the method you used to determine the area of each region. If you used formulas, note them in your descriptions and explain how they were used.

c. Which of your methods will work for all plane regions? Why won't the other methods work for all regions?

Checkpoint

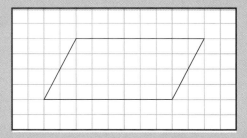

a Describe two ways in which you can find the perimeter of the parallelogram shown here. Use each method to find the perimeter.

b Describe two ways in which you can find the area of the parallelogram. Find the area using both methods.

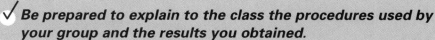

✓ *Be prepared to explain to the class the procedures used by your group and the results you obtained.*

On Your Own

Consider this scale drawing of Mongoose Lake. Using the given scale, estimate the perimeter to the nearest 10 meters and the area to the nearest 100 square meters.

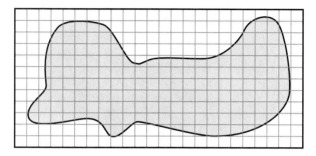

Mongoose Lake
Scale: ⊢—⊣ = 10 meters

Formulas used to calculate the perimeter and area of common plane shapes are summarized below. You should be familiar with these from your previous mathematics coursework.

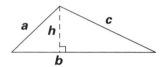

Triangle	**Parallelogram**	**Circle**
Perimeter: $P = a + b + c$	$P = 2(a + b)$	$P = 2\pi r$
Area: $A = \frac{1}{2}bh$	$A = bh$	$A = \pi r^2$

6. a. For each formula above, what is the meaning of the letters a, b, c, h, or r?

 b. Use the formulas above to compute the areas of figures A, C, E, G, and H of activity 4. Recall that each grid square has side length 0.5 cm.

 c. Compare your results in part b with those you obtained for part b of activity 5.

 d. Illustrate how you could use the formulas above to compute the areas of figures B and D of activity 4. Compare your results with those obtained previously.

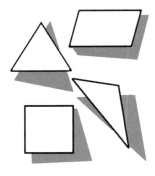

7. Now examine more closely the formulas for the perimeter and area of a triangle and of a parallelogram.

    a. Write a formula for the perimeter of an equilateral triangle which is different from the formula for a general triangle. Write a similar formula for the perimeter of a square.

    b. If you only remembered the area formula for a parallelogram, how could you figure out the area formula for a triangle?

    c. How could you modify the formula for the area of a parallelogram so that it applies only to squares? Illustrate with a sketch.

8. In your group, investigate whether each of the following statements is true.

    – If two rectangles have the same perimeter, then they must have the same area.

    – If two rectangles have the same area, then they must have the same perimeter.

    a. Begin by dividing your group into two approximately equal subgroups: A and B.

        Subgroup A: Develop an argument supporting the first statement or provide a counterexample. (A **counterexample** is an example for which a statement is not true.) Use rectangles with the same perimeter (such as 40 cm) and make a data table showing length, width, and area.

        Subgroup B: Develop an argument supporting the second statement or give a counterexample. Use rectangles with the same area (such as 48 cm^2) and make a data table showing length, width, and perimeter.

    b. Share and check the findings of each subgroup. Then compare your group's final conclusions with those of other groups.

    c. Would your group's views on the two statements be the same or different if "rectangle" was replaced by "square"? Explain.

9. Jacob has 30 meters of fencing to enclose a garden plot in the shape of a rectangle.

    a. Find the dimensions of all possible gardens Jacob could make using whole number sides.

    b. Find the areas of the gardens in part a. Put all your information in a table. Of your sample garden dimensions, which give the largest garden?

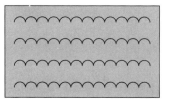

c. Let x represent the width of a garden whose perimeter is 30 meters.

  – Write an expression for the length of the garden.

  – Write an expression for the area of the garden.

d. Use your graphing calculator or computer to find the dimensions of the largest rectangular garden that can be enclosed with 30 meters of fencing. Find the dimensions to the nearest 0.1 meter.

e. Did you use tables of values or graphs in part d? Verify your answer to part d using the other form of representation.

f. Suppose the fencing available to Jacob is 75 meters long. What is the largest rectangular garden he can enclose? Support your position.

g. What is similar about the shape of the two largest garden plots in this activity?

Checkpoint

Look back at your work calculating perimeters and areas of rectangles.

a If two rectangles have equal areas, can you conclude anything about their perimeters? If so, what?

b If two rectangles have equal perimeters, can you conclude anything about their areas? If so, what?

c For a given perimeter, can you say anything about the shape of the rectangle having the largest possible area? If so, what?

✓ *Be prepared to share and defend your group's conclusions.*

On Your Own

a. How many different rectangles with whole number dimensions and a perimeter of 126 units can you create?

b. Of the rectangles in part a, which has the maximum area?

c. To the nearest 0.1 unit, find the dimensions of the rectangle with a perimeter of 126 units that has the largest possible area.

Investigation (2.2) Television Screens and Pythagoras

Television manufacturers often describe the size of their rectangular picture screens by giving the length of the diagonal. The set pictured here has a 25-inch diagonal screen. Several companies also advertise a 50-inch diagonal color stereo television. How well does giving the measure of the diagonal describe the rectangular screen?

1. For this activity, consider a 20-inch TV picture screen.

    a. Model the 20-inch diagonal by drawing a 5-inch segment on your paper. (Each member of your group should do this.) In your drawing, each inch represents 4 inches on the picture screen. This is done so that the drawing will fit on your paper. Your drawing has a 1 to 4 (1:4) scale.

    b. Draw a rectangle with the segment you drew as its diagonal. One way to do this is to place a piece of notebook paper with a 90° corner over the segment. Carefully position the paper so that its edges just touch the ends of the segment. Mark the corner. Describe how the total rectangle can be drawn from this one point and the segment.

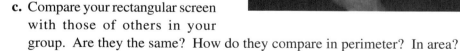

    c. Compare your rectangular screen with those of others in your group. Are they the same? How do they compare in perimeter? In area?

    d. Draw a scale model of the TV screen that is 4 inches wide and has a diagonal of 20 inches. What are the lengths of the other sides? What is its area?

    e. Make a scatterplot of at least eight (*width*, *area*) data pairs for 20-inch diagonal screens. Use your plot to estimate the 20-inch diagonal screen with the greatest viewing area.

f. How well does the length of the diagonal of a TV screen describe the screen? Give reasons for your opinion.

2. A manufacturer of small personal TVs thinks that a screen measuring 6 by 8 inches is a nice size for good picture quality. What diagonal length should be advertised?

3. You can calculate the diagonal length of screens by considering the right triangle formed by the sides. To see how to do this, examine the figures below in which squares have been constructed on the sides of right triangles.

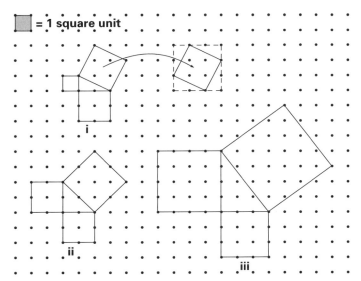

a. For each figure, calculate the areas of the squares on the sides. Use the unit of area measure shown. To calculate areas of squares on the longest side (the diagonal), you may have to be creative as suggested by the first figure. Record your data in a table like the one below.

Area of Square on Short Side 1	Area of Square on Short Side 2	Area of Square on Longest Side

b. Describe any pattern you see in the table. Check to see if the pattern holds for other right triangles. Have each member of your group draw a different test case on a sheet of square dot paper. Record this data in your table as well.

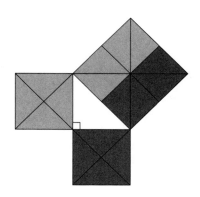

c. Now examine the more general figure at the right. Explain how this figure illustrates the general pattern in the table of data you prepared in part b.

d. In general, how are the areas of the squares constructed on the two shorter sides of a right triangle related to the area of the square on the longest side? Compare your discovery with those made by other groups.

e. Represent the lengths of the two shorter sides of the right triangle by a and b. How could you represent the area of each of the two smaller squares? If the length of the longest side is c, what is the area of the largest square?

f. Write an expression for the conjecture you made in part d using a, b, and c.

The discovery you made in activity 3 was based on a careful study of several examples. The Greek philosopher Pythagoras is credited with first demonstrating that this relationship is true for all right triangles. The relationship is called the **Pythagorean Theorem**. Historians believe that special cases of this relationship were earlier discovered and used by the Babylonians, Chinese, and Egyptians.

4. Now investigate how the Pythagorean Theorem can help in sizing television screens.

a. Recall the 6-by-8 inch TV screen.

- Find the square of the diagonal.

- How can you find the length of the diagonal when you know its square? What do you get in this case?

- How do you think the manufacturer advertises the size of the 6-by-8 inch TV set? Compare this answer to what you proposed in activity 2.

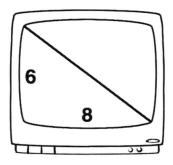

b. Use your calculator or computer to find the length of a diagonal whose square is 56.

c. In activity 1, the diagonal of the TV screen was 20 inches. Suppose one of the sides of the screen is 13 inches. Find, to the nearest 0.1 inch, the length of the other side.

d. For a 50-inch TV, find five possible length-width pairs that would be reasonable dimensions for a rectangular screen.

5. Jonathan wondered if the Pythagorean Theorem is true for triangles without a right angle. Draw several triangles, measure the sides, and apply the Pythagorean Theorem. Does it work for such triangles? Divide the work among your group and summarize your findings.

6. a. Do the numbers 8, 15, and 17 satisfy your statement of the Pythagorean Theorem in part f of activity 3? Use tools such as a compass or piece of spaghetti to draw a triangle whose lengths, in centimeters, are 8, 15, and 17. What kind of triangle is formed?

b. Find four more sets of three numbers that satisfy the Pythagorean Theorem. Make triangles with these lengths as sides. Divide the work and report the kind of triangles you get.

Checkpoint

ⓐ Write a calculator keystroke sequence to compute the length of the longest side of a right triangle with shorter sides of lengths 7 cm and 10 cm.

ⓑ Write a keystroke sequence to compute the length of the third side of a right triangle when the longest side is 25 cm and one other side is 7 cm.

ⓒ Given the lengths of the sides of any triangle, how can you tell if the triangle is a right triangle?

✓ *Be prepared to share and defend your group's procedures and right-triangle test.*

In a right triangle, the longest side (the one opposite the right angle) is called the **hypotenuse** and the shorter sides are called **legs**. The Pythagorean Theorem can be stated in the following form:
The sum of the squares of the legs of a right triangle equals the square of the hypotenuse.

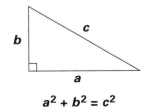

$$a^2 + b^2 = c^2$$

On Your Own

The Morgan family made a garden for perennial flowers in the corner of their lot. It was a right triangle with legs of 8 and 10 meters.

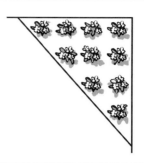

a. Find the perimeter of the garden and explain how this information might be used by the Morgans.

b. Find the area of the garden and explain how this information might be used in care of the garden.

Modeling **O**rganizing **R**eflecting **E**xtending

Modeling

1. A TV manufacturer plans to build a picture screen with a 15-inch diagonal.

   a. Find the dimensions of 4 possible rectangular picture screens.

   b. Find all picture screens with whole number dimensions. Describe the procedure you used to do this.

   c. Of all possible 15-inch screens, which design would give the largest viewing area? Do you think this would be a good design? Why or why not?

2. The Alvarez family purchased twenty 90-cm length sections of fencing to protect their planned garden from the family dog. They plan to use an existing wall as one of the borders. The 90-cm sections can not be cut or bent.

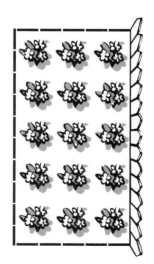

   a. Make a table of the dimensions and areas of gardens that can be enclosed by the 90-cm length sections.

   b. What is the largest garden area that can be enclosed with these sections of fence?

   c. For a garden with the largest area, how many sections of fence should be used for each width of the border? For the length of the border?

d. The Alvarez family could have purchased 15 sections of 120-cm length fencing for the same price as the shorter sections they bought. Could they have enclosed a larger garden area using these sections? Explain your response.

e. What else might influence the decision about how to set up the garden?

3. A historical museum plans to paint a mural on its walls illustrating different flags of the world. The flags of the Czech Republic, Switzerland, Thailand, and Japan use some combination of red, white, or blue as shown on the following page. Each of the flags is to be 3 yards long and 2 yards wide. A quart (32 ounces) of paint covers approximately 110 square feet. Paint can be purchased in cans of 32, 16, 8 and 4 ounces. How much paint of each color should be purchased to paint these flags?

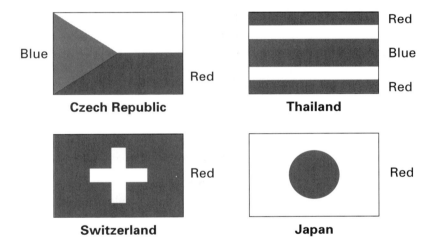

Czech Republic   **Thailand**

Switzerland   **Japan**

4. Materials tend to expand when heated. This expansion needs to be considered carefully when building roads and railroad tracks. Each 220-foot long rail is anchored solidly at both ends. Suppose that on a very hot day it expands 1.2 inches, causing it to buckle as shown below.

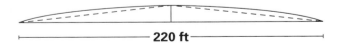

220 ft

a. At what point along the rail do you think the buckling will occur?

b. Do you think you could slide a gym bag between the raised rail and the track bed?

c. Model this situation using right triangles and then calculate an estimate of the height of the buckle.

d. Would you expect your estimate of the height of the buckle to be more or less than the actual value? Explain your reasoning.

e. Research *expansion joints*. How does the use of these joints in railroad tracks and concrete highways minimize the problem you modeled in part c?

5. In Investigation 1.1, you used an 11-inch long sheet of paper to model a rectangular prism column.

a. If 0.5 inches is used for overlapping before taping the seam, how should the paper be folded to make the area of the rectangular base as large as possible?

b. Does the paper folded as in part a produce the rectangular prism column with the largest possible surface area? Organize your work and provide evidence to support your answer.

O*rganizing*

1. Carefully trace the figure shown here.

a. Cut out the square labeled *A* and the labeled pieces of the other square.

b. Can you use the five labeled pieces to cover the square on the hypotenuse of the right triangle? If so, draw a sketch of your covering.

c. This puzzle was created by Henry Perigal, a London stockbroker who found recreation in the patterns of geometry. How is Perigal's puzzle related to the Pythagorean Theorem?

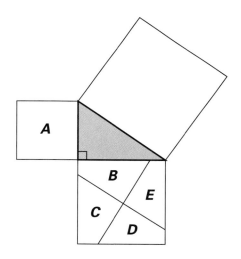

d. After studying the puzzle, Anne conjectured: "Every square can be dissected into 5 pieces which can be reassembled to form two squares." Do you think Anne is correct? Explain your reasoning.

2. The television industry has set a standard for the sizing of television screens. The ratio of height h to width w, called the *aspect ratio*, is 3:4. That is $\frac{h}{w} = \frac{3}{4}$.

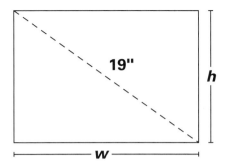

a. Write an equation expressing h as a function of w.

b. Use the Pythagorean Theorem to write an equation relating h, w, and the diagonal length 19.

c. Use your equations in parts a and b to find the standard dimension of a 19" TV screen.

d. Check the dimensions you obtained against actual measurements of a 19" screen.

3. Draw squares of side lengths 2, 4, 7, 8, 10, and 11 centimeters on centimeter grid paper.

a. Measure the diagonals to the nearest 0.1 cm. Record your data in a table.

b. Make a plot of your (*side length*, *diagonal*) data.

c. Does the plot appear to have a linear pattern? If so, find a linear model that fits the data well.

d. Find an equation for your line.
   – What is the slope? What does it mean?
   – What is the *y*-intercept? Does it make sense? Explain.

e. Predict the length of the diagonal of a square with side length of 55 cm.

f. Compare your predicted length to that computed by using the Pythagorean Theorem. Explain any differences.

4. Locate six cylindrical shapes of different sizes. Cans and jar lids work well.

a. Measure the circumference of each cylinder to the nearest 0.1 cm. Record your data in a table.

b. On a sheet of paper, trace around the base of each cylinder. Then measure, to the nearest 0.1 cm, the diameter of each tracing and record it in your table.

c. Make a plot of your (*diameter*, *circumference*) data.

d. Find a line and its equation that model this data well.

- What is the slope of the line? What does it mean?

- What is the *y*-intercept? Does it make sense? Explain.

e. The diameter of a small fruit-juice can is approximately 5.5 cm. Use your linear model to predict the circumference of the can.

f. Compare your predicted circumference to that computed by using the formula for circumference of a circle. Explain any differences.

5. Imagine a plane intersecting a cube.

a. Describe the shape of the intersection of a cube and a plane that has the largest possible area.

b. Describe the shape of the intersection of a cube and a plane that has the smallest possible area.

c. Find the least and greatest possible areas of shapes formed by the intersection of a plane with a cube 5 cm on a side.

6. Draw a segment 10 cm long on your paper.

a. Imagine a right triangle that has the segment as its hypotenuse. If one side is 0.5 cm long, where would the vertex of the right angle be? Locate that point and make a mark there. (Use a technique similar to the one in activity 1 of Investigation 2.2, page 362.) Where would that vertex be if the side is 1 cm long? Mark that point. Now increase the side length in steps of 0.5 cm and plot those vertices of the resulting triangles. Stop when the side length is 10 cm.

b. Examine your plot of the points. What shape do they appear to form?

c. Support your view by citing appropriate measurements from your model.

Reflecting

1. Architects use many design principles. For example, tall buildings will always provide more daylight, natural ventilation, and openness than low buildings of the same floor area. Explain why this is the case.

2. Which shape encloses more area: a square with perimeter 42 or a circle with perimeter 42? Justify your reasoning.

3. In what kind of units is area measured? How can you use this fact to avoid confusing the formulas $2\pi r$ and πr^2 when computing the area of a circle?

4. Experimenting, collecting data, and searching for patterns is a powerful way to discover important mathematical relationships. However, it also has limitations. Consider the following example.

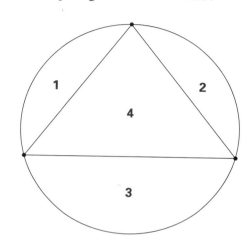

On the circle at the right, three points are marked. Each point is connected to all the others. Four nonoverlapping regions are formed.

Anthony investigated what happened when differing numbers of points were marked on a circle and each was connected to all the others. He summarized his findings in the table below.

Number of Points	1	2	3	4	5
Number of Regions	1	2	4	8	16

a. Do you see any pattern in the table?

b. Anthony predicted that the number of nonoverlapping regions formed by six points would be 32. Check his prediction.

c. What lesson can be learned from this example?

Extending

1. Examine more closely the *dissection* method of "proof" of the Pythagorean Theorem in Organizing task 1. Will this method establish the relation for *any* right triangle?

a. There are two "cut lines" dividing the square on the longer leg of the triangle. Is one of those lines related in a special way to the hypotenuse of the right triangle? Explain.

b. How are the two "cut lines" related to each other?

2. The circle at the right has been dissected into 8 sections. These sections can be reassembled to form an "approximate" parallelogram.

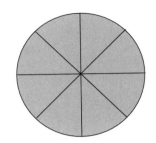

a. How is the base of this "approximate" parallelogram related to the circle?

b. What is the height of the "approximate" parallelogram?

c. How could you dissect the circle into sections to get a better approximation of a parallelogram?

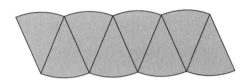

d. Use the above information to produce the formula for the area of a circle.

3. a. How much decorative fencing is needed to enclose a regular hexagonal flower garden which measures 4 meters between opposite vertices?

b. Suppose the distance between opposite sides were 4 meters. How much fencing is needed?

c. How many flowers can be planted in the garden described in part a if each flower requires 225 square centimeters?

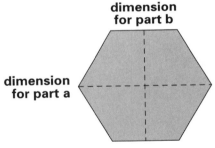

d. How many flowers can be planted in the garden described in part b?

e. Suppose the 4-meter length measured the length of other segments through the center of the hexagon. What can you say about the amount of fencing needed? Explain your reasoning.

4. In order for kites to fly well, they need to have a high ratio of *lift area* to weight. For two-dimensional kites, the lift area is just the area of the kite. Find the lift area of the traditional kite shown with cross pieces of lengths 0.8 m and 1.0 m.

Investigation 2.3 | Size Measures for Space–Shapes

Prisms model the shape of most buildings we construct. Among the prisms, the rectangular prism is the most common. This fact is demonstrated in an aerial photo of a portion of New York City. Other prisms well suited to architecture generally have numbers of sides that are multiples of four. One building in the Crown Zellerbach Plaza in San Francisco (shown below) is based on a 40-gon prism. (A 40-gon is a polygon with 40 sides.) Regardless of the shape of the base, the other faces (*lateral faces*) of a prism are rectangles. These facts permit easy measuring of the surface area and volume of space-shapes commonly found in architecture.

1. In your group, discuss possible real-life situations where you would want to know

   a. the areas of the lateral faces of a prism.

   b. the surface area (total area of the bases and lateral faces) of a prism.

   c. the volume of a prism.

2. Now try to discover a formula for calculating the total area of the lateral faces of a prism.

   a. Refer to the skeleton models of five prisms that you made in activity 8 of Investigation 1.2 (page 333). Imagine covering each prism with paper. Describe how you would find the total area of the lateral faces of each of those prisms.

   b. Based on your descriptions in part a, write a general formula for finding the total area of the lateral faces of any prism. Describe what each variable in your formula represents.

   c. Suppose you have a regular octagonal prism whose bases have sides of length 4 cm. The edges connecting the bases are 10 cm long. Apply your formula to this prism.

   d. Could you use the concept of perimeter to simplify your formula in part b? If you can, do so; if not, explain why not.

   e. How could you simplify your formula for the special case of a cube?

3. Modify your formula of activity 2 to give a formula for the surface area of a prism.

   a. Apply your formula to find the surface area of one of the boxes you analyzed in activity 1 of Investigation 2.1 (page 356).

   b. Apply your formula for surface area to the following prisms.

     – Square prism: 5 cm edges on bases, 6 cm height

     – Triangular prism: 5 cm edges on bases, 6 cm height

   c. The base of a hexagonal prism with 4 cm edges can be divided into 6 equilateral triangles as shown here.

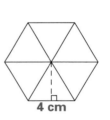
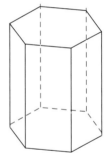

     – How can you calculate the altitude of one of the equilateral triangles?

     – Calculate the area of a base.

     – Find the surface area of this prism if the height is 9 cm.

4 cm

Surface area gives you one measure of the size of a space-shape. *Volume* gives you another. Just as area can be found by counting squares (hence square units), volume can be found by counting cubes (hence cubic units).

4. Look at the figure below showing one layer of unit cubes in a prism.

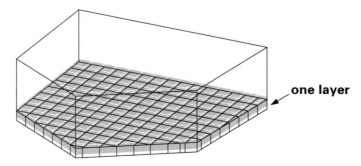

one layer

a. If that layer has a base area of 84 square units, how many unit cubes are in it?

b. If there are 6 such layers, what is the volume of the prism? What is the volume if there are 134 layers?

c. Suppose the layer has a base area of 13 square units. How many unit cubes are in it? If there are h such layers, what is the total volume?

d. Write a formula for calculating the volume V of a prism which has a base area of B square units and a height of h units. Compare your formula with that of other groups. Resolve any differences.

5. Make a sketch of each prism with the given dimensions and then find its volume.

   a. Rectangular prism: base is 4 cm by 5 cm, height is 6 cm.

   b. Cube: edge is 8 cm.

   c. Equilateral triangular prism: base edges are 3 cm, height is 8 cm.

   d. Regular hexagonal prism: base edges are 6 cm, height is 3 cm.

6. Find the surface area of each prism in activity 5.

7. Some products like vegetables or fruit juice are packaged in cylindrical cans. A cylinder (shown here) can be thought of as a special prism-like shape.

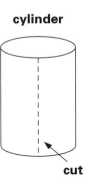

cylinder

cut

   a. What shape are its bases? Imagine removing the bases and cutting the lateral face from base to base. (Cut along the dotted line in the diagram.) If you flatten the cut lateral face, what shape is it?

   b. Find the surface area and volume of a cylinder if the base has a radius of 4 cm and the height is 7 cm.

   c. Write a formula for the surface area S of a cylinder with radius r and height h.

   d. Write an equivalent expression for your formula for surface area. Which expression will be easier to remember?

   e. Write a formula for the volume V of a cylinder with radius r and height h.

8. A can of diced tomatoes has a base with a diameter 7.5 cm and a height of 11 cm. These cans are usually packaged for shipping in boxes of 24 (two layers of 12).

   a. What space-shape usually is used for the shipping boxes?

   b. What arrangements of the cans are possible for a box holding 12 in a layer?

   c. For each arrangement of 12 cans, determine the dimensions of the smallest shipping box possible.

   d. What arrangement of cans uses the greatest amount of available space in the box?

   e. Which arrangement of cans requires the smallest amount of cardboard to make the box?

9. A $10\frac{3}{4}$ ounce can of soup has a height of 10 cm and a base with radius 3.3 cm. A $6\frac{1}{8}$ ounce can of tuna has a height of 4 cm and a base with radius 4 cm. Which can is most efficient in its use of tin for the weight of its contents?

Checkpoint

   a How is the perimeter of a base of a prism useful in finding the area of the lateral faces?

   b How are the formulas you developed for surface area and volume of cylinders similar to the corresponding formulas for prisms? How are they different?

   c How is the Pythagorean Theorem helpful in computing surface areas and volumes of prisms with equilateral triangles or regular hexagons as bases?

   ✓ *Be prepared to share your group's ideas with the entire class.*

On Your Own

A decorative candy tin used by Sorby's Candies and Nuts has a regular hexagonal base with dimensions as shown. These tins are shipped from the manufacturer in boxes 20 cm by 17.5 cm.

   a. How many tins can be put in one layer of a box?

   b. If the box and tin have the same height, how much of the available volume of the box is used by the candy tins?

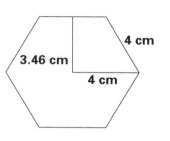

3.46 cm

4 cm

4 cm

Modeling Organizing Reflecting Extending

Modeling

1. Susan and John Sitzman are farmers who specialize in raising cattle. They need to build a new feed storage silo with an estimated volume of 20,000 cubic feet for the cylinder portion. They have prepared a square piece of land, 20 feet on each side, on which to build the silo.

   a. After shopping around, the Sitzmans found the "best buy" comes from a company which makes a type of silo with a diameter of 18 feet and a height of 55 feet. Would this type fit their needs? Why or why not?

   b. ACME Equipment Company makes silos with a range of diameters from 16 to 21 feet. They will custom-build their silos to any height the customer desires. If the Sitzmans require a volume of 20,000 cubic feet, how high would a silo of a given diameter have to be? Make a table like the one below to help organize your work.

Diameter (in feet)	16	17	18	19	20	21
Height (in feet)						

   c. The Sitzmans want to keep the height of their new silo below 75 feet, since they often have strong wind storms in their area. Which of the silos in your table would be suitable for these conditions?

2. A computer disk box measures 9.7 cm by 4.8 cm by 9.7 cm (from inside edge to inside edge). Inside, the bottom half of the box is an open-ended cardboard protective liner which measures 7.2 cm high at its back and 5.8 cm high at its front. The thickness of all material is 0.1 cm.

   a. Sketch the liner and give its dimensions.

   b. How much cardboard is needed to make the disk box and its liner?

   c. What is the volume of the box?

   d. What is the volume of the liner?

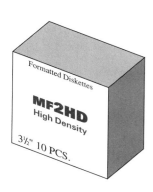

Formatted Diskettes

MF2HD
High Density

3½" 10 PCS.

3. A container manufacturing company makes open-top storage bins for small machine parts. One series of containers is made from a square sheet of tin 24 cm on a side. Squares of the same size are cut from each corner. The tabs are then turned up and welded.

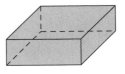

a. Using centimeter graph paper, make model bins by cutting out squares 24 cm on a side. Then, cut squares of one and two centimeters on a side from the corners of the 24 × 24 square. Fold up and tape the tabs. What are the dimensions of the model which has the larger volume?

b. Let x represent the side-length of the cutout square. Write an expression
- for the length of each side of the storage bin;
- for the volume of the bin.

c. What is the possible range of values for x, the side-length of the cutout squares?

d. Use the table-building capability of your graphing calculator or software to help find the dimensions of the container with the largest possible volume.

4. A particular swimming pool is 28 feet long and 18 feet wide. The shallow 3-foot end extends for 6 feet. Then for 16 feet horizontally, there is a constant decline toward the 9-foot deep end.

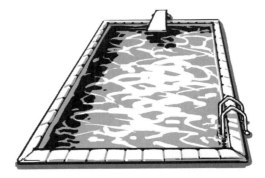

a. Sketch the pool and indicate the measures on the sketch. Is this a prism? If so, name it.

b. How much water is needed to fill the pool within 6 inches of the top?

c. One gallon of paint covers approximately 75 square feet of surface. How many gallons of paint are needed to paint the inside of the pool? If the pool paint comes in 5-gallon cans, how many cans should be purchased?

d. How much material is needed to make a pool cover that extends 2 feet beyond the pool on all sides?

e. About how many six-inch ceramic square tiles are needed to tile the top 18 inches of the inside edge of the pool?

Organizing

1. Imagine a rectangular gift box that has a volume of 60 cubic centimeters and whole number dimensions.

> **a.** Find the dimensions of all possible boxes. Use a table to organize your findings.
>
> **b.** What is the surface area of each gift box?
>
> **c.** What are the dimensions of the gift box that uses the least amount of paper?
>
> **d.** Express your view on the statement: *If two prisms with the same kind of bases (the same shape not same size) have identical volumes, then their surface areas are identical.* Explain your position.

2. To use the formula for the area of a triangle, you need to know the length of a side (the base) and the length of the altitude to that side (the height). In the case of some special triangles, it's sufficient to know the length of a side.

> **a.** Develop a formula for calculating the area A of an equilateral triangle with side-length s.
>
> **b.** Develop a formula for calculating the area A of a regular hexagon with side-length s.

3. Ian's class had two prisms that were 20 cm high. One had a square base with 5 cm sides. The other had an equilateral triangular base with 5 cm sides. The class collected data on the amount of water needed to raise the water level to various heights in each prism. The data is summarized in the following table.

Height in cm	0	2	4	6	8	10	12	14	16	18	20
Volume of Square Prism (5 cm sides)	0	49	102	150	199	252	300	347	398	452	500
Volume of Triangular Prism (5 cm sides)	0	21	44	65	86	107	130	152	172	196	216

> **a.** Produce a scatterplot of the (*height, volume*) data for each prism.
>
> **b.** For which scatterplots would a linear model fit the data well? Where appropriate, find an equation for the linear model.
>
> **c.** Describe the rate of change in the volume for each prism.
>
> **d.** How is the rate of change related to the base of the space-shape?

4. Ian's class found the results of modeling the volumes of the prisms being filled with water (Organizing task 3) very interesting. They extended the investigation and collected (*height*, *volume*) data for other 20 cm tall space-shapes. The results are summarized in the following table.

Height in cm	0	2	4	6	8	10	12	14	16	18	20
Volume of Square Pyramid (5 cm sides)	0	17	33	50	66	84	99	115	133	149	167
Volume of Triangular Pyramid (5 cm sides)	0	7	16	22	28	36	44	50	57	66	72
Volume of Cylinder (2 cm radius)	0	25	49	75	101	123	149	177	200	227	252
Volume of Cone (2 cm radius)	0	8	17	26	34	41	49	59	66	76	84

a. Produce four scatterplots of the (*height*, *volume*) data in the table.

b. If appropriate, find a linear model for each scatterplot.

c. Compare the linear models for the cone and the cylinder. Make a conjecture about the relationship between the volumes of a cylinder and a cone with identical bases and identical heights.

d. Compare the linear models for the pyramids with those of a prism with a similar base in Organizing task 3. Make a conjecture regarding the relation between the volumes of a prism and a pyramid with identical bases and identical heights.

Reflecting

1. Commodities sold in grocery stores come in many kinds of packages. Packages made of cardboard tend to be rectangular prisms. Packages made of metal or glass are more often cylinders. What reasons might you give for these trends?

2. What changes the volume of a cylinder more: doubling its diameter or doubling its height? Explain your reasoning.

3. In Investigation 2.3, you saw that the volume of a prism or a cylinder is found simply by multiplying the area of the base by the height. Explain why it would not be reasonable to calculate volumes of pyramids or cones in the same way.

4. In Chapter 4, "Graph Models," you developed *algorithms* for finding Euler circuits and coloring the vertices of a graph. In this investigation you developed *formulas* for calculating volumes of space-shapes. How is a formula similar to an algorithm? How is it different?

Extending

1. The U. S. Postal Service has requirements on the size of packages it will ship within the United States. The maximum size for parcel post packages is 108 inches in combined length and *girth*.

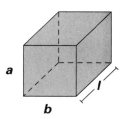

Girth = 2a + 2b

   a. Suppose you are shipping goods via parcel post that do not require a specific length shipping box. What are the dimensions of a square prism package that would allow you to ship the greatest volume of goods?

   b. Could you ship a greater volume of goods using a rectangular prism package? Explain your reasoning.

2. A cone has a circular base with a radius of 4 cm. To cut it open, you need to make a 12 cm cut from bottom to top.

   a. Sketch the shape of the cone when cut and flattened.

   b. The flattened shape is part of what larger shape? What fractional part of the larger shape is this surface?

   c. Find the area of the surface of the cone.

3. The volume formulas in this chapter can be viewed as special cases of the *prismoidal formula*:

$$V = \frac{B + 4M + T}{6} \cdot h$$

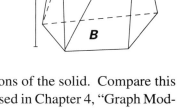

   B is the area of the cross section at the base. *M* is the area of the cross section at the "middle." *T* is the area of the cross section at the top, and *h* is the height of the space-shape.

   a. Explain why $\frac{B+4M+T}{6}$ can be thought of as the "weighted" average area of the cross sections of the solid. Compare this formula for "weighted average" with the one used in Chapter 4, "Graph Models" (page 313).

   b. Use the prismoidal formula and the diagram here to show that the volume of a triangular prism is $V = Bh$ where *B* is the area of the base and *h* is the height.

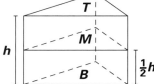

c. Examine the cylinder shown here.

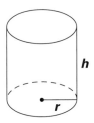

- What is the shape of any cross section of a cylinder (parallel to the base)?

- Use the prismoidal formula to show that the volume of a circular cylinder with radius r and height h is given by $V = \pi r^2 h$.

d. Examine the sphere shown at the right.

- What is the shape of the cross section at the middle? At the top? At the base (bottom)?

- Use the prismoidal formula to develop a formula for the volume of a sphere with radius r.

e. Examine the cone shown here. Use the prismoidal formula to help you discover a formula for the volume of a cone with base radius r and height h.

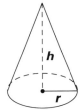

f. Locate an irregular shaped vase or bottle. Use the prismoidal formula to estimate the volume of the container. Check your estimate by filling the container with water, then pouring it into a measuring cup.

4. a. One large juice can has dimensions twice those of a smaller can. How do the volumes of the two cans compare?

b. One cereal box has dimensions 3 times those of another. How do the volumes of the two boxes compare?

c. If the dimensions of one prism are 5 times those of another, how do the volumes compare?

d. If the dimensions of one prism are k times those of another, how do the volumes compare?

5. a. The dimensions of a model of a building are one-hundredth of the dimensions of the actual building. How does the volume of the model compare to the volume of the actual building?

b. How does the surface area of the model compare to the surface area of the building?

3 *The Shapes of Plane Figures*

Space-shapes come in a wide variety of forms. Many of those forms are based on some very common shapes such as the rectangular prism, the pyramid, the cylinder, and the cone. All the faces of prisms and pyramids, as well as the bases of cylinders and cones are *plane-shapes*. The most common shape of a face is the *polygon*. In this lesson you will study the characteristics of polygons and explore how they are used in art, design, and other ways.

Think about this situation

Examine the portion of a floor tiling shown above.

a What is most striking about the pattern visually?

b What shapes make up the pattern?

c What symmetry is evident in the pattern?

d Some seams appear to be parallel. Why is this?

e Are there any gaps or overlaps in the tiling? Explain.

Investigation 3.1 Polygons and Their Properties

The word "polygon" comes from Greek words *poly* meaning "many" and *gon* meaning "angle." This is descriptive, but it describes shapes that are not polygons as well as those that are. It will be helpful to have a more precise definition of "polygon" before investigating properties of various polygons.

1. Shown below are twelve plane-shapes.

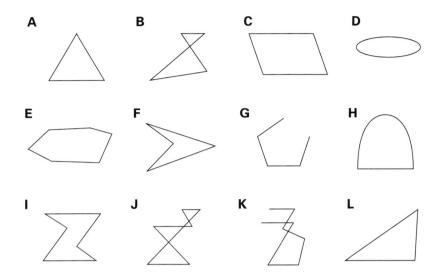

   a. Working individually, sort these shapes into groups of shapes that are "alike" in some manner.

   b. Share with your group the criteria you used to sort the twelve shapes.

   c. Choose another set of sorting criteria for sorting the shapes. Re-sort and describe the criteria you used.

   d. As a group, determine a criterion for sorting which would put all shapes except shapes D and H in one group.

   e. What criterion would put shapes A, B, C, E, F, I, J, and L (no others) into one group?

   f. What criterion would put shapes A, C, E, F, I, and L (no others) into one group?

   g. What criterion would put shapes A, C, E, and L (no others) into one group?

   h. What criterion would put shapes A and L in one group; B, C, F, and G in another group; and E, I, and J in a third group?

   i. What criterion would put shapes A, D, G, and H (no others) into one group?

   j. What criterion would put shapes A, C, and D (no others) into one group?

Your work in activity 1 suggests that there are many ways that plane-shapes can be grouped or classified. One commonly used classification puts *polygons* into one group and all other shapes into another group (non-polygons). The criterion you developed for part f above should have identified only shapes which are polygons.

2. Review the shapes that were grouped together in part f of activity 1.

    a. Are there shapes in that group that did not fit your idea of a polygon? If so, which ones?

    b. What is it about these shapes that made you think they were not polygons?

    c. Draw a shape, either a polygon or not a polygon. Trade shapes with a partner and have each person identify the shape as a polygon or not. Explain why that choice was made.

One special class of polygons commonly seen in architectural designs is the **quadrilaterals**, the four-sided polygons.

3. You are familiar with many quadrilaterals from your previous work in mathematics. The diagram at the right shows a general quadrilateral. It has no special properties; just four sides and four angles.

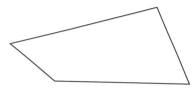

    a. You may recall that there are six special kinds of quadrilaterals. They are the *square, rectangle, parallelogram, rhombus, trapezoid,* and *kite.* Draw a sketch of each of these polygons.

    b. For each quadrilateral sketched in part a, list all the special properties you think it has. For example, are opposite sides parallel or equal in length? Are adjacent angles equal or supplementary (sum of their degree measures is 180)?

    c. Which of your shapes has the greatest number of special properties? Which has the least?

Checkpoint

    a Write a criterion (a definition) that will put all polygon shapes in one group and any other plane-shape in another group.

    b Write criteria you would use to categorize a quadrilateral as the following:

A kite	A trapezoid	A rhombus
A parallelogram	A rectangle	A square

    ✓ **Be prepared to compare your group's sorting criteria with those of other groups.**

On Your Own

Classify each statement as true or false. Give a justification for your conclusion.

a. Shape A is a polygon.

b. Shape B is a polygon.

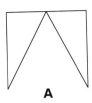

A

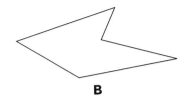

B

c. Every parallelogram is a rectangle.

d. Every rhombus is a kite.

e. Every trapezoid is a parallelogram.

A polygon with *n* angles and *n* sides is often called an *n-gon*. So another name for a quadrilateral is a *4-gon*. In the next activity you will explore connections between the number of sides of a polygon and the measures of its angles.

4. Carefully draw polygons having 4, 5, 6, 7, 8, 9, and 10 sides. Share the work in your group.

  a. Subdivide each polygon into *nonoverlapping* triangles by drawing line segments from one vertex to another. Try to make the *fewest* possible triangles in each polygon.

  – Record your results in a table like the one below. Compare the number of sides of a polygon and the number of triangles into which it can be subdivided.

Number of Sides	Number of Triangles
4	

  – Examine your table to find a pattern. Draw and test more polygons, if needed.

  – Suppose a polygon has *n* sides. Into how many nonoverlapping triangles can it be subdivided? Use the pattern you discovered in your table to write a rule (formula) relating the *number of sides n* to the *number of triangles T*.

b. Recall that the sum of the measures of the angles of a triangle is 180 degrees.

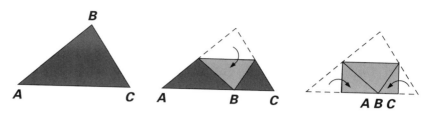

Use this fact to find the sum of the measures of the angles of each polygon listed in your table. Add a column "Angle Sum" to your table and record your results.

- Write a rule relating the number of sides of an *n*-gon to the sum of the measures of its angles.

- Use your rule to predict the sum of the measures of the angles of a 12-gon. Check your prediction with a sketch.

c. Can the (*number of sides, angle sum*) data be modeled well with a line? If so, what is the slope and what does it mean in terms of the variables? Does the *y*-intercept make sense? Why or why not?

5. Now investigate how to predict the measure of one angle of a **regular polygon**. In a regular polygon, all angles are the same size and all sides are the same length.

a. Determine the measure of one angle of a regular hexagon. Apply your procedure to a regular 10-gon.

b. Write a rule relating the *number of sides n* to the *measure of an angle A* of a regular *n*-gon.

6. Polygons and other plane shapes also may have other properties. For example, look at your grouping rules for parts i and j of activity 1, page 384.

a. Shapes A, D, G, and H could be grouped together because they each have **reflection** or **line symmetry**. On a copy of each shape, draw a line through it so that one half is the reflection of the other.

b. Shapes A, C, and D could be grouped together because they have **rotational symmetry**. This is also called **turn symmetry** because the amount of rotation is given as an angle in degrees. Locate the center of each shape and determine through what angles it can be turned so that it coincides with itself.

c. Which of the following figures have reflection (line) symmetry?

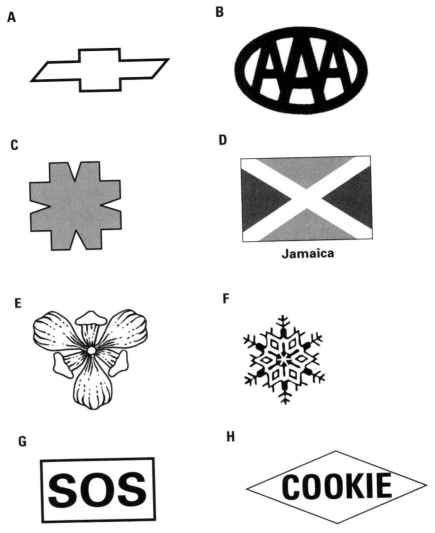

A

B

C

D

Jamaica

E

F

G

SOS

H

COOKIE

d. Which of the figures in part c have rotational (turn) symmetry? Estimate the angles through which each can be turned to coincide with itself.

e. In parts c and d, how did you determine which figures had reflection or rotational symmetry?

f. Which of the quadrilaterals that you drew in activity 3 (page 385) have reflection (line) symmetry? Which have rotational (turn) symmetry?

Checkpoint

a Does the logo shown at the right have reflection or rotational symmetry? If so, trace the logo and sketch lines of symmetry or give angles of rotation.

b Describe what is meant by reflection or line symmetry.

c Describe what is meant by rotational or turn symmetry.

d The corner angles of this logo are the same size. Describe how you would determine the measure of any one of these angles without measuring.

✓ *Be prepared to share your group's responses with the entire class.*

On Your Own

The plane-shape depicted is a drawing of a stop sign (without the word "stop").

a. Is it a polygon? Explain.

b. What is the *sum* of the measures of its angles?

c. Using what you believe to be true about the shape of stop signs, determine the measure of *each* of its angles.

d. What symmetry, if any, does the shape have?

e. Identify another traffic sign that is in the shape of a regular polygon. Describe the shape and its symmetry.

Investigation 3.2 Patterns with Polygons

In a regular polygon all sides are the same length and all angles are the same size. Because of these characteristics, regular polygons have many useful applications. Prism-like packages are often designed with regular polygons as bases. If you think about tiled walls or floors you have seen, it is likely they were tiled with regular polygon-shaped tiles.

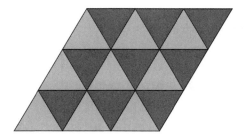
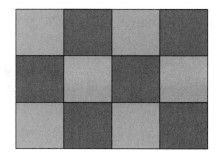

1. The figures above show portions of **tilings** of equilateral triangles and squares. The tilings are made of repeated copies of a shape placed edge-to-edge. In this way, the tilings completely cover a region without overlaps or gaps.

   a. Assume that the tilings are extended indefinitely in all directions to cover the plane. Describe the symmetries of each tiling.

   b. For each tiling:

   – What is the total measure of the angles at a common vertex?

   – What is the measure of each angle at a common vertex?

   c. Using the tiling with equilateral triangles, identify other common polygons formed by two or more triangles. Sketch each and show the equilateral triangles that form the shape.

2. You have seen that equilateral triangular regions tile a plane. In this activity you will explore other kinds of triangular regions that can be used as tiles.

   a. Each member of your group should cut from poster board a small triangle that is *not* equilateral. Each member's triangle should have a shape different from the other members' triangles. Individually, explore whether a tiling of a plane can be made by using repeated tracings of your triangular region. Draw and compare sketches of the tilings you made.

   b. Can more than one tiling pattern be made by using copies of one triangular shape? If so, illustrate with sketches.

   c. Do you think any triangular shape could be used to tile a plane? Explain your reasoning.

3. Square regions also can tile a plane. In this activity, you will explore other quadrilaterals that can be used to make a tiling.

   a. Each member of your group should cut a non-square quadrilateral from poster board. Again, each of the quadrilaterals should be shaped differently. Individually, investigate whether a tiling of a plane can be made. Draw sketches of the tilings you made.

b. For those quadrilaterals that tile, can more than one tiling pattern be made using the same shape? If so, illustrate and explain.

c. Make a conjecture about which quadrilaterals can be used to tile a plane.

4. You have seen two regular polygons which tile the plane. Now explore other regular polygons that could be used to make a tiling.

a. Does a regular pentagon tile the plane? Explain your reasoning.

b. Does a regular hexagon tile the plane? Explain.

c. Will any regular polygon of more than 6 sides tile the plane? Provide an argument supporting your view.

Checkpoint

a Write a summarizing statement describing which triangles and which quadrilaterals tile the plane.

b Which regular polygons tile the plane? Justify your choices.

✓ *Be prepared to share your group's conclusions and thinking with the entire class.*

On Your Own

Using a copy of the figure at the right, find a pentagon in the figure that will tile the plane. Shade it. Show as many different tiling patterns for your pentagon as you can.

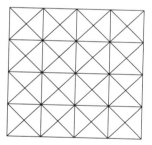

5. Tilings which use only one type of shape are called **pure tessellations.** Those that use more than one type of shape are called **semi-pure tessellations.** Two examples are shown at the top of the following page. The pattern on the left is from a Persian porcelain painting. The pattern on the right is from the Taj Mahal mausoleum in India.

a. Examine carefully each of these patterns. How many different shapes are used in the tessellation on the left? How many different shapes are used in the pattern on the right?

b. Examine the semi-pure tessellation shown here.

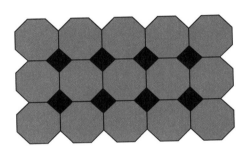

  – Use angle measure to explain
    why the polygons will fit to-
    gether with no overlaps or
    gaps.

  – At each vertex, is there the
    same combination and order
    of polygons?

c. In some semi-pure tessellations of regular polygons, at each vertex there is the same arrangement of polygons. These tilings are called **semi-regular tessellations**. Test whether a regular hexagon, two squares, and an equilateral triangle can be used to make a semi-regular tessellation. If possible, draw a sketch of the tessellation.

d. Semi-regular tessellations are coded by listing the number of sides of the polygons at each vertex. The numbers are arranged in order with the smallest number first. The tessellation in part b is 4, 8, 8. Use this code to describe:

  – the tessellation of equilateral triangles and regular hexagons at the beginning of this lesson (page 383);

  – the tessellation you drew in part c;

  – each of the three possible pure edge-to-edge tessellations of regular polygons.

A **net** is a two-dimensional pattern which can be folded to form a three-dimensional shape. Buckminster Fuller, inventor of the geodesic dome (see Extending task 4 on page 353), created a net for a "globe" of the earth. In the modified version below, each equilateral triangle contains an equal amount of the earth's surface area.

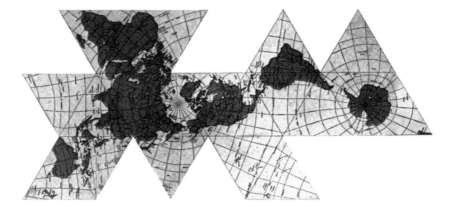

6. a. Examine the three nets shown below. Which of these nets can be folded to make a cube?

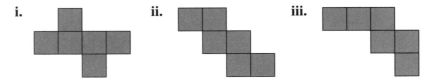

b. Make a new net of your own that can be folded to make a cube.

c. Which die could be formed from the net on the left?

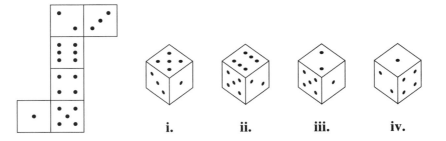

The equilateral triangle is more versatile than the square when it comes to making nets for space-shapes. You can make three different space-shapes using nets of only equilateral triangles attached to each other. Use copies of congruent equilateral triangles to complete the next activity.

7. a. Attach four equilateral triangles edge-to-edge. What space-shapes can you form by folding your pattern? What *complete* (with no open faces) space-shapes can you form? Sketch the net and the complete space-shape formed. Find another pattern of the four triangles that can be folded into the same shape. Sketch your net. You have made a **tetrahedron.**

b. Now try your hand at making a space-shape with 8 equilateral triangular faces. Draw a net of eight equilateral triangles that will fold into a space-shape. Sketch the net and the space-shape. You have made an **octahedron.**

c. Examine the net of a "globe" shown on the previous page.

- How many equilateral triangles are in this net?

- When the net is folded to form the "globe," how many triangles are at each vertex?

- Fuller's globe shown at the right is an example of a space-shape called an **icosahedron.** Make an icosahedron model.

Checkpoint

a Sketch a net of squares that can be folded into an open-top box.

b How could you modify your net in part a so that it could be folded into a model of a house with a peaked roof?

c Compare the sum of angle measures at a common vertex of a tiling with those of a net.

✓ *Be prepared to share your sketches, findings, and reasoning with the class.*

On Your Own

A cereal box is shown at the left. Draw a net for a model of it. Cut out your net and verify that it can be folded into a model of the box.

Modeling Organizing Reflecting Extending

Modeling

1. Examine the picture at the right of a Native American rug.

   a. Are there any designs in this rug that have rotational symmetry? Sketch each design and describe the angles through which it can be turned.

   b. Are there any designs in this rug that have line symmetry? Sketch each design and the lines of symmetry.

   c. Are there any designs which have both rotational and line symmetry? If so, identify them. Where is the center of rotation in relation to the lines of symmetry?

2. Polygons and symmetry are an important part of the arts and crafts of many cultures.

   a. The design of the quilt below is called "Star of Bethlehem". What rotational symmetry do you see in the fundamental "stars"? List the degree measure of each turn that will rotate the shape onto itself.

   b. What line symmetry do you see in the "stars"? Sketch to illustrate.

   c. Does the quilt as a whole have rotational or line symmetry? Describe each symmetry you find.

3. This two-person game can be played on any regular polygon. To play, place a penny on each vertex of the polygon. Take turns removing one or two pennies from adjacent vertices. The player who picks up the last coin is the winner.

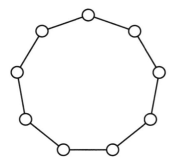

   a. Suppose the game is played on a 9-sided polygon as shown at the left. Try to find a strategy using symmetry that will permit the second player to win always. Write a description of your strategy.

   b. Will the strategy you found work if the game is played on any polygon with an odd number of vertices? Explain your reasoning.

   c. Suppose the game is played on a polygon with an even number of vertices, say an octagon. Try to find a strategy that will guarantee that the second player still can win always. Write a description of this strategy.

4. a. Objects in nature are often symmetric in form. The shapes below are single-celled sea plants called *diatoms*.

   – Identify all of the symmetries of these diatoms.

   – For those with reflection symmetry, sketch the shape and show the lines of symmetry.

   – For those with rotational symmetry, describe the angles of rotation.

A 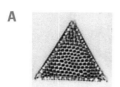   B   C   D

   b. Identify all of the symmetries of the two flowers shown below.

   – If the flower has line symmetry, sketch the shape and draw the lines of symmetry.

   – If the flower has rotational symmetry, describe the angles of rotation.

A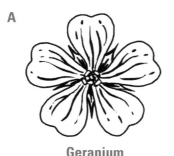

Geranium

B

Periwinkle

c. It has been said that no two snowflakes are identical.

    – Identify the symmetries of the snowflakes below.

    – In terms of their symmetry, how are the snowflakes alike?

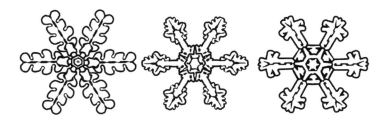

5. Great Lakes Packaging manufactures boxes for many different companies. Shown at the right is the net for one type of box manufactured for a candy company.

a. Sketch the box.

b. Sketch two other possible nets that could be used to manufacture the same box.

c. Find the volume of the box.

d. Find the surface area of the box.

e. Does the box have any symmetries? If so, explain how the symmetries are related to the symmetries of its faces.

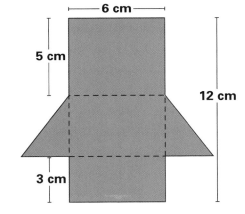

O*rganizing*

1. In Investigation 3.1, Ellen invented the rule $A = \frac{(n-2)180}{n}$ to predict the measure A of one angle of a regular n-gon.

a. Do you think Ellen's rule is correct? Explain your reasoning.

b. As the number of sides of a regular polygon increases, how does the measure of one of its angles change? Is the rate of change constant? Explain.

c. Use Ellen's rule to predict the measure of one angle of a regular 20-gon. Could a tessellation be made of regular 20-gons? Explain your reasoning.

    d. When will the measure of each angle of a regular polygon be a whole number?

    e. Use your calculator or computer software to produce a table of values for angle measures of various regular polygons. Use your table to help explain why only regular polygons of 3, 4, or 6 sides will tile a plane.

2. a. Locate any lines of symmetry for the two histograms below.

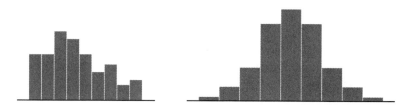

    b. On each histogram, estimate the location of the median and mean.

    c. If a distribution is symmetric, what can you conclude about its median and mean? Explain your reasoning.

    d. If a distribution is symmetric, what, if anything, can you conclude about its mode? Explain your reasoning.

3. Shown below are graphs of various functions. The scale on the axes is 1.

    a. For each graph, locate any line of symmetry. Write the equation of the symmetry line.

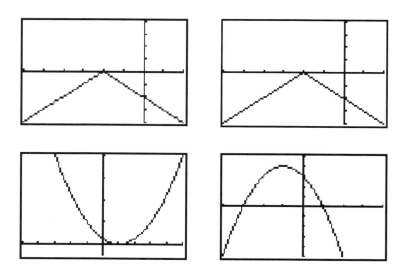

b. Suppose you have a graph and its line of symmetry is the *y*-axis. If one point on the graph has coordinates (-8, -23), what is the *y*-coordinate of the point on the graph with *x*-coordinate 8? Explain your reasoning.

4. In general, how many lines of symmetry does a regular *n*-gon have? How many rotational symmetries?

5. a. Describe all the line and rotational symmetries of a circle as completely as possible.

b. If you are given a circle, how can you find its center? Describe as many different ways as you can.

c. How can you use a method for finding the center of a circle to help you find the point of rotation for a shape that has rotational symmetry?

6. The following two figures come from a branch of mathematics called *fractal geometry*. Describe all the line and rotational symmetries of each figure as completely as you can.

Tree Curve   **Dragon Curve**

Reflecting

1. Thumb through the yellow pages of a phone directory noting the shape of company logos. Why do you think so many of the logo designs are symmetric?

2. Do you find it easier to recognize line symmetry or rotational symmetry in a shape? What do you think might explain this fact?

3. Cross-cultural studies suggest that symmetry is a fundamental idea that all people use to help understand, remember, compare, and reproduce forms. However, symmetry preferences have been found across cultures. One study found that symmetry about a vertical line was easier to recognize than symmetry about a horizontal line. The study also found that symmetry about a diagonal line was the most difficult to detect.

   Source: Palmer, S.E. and K. Henenway. 1978. Orientation and symmetry: effects of multiple, rotational, and near symmetries. *Journal of Experimental Psychology* 4(4): 691–702.

   a. Would the findings of the study apply to the way in which you perceive line symmetry?

   b. Describe a simple experiment that you could conduct to test these findings.

4. Tiling patterns often are found on floors and walls. What tiling patterns are most common in homes, schools, and shopping malls? What might explain this?

5. In Investigation 3.2 you examined shapes that tessellate a plane—a flat surface. Examine at least three of the following balls: baseball, softball, basketball, tennis ball, volleyball, and soccer ball.

   a. Is it possible to tessellate a sphere?

   b. If so, is the tessellation pure or semi-pure? Is it semi-regular?

   c. Find a National Geographic magazine with a world map in it. How do the map-makers use the idea of tessellations in their production of world maps reproduced on a flat surface?

Extending

1. **a.** Using a computer drawing utility or a straight edge and compass, design a simple quilt pattern. Try to use polygonal shapes which were not used in the designs shown in this lesson.

   b. Print or draw your pattern and indicate all symmetry lines of the design.

2. **a.** How is a polygon with rotational symmetry related to a circle?

   b. How could you use a circle to draw a 10-sided polygon with equal length sides? Try it. Does the polygon have rotational symmetry? If so, through what angles can it be turned? Where is the center?

3. Find as many nets of six squares as you can that will fold to make a cube. Sketch each. (**Hint:** There are more than ten!)

4. The space-shape shown here is a **dodeca-hedron**. It is made of 12 regular pentagons.

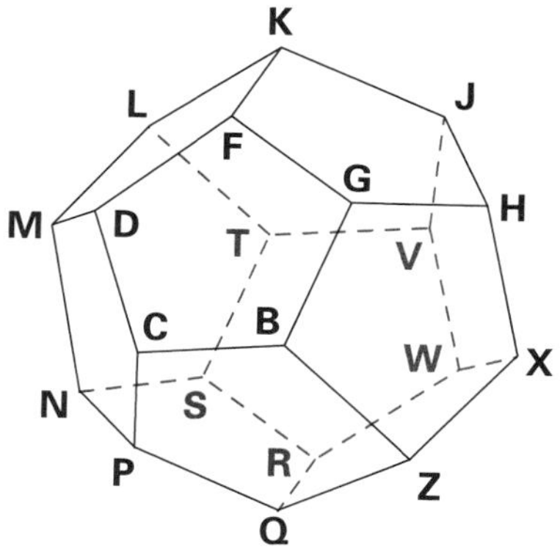

   a. Use a net of pentagons to make a dodeca-hedron shell.

   b. Make a die by numbering the faces.

   c. Toss the die 100 times. Record the number of times each face lands up.

   d. Make a histogram of your data in part c. What do you observe?

   e. Repeat parts a through d for a dodecahedral die for which the opposite faces add to 13. Compare your histograms.

5. The **diagonals** of a polygon are segments connecting pairs of vertices which are not endpoints of the same side.

   a. Examine the diagonals of each type of quadrilateral. For which quadrilaterals are the diagonals lines of symmetry?

   b. Develop a formula for the number of diagonals in any n-gon.

6. A *kapa pohopoho* is a Hawaiian quilt made from twelve or more unique designs. The original designs exhibit reflection and rotational symmetry. Each design is cut from one piece of fabric and sewn onto a square piece of background fabric. The following steps illustrate one way to create a Hawaiian quilt design.

   a. Fold a piece of square paper in half by bringing the bottom side up to meet the top. Fold this half portion into a square. Note which corner of the new square is the center of the original square. Fold along the diagonal that has this corner as one vertex. You now should have a right triangle with one end of the hypotenuse at the center of the original square. The other end is at the point where the four corners of the original square meet. Sketch a design along the leg of the right triangle adjacent to the four corners of the original square. Cut along your design.

   b. Unfold your pattern. If the design has reflection symmetry, sketch in the lines of symmetry. If the design has rotational symmetry, identify the center and angles of rotation.

   c. If you open up the folded square before making any cuts, what lines should your folds represent? (You can repeat part a to check.)

   d. How does your design compare with those of your classmates?

   e. What would happen if you started with a circle or an equilateral triangle instead of a square? Can you make designs with only one line of symmetry? With two lines? With more than two lines? Explain your reasoning.

Investigation 3.3 Symmetry Patterns in Strips

Many plane-shapes and space-shapes have symmetry, either about a line, a point, or a plane. Artists have used these types of symmetry for centuries. For example, from earliest history, space-shapes often have been decorated with *strip patterns*. Imagine slicing the Native American jar at the right by a symmetry plane and then "flattening out" the shape.

1. **a.** Draw what you think would be the strip pattern along the center of the plane-shape.

   b. What is it about the pattern that permitted you to draw the full pattern without seeing the back of the jar?

2. Shown below are some general strip patterns commonly used for decorative art. Imagine that each strip pattern extends indefinitely to the right and to the left.

   a. Examine each pattern and make a sketch of the next two shapes to the right in the pattern.

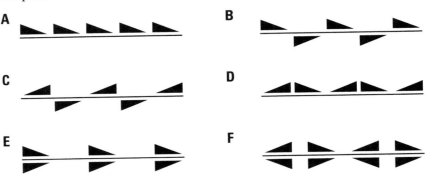

   b. Examine the design symmetries of the two bracelet patterns below. Match each pattern with the strip pattern in part a which it most resembles.

A

B

c. Each of the strip patterns in parts a and b exhibit slide or *translational symmetry*. What are two essential characteristics of the patterns that ensure translational symmetry?

d. Write a definition of translational symmetry for strip patterns. Compare your group's definition with that of other groups. Work out any differences.

3. The portions of the strip patterns below came from artwork on the pottery of San Ildefonso Pueblo, New Mexico.

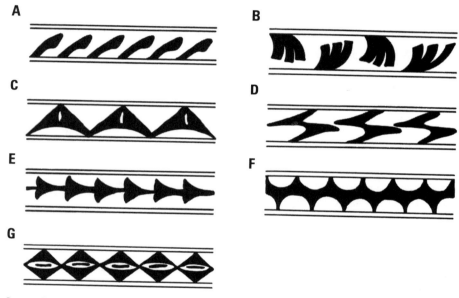

Source: Crowe, D.W. and D.K. Washburn. "Groups and Geometry in the Ceramic Art of San Ildefonso." *Algebras, Groups and Geometries* 2, no. 3 (September 1985): 263–277.

a. Confirm that each pattern has translational symmetry.

b. Examine each strip for reflection and rotational symmetries. If a strip has such a symmetry, it appears the same before and after it is reflected across a line or rotated about a point. Systematically record your results.

c. Look again at strip pattern B. It has neither rotational nor reflection symmetry. However, consider the following *transformation*:

Slide the strip to the right so the first "shape" is above the second "shape." Now reflect the entire strip over the horizontal line through the middle of the strip.

Does the pattern of the strip transform onto itself?

d. Make a sketch of your footprints as they would appear if you walked a straight line in snow or damp sand. How is your footprint strip pattern related to the transformation described in part c?

e. Using the shape at the right, draw a strip pattern that has the type of symmetry described in part c.

The tranformation described in part c of activity 3 is called a **glide reflection** because you glide (translate) and reflect.

4. Re-examine the 7 strip designs of the San Ildefonso Pueblo. Do any other of these patterns have glide reflection symmetry? If so, record it with your other results from part b of activity 3.

Checkpoint

> **ⓐ** What symmetries, other than translational symmetry, are evident in some strip patterns?
>
> **ⓑ** Write a description of a glide reflection.
>
> ✓ *Be prepared to share and explain your group's descriptions.*

On Your Own

Design an interesting strip pattern that has reflection symmetry about a horizontal line and translational symmetry.

Investigation (3.4) Symmetry Patterns in Planes

Strip patterns often form a decorative border for other designs that cover part of a plane. Plane tiling patterns are far more numerous than strip designs. They can be found in the floor coverings, ceramic tile work, and textiles of many cultures. The walls and floors of the Alhambra, a thirteenth-century Moorish palace in Granada, Spain, contain some of the finest early examples of this kind of mathematical art. Note the variety of their patterns in the following photo.

Recently, the tessellation artwork of the Dutch artist, M.C. Escher, has become very popular. Escher was deeply influenced by the work of the ancient Moors. Examine the following Escher pattern.

1. As a class, imagine that this pattern is extended indefinitely to cover the plane.

   a. Describe all translational symmetries that you see.

   b. Does the pattern have reflection or rotational symmetries? If so, describe them.

   c. Does the pattern have glide reflection symmetry? If so, describe them.

   d. On what type of polygon do you think this pattern is based?

Tessellations such as that above are based on polygon tilings of the plane. The polygon is modified carefully so that the new shape will tile the plane when certain transformations are applied. Rotations and translations are two of the most common transformations. Escher was a master at these modifications.

Knowing which polygonal regions tile is one important part of understanding Escher-like tilings. Another important aspect is understanding which transformations will take an individual tile into another tile within the entire tiling pattern. Applying these ideas leads to beautiful patterns.

2. A tiling based on squares is shown in the figure here. Adjacent squares have a different color. Think of the square labeled "0" as the beginning tile. How many squares surround square 0?

		1	2	3	
		8	0	4	
		7	6	5	

a. Which transformations (reflection, rotation, translation, or glide reflection) will move square 0 to a surrounding square of the *same* color? Illustrate with diagrams.

b. Which transformations will move square 0 to a surrounding square of the *other* color? Illustrate with diagrams.

c. If *translation* is the only motion permitted, can square 0 be translated to each of squares 1–8? On a copy of the tiling, represent each such translation by drawing an arrow which shows its direction and how far square 0 must be translated.

d. Using only *rotation* about a vertex of square 0, can square 0 be moved onto each of squares 1–8? Describe each such rotation on the copy of the tiling by marking its center and giving its angle. If some squares can be reached in more than one way, describe each way.

Escher used the square tiling and knowledge of the translations that move square 0 to the adjacent positions to help him design some of his art. In the remainder of this investigation, you will explore some of the mathematics behind Escher's art.

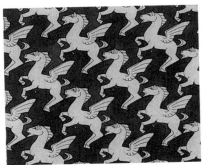

3. If you were to replace square 0 with the shape at the right, could you make a tiling? If so, sketch the resulting pattern on a sheet of paper.

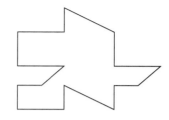

a. The shape you used is a modification of square 0. Describe as accurately as you can how you think square 0 was modified to obtain this shape.

b. How do the areas of square 0 and the modified shape compare?

The above shape, like most of Escher's shapes, is an example of an **asymmetric** shape that tiles the plane. It was created by modifying a symmetric shape, the square, that also tiled. This technique can be used to create an unlimited number of interesting tessellations.

4. Working alone, modify the sides of square 0 to create a shape that is asymmetric and that will tile the plane by translation to the 8 adjacent positions. Sketch or make a computer-generated nine-square version of your tessellation. Compare your tessellation with those of the other members of your group.

Checkpoint

ⓐ Suppose that by translation alone, you create a tessellation of an asymmetric shape based on a square.

– How must the "sides" of the shape be related?

– How are the areas of the original square and the transformed asymmetric shape related? Why?

ⓑ Describe an algorithm for transforming any parallelogram shape into an Escher-like shape that will tile the plane.

✓ *Be prepared to discuss your group's ideas with the class.*

On Your Own

Recall that a rhombus is a parallelogram, all of whose sides are the same length. Can a rhombus be made into an Escher-like asymmetrical tile that will tessellate by translation alone? Explain and illustrate your answer.

Modeling Organizing Reflecting Extending

Modeling

1. Archeologists and anthropologists use symmetry of designs to study human cultures. The table below gives frequency of strip designs on a sampling of pottery from two cultures on two different continents: the Mesa Verde (U.S.A.) and the Begho (Ghana, Africa).

Strip Pattern Symmetry Type	Mesa Verde		Begho	
	Number of Examples	Percentage of Total	Number of Examples	Percentage of Total
Translation Symmetry Only	7		4	
Horizontal Line Symmetry	5		9	
Vertical Line Symmetry	12		22	
180° Rotational Symmetry	93		19	
Glide Reflection Symmetry	11		2	
Glide Reflection and Vertical Line Symmetry	27		9	
Both Horizontal and Vertical Line Symmetry	19		165	
Total	174		230	

Source: Washburn, Dorothy K. and Donald W. Crowe. *Theory and Practice of Plane Pattern Analysis.* Seattle: University of Washington Press, 1988.

a. Fill in the two "percentage of total" columns.

b. Which types of symmetry patterns appear to be preferred by the Mesa Verde? By the Begho?

c. Examine the strips shown below. In which place is each strip more likely to have been found? Use the data from the table to explain your answer.

i.    ii.    iii.

2. Examine the eighteenth-century embroidered-cloth strip patterns of Kuba, Zaire shown below.

a. Identify those patterns that exhibit reflection symmetry about a vertical line.

b. Identify those patterns that exhibit reflection symmetry about a horizontal line.

c. Identify those patterns that exhibit rotational symmetry.

d. Identify those patterns that exhibit glide reflection symmetry.

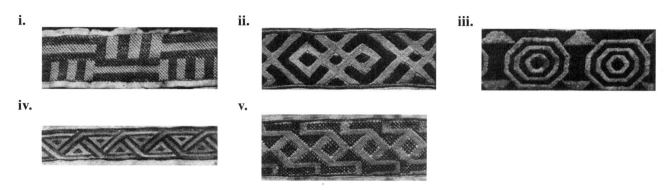

3. The fourteen Japanese border designs pictured below seem to have great variability. Sort them into groups. Describe the characteristics used to determine membership in the groups you create.

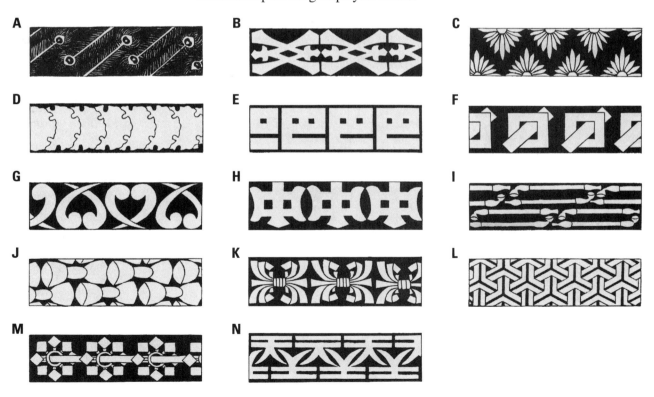

4. Shown here is an example of a common first step used to create a tessellation. This example could become the "flying-horse" tessellation shown on page 406.

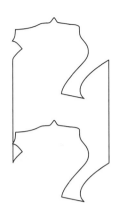

a. Trace the modified square. Complete the modification to obtain the horse shape.

b. Test by repeated tracings that the shape will tessellate. If necessary, make further adjustments for a good fit.

c. What kinds of symmetry does your tessellation have?

5. Create an Escher-like tessellation of your own by modifying a square so that it will tessellate the plane by translation alone. Try to construct your shape so that it can be enhanced to look like a common object or animal. (You may use both curved and straight segments.)

Organizing

1. For each of the following descriptions, construct a strip pattern that has translational symmetry and the given symmetry or symmetries. Use a computer drawing utility if it is available.

   a. vertical line symmetry   b. horizontal line symmetry
   c. 180° rotational symmetry   d. horizontal and vertical line symmetry
   e. glide reflection symmetry   f. glide reflection and vertical line symmetry

Source: Washburn, D. and D. Crowe. *Symmetries of Culture.* Seattle: Washington University Press, 1988.

2. Use the chart below to help organize your thinking about classifying strip patterns.

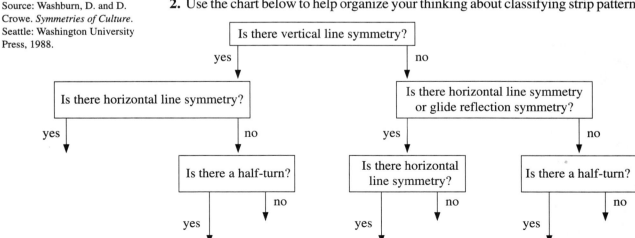

a. Make or obtain an enlarged copy of this chart. For each of the triangle strip patterns in activity 2 of Investigation 3.3, sketch the pattern at the point on the chart that describes its characteristics.

b. The chart suggests that there are 7 different possible one-color strip patterns. Which pattern was not included in activity 2? Draw an example of the missing strip pattern at the appropriate place on the chart.

3. Suppose the following graphs extend indefinitely in the pattern illustrated. Which have translational symmetry? For those that do, identify any other symmetries of the graph.

a.

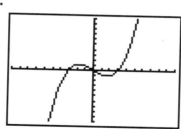

b.

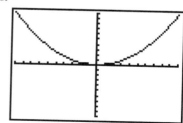

c.

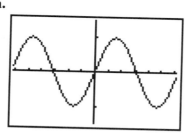

d.

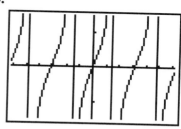

4. Suppose each polygon below is modified as shown.

a. Explain why you think the shape will or will not tessellate the plane.

b. If the shape will tessellate, describe the symmetries, if any, of the resulting tessellation.

A   **B**   **C**   **D**

Reflecting

1. Juan has been trying to make a strip pattern which has both horizontal and vertical symmetry, but no 180° rotational symmetry. He asks your advice. What do you suggest and why?

2. The chart in Organizing task 2 provides a systematic way of analyzing strip patterns. On the basis of the chart, why can you conclude there are exactly 7 essentially different strip patterns?

3. In your home or neighborhood, find examples of strip patterns. Investigate why the patterns were chosen or if the patterns have special meaning. Make a sketch of each design. Describe the symmetries evident in the designs.

4. Dorothy Washburn is an archeologist at the University of Rochester. She discovered that the pattern found in Escher's tessellation of lizards is strikingly similar to that found in a Fiji basket lid and an Egyptian wall mosaic. Why do you think patterns of this sort are found in different cultures?

5. In 1970, M.C. Escher wrote: "Although I am absolutely innocent of training or knowledge in the exact sciences, I often seem to have more in common with mathematicians than with my fellow artists."

   Source: Escher, M.C. *The Graphic Work of M.C. Escher*, trans. John E. Brigham. New York: Ballantine Books, 1971.

   a. What is it about mathematics, geometry in particular, that permits people with little mathematical training to discover, on their own, many of its basic principles?

   b. Based on what you have seen of Escher's work, why do you think he felt as he did about himself?

Extending

1. a. Investigate how the decimal representation of numbers between 0 and 1 might be related to strip patterns. Identify any characteristics of the numbers that make the analogy fail.

   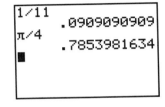

   b. What would be the fundamental unit for the strip pattern for $\frac{2}{11}$? For $\frac{1}{13}$? For $\frac{1}{3}$?

   c. What would you say about the strip pattern representation of $\frac{1}{2}$?

2. The strip patterns you have investigated are often identified with several coding schemes. The following one seems useful. It is made up of 3 characters in order. The first character is **m** if there is a vertical reflection and **1** (one) if there is none; the second character is **m** if there is a horizontal reflection, **a** if there is a glide reflection, and **1** if there is neither; the third character is **2** if there is 180° rotational symmetry and **1** otherwise.

   a. Assign a symbol to each of the 7 San Ildefonso Pueblo designs studied in activity 3 of Investigation 3.3.

   b. Assign a symbol to each of the Japanese border patterns in task 3 of the Modeling section.

   c. Assign a symbol to each of the strip patterns shown below.

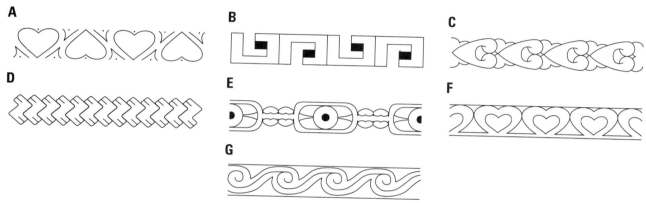

3. Shown here and on the following page are two sketches that M.C. Escher used in his lectures about ways to regularly fill or divide the plane. Each of these patterns is based on a square. Where are the vertices of the squares located?

   a. In this first display, what transformations will move a tile of one color onto a tile of the same color?

   b. What transformations will move a tile of one color onto a tile of the other color?

   c. Make your own tile with characteristics similar to those found in this first display. Use it to make a tiling of the plane.

verschuiving en assen.

d. In this second display, what transformations will move a tile of one color onto a tile of the same color?

e. What transformations will move a tile of one color onto a tile of the other color?

f. Make a personal tile with characteristics similar to those found in this second display. Use it to make a tiling of the plane.

verschuiving en glijspiegeling.

4. The Escher tessellation at the right is based on a regular hexagon.

a. What characteristic of the tessellation helps you locate each vertex of the hexagon?

b. Draw a regular hexagon on poster board. Modify it to make an Escher-like shape. Describe the modifications which you made. Show by repeated tracings of the shape that it will cover the plane.

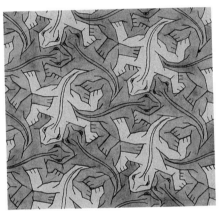

5. Study this tessellation of light and dark-colored lizards.

a. What is the fundamental polygonal shape on which this tessellation is based? Justify your choice and discuss it with a classmate.

b. Make a poster board model of the polygon on which the tessellation is based. Show the modifications needed to make the shape used in the design.

c. Compare the areas of the polygon and the lizard tiles.

d. What transformation will move a light-colored lizard with its head facing upward to

- a light-colored lizard with its head pointing down?
- a dark-colored lizard with its head toward the right?
- a dark-colored lizard with its head toward the left?

4 *Looking Back*

In this chapter, you saw how space-shapes and plane-shapes are related. You also saw how they are constructed and visualized, and how they may be drawn in two dimensions. You learned ways to measure them and what sorts of symmetry they have. You even saw how they may be used in art and design to make our lives more productive and enjoyable, both visually and physically. The landscape architects who designed this mall garden area made extensive and integrated use of these fundamental ideas of geometry.

This final lesson of the chapter gives you the opportunity to pull together and apply what you have learned. You will use your visualization skills and knowledge of shapes, symmetry, tessellations, and measurement in new situations.

1. Shown below is a net for a decorative box. Some of its dimensions are given.

10 cm

5 cm

4 cm

    a. Name the space-shape for which this is a net.

    b. Make a paper model of the space-shape.

    c. Sketch the space-shape showing its hidden edges. Give the lengths of each edge.

    d. Describe any planes of symmetry for the space-shape.

    e. Draw and name each face of the space-shape.

    f. Describe all symmetries for each face.

    g. Find the surface area and the volume of the space-shape. How is the surface area related to the area of the net?

    h. Will a pen 11 cm long fit in the bottom of the box? Explain why or why not in at least two different ways.

    i. Estimate the length of the longest pencil that will fit inside the box. Illustrate and explain how you found your answer.

    j. Draw a different net for the same space-shape.

2. As an art project, Tmeeka decided to make a decorative baby quilt for her newborn sister Kenya. She chose the quadrilateral below and modified it as shown. Her completed pattern is shown next to the fundamental tile.

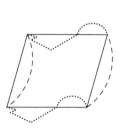

    a. Does this quadrilateral have a special name? If so, give it; if not, explain.

    b. Describe how Tmeeka modified the sides of the quadrilateral to make the fundamental tile. What transformations did she use?

    c. Use the geometric ideas and language developed in this chapter to describe how Tmeeka made the quilt pattern.

    d. Assuming the pattern continues in all directions, describe all the symmetries you can find.

e. Consider only the bottom row of shapes. Does this row form a strip pattern? If so, describe its symmetries including any centers of rotation and any lines of reflection.

f. Create a strip pattern with both horizontal and vertical line symmetry that could be used as a border for Tmeeka's quilt. Describe all symmetries in your strip pattern.

Checkpoint

In this chapter, you have developed ways for making sense of situations involving shapes and spatial relationships.

ⓐ Compare and contrast prisms, pyramids, cylinders, and cones.

ⓑ Compare and contrast the six special quadrilaterals.

ⓒ For each shape in parts a and b, describe a real-life application of that shape. What properties of the shape contribute to its usefulness?

ⓓ Describe a variety of ways you can represent (draw or construct) space-shapes.

ⓔ Pose a problem situation which requires use of cubic, square, and linear units of measure. Describe how you would solve it.

ⓕ Summarize what you know about how to make a strip pattern or tiling.

✓ *Be prepared to share your descriptions with the entire class.*

Chapter **6** *Exponential Models*

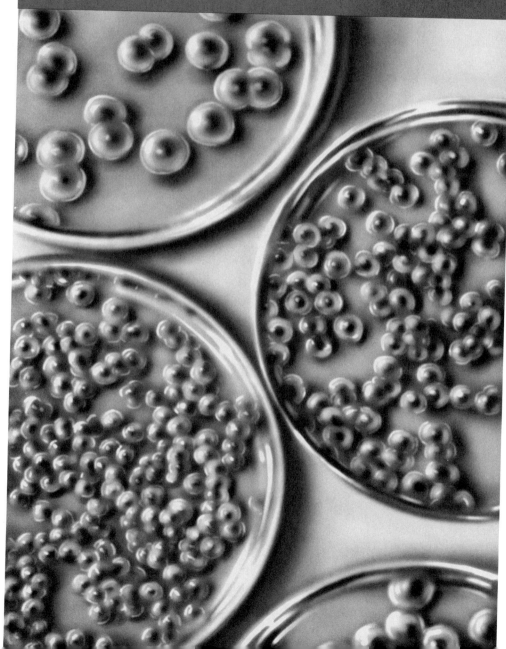

1 *Exponential Growth*

News stories spread rapidly in modern society. With broadcasts over television and radio, millions of people hear about important events within hours. The major television and radio news networks try hard to report only stories that they know are true. But quite often, rumors get started and spread around a community by word of mouth alone.

Suppose that to study the spread of information through rumors, two students started this rumor at 5 PM one evening:

Because of the threat of a huge snowstorm, there will be no school tomorrow and probably for the rest of the week.

The next day, they surveyed students at the school to find out how many heard the rumor and when they heard it. How fast do you think this rumor would spread?

Think about this situation

The graphs at the right show three possible patterns in the rate at which the school-closing rumor could spread.

a How would you describe the rate of rumor spread in the case of each graph?

b Which pattern of spread is most likely if the students plant the story on the 5 o'clock television or radio news? Explain your reasoning.

c Which pattern of spread is most likely if the rumor spreads only by word of mouth around the community? Why?

In many problems, key variables are related by linear models. But there are many other important situations in which variables are related by nonlinear patterns. Some examples include spread of information and disease, change in populations, pollution, temperature, bank savings, drugs in the bloodstream, and radioactivity. These problems often require mathematical models with graphs that are curves. Equations for the models use forms other than the familiar $y = a + bx$. In this chapter you will learn to use the family of nonlinear models that describes *exponential* patterns of change.

Investigation 1.1 Have You Heard About ... ?

Some organizations need to spread accurate information to many people quickly. One way to do this efficiently is by a telephone calling tree. For example:

> The Silver Spring Soccer Club has boys and girls from about 750 families who play soccer each Saturday in the fall. When it is rainy, everyone wants to know if the games are canceled. The club president makes a decision and then calls two families. Each of them calls two more families. Each of those families calls two more families, and so on.

This calling pattern can be represented by a **tree graph** that starts like this:

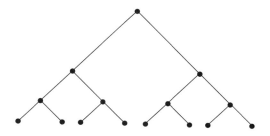

1. What do the vertices of this tree graph represent? What do the edges represent?

2. At the start of the calling process, only the president knows whether the games are on or not. In the first stage of calling, two new families get the word. In the next stage, four others hear the decision, and so on.

   a. Make a table showing the number of families who will hear the decision at each of the next 8 stages of the calling process. Then plot the data.

Stage of Calling Tree	0	1	2	3	4	5	6	7	8	9	10
Families Informed		1	2	4							

b. How does the number of families hearing the message grow as the calling tree progresses in stages? How is that pattern of change shown in the plot of the data?

c. How many stages of the tree will be needed before all 750 families know the decision? How many telephone calls will be required?

3. How will word pass through the club if each person in the tree calls three other families, instead of just two?

   a. Make a tree graph for several stages of this calling plan.

   b. Make a table showing the number of families who will hear the decision at each of the first ten stages of the calling process. Then plot the data.

Stage of Calling Tree	0	1	2	3	4	5	6	7	8	9	10
Families Informed	1	3									

   c. How does the number of families hearing the message increase as the calling tree progresses in stages? How is that pattern of change shown in the plot of the data?

   d. How many stages of the tree will be needed before all 750 families know the decision? How many telephone calls will be required?

4. In each of the two calling trees, you can use the number of phone calls at any stage to calculate the number of calls at the next stage.

   a. Use the words *NOW* and *NEXT* to write equations showing the two patterns.

   b. Explain how the equations match the patterns of change in the tables of (*stage, number of families informed*) data.

   c. Describe how the equations can be used with your calculator or computer to produce the tables you made in activities 2 and 3.

   d. Write an equation relating *NOW* and *NEXT* that could be used to model a telephone calling tree in which each family calls four other families.

Checkpoint

ⓐ Compare the two calling trees by noting similarities and differences in the following:

- Patterns of change in the tables of (*stage, number of families informed*) data

- Patterns in the graphs of (*stage, number of families informed*) data

- The equations relating *NOW* and *NEXT* numbers of calls

ⓑ Below are a table and a graph for a linear model. In what ways are the table, graph, and equation patterns for the calling trees different from those of linear models?

x	y
0	1
1	2
2	3
3	4
4	5

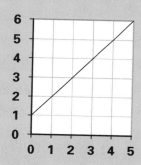

✓ **Be prepared to share your ideas with the rest of the class.**

On Your Own

The patterns of change in information spread by calling trees occur in many other situations. For example, when bacteria infect some part of your body, they grow and split into two genetically equivalent cells again and again.

a. Suppose a single bacterium lands in a cut on your hand. It begins spreading an infection by growing and splitting into two bacteria every 20 minutes.

- Make a table showing the number of bacteria after each 20-minute period in the first three hours. (Assume none of the bacteria are killed by white blood cells.)

- Plot the (*number of 20-minute time periods, bacteria count*) data.

- Describe the pattern of growth of bacteria causing the infection.

b. Use *NOW* and *NEXT* to write an equation relating the number of bacteria at one time to the number 20 minutes later. Then use the equation to find the number of bacteria after fifteen 20-minute periods.

c. How are the table, graph, and equation of bacteria growth similar to, and different from, the calling tree examples? How are they similar to, and different from, typical patterns of linear models?

Investigation  1.2   Shortcut Calculations

Everyone knows that mathematics is useful in solving business, engineering, or science problems. It is also used to design works of music and art. Sometimes it even plays a role in the plots of stories and books. For example, an old Persian legend illustrates the speed of exponential growth.

A wealthy king was rescued from danger by the quick thinking and brave action of one of his soldiers. The king wanted to honor the poor soldier, so he offered a very generous reward: a beautiful chessboard made of ivory and ebony and a set of gold chess pieces.

While the chess set was beautiful and valuable, the young man asked for a different reward. To help the poor people in his country, he asked the king to distribute rice from his storehouse—two grains for the first square of the chessboard, four grains for the second square, eight grains for the third square, sixteen grains for the fourth square, and so on. The king was pleased that he could keep his beautiful chessboard and repay the brave soldier with such a simple grant of rice to the poor. But he soon discovered that the request was not as simple as he thought.

1. Use your calculator to find the number of grains of rice for each of the squares 10, 20, 30, 40, 50, 60, and 64.

2. The national debt of the United States in 1994 was about $4,600,000,000,000. How does this number compare to the number of grains of rice for square 64 of the king's chessboard?

3. For some kinds of rice it takes about 2000 grains to fill one cubic inch of space. Consider the number of grains that the king owed for the 64th square alone.

   a. How many cubic inches would that rice occupy?

   b. How many cubic feet?

   c. How many cubic yards?

   d. How many cubic miles?

4. A cubic inch of rice costs about $0.05. What would this mean for the present-day value of the rice on square 64 alone?

5. To calculate the number of grains of rice for each square of the king's chessboard, you could use the equation $NEXT = NOW \times 2$, beginning at 2 grains for the first square. So the number of grains of rice for square 2 could be represented as 2×2.

   a. Why can the number of grains of rice for square 3 be expressed as $(2 \times 2) \times 2$?

   b. Write expressions for the number of grains of rice for squares 5, 10, and 20.

   c. What is the shorthand way of writing the calculations in part b using *exponents*?

   d. Write an exponential expression for the number of grains of rice for square 64. For any square x.

   e. Compare your exponential expressions in parts c and d with those of another group. Resolve any differences.

6. You can use your graphing calculator or computer and the exponential rule for any square x to make tables and graphs of the pattern formed by counting rice grains. Enter the rule in the "Y=" list of your calculator or computer, using the ⌷^⌷ key before the exponent. (With some tools, you may need to use the y^x or a^b key or a different symbol instead.)

   a. Make a table showing the number of grains of rice for squares 1 through 10. You may use the calculator program *TablePlot* (AATBLPLT), if available. The program allows you to switch easily between the table and a scatterplot of the table's values.

b. Use *TablePlot* or similar software to plot the (*square number, number of grains of rice*) data.

c. Explain why the table and plot produced using your exponential rule are the same as those from using the equation *NEXT = NOW* × 2.

7. Suppose the wealthy Persian king offered his soldier a more generous deal: 3 grains of rice for the first square, 9 for the second, 27 for the third, 81 for the fourth, and so on.

a. Use an equation relating *NOW* and *NEXT* and your calculator or computer to find the number of grains of rice for each of the first 10 squares of the chessboard in this case.

b. Write a rule using exponents that could be used to calculate the number of grains of rice for any square, without starting from the first square.

c. Enter your rule for part b in the "Y=" list of your graphing calculator or computer. Find the number of grains of rice for squares 15, 25, and 35.

d. For which square will the number of grains of rice first exceed 1 billion?

Checkpoint

> **ⓐ** How are the patterns of change in the tables for the king's chessboard similar to, and different from, those in the telephone trees and bacterial growth problems in Investigation 1.1?
>
> **ⓑ** How are the graphs of those relations similar to each other and how are they different?
>
> **ⓒ** Compare the equations modeling the three situations from part a.
>
> – How are the rules using *NOW* and *NEXT* similar and how are they different?
>
> – Write exponential rules (*y* = …) that model the telephone trees. Write a rule that models the bacterial growth problem.
>
> – How are these rules similar and how are they different?
>
> ✓ *Be prepared to share your ideas with the entire class.*

The patterns of change in the situations involving the king's chessboard, bacterial growth, and telephone trees are called **exponential growth**. Exponential growth patterns of change can be modeled using rules involving exponents.

On Your Own

The sketch below shows the first stages in the formation of a geometric figure. This figure is an example of a *fractal*. At each stage in growth of the figure, the middle of every segment is replaced by a triangular tent. The new figure is made up of more, but shorter, segments.

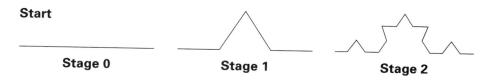

Start

Stage 0   **Stage 1**   **Stage 2**

a. Make a sketch showing at least one more stage in the growth of this fractal. Describe any symmetries that the fractal has at *each* stage.

b. Continue the pattern begun in this table:

Stage of Growth	0	1	2	3	4	5	6	7
Segments in Design	1	4						

c. Write an equation showing how the number of segments at any stage of the fractal can be used to find the number of segments at the next stage.

d. Write an exponential rule that can be used to find the number of segments in the pattern at any stage *x*, without finding the numbers at each stage along the way. Begin your rule, "$y = \ldots$"

e. Use the rule from part d to produce a table and a graph showing the number of segments in the fractal pattern at each of the first 10 stages of growth. Do the same for the first 20 stages. (The calculator program *TablePlot* is helpful here.)

f. At what stage will the number of small segments first reach 1 million?

Investigation **1.3** Getting Started

Bacterial infections seldom start with a single bacterium. Suppose that you cut yourself on a rusty nail that puts 25 bacteria cells into the wound. Suppose also that those bacteria divide in two after every quarter of an hour.

1. Use *NOW* and *NEXT* to write an equation showing how the number of bacteria changes from one quarter-hour to the next.

2. Make a table showing the number of bacteria in the cut for each quarter-hour over the first three hours. Then plot a graph of the (*number of quarter-hours, bacteria count*) data.

3. In what ways are the table, graph, and equation of bacteria counts in this case similar to, and different from, the simple case (pages 423–24) that started from a single one-celled bacterium?

You could use the equation from activity 1 to find the number of bacteria after 8 hours. (That would assume your body did not fight off the infection and you did not apply any medication.) Activity 4 will help you find a way to get that answer directly, without finding the bacteria count at each quarter-hour along the way.

4. **a.** What is your estimate of the number of bacteria after 8 hours?

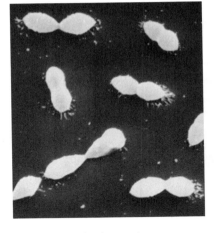

   b. What arithmetic operations are required to calculate the bacteria count after 8 hours (32 quarter-hours) if the equation relating *NOW* and *NEXT* is used?

   – How can those operations be written in short form using exponents?

   – What set of calculator keystrokes will give the result quickly?

   – What is the number of bacteria after 8 hours? How close was your estimate in part a?

   c. Write a rule using exponents that could help calculate the bacteria count.

5. Investigate the number of bacteria expected after 8 hours if the starting number of bacteria is 30 or 40 or 60 or 100, instead of 25. For each starting number, do the following. (Divide the work among your group members.)

   a. Find the number of bacteria after 8 hours.

   b. Write two equations that model the bacterial growth. One should use *NOW* and *NEXT*. The other should begin "$y = ...$"

   c. Make a table and plot of (*number of quarter-hours, bacteria count*) data.

d. Compare your results:

- How were your calculations of the number of bacteria after 8 hours similar and how were they different?

- How are the equations relating *NOW* and *NEXT* and the equations beginning "*y* = ..." for bacteria counts similar and how are they different?

- How are the tables and graphs of (*number of quarter-hours, bacteria count*) data similar and how are they different?

Just as bacterial growth won't always start with a single cell, other exponential growth processes can start with different initial numbers. Think again about the telephone calling tree for the Silver Spring Soccer Club in Investigation 1.1.

6. Suppose that before deciding to call off play because of bad weather, the president must talk with the club's four-member board of directors. When the calling tree is started, there are already 5 people who know the news to be spread. The president and each member of the board begin the calling tree by calling three other families apiece. Each family then calls three other families, and so on.

a. Draw a tree graph illustrating this pattern of calling.

b. Write an equation showing how the number of calls at any stage of the calling process can be used to find the number of calls at the next stage.

c. Use the equation from part b to make a table and a plot showing how the number of calls increases as the process moves to further stages.

d. What arithmetic operations are required to find the number of calls at the 8th stage of the tree, using the equation relating *NOW* and *NEXT*?

- How can those operations be written in short form using exponents?

- What set of calculator keystrokes will give the result quickly?

- What is the number of calls at stage 8?

e. What rule using exponents could help with the number of call calculations?

7. a. Suppose the board of directors had only three members (so four people know the news at the start), and each caller in the tree is expected to call five other families. How would your answers to activity 6 change?

b. Which phone tree should reach all families in the least amount of time? Why?

In studying exponential growth it is common to refer to the *starting point* of the pattern as **stage 0** or the **initial value**.

8. a. Use your calculator and the $\boxed{\wedge}$ key to find each of the following values: 2^0, 3^0, 5^0, 23^0.

b. What seems to be the calculator value for b^0, for any positive value of b?

c. Recall the examples of exponential patterns in bacterial growth and telephone calling trees. How is your conclusion for part b supported by these examples?

9. a. Now use your calculator to make tables of (x, y) values for each of the following equations. Use values for x from 0 to 10. Share the work among members of your group.

  i. $y = 5(2^x)$ **ii.** $y = 4(3^x)$

  iii. $y = 3(5^x)$ **iv.** $y = 7(23^x)$

b. What patterns do you see in your tables that show how to model exponential growth from any starting point?

c. If you see an equation of the form $y = a(b^x)$ relating two variables x and y, what will the values of a and b tell you about the relation?

Checkpoint

The tables that follow show variables changing in a pattern of exponential growth.

I.
x	0	1	2	3	4	5	6
y	1	2	4	8	16	32	64

II.
x	0	1	2	3	4	5	6
y	3	6	12	24	48	96	192

a What equation relating *NOW* and *NEXT* shows the common pattern of growth in the tables?

b How are the patterns of change in the tables different? How will that difference show up in plots of the tables?

c What equations ($y = \ldots$) will give rules for the patterns in the tables?

d How do the numbers used in writing those rules relate to the patterns of entries in the table? How could someone who knows about exponential growth examine the equation and predict the pattern in a table of (x, y) data?

✓ *Be prepared to share your equations and observations with the entire class.*

On Your Own

Jurassic Park is a popular book and movie about a dinosaur theme park. It is based on the idea that dinosaur DNA might be recovered from fossils and copied in laboratories until the genetic material for dinosaurs is available. The possibility of actually "recreating" dinosaurs is remote. But chemists *have* invented processes for copying genetic materials. The 1993 Nobel Prize for chemistry was shared by two scientists who developed such processes. In the PCR (polymer chain reaction) process invented by Kary Mullis, a sample of DNA is doubled. The process takes about 5 minutes.

a. Suppose a chemist starts the PCR process with a sample that holds only 7 copies of a special piece of DNA.

– Write two different equations that can be used for calculating the number of copies of the DNA on hand after any number of 5-minute periods.

– Use your equations from above to find the number of copies of the DNA produced after 2 hours.

– Use your equations to find the number of 5-minute periods required to first produce 1 billion copies of the DNA.

b. How would your answers to part a change if the starting DNA sample held 1, 2, or 3 copies of the DNA to be copied?

c. From your earlier study of linear models, you know that the exponential growth pattern common in living organisms is not the way all things change. For example, think about a car that accelerates quickly to the speed limit of 55 mph on a highway and keeps going at that speed for some time.

– How long will it take the car to cover a distance of 250 miles?

– What equations allow you to calculate the distance traveled by this car for any time? How are those equations different from what you expect to find with exponential growth?

– What patterns do you expect to find in tables and graphs of (*time, distance*) data for this car? How are those patterns different from what you find with exponential growth?

Modeling **O**rganizing **R**eflecting **E**xtending

Modeling

1. Suppose a single bacterium lands in an open cut on your leg and begins doubling every 15 minutes.

   a. How many bacteria will there be after 15, 30, 45, 60, and 75 minutes have elapsed (if no bacteria die)?

   b. Write rules that can be used to calculate the number of bacteria in the cut after any number of 15-minute periods.
   - Make the first an equation relating *NOW* and *NEXT*.
   - Make the second a rule using exponents, beginning "$y = ...$"

   c. Use your rules from part b to make a table showing the number of bacteria in the cut at the end of each 15-minute period over 3 hours. Then describe the pattern of change in number of bacteria from each quarter hour to the next.

   d. Use the rules from part b to find the predicted number of bacteria after 5, 6, and 7 hours. (Hint: How many 15-minute periods will that be?)

2. Suppose the wealthy Persian king in Investigation 1.2 offered his soldier an even more generous deal. The king will distribute 5 grains of rice for the first square, 25 for the second, 125 for the third, 625 for the fourth, and so on.

   a. Use an equation relating *NOW* and *NEXT* rice grain counts to find the number of grains of rice for each of the first 5 squares of the chessboard.

   b. Write a rule using exponents that could be used to calculate the number of grains of rice for any square, without starting from the first square.

   c. Use the rule in part b to make a table showing the number of grains of rice for each of the first 10 squares. Describe the pattern of change in this table, from one square to the next.

   d. How would your answers to parts a through c change if the king offered 5 grains for square 1, 10 grains for square 2, 15 grains for square 3, 20 grains for square 4, and so on?

3. The next sketches show several stages in the growth of a *fractal tree*.

Stage 1   Stage 2   Stage 3   Stage 4   Stage 5

a. Suppose at Stage 0 there is one branch. Each year the tree grows exactly two new branches at the end of each branch. Make a table showing the number of new branches in each year from 0 to 10.

b. How many new branches will there be on this tree in year 20?

c. At what age will this sort of tree first produce at least 1 billion new branches?

d. Explain how you could find the answers to parts a through c in three different ways using your calculator or computer.

e. Describe any symmetries that the fractal tree has at each stage. How could this information be used in drawing the next stage of the tree?

4. The drug penicillin was discovered by observation of mold growing on biology laboratory dishes. Suppose a mold begins growing on a lab dish. When first observed, the mold covers only $\frac{1}{8}$ of the dish surface, but it appears to double in size every day. When will the mold cover the entire dish?

O*rganizing*

1. Write each of the following calculations in shorter form using exponents.

a. $5 \times 5 \times 5 \times 5$

b. $3 \times 3 \times 3 \times 3 \times 3 \times 3 \times 3 \times 3$

c. $1.5 \times 1.5 \times 1.5 \times 1.5 \times 1.5 \times 1.5$

d. $(-10) \times (-10) \times (-10) \times (-10) \times (-10) \times (-10) \times (-10) \times (-10)$

e. $\underbrace{6 \times 6 \times \ldots \times 6}_{n \text{ factors}}$

f. $\underbrace{a \times a \times \ldots \times a}_{n \text{ factors}}$

2. a. Do each of the following calculations without use of the exponent key ($\boxed{\wedge}$ or $\boxed{y^x}$) on your calculator.

   i. 5^4 **ii.** $(-7)^2$ **iii.** 10^0

   iv. $(-8)^3$ **v.** 2^8 **vi.** 2^{10}

b. Suppose b is any number and x is some positive whole number. Describe two ways in which you can calculate the value of b^x .

3. a. Compare the patterns of (x, y) values produced by these two rules: $y = 3^x$ and $y = 1 + 3x$.

- For each rule, make a table of (x, y) values for x from 0 to 10 in steps of 1.
- For each rule, plot the data obtained. The program *TablePlot* would be helpful here.
- For each rule, write an equation using *NOW* and *NEXT* that could be used to produce the same pattern of (x, y) data.
- For each rule, describe the way that y changes as x increases. Explain how that pattern shows up in the table and the graph.

b. Now think about any two relations with rules $y = b^x$ and $y = a + bx$ where $b > 1$.

- What patterns are you sure to find in any table of (x, y) values in each case? What will the values of a and b tell about those patterns?
- What patterns are you sure to find in graphs of the two relations? What will the values of a and b tell about those patterns?
- What equations relating *NOW* and *NEXT* will give the same patterns of (x, y) values as the equations $y = b^x$ and $y = a + bx$?

4. Shown below are partially completed tables for four relations between variables. In each case, decide if the table shows an exponential or a linear pattern of change. Based on that decision, complete the table as the pattern suggests. Then write equations for the patterns in two ways: using rules relating *NOW* and *NEXT* y values and using rules beginning "$y = \ldots$" for any given x value.

a.

x	0	1	2	3	4	5	6	7	8
y				8	16	32			

b.

x	0	1	2	3	4	5	6	7	8
y				40	80	160			

c.

x	0	1	2	3	4	5	6	7	8
y				48	56	64			

d.

x	0	1	2	3	4	5	6	7	8
y				125	625	3125			

5. For each pair of equations relating *NOW* and *NEXT y* values, produce tables and scatterplots of data. Then compare the patterns of growth by describing similarities and differences in the tables and graphs produced and in the rates of change.

   a. Compare change patterns produced by the equations *NEXT = NOW* × 3 and *NEXT = NOW* × 5, starting at 10 in each case.

   b. Compare change patterns produced by *NEXT = NOW* × 3 (starting at 5) and *NEXT = NOW* × 5 (starting at 3).

   c. Compare change patterns produced by *NEXT = NOW* × 3 (starting at 5) and *NEXT = NOW* + 3 (starting at 5).

   d. Compare change patterns produced by *NEXT = NOW* × 3 (starting at 5) and *NEXT = NOW* + 10 (starting at 100).

R*eflecting*

1. One common illness in young people is *strep throat*. This bacterial infection can cause painful sore throats. Have you or anyone you know ever had strep throat? How does what you have learned about exponential growth explain the way strep throat seems to develop very quickly?

2. Suppose you are asked to design a telephone calling tree for a school chorus that has 30 members. The purpose of the tree will be to help the director reach families of all chorus members as quickly and reliably as possible with information about trips, performances, and practices.

   a. Sketch diagrams of several different possible calling trees.

   b. Explain the advantages and disadvantages of each design.

3. You've now worked on many different problems involving exponential growth patterns.

   a. What are the key features of a relation between variables that are hints that exponential growth will be involved?

   b. How are the patterns of exponential growth models different from those of linear models?

4. Which of the two models for growth by doubling do you prefer: *NEXT = NOW* × 2 or $y = 2^x$? Give reasons for your preference and explain how the two models are related to each other.

5. The population of our world is now about 5 billion. At the present rate of growth, that population will double every 40 years.

　a. If this rate continues, what will the population be 40, 80, 120, and 160 years from now?

　b. How would that growth pattern compare to a pattern that simply added 5 billion people every 40 years?

　c. Do you think the population is likely to continue growing in the "doubling every 40 years" pattern? Explain your reasoning.

　d. What do you think the effect of rapid population growth will be on your life in the 21st century?

Extending

1. Here are five stages in growth of another fractal design called the *dragon fractal*.

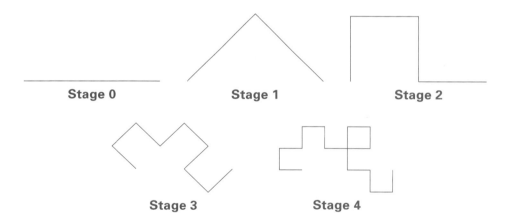

a. Draw the next stage of growth in the dragon fractal.

b. What pattern of change do you see in the number of segments of the growing fractal?

c. Make a table and a plot of the data showing that pattern of change.

d. Write an equation relating *NOW* and *NEXT* and an equation beginning "*y* = ..." for finding the number of segments in the figure at each stage of growth.

e. How many segments will there be in the fractal design at stage 16?

f. At what stage will the fractal design have more than 1000 segments?

2. One of the most famous fractal forms is the *Koch snowflake*. It grows in much the same way as the tent-like fractal you explored in "On Your Own" on page 427, except it starts with an equilateral triangle. In the first growing step, divide each segment into three equal pieces. Raise a "tent" over the center section with segments equal in length to the two remaining pieces on each side of the center section. Then the next stage repeats that process on each segment of the pattern at stage one, and so on.

a. Draw stages 0–2 of the Koch snowflake.

b. Make a table showing the number of segments, the length of each segment, and the perimeter of the total figure at each stage through stage 6. Assume the length at stage 0 is 1.

c. Write equations in two ways for each of the following relations: (*stage, number of segments*); (*stage, segment length*); (*stage, perimeter*).

d. Study the pattern in each variable (*number of segments, segment length,* and *perimeter*) as the number of growth stages increases to a very large number. Write a report describing your observations, making sure to comment especially on any surprising patterns.

3. Create a fanciful fractal of your own. Use color, or simply create it in black and white. Draw at least five stages of your fractal. Analyze it mathematically. Be sure to include a table, a graph, an equation relating *NOW* and *NEXT*, and an equation beginning "$y = \ldots$."

4. In this task you will examine more closely the tent-like fractal from page 427.

Stage 0   Stage 1   Stage 2

Recall that in moving from one stage to the next, each segment is divided into three equal-length parts. A tent is raised over the middle section with sides equal in length to the parts on each side.

a. If the original line segment is one inch long, how long is each segment of the pattern in stage 1?

b. How long is each segment of the pattern in stage 2?

c. Complete the following table showing the length of segments in the first ten stages.

Stage	0	1	2	3	4	5	6	7	8	9
Length	1	$\frac{1}{3}$	$\frac{1}{9}$							

d. Look back to parts c and d of task 2 (on page 437) where you wrote equations giving the number of short segments at each stage of the pattern. Then use that information and the results of part c to complete the following table giving the length of the total pattern at each stage.

Stage	0	1	2	3	4	5	6	7	8	9
Length	1	$\frac{4}{3}$	$\frac{16}{9}$							

e. What appears to be happening to the length of the total pattern as the number of segments in the pattern increases?

5. In the king's chessboard problem described in Investigation 1.2, it was easy to calculate the number of grains of rice for any given square. In this task, you will investigate the total number of grains for all squares taken together.

a. Find these sums:

$$1 + 2 + 4 + 8$$
$$1 + 2 + 4 + 8 + 16$$
$$1 + 2 + 4 + 8 + 16 + 32$$
$$1 + 2 + 4 + 8 + 16 + 32 + 64$$

b. What pattern do you see in the results of part a that would allow you to predict the sum of any number of terms of this sequence? Test your conjecture on the sum: $1 + 2 + 4 + 8 + 16 + 32 + 64 + 128 + 256 + 512 + 1024$. Revise your conjecture and test again if necessary.

c. Plan and carry out an investigation that would allow you to quickly calculate the sum of terms in a tripling sequence: $1 + 3 + 9 + 27 + 81 + 243 + ... + N$.

d. Try to find a pattern in your work in parts b and c that would allow you to quickly calculate the sum of terms in any exponential sequence: $1 + r + r^2 + r^3 + r^4 + ... + r^n$.

2 *Exponential Decay*

In 1989 the oil tanker Exxon Valdez ran aground in waters near the Kenai peninsula of Alaska. Over 10 million gallons of oil spread on the waters and shoreline of the area, endangering wildlife. That oil spill was eventually cleaned up—some of the oil evaporated, some was picked up by specially equipped boats, and some sank to the ocean floor as sludge.

For scientists planning environmental cleanups, it is important to be able to predict the pattern of dispersion in such contaminating spills. *Think about* the following experiment that simulates pollution and cleanup of a lake or river by some poison.

- Mix 20 black checkers (the pollution) with 80 red checkers (the clean water).

- On the first "day" after the spill, remove 20 checkers from the mixture (without looking at the colors) and replace them with 20 red checkers (clean water). Count the number of black checkers remaining. Then shake the new mixture. This simulates a river draining off some of the polluted water and a spring or rain adding clean water to a lake.

- On the second "day" after the spill, remove 20 checkers from the new mixture (without looking at the color) and replace them with 20 red checkers (more clean water). Count the number of black checkers remaining. Then stir the new mixture.

- Repeat the remove/replace/mix process for several more "days."

Think about this situation

The graphs at the right show two possible outcomes of the pollution and cleanup simulation.

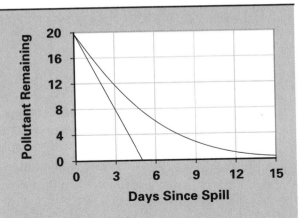

a What pattern of change is shown by each graph?

b Which graph shows the pattern of change that you would expect for this situation? Test your idea by running the experiment several times and plotting the (*time, pollutant remaining*) data.

c What sort of equation relating pollution *P* and time *t* would you expect to match your plot of data? Test your idea using a graphing calculator or computer.

The pollution cleanup experiment gives data in a pattern that occurs in many familiar and important problem situations. That pattern is called **exponential decay**.

Investigation 2.1 — More Bounce to the Ounce

Most popular American sports involve balls of some sort. In playing with those balls one of the most important factors is the bounciness or *elasticity* of the ball. For example, if a new golf ball is dropped onto a hard surface, it should rebound to about $\frac{2}{3}$ of its drop height.

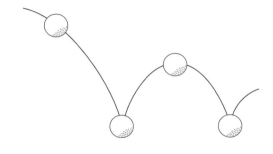

Suppose a new golf ball drops downward from a height of 27 feet onto a paved parking lot and keeps bouncing up and down, again and again.

1. a. Make a table and plot of the data showing expected heights of the first ten bounces.

Bounce Number	0	1	2	3	4	5	6	7	8	9	10
Rebound Height	27										

b. How does the rebound height change from one bounce to the next? How is that pattern shown by the shape of the data plot?

c. What equation relating *NOW* and *NEXT* shows how to calculate the rebound height for any bounce from the height of the preceding bounce?

d. Write an equation beginning "$y = \ldots$" to model the rebound height after any number of bounces.

e. How will the data table, plot, and equations for calculating rebound height change if the ball drops first from only 15 feet?

As is the case with all mathematical models, data from actual tests of golf ball bouncing will not match exactly the predictions from equations of ideal bounces. You can simulate the kind of quality control testing that factories do by running some experiments in your classroom.

2. a. Get a golf ball and a tape measure or meter stick for your group. Decide on a method for measuring the height of successive rebounds after the ball is dropped from a height of at least 8 feet. Collect data on the rebound height for successive bounces of the ball.

b. Compare the pattern of your data to that of the model that predicts rebounds which are $\frac{2}{3}$ of the drop height. Would a rebound height factor other than $\frac{2}{3}$ give a better model? Explain your reasoning.

c. Write an equation using *NOW* and *NEXT* that relates the rebound height of any bounce of your tested ball to the height of the preceding bounce.

d. Write an equation beginning "$y = \ldots$" to predict the rebound height after any number of bounces.

3. a. Repeat the experiment of activity 2 with some other ball such as a tennis ball or a basketball. Study the data to find a reasonable estimate of the rebound height factor for your ball.

b. Write an equation using *NOW* and *NEXT* and an equation beginning "$y = \ldots$" that model the rebound height of your ball on successive bounces.

Checkpoint

Different groups might have used different balls and dropped the balls from different initial heights. However, the patterns of (*bounce number, rebound height*) data should have some similar features.

a Look back at the data from your two experiments.

- How do the rebound heights change from one bounce to the next in each case?

- How is the pattern of change in rebound height shown by the shape of the data plots in each case?

b List the equations relating *NOW* and *NEXT* and the rules (*y* = ...) you found for predicting the rebound heights of each ball on successive bounces.

- What do the equations relating *NOW* and *NEXT* bounce heights have in common in each case? How, if at all, are those equations different and what might be causing the differences?

- What do the rules beginning "*y* = ..." have in common in each case? How, if at all, are those equations different and what might be causing the differences?

c What do the tables, graphs, and equations in these examples have in common with those of the exponential growth examples in the beginning of this chapter? How, if at all, are they different?

✓ *Be prepared to share and compare your data, models, and ideas with the rest of the class.*

On Your Own

When dropped onto a hard surface, a brand new softball should rebound to about $\frac{2}{5}$ the height from which it is dropped. If a foul-tip drops from a height of 25 feet onto concrete, what pattern of rebound heights can be expected?

a. Make a table and plot of predicted rebound data for 5 bounces.

b. What equation relating *NOW* and *NEXT* and what rule (*y* = ...) giving height after any bounce match the pattern of rebound heights?

c. Here are some data from bounce tests of a softball dropped from a height of 10 feet.

Bounce Number	1	2	3	4	5
Rebound Height	3.8	1.5	0.6	0.2	0.05

– What do these data tell you about the quality of the tested softball?

– What bounce heights would you expect from this ball if it were dropped from 20 feet instead of 10 feet?

d. What equation would model rebound height of an ideal ball if the drop was from 20 feet?

Investigation **2.2** **Sierpinski Carpets**

One of the most interesting and famous fractal patterns is named after the Polish mathematician Waclaw Sierpinski. The first two stages in forming that fractal are shown here.

Start

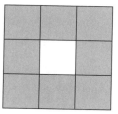

Cutout 1

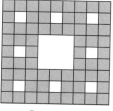

Cutout 2

Starting with a solid square "carpet" one meter on a side, smaller and smaller squares are cut out of the original in a sequence of steps. Notice how, in typical fractal style, small pieces of the design are similar to the design as a whole.

At the start of a Sierpinski carpet there is one square meter of carpet. But as cutting proceeds, there seems to be less and less carpet, and more and more hole.

1. Make a sketch showing the new holes that will appear in the third cutout from the carpet.

2. The carpet begins with an area of 1 square meter.

    a. How much of the original carpet is left after the first cutout?

    b. What fraction of the carpet left by the first cutout remains after the second cutout? How much of the original 1 square meter of carpet remains after the second cutout?

    c. What fraction of the carpet left by the second cutout remains after the third cutout? How much of the original 1 square meter of carpet remains after the third cutout?

    d. Following the pattern in the first three stages, how much of the original 1 square meter of carpet will remain after cutout 4? After cutout 5?

3. **a.** Write an equation showing the relation between the area of the remaining carpet at any stage and the next stage.

    b. What area would you predict for the carpet left after cutout 10? After cutout 20? After cutout 30?

4. **a.** Write an exponential equation that would allow you to calculate the area of the remaining carpet after any number of cutouts x, without going through all the cutouts from 1 to x.

    b. Make a table giving the area of the Sierpinski carpet from the start through cutout 10. Use *TablePlot* or similar software to make a plot of this data.

    c. How many cutouts are needed to get a Sierpinski carpet in which there is more hole than carpet remaining?

Checkpoint

Summarize the ways in which the table, graph, and equations for the Sierpinski carpet pattern are similar to, and different from, those for the following patterns:

ⓐ The bouncing ball patterns of Investigation 2.1

ⓑ The calling tree, king's chessboard, and bacteria growth patterns of Lesson 1

✓ *Be prepared to share your summaries of similarities and differences with the entire class.*

On Your Own

Suppose you started working on a very large Sierpinski carpet—a square that is 3 meters long on each side. Its starting area would be 9 square meters.

a. Find the area of the remaining carpet after each of the first 10 cutouts.

b. Make a plot of the (*cutout number, area*) data from part a.

c. Write an equation that shows the change in area from one cutout to the next.

d. Write an exponential equation showing how to calculate the area of the carpet after any number *x* of cutouts.

e. How many cutouts are needed to get a Sierpinski carpet in which there is more hole than carpet remaining?

 – Show how the answer to this question can be found in a table of (*cutout number, area*) data.

 – Show how the answer to this question can be found in a plot of (*cutout number, area*) data.

f. How do your answers to parts a through e compare to those for the first Sierpinski carpet with original area 1 square meter?

Investigation **2.3** Medicine and Mathematics

Drugs are a very important part of the human health equation. Many drugs are essential in preventing and curing serious physical and mental illnesses.

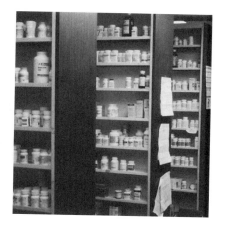

Diabetes, a disorder in which the body cannot metabolize glucose properly, affects people of all ages. In 1995, there were about 8 million diagnosed cases of diabetes in the United States. It was estimated that another 8 million cases remained undiagnosed.

In 5–10% of the diagnosed cases, the diabetic's body is unable to produce insulin, which is needed to process glucose. To provide this essential hormone, these diabetics must take injections of a medicine containing insulin. The medications used (called insulin delivery systems) are designed to release insulin slowly. The insulin itself breaks down rather quickly. The rate varies greatly between individuals, but the following graph shows a typical pattern of insulin decrease.

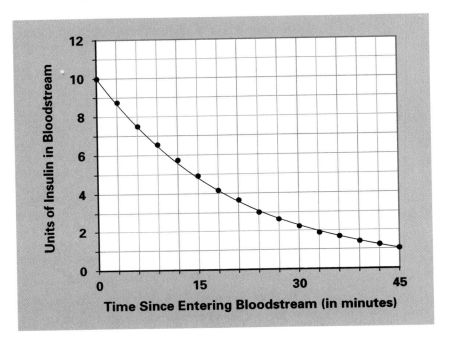

1. Medical scientists usually are interested in the time it takes for a drug to be reduced to one half of the original dose. They call this time the **half-life** of the drug. What appears to be the half-life of insulin in this case?

2. The pattern of decay shown on this graph for insulin can be modeled well by the equation $y = 10(0.95)^x$. Experiment with your calculator or computer to see how well a table of values and graph from this rule fit the pattern in the given graph. Then explain what the values 10 and 0.95 tell about the amount of insulin in the bloodstream.

3. What equation relating *NOW* and *NEXT* shows how the amount of insulin in the blood changes from one minute to the next, once 10 units have entered the bloodstream?

4. The insulin graph shows data points for each minute following the original insulin level. But the curve connecting those points reminds us that the insulin breakdown does not occur in sudden bursts at the end of each minute! It occurs *continuously* as time passes.

What would each of the following calculations tell about the insulin decay situation? Based on the graph on the previous page, what would you expect as reasonable values for those calculations?

a. $10(0.95)^{1.5}$ **b.** $10(0.95)^{4.5}$ **c.** $10(0.95)^{18.75}$

5. Mathematicians have figured out ways to do calculations with fractional or decimal exponents so that the results fit in the pattern for whole number exponents. One of those methods is built into your graphing calculator or computer.

a. Enter the rule $Y = 10(0.95^X)$ in the "Y=" list of your calculator or computer. Then complete the following table of values showing the insulin decay pattern at times other than whole minute intervals.

Time in Minutes	0	1.5	4.5	7.5	10.5	13.5	16.5	19.5
Units of Insulin in Blood	10							

b. Compare the entries in this table with data shown by points on the graph on page 446.

c. Use your rule to estimate the half-life of insulin.

Checkpoint

In this chapter you have seen that patterns of exponential change can be modeled by equations of the form $y = a(b^x)$.

ⓐ What equation relates *NOW* and *NEXT* y values of this model?

ⓑ What does the value of a tell about the situation being modeled? About the tables and graphs of (x, y) values?

ⓒ What does the value of b tell about the situation being modeled? About the tables and graphs of (x, y) values?

ⓓ How is the information provided by values of a and b in exponential equations like $y = a(b^x)$ similar to, and different from, that provided by a and b in linear equations like $y = a + bx$?

✓ *Be prepared to compare your responses with those from other groups.*

On Your Own

The most famous antibiotic drug is penicillin. After its discovery in 1929, it became known as the first *miracle drug*, because it was so effective in fighting serious bacterial infections.

Drugs act somewhat differently on each person, but on average, a dose of penicillin will be broken down in the blood so that one hour after injection only 60% will remain active. Suppose a hospital patient is given an injection of 300 milligrams of penicillin at noon.

a. Make a table showing the amount of that penicillin that will remain at hour intervals from noon until 5 PM.

b. Make a plot of the data from part a. Explain what the pattern of that plot shows about the rate at which penicillin decays in the blood.

c. Write an equation of the form $y = a(b^x)$ that can be used to calculate the amount of penicillin remaining after any number of hours x.

d. Use the equation from part c to produce a table showing the amount of penicillin that will remain at *quarter-hour* intervals from noon to 5 PM. What can you say about the half-life of penicillin?

e. Use the equation from part c to graph the amount of penicillin in the blood from 0 to 10 hours. Find the time when less than 10 mg remain.

Modeling **O**rganizing **R**eflecting **E**xtending

Modeling

1. If a basketball is properly inflated, it should rebound to about $\frac{1}{2}$ the height from which it is dropped.

   a. Make a table and plot showing the pattern to be expected in the first ten bounces after a ball is dropped from a height of 10 feet.

   b. At which bounce will the ball first rebound less than 1 foot? Show how the answer to this question can be found in the table and on the graph.

   c. Write two different forms of equations that can be used to calculate the rebound height after many bounces.

   d. How will the data table, plot, and equations change for predicting rebound height if the ball is dropped from a height of 20 feet?

2. The sketch below shows the start and two cutout stages in making a triangular Sierpinski carpet. Assume that the area of the original triangle is 3 square meters.

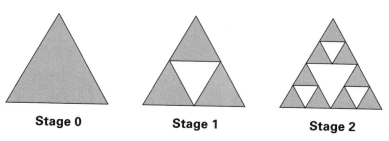

| Stage 0 | Stage 1 | Stage 2 |

a. Sketch the next stage in the pattern.

b. Make a table showing (*cutout number, area remaining*) data for cutout stages 0 to 5 of this process.

c. Make a plot of the data in part b.

d. Write two different equations that can be used to calculate the area of the remaining carpet at different stages. One equation should show change from one stage to the next. The other should be in the form "$y = ...$"

e. How many stages are required to reach the points where there is:

 – more hole than carpet remaining?

 – less than 0.1 square centimeters of carpet remaining?

f. How are the pattern, table, graph, and equations for this triangular carpet similar to, and different from, those of the square carpets in Investigation 2.2?

g. Describe any symmetries that the triangular carpet has at each stage.

3. You may have heard of athletes being disqualified from competitions because they have used anabolic steroid drugs to increase their weight and strength. These steroids can have very damaging side effects for the user. The danger is compounded by the fact that these drugs leave the human body slowly. With an injection of the steroid *ciprionate*, about 90% of the drug and its by-products will remain in the body one day later. Then 90% of that amount will remain after a second day, and so on. Suppose that an athlete tries steroids and injects a dose of 100 milligrams of ciprionate. Analyze the pattern of that drug in the athlete's body by completing the following tasks.

a. Make a table showing amount of the drug remaining at various times.

Time Since Use (in days)	0	1	2	3	4	5	6	7
Steroid Present (in mg)	100	90	81					

b. Make a plot of the data in part a and write a short description of the pattern shown in the table and the plot.

c. Write two equations that describe the pattern of amount of steroid in the blood.

   – Write one equation showing how the amount of steroid present changes from one day to the next.

   – Write a second equation in the form $y = a(b^x)$ that shows how one could calculate the amount of steroid present after any number of days.

d. Use one of the rules in part c to estimate the amount of steroid left after 0.5 and 8.5 days.

e. Estimate, to the nearest tenth of a day, the half-life of ciprionate.

f. How long will it take the steroid to be reduced to only 1% of its original level in the blood? That is, how many days will it take for only 1 milligram of the original dose to be left in the bloodstream?

4. When people suffer head injuries in accidents, emergency medical personnel sometimes administer a paralytic drug to keep the patient immobile. If the patient is found to need surgery, it's important that the immobilizing drug decay quickly.

For one typical paralytic drug the standard dose is 50 micrograms. One hour after the injection, half the original dose has decayed into other chemicals. The halving process continues the next hour, and so on.

a. How much of the 50 micrograms will remain in the patient's system after 1 hour? After 2 hours? After 3 hours?

b. Write an equation for calculating the amount of drug that will remain x hours after the initial dose.

c. Use the equation from part b to make a table showing the amount of drug left at half-hour intervals from 0 to 5 hours.

d. Make a plot of the data from part c and then a continuous graph using the ⌐Y=⌐ and ⌐GRAPH⌐ commands.

e. How long will it take the 50 microgram dose to decay to less than 0.05 micrograms?

5. In Chapter 1 "Patterns in Data," you studied growth charts as you learned about percentiles. For children who fall under the 5 percentile level on these charts, a growth hormone may be used to help them grow at a more normal rate. If 10 milligrams of one particular growth hormone is introduced to the bloodstream, as much as 70% will still be present the next day. After another day, 70% of that amount will remain, and so on.

a. Write two different equations that can be used to calculate the amount of a 10 milligram dose of growth hormone remaining after any number of days.

b. How long will it take for the original 10 milligram dose to be reduced to 0.1 milligrams? Show how the answer to this question can be found in a table of (*time*, *drug amount*) data and in a graph of that data.

c. What is the half-life of this growth hormone?

d. Suppose half the amount (5 milligrams) of the drug is introduced to the bloodstream. Compare the half-life of this dosage with that in part c.

6. Radioactive materials have many important uses in the modern world, from fuel for power plants to medical x-rays and cancer treatments. But the radioactivity that produces energy and tools for "seeing" inside our bodies has some dangerous effects too, for example, it can cause cancer in humans.

The radioactive chemical strontium-90 is produced in many nuclear reactions. Extreme care must be taken in transportation and disposal of this substance. It decays rather slowly—if any amount is stored at the beginning of a year, 98% of that amount will still be present at the end of that year.

a. If 100 grams (about 0.22 pounds) of strontium-90 are released due to an accident, how much of that radioactive substance will still be around after 1 year? After 2 years? After 3 years?

b. Write two different equations that can be used to calculate the amount of strontium-90 remaining at any year in the future, from an initial 100 grams.

c. Make a table and a scatterplot showing the amount of strontium-90 that will remain from an initial amount of 100 grams at the end of every 10-year period during a century:

Years	0	10	20	30	40	50	...
Amount Left (in g)	100						

d. Use one of the equations in part b to find the amount of strontium-90 left from an initial amount of 100 grams after 15.5 years.

   e. Use one of the equations from part b to find the number of years that must pass until only 10 grams remain.

   f. Estimate to the nearest tenth of a year, the half-life of strontium-90.

Organizing

1. The following graphs, tables, and equations model four exponential growth and decay situations. For each graph, there is a matching table and a matching equation. Use what you know about the patterns of exponential relations to pair each graph with its corresponding table and equation. In each case, explain the clues that can be used to match the items without any use of a graphing calculator or computer.

Graphs

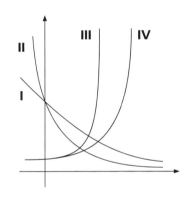

Tables

A.

x	1	2	3	4
y	40	16	6.4	2.56

B.

x	1	2	3	4
y	30	90	270	810

C.

x	1	2	3	4
y	60	36	21.6	12.96

D.

x	1	2	3	4
y	20	40	80	160

Equations

a. $y = 100(0.6^x)$

b. $y = 100(0.4^x)$

c. $y = 10(2^x)$

d. $y = 10(3^x)$

2. This task will help you develop a better understanding of fractional or decimal exponents.

   a. Use your calculator or computer to produce a table of values for $y = 4^x$. Use values of x from 0 to 3 in steps of 0.1.

   b. Use your calculator or computer to produce a table of values for $y = (0.36)^x$. Use values of x from 0 to 4 in steps of 0.25.

   c. Suppose you have an exponential model of the form $y = b^x$ where $b > 0$ and $b \neq 1$. If x is a decimal number between two numbers s and t, how is b^x related to b^s and b^t? Test your conjecture using exponential models different from those in parts a and b.

   d. Without using your calculator, estimate $3^{1.5}$. Explain the method you used.

3. For an equation of the form $y = a(b^x)$, what conclusions can you draw about the tables and the graphs of (x, y) values when b is

    a. between 0 and 1?

    b. greater than 1?

4. Suppose two equations $y = 100(b^x)$ and $y = 100(c^x)$ model the decay of 100 grams of two different radioactive substances. How can you tell which substance will have the shorter half-life by comparing the values of b and c? How will this difference appear in the graphs of the two equations?

Reflecting

1. Which example of an exponential decay pattern seems to you to be the most interesting or important example of exponential decay—the Sierpinski carpets, metabolizing of drugs in the body, bouncing of a golf ball, or decay of radioactive chemicals? Give reasons for your choice.

2. Suppose the makeup of a drug is such that one hour after a dose is administered to an individual's bloodstream, 70% remains active. Does it follow that one-half hour after administration of the same dose to the same person, 85% will remain active? Explain your reasoning.

3. When an exponential equation models a situation such as in the metabolizing of drugs in the body, fractional or decimal exponents are useful. In other situations they may not be particularly meaningful.

    a. Give an example of an exponential growth or decay situation where use of fractional exponents would not make sense.

    b. What are some characteristics of exponential growth or decay situations that would suggest that use of fractional exponents is sensible?

4. Suppose a problem situation is modeled by the equation $y = 500(0.6^x)$. Tell as much as you can about the nature of the situation.

5. Suppose a person taking steroid drugs is hospitalized due to a side effect from the drug. Tests taken upon admittance show a steroid concentration of 1.0. The next test one day later shows a concentration of 0.75. Based on these results the person's family and friends assume that in three days the drug will be out of the person's system.

    a. What pattern of change are the family and friends assuming?

    b. What might be a more accurate pattern prediction? Why is this pattern more reasonable?

Extending

1. Fleas are one of the most common pests for dogs. If your dog has fleas, you can buy many different kinds of treatments, but those wear off over time. Suppose the half-life of one such treatment is 10 days.

   a. Make a table showing the fraction of an initial treatment that will be active after 0, 10, 20, 30, and 40 days.

   b. Experiment with your calculator or computer to find an equation of the form $y = b^x$ that matches the pattern in your table of part a.

2. In Chapter 3, "Linear Models," you solved linear equations of the form $ax + b = c$ and $ax + b = cx + d$ using several different methods. Solve each of the following *exponential equations* in at least two different ways.

   a. $2^x = 6$

   b. $2x = 2^x$

3. The following program creates a drawing of the Sierpinski Triangle (Modeling task 2) in an interesting way. This program is from the *TI-82 Graphics Calculator Guidebook.*

Program: SIERPINS

:FnOff	:For(K,1,3000)	:.5(1+Y)→ Y
:ClrDraw	:rand→N	:End
:PlotsOff	:If N≤1/3	:If 2/3<N
:AxesOff	:Then	:Then
:0→Xmin	:.5X→X	:.5(1+X)→ X
:1→Xmax	:.5Y→Y	:.5Y→Y
:0→Ymin	:End	:End
:1→Ymax	:If 1/3<N and N≤2/3	:Pt - On(X,Y)
:rand→X	:Then	:End
:rand→Y	:.5(.5+X)→ X	:StorePic Pic6

Reprinted by Permission of Texas Instruments.

   a. Enter the program in your calculator.

   b. After you execute the program, recall and display the picture by pressing RecallPic Pic6.

   c. How is the idea of *NOW* and *NEXT* used in the design of this program?

3 *Compound Growth*

Every now and then we hear about somebody winning a big payoff in a state lottery somewhere. The wins can be 1, 2, 5, or even as large as 50 million dollars. Those big money wins are usually paid off in annual installments for about 20 years. But some smaller prizes like $10,000 are paid at once. How would you react if this news report was actually about you?

Kalamazoo Teen Wins Big Lottery Prize—$20,000

A Kalamazoo teenager has just won $20,000 from a Michigan lottery ticket that she got as a birthday gift from her uncle. In a new lottery payoff scheme, the teen (whose name has been withheld) has two payoff choices: One option is to receive $1,000 payments each year for the next 20 years. In the other plan, the game show will invest $10,000 in a special savings account that will earn 8% compound interest yearly for 10 years. At the end of that time she can withdraw the balance of the account.

Think about this situation

a Which of the two payoff methods would you choose, if you had just won the lottery?

b Which method do you think would give the greatest total payoff?

c About how much money do you think would be in the special savings account at the end of 10 years?

Investigation **3.1** | **Just Like Money in the Bank**

Of the two lottery payoff methods, one has quite a simple rule: $1,000 per year for 20 years, giving a total payoff of $20,000. The plan to put $10,000 in a savings account paying 8% **compound interest** might not be as familiar.

- After one year your balance will be:
    $10,000 + (0.08 \times 10,000) = 1.08 \times 10,000 = 10,800$.

- After the second year your balance will be:
    $10,800 + (0.08 \times 10,800) = 1.08 \times 10,800 = 11,664$.

During the next year the savings account balance will increase in the same way, starting from $11,664, and so on.

1. Write equations that will allow you to calculate the balance of this deposit
   a. for any year, using the balance from the year before.
   b. after any number of years x.

2. Use the equations to make a table and a plot showing the growth of this special savings account for a period of 10 years.

Time (in years)	0	1	2	3	4	...	9	10
Balance ($)	10,000	10,800	11,664					

3. Describe the pattern of growth in this savings account as time passes.
   a. Why is the balance not increasing at a constant rate?
   b. How could the pattern of increase be predicted from the shape of the graph of the modeling rules?

4. How long would it take to double the $10,000 savings account?

5. Compare the pattern of change and the final account balance in activity 2 to that for each of the following possible savings plans over 10 years. Write a summary of your findings.
   a. Initial investment of $15,000 earning only 4% annual interest.
   b. Initial investment of $5,000 earning 12% annual interest.

Checkpoint

Most savings plans operate in a manner similar to the special lottery savings account. They may have different starting balances, different interest rates, or different periods of investment.

a Describe two ways to find the value of such a savings account at the end of each year from the start to year 10. Use methods based on
  – an equation relating *NOW* and *NEXT*.
  – an exponential equation $y = a(b^x)$.

b What is the shape of the graphs that you would expect?

c How will the rules change as the interest rate changes? As the amount of initial investment changes?

d Why does the dollar increase in the account get larger from one year to the next?

✓ *Be prepared to explain your methods and ideas to the entire class.*

On Your Own

The world population and populations of individual countries grow in much the same pattern as money earning interest in a bank.

   i. Brazil is the most populous country in South America. In 1995, its population was about 161 million. It is growing at a rate of about 1.2% per year.

   ii. Nigeria is the most populous country in Africa. Its 1995 population was about 119 million. It is growing at a rate of about 3.2% per year.

a. Assuming these growth rates continue, make a table showing the predicted populations of these two countries in each of the 10 years after 1995. Then make a scatterplot of the data for each country.

   – Describe the patterns of growth expected in each country.

   – Explain how the different patterns of growth are shown in the scatterplots.

b. Write equations to predict the populations of these countries for any number of years *x* in the future. Use the equations

   – to estimate when Brazil's population might reach 300 million.

   – to estimate when Nigeria's population might reach 200 million.

Modeling **O**rganizing **R**eflecting **E**xtending

Modeling

1. Suppose that a local benefactor wants to offer college scholarships to every child born into a community. When a child is born, the benefactor puts $5,000 in a special savings fund earning 5% interest per year.

   a. Make a table and graph of an account showing values each year for 18 years.

   b. Compare the pattern of growth of the account in part a to one in which the initial deposit was $10,000. Compare values of each account after 18 years.

c. Compare the pattern of growth of the account in part a to one in which the interest rate was 10% and the initial deposit was $5,000. Compare values of each account after 18 years.

d. Compare values of the accounts in parts b and c after 18 years. Explain why your finding makes sense.

2. In 1995 the population of Iraq was 20.6 million and was growing at a rate of about 2.9% per year, one of the fastest growth rates in the world.

a. Make a table showing the projected population of Iraq in each of the eight years after 1995.

b. Write two different kinds of equations that could be used to calculate population estimates for Iraq at any time in the future.

c. Estimate the population of Iraq in 2020.

d. What factors might make the estimate of part c an inaccurate forecast?

3. In Chapter 2, "Patterns of Change," you studied growth in the population of Arctic bowhead whales. The natural growth rate was about 3.1% and estimates place the 1994 population between 5,700 and 10,600. The harvest by Inuit people is very small in relation to the total population. Disregard the harvest for this task.

a. If growth continued at 3.1%, what populations would be predicted for each year to 2000? Make tables based on both 1994 population estimates.

b. How would the pattern of results in part a change if the growth rate were and continued to be 7%, as some scientists believe it is?

c. Write two different types of equations that can be used to calculate population estimates for the different possible combinations of initial population and growth rate estimates.

d. Find the likely time for the whale population to double in size under each set of assumptions.

Organizing

1. Consider the four exponential equations:

i. $y = 5(1.2^x)$ **ii.** $y = 5(1.75^x)$

iii. $y = 5(2.5^x)$ **iv.** $y = 5(3.25^x)$

a. Sketch the patterns of graphs you expect from these four equations; then check your estimates with your calculator or computer.

b. Make tables of (x, y) values for the four equations and explain how the patterns in those tables fit the shape of the graphs in part a.

2. a. Sketch the graph shape you would expect from an exponential equation $y = a(b^x)$ when $0 < b < 1$. Sketch the shape you would expect when $b > 1$.

b. How does the value of a affect the graph?

3. One way to think about rates of growth is to calculate the time it will take for a quantity to double in value. For example, it is common to ask how long it will take a bank investment or a country's population to double.

a. If the U.S. population in 1994 was about 250 million and growing exponentially at a rate of 1% per year, how long will it take for the U.S. population to double?

b. One year's growth is 1% of 250 million, or 2.5 million. How long would it take the U. S. population to double if it increased *linearly* at the rate of 2.5 million per year?

c. How long does it take a bank deposit of $5,000 to double if it earns interest compounded yearly at the rate of 2%? At a 4% rate? At a 6% rate? At an 8% rate? At a 12% rate?

d. Examine your (*rate, time to double*) data in part c. Do you see a pattern that would allow you to predict the doubling time for an investment of $5,000 at an interest rate of 3% compounded annually? Check your prediction. If your prediction was not close, search for another pattern for predicting doubling time and check it.

4. What property of addition and multiplication justifies each of the following calculations in figuring compound interest?

$$10,000 + 0.06(10,000) = 1.06(10,000)$$
$$10,600 + 0.06(10,600) = 1.06(10,600)$$
$$P + rP = (1 + r)P$$

Reflecting

1. What characteristic of money earning interest in the bank and growth of human or animal populations makes them grow in similar exponential patterns?

2. Which of these two offers would you take to invest a $500 savings? Justify your choice.

i. 4% interest paid each year on the balance in that year

ii. $20 interest paid each year (Notice: $20 = 4% of $500.)

3. Refer to the savings fund description in Modeling task 1 and complete part a if you have not already done so. Calculate *differences* between the value of the account at the beginning and end of years 1, 5, 11, and 18. What do these four differences say about the rate at which the savings account grows?

Extending

1. Banks frequently pay interest more often than once each year. Suppose your bank pays interest compounded *quarterly*. If the annual percentage rate is 4%, then the bank pays 1% interest at the end of each 3-month period.

   a. Explore the growth of a $1000 deposit in such a bank over 5 years.

   b. Compare the quarterly compounding with annual compounding at 4%.

   c. Repeat the calculations and comparisons if the annual rate is 8%.

2. Many people borrow money from a bank to buy a car, a home, or to pay for a college education. However, they have to pay back the amount borrowed plus interest. To consider a simple case, suppose that a car loan of $9,000 charges 6% annual rate of interest and the repayment is done in quarterly installments. One way to figure the balance on this loan at any time is to use the equation:

$$new\ balance = 1.015 \times old\ balance - payment$$

   a. Use this equation to find the balance due on this loan for each quarterly period from 0 to 20, assuming that the quarterly payments are all $250.

   b. Experiment with different payment amounts to see what quarterly payment will repay the entire loan in 20 payments (5 years).

   c. Experiment with different loan amounts, interest rates, and quarterly payments to see how those factors are related to each other. Write a brief report of your findings.

3. The value of purchased products such as automobiles *depreciates* from year to year.

   a. Would you suspect the pattern of change in value of an automobile from year to year is linear? Exponential?

   b. Select a 1990 automobile of your choice. Research the initial cost of the car and its value over the years since 1990.

   c. Does the plot of (*time since purchase, value*) data show an exponential pattern? If so, find an exponential model that fits the data well. Use your model to predict the value of the car when it is 10 years old.

   d. Compare your findings with those of other classmates who completed this task. Which 1990 automobile researched held its value best? Explain your reasoning.

4 *Modeling Exponential Patterns in Data*

Our planet Earth is home for millions of different species of animal and plant life. Many species of life become *extinct* every day. Much loss is due to human actions that change the environment for animal and plant life. The endangerment of life forms often can be reversed by protection of species and their habitats.

For example, the Kenai Peninsula of Alaska is a natural home for wolves, moose, bear, and caribou. When a gold rush in 1895–96 brought thousands of prospectors to the area, hunting and changes to the environment reduced all those populations. Wolves disappeared from the Kenai Peninsula by about 1915.

In the late 1950s a few wolves reappeared on the Kenai Peninsula. They were protected from hunting in 1961. The graph at the right shows Kenai wolf population growth as a protected species.

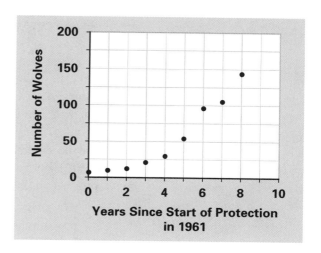

Think about this situation

ⓐ What sort of graph model do you think would best fit the trend in wolf population data?

ⓑ How would you find equations modeling the growth of the wolf population on the Kenai Peninsula over time?

ⓒ How might a Natural Resources Department use your equations?

Investigation 4.1 — Popcorn and Thumbtacks

This investigation includes four experiments that give you practice in modeling exponential patterns in data. In each case you will collect some data showing how a variable changes over time. Then you will make a table and a scatterplot of that data. Next you will experiment to find an equation relating x and y to fit the pattern in your data. Finally, you will use the equation to make predictions. The main steps are outlined in Experiment 1. Apply the same steps in the other three experiments.

Share the work so that each group does Experiment 1 and one of the remaining three experiments. Compare results to see similarities and differences in outcomes of the same and different experiments.

Experiment 1

Begin this experiment with a paper plate divided into four equal sections. Shade one of the sections, as shown here. You also need a paper cup containing 200 kernels of unpopped popcorn.

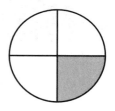

Pour the kernels of corn from the cup onto the plate at its center. Shake the plate gently to spread the kernels around. Then *remove* and count all kernels that end up on the shaded sector. (This ends Stage 1 of the experiment.) For the next stage, repeat the shake-remove process with the kernels that remain.

1. **Collect Data** Collect the data from your experiment in a table like this:

Stage Number	0	1	2	3	4	5	6	7
Kernels Left	200							

2. **Display Data** Make a scatterplot of the (*stage, kernels left*) data.

3. **Analyze Data** Write a short description of the pattern in the data table and scatterplot.

   a. Experiment entering different equations in the "Y=" function list. See if you can find one that fits the pattern well.

   b. Use your calculator or computer to find the equation of the best-fitting exponential model. The **exponential regression** "Technology Tip" handout will be very helpful.

c. Write the exponential equation $y = a(b^x)$ that you believe fits your data best.

d. Explain how the values of a and b relate to the experiment you have done. What do they tell about stages and kernels of corn?

4. Apply Model Use your exponential equation to do the following.

a. Predict the number of kernels of corn left after stage 3 and stage 7. Compare your predictions with the data table. Explain any differences you observe.

b. Write a question about the experiment that can be answered by using your modeling equation. Then show how you would use the equation to find the answer.

Experiment 2

Begin this experiment by pouring 20 kernels of corn onto the plate that has been divided into quarters. After shaking the plate to spread the kernels, count the number of kernels that land on the shaded sector of the plate. *Add that number of kernels to the test supply.* (This ends Stage 1.) Repeat the shake-count-add process several times.

Record the data n a table of (*stage, supply of kernels after adding*) data. Plot that data. Find an equation that models the relation between stage number and number of kernels. Explain the relation between the equation and the experiment. Compare values predicted by your model with data table entries. Write a question about the experiment. Use your equation to answer the question.

Experiment 3

Begin this experiment with a collection of 200 identical thumbtacks. Toss those tacks onto a flat surface and *remove* all tacks that land with the point up. Count and record the number of tacks remaining. (This ends Stage 1.)

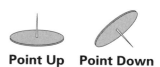

Point Up   Point Down

Toss the remaining tacks again and *remove* all tacks that land with their point up. Record the number of tacks left. Repeat the toss-remove-count process several times.

Record the data in a table of (*stage, tacks left*) data. Plot that data. Find an equation that models the relation between stage number and number of tacks. Explain the relation between the equation and the experiment. Compare values predicted by your model with data table entries. Write a question about the experiment. Use your equation to answer the question.

Experiment 4

Begin this experiment by tossing 10 tacks onto a flat surface. Count the number of tacks that land with their point down and *add* that number of tacks to the test supply. (This ends stage 1.) Repeat the toss-count-add process several times.

Record the data in a table of (*stage, supply of tacks after adding*) data. Plot that data. Find an equation that models the relation between the stage and the number of tacks. Explain the relation between the equation and the experiment. Compare values predicted by your equation with data table entries. Write a question about the experiment. Use your equation to answer the question.

Checkpoint

After each experiment has been reported to your class, consider the following questions about exponential patterns in data, their graphs, and their equations $y = a(b^x)$.

a What does the value of a indicate about each of the experiments? What does it indicate about the table of values for any exponential relation?

b What does the value of b indicate about each of the experiments? What does it indicate about the table of values for any exponential relation?

c In what sorts of problem situations can you expect an exponential model for which the value of b is between 0 and 1?

d In what sorts of problem situations can you expect an exponential model for which the value of b is greater than 1?

e What changes in data, graphs, and equation models would you expect if the experiments were changed

   – by dividing the paper plate differently in the corn kernel experiment?

   – by using different tacks, with shorter or longer points, in the tack experiment?

✓ *Be prepared to explain your ideas to the entire class.*

On Your Own

Suppose you have a collection of 300 dice. You toss them and remove all that show ones or sixes. Then you count and record the number of dice remaining. You repeat this procedure until you have only a few dice left.

a. What pattern of (*toss number*, *dice remaining*) data would you expect?

b. What would a scatterplot of the (*toss number*, *dice remaining*) data look like?

c. What equation would you expect as a good model of the data?

d. Suppose your teacher gives a homework assignment to conduct the dice-tossing experiment for ten tosses. If you were the teacher, what would you think:
  - If two students reported exactly the same data?
  - If one student's data fit exactly the equation $y = a(b^x)$ that was reported as the most likely model for that data pattern?

Investigation  **4.2** **Another Day Older ... and Deeper in Debt**

By the end of 1995, the national debt of the United States government was about $5,000,000,000,000. The debt was growing by nearly $900,000,000 every day. The numbers may seem too large to comprehend and the national debt may seem unrelated to your life. But on February 17, 1993, the *Chicago Tribune* reported that a large group of young people had gathered to make their position on the national debt known. These young people were concerned about government spending in this country and its long range implications. How will the national debt affect your financial future? Is the damage to the financial health of future generations beyond repair?

1. Consider the data table below which gives the federal debt in trillions of dollars from 1988 to 1993.

Year	1988	1989	1990	1991	1992	1993
Debt in $ trillion	2.6	2.9	3.2	3.6	4.0	4.4

Source: U.S. Bureau of the Census, *Statistical Abstract of the United States: 1995* (115th edition.) Washington, DC, 1995.

 a. Enter these data in your calculator or computer using 0 for 1988, 1 for 1989, and so on. Make a scatterplot.

 b. What patterns in the data and the plot suggest that a linear model might fit the trend in national debt? What patterns in the data are unlike linear models?

 c. Use your calculator or computer to find a linear rule for the (*year*, *debt*) data that you believe fits well. Find an exponential rule that seems to fit well, also.

 – Use the two rules to make tables and graphs. Describe the similarities and differences.

 – Use each model equation to estimate the national debt in the years 1995–2000, 2010, 2020, and 2030.

 d. Which of the two models do you think is better for describing and predicting the American national debt? Compare your choice with those of other groups. Resolve any differences between groups.

2. Early estimates of the national debt data for 1994 indicated that the rate of increase might be slowing. The debt figure for 1994 actually turned out to be around 4.6 trillion.

 a. How does this change affect the pattern of the data plot?

 b. How might it affect equations of good linear and exponential models?

 c. How might it affect the long-range projection of the national debt?

Checkpoint

Consider your studies of tables and graphs of data from two related variables.

ⓐ What patterns suggest use of a linear model? What patterns suggest an exponential model?

ⓑ If you think a linear model is probably a good one to use, how can you find values of a and b for the modeling equation $y = a + bx$?

ⓒ If you think an exponential model is probably a good one to use, how can you find values of a and b for the modeling equation $y = a(b^x)$?

✓ *Be prepared to share your thinking and methods for fitting models to data with the entire class.*

On Your Own

Earthquakes are among the most damaging kinds of natural disasters. The size of an earthquake is generally reported as a rating on the *Richter scale*—usually a number between 1 and 9. That Richter scale rating indicates the energy released by the shaking of the ground and the height of the shock waves recorded on seismographs.

The data in the following table show Richter scale ratings and amount of energy released for six earthquakes.

Earthquake Location	Richter Scale Rating	Energy (in sextillion ergs)
San Francisco, CA 1906	8.25	1500
Yugoslavia, 1963	6.0	0.63
Alaska, 1964	8.6	5000
Peru, 1970	7.8	320
Italy, 1976	6.5	3.5
Loma Prieta, CA 1989	7.1	28

a. Use your calculator or computer to make a scatterplot for this data.

b. What pattern makes it reasonable to think that this is an exponential relation?

c. Use your calculator or computer to find an algebraic model that fits the data pattern well.

d. Use the model to estimate energy released by earthquakes listed in the following chart.

Earthquake Location	Richter Scale Rating	Energy (in sextillion ergs)
Quetta, India 1906	7.5	
Kwanto, Japan 1923	8.2	
Chillan, Chile 1939	7.75	
Agadir, Morocco 1960	5.9	
Iran 1968	7.4	
Tangshan, China 1976	7.6	
Northridge, CA 1994	6.7	
Kobe, Japan 1995	7.2	

Modeling **O**rganizing **R**eflecting **E**xtending

Modeling

1. Suppose you are given a collection of 200 new pennies and directed to perform this experiment: Shake the pennies and drop them on a flat surface. *Remove* all pennies that land heads up. Count and record the number of pennies remaining. Repeat the shake-drop-remove-count process several times.

   a. What pattern of (*drop number*, *pennies left*) data would you expect from this experiment?

   b. What pattern would you expect in a scatterplot of the data?

   c. What equations would you expect to be good models of the data?

   d. Conduct the experiment to test your predictions.

2. Suppose you are given a collection of new pennies and directed to perform this experiment: Start with a cup holding 10 pennies. Shake the pennies and drop them on a flat surface. Count the pennies that turn up tails. *Add* that number of pennies to your cup and record the number of pennies now in the cup. Repeat the shake-drop-count-add process several times.

   a. What pattern of (*drop number*, *number of pennies*) data would you expect from this experiment?

b. What pattern would you expect in a scatterplot of the data?

c. What equations would you expect to be good models of the data?

d. Conduct the experiment to test your predictions.

3. Try this experiment with a supply of about 200 plastic spoons. Toss the spoons onto a flat surface and *remove* all spoons that land right side up. Count and record the number of spoons remaining. Repeat this toss-remove-count process several times.

a. Record the (*toss number, number of spoons*) data in a table.

b. Make a scatterplot of the data.

c. Find an equation that models the relation between toss number and number of spoons. Explain the relation between the equation and the experiment.

d. Write a question about this experiment. Use your model to answer the question.

4. Try this spoons experiment: Start with a supply of about 15 plastic spoons. Toss the spoons onto a flat surface and count the spoons that land right side up. *Add* that number of new spoons to your test collection. Then repeat the toss-count-add process several times.

a. Record the (*toss number, number of spoons*) data in a table.

b. Plot the data.

c. Find an equation that models the relation between toss number and number of spoons.

d. Explain the relation between the equation and the experiment. How is the equation related to the experiment in Modeling task 3?

5. With improved health care and advances in medicine, people continue to live longer. The American Hospital Association has predicted that the nursing home population will increase rapidly. It has made the following projections.

Projected Nursing Home Population								
Year	1985	1990	2000	2010	2020	2030	2040	2050
Population (millions)	1.30	1.45	1.80	2.30	2.55	3.35	4.30	4.80

Source: Person, J.E. Jr., ed., *Statistical Forecasts of the United States*. Detroit: Gale Research, Inc. 1993.

a. Find linear and exponential models that fit these data well. Use 0 for 1985, 5 for 1990, 10 for 2000, and so on.

b. In the equation $y = a + bx$ for the linear model, what do the values of a and b indicate about the projected pattern of change in nursing home populations?

c. In the equation $y = a(b^x)$ for the exponential model, what do the values of a and b indicate about the projected pattern of change in nursing home populations?

d. Which model do you believe was used to make the projections in the table?

e. What is the projected number of elderly who will be receiving nursing home care when you are eighty years old?

6. Life began on earth millions of years ago. Our species, *Homo Sapiens*, dates back only 300,000 years. The black rhinoceros, the second largest of all land mammals, has walked the earth for 40,000,000 years. In less than a century, the very existence of this species has been threatened. Prior to the 19th century, over 1,000,000 black rhinos roamed the plains of Africa. That number has been drastically reduced by hunting over the years. Recent data on the black rhino population is shown in the table below.

African Black Rhino Population

Year	1970	1980	1984	1986
Population (in 1000s)	65	15	9	3.8

Source: Nowak, R.M. *Mammals of the World*, fifth ed., vol. 2. Johns Hopkins University Press: Baltimore, 1991.

a. Make a scatterplot of these data and find an exponential equation that models the pattern in the data well. Use 0 for 1970, 10 for 1980, and so on.

b. Use the model from part a to predict the black rhino population in the year 2000.

c. Use your model to predict the time when the black rhino population will be less than 1000.

d. Find a linear model for the black rhino data that you believe fits the data well. Answer parts b and c with that model.

e. A model based on very few data points is sometimes inaccurate, especially if one data point has an incorrect value. Suppose the 1970 black rhino population was actually only 30,000. Find what you believe is a good-fitting model in that case.

Organizing

1. Without using your calculator or computer, sketch graphs for each of the following equations. Explain the reasoning you used in making each sketch.

a. $y = 3x + 5$

b. $y = 5(3^x)$

c. $y = 5\left(\frac{1}{3}\right)^x$

2. Make tables of sample (x, y) data that fit the conditions below. Use values for x from 0 to 8. Explain your reasoning in making each table.

a. The y values increase exponentially from initial value of 5.

b. The y values increase exponentially from initial value of 5 at a greater rate than the example in part a.

c. The y values increase linearly from an initial value of 5.

d. The y values decrease exponentially from an initial value of 25.

e. The y values decrease linearly from an initial value of 25.

3. Complete a table like the one here so that it shows

a. a pattern of linear growth. Write a linear equation that describes the pattern.

b. a pattern of exponential growth. Write an exponential equation that describes the pattern.

x	0	1	2	3	4	5
y	10	20				

4. When a fair coin is flipped, the outcome of "heads" or "tails" is equally likely. So the probability of a flipped coin landing heads up is $\frac{1}{2}$ or 0.5. Refer back to Experiment 3 of this lesson.

   a. If one of the thumbtacks is tossed in the air, what do you think is the probability that it will land with the point up?

   b. Toss a thumbtack in the air 100 times and count the number of times the tack lands with the point up. Use the results of your experiment to get a better estimate of the probability in part a.

   c. What do the results of your experiment in part b tell you about the probability that a tack tossed in the air will land point down?

   d. How, if at all, is the probability of a tack landing point up reflected in the equation model for Experiment 3?

Reflecting

1. A thousand-dollar bill is about 0.0043 inches thick. Imagine a stack of thousand-dollar bills whose total value is a trillion dollars. How high would the stack of bills be? If you created a stack of thousand-dollar bills whose value is that of the current national debt, about how many miles high would the stack be? Does this help show the seriousness of the debt you and your classmates will be inheriting?

2. Prison overcrowding is an issue in many states. Drug use and drug-related crime have contributed to the problem. Average operating costs of $25,000 per inmate and construction costs of $50,000 per cell will be an incredible burden on these prison systems. Examine the data in the following table, which gives the total prison population in twelve states for the years 1989 through 1993.

U. S. Prison Population					
Year	1989	1990	1991	1992	1993
Prison Population	271,787	329,459	367,832	400,713	430,681

Source: Person, J.E. Jr., ed., *Statistical Forecasts of the United States*. Detroit: Gale Research, Inc. 1993.

   a. What sort of model seems best for projecting this growth pattern into the future—linear, exponential, or some other type?

b. Assume that the prisons in these states were all full in 1993. Make a reasonable estimate of the number of additional cells that would have been needed in 1996. Estimate the construction and operating costs for the additional cells.

c. Where might the money for the increased costs come from?

3. Health care spending has been another factor in American life which has shown exponential growth. Using the data below, create a scatterplot and find an algebraic model to closely fit this data.

Total U. S. Spending on Health Care

Year	1975	1980	1985	1990
Spending in $ Billions	132	249	420	671

Source: Person, J.E. Jr., ed., *Statistical Forecasts of the United States*. Detroit: Gale Research, Inc. 1993.

a. Predict the health care spending total for 1995 and 2000.

b. Besides inflation, what factors do you think would cause this dramatic rise in the cost for health care?

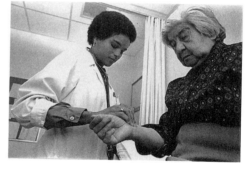

c. "Cost per capita" indicates the expense per person and therefore adjusts to reflect changes in population. The population of the U.S. for the given years is indicated in the following table. Calculate the health care cost per capita.

U. S. Population

Year	1975	1980	1985	1990
Population in Millions	216	227	238	249

Source: U.S. Bureau of the Census, *Statistical Abstract of the United States: 1995* (115th edition.) Washington, DC, 1995.

d. Is the cost per capita for health care also growing exponentially? What implications does this have for the future of health care in this country?

Extending

1. The following data were collected using a Geiger counter and a sample of radioactive barium-137. A Geiger counter measures the radioactivity level of the sample.

Geiger Counter Readings for Barium-137

Time in Minutes	0	1	2	3	4	5	6
Counts per Minute	10,094	8,105	5,832	4,553	3,339	2,648	2,035

a. Make a scatterplot of the data.

b. Use your calculator or computer and what you know about exponential models to determine the half-life of this radioactive substance.

2. The following data is from the *HIV/AIDS Surveillance Report*.

AIDS Cases and Fatalities by Age Group

Year	1981	1982	1983	1984	1985	1986	1987	1988	1989	1990	1991	1992
Cases Diagnosed Adult/Adolescents	308	1,115	2,964	5,985	11,327	18,430	27,604	34,113	40,126	43,905	51,423	57,023
Fatalities Adult/Adolescents	124	444	1,463	3,383	6,730	11,682	15,623	20,134	26,563	29,557	33,001	33,399
Cases Diagnosed Children <13	16	29	75	112	228	325	480	597	684	730	652	649
Fatalities Children <13	9	13	29	48	115	156	286	308	357	382	350	346

Source: U.S. Department of Heath and Human Services. *HIV/AIDS Surveillance Report 5, no. 2* (July 1993).

a. Make a scatterplot for each of the four sets of data included in the table, showing how those variables have changed over time. Make notes of any interesting patterns in the scatterplots and your explanations for those patterns.

b. What kind of model will help you make the best predictions about the number of adult/adolescent AIDS cases in the future?

c. Find a model for the adult/adolescent AIDS cases data. Assuming the pattern will continue, use your model to predict the number of AIDS cases for adults and adolescents that will be diagnosed in the year 2004.

d. Suppose you were making the same prediction in 1988.

   – What model would you have used based on only the data available at that time?

   – Does that model give you the same prediction for AIDS cases in 2004?

   – What changes in conditions might explain the differences?

3. Cigarette smoke contains nicotine, a very addictive and harmful chemical that affects the brain, nervous system, and lungs. The productivity losses and health care costs associated with cigarette smoke are considerable.

   Suppose an individual smokes one cigarette every 40 minutes over a period of three hours and that each cigarette introduces 100 units of nicotine into the bloodstream. The half-life of nicotine is 20 minutes.

a. Create a chart that keeps track of the amount of nicotine which remains in the body over the three-hour time period in 20-minute intervals. Plot these totals over time. Then describe the pattern of nicotine build-up in the body of a smoker.

b. How would the data change if the individual smokes a cigarette every twenty minutes?

c. Because nicotine is a very addictive drug, it is difficult for a smoker to break the habit. Suppose a long-time smoker decides to quit "cold turkey." That is, rather than reducing the number of cigarettes smoked each day, the smoker resolves never to pick up another cigarette. How will the level of nicotine in that smoker's bloodstream change over time?

4. Alcohol is another dangerous drug. Driving after excessive drinking is not only dangerous but also punishable by law. The National Highway Traffic Safety Administration estimated about 427,000 alcohol-involved traffic accidents in 1993—an average of almost 1,200 accidents each day. While legal limits of blood alcohol concentration (BAC) are different in each state, the American Medical Association recommends that a limit of 0.05% be used.

   There are many factors that affect a person's BAC. Some factors include body weight, gender, and the amount of alcohol drunk. The following chart contains typical data relating body weights and number of drinks consumed to approximate blood alcohol concentration. (Because of individual differences, this chart should not be considered to apply to everyone.)

Approximate Blood Alcohol Concentration

Weight (in pounds)	1 Drink	2 Drinks	3 Drinks	4 Drinks	5 Drinks
100	0.05	0.09	0.14	0.18	0.23
120	0.04	0.08	0.11	0.15	0.19
140	0.03	0.07	0.10	0.13	0.16
160	0.03	0.06	0.09	0.11	0.14
180	0.03	0.05	0.08	0.10	0.13

Source: National Highway Traffic Safety Administration, *Driving under the influence: A report to Congress on alcohol limits*, Washington, DC. 1992.

a. As time passes since alcohol was consumed, a person's body metabolizes the drug. Again, the rate at which this happens is different for each person. For most people, their BAC would drop at a rate of at least 0.01 each hour. Suppose a 120 lb. person had consumed 3 drinks. Using the table above and a burnoff rate of 0.01 per hour, when would this person satisfy the AMA's suggested limit of 0.05? How would this change if the person weighed 180 pounds and had consumed 4 drinks?

b. Prepare a graphical display of the data in the chart. Describe any patterns you see in the display.

c. Create a table showing the change in blood alcohol level over time, for a 140 lb. person who has consumed 5 drinks. Make a scatterplot of this data.

d. What type of model would best fit the scatterplot in part c?

e. Based on your work in Investigation 2.3 and in Extending task 3 on the previous page, what type of model best describes the amount of substance in the body over time for steroids, nicotine, and penicillin?

5 *Looking Back*

Many interesting and important patterns of change involve quantities changing as time passes. Populations of animals, bacteria, and plants grow over time. Drugs in the blood and radioactive chemicals in the environment decay over time. Most people hope that their bank savings account grows quickly over time. In many of the examples, the change is modeled well by exponential rules of the form $y = a(b^x)$.

When you find an exponential model for change in a variable, that model can be used to make useful predictions of events in the future. Test your understanding of exponential models on the following problems.

1. Code numbers are used in hundreds of ways every day—from student and social security numbers to product codes in stores and membership numbers in clubs.

   a. How many different 2-digit codes can be created using the digits 0, 1, 2, 3, 4, 5, 6, 7, 8, and 9 (for example, 33, 54, 72 or 02)?

   b. How many different 3-digit codes can be created using those digits?

   c. How many different 4-digit codes can be created using those digits?

   d. Using any patterns you may see, complete a table like the one below showing the relation between number of digits and number of different possible codes.

Number of Digits	1	2	3	4	5	6	7	8	9
Number of Codes									

   e. Write an equation using *NOW* and *NEXT* to describe the pattern in the table of part d.

   f. Write an equation that shows how to calculate the number of codes C for any number of digits D used.

g. Kitchenware stores stock thousands of different items. How many digits would you need in order to have code numbers for up to 8,500 different items?

h. How will your answers to parts a through f change if the codes were to begin with a single letter of the alphabet (A, B, C, ... , or Z) as in A23 or S75?

2. In one professional golf tournament, the money a player wins depends on her finishing place in the standings. The first place finisher wins $\frac{1}{2}$ of the $1,048,576 in total prize money. The second place finisher wins $\frac{1}{2}$ of what is left; then the third place finisher wins $\frac{1}{2}$ of what is left, and so on.

a. What fraction of the *total* prize money is won

– by the second place finisher?

– by the third place finisher?

– by the fourth place finisher?

b. Write a rule showing how to calculate the share of the prize money won by the player finishing in nth place, for any n.

c. Make a table showing the actual prize money in dollars (not fraction of the total prize money) won by each of the first ten place finishers.

Place	1	2	3	4	5	6	7	8	9	10
Prize (dollars)										

d. Write a rule showing how to calculate the actual prize money in dollars won by the player finishing in place n. How much money would be won by the 15th place finisher?

e. How would your answers to parts a through d change if

– the total prize money was reduced to $500,000?

– the fraction used was $\frac{1}{4}$ instead of $\frac{1}{2}$?

f. When prize monies are awarded using either fraction, $\frac{1}{2}$ or $\frac{1}{4}$, could the tournament organizers end up giving away more than the stated total prize amount? Explain your response.

3. Growth of protected wild animal populations like the Alaskan wolves can be simulated as follows:

– Assume that the population starts with 4 adult wolves, 2 male and 2 female.

– Assume that each year, each female produces 4 pups who survive (assume 2 male and 2 female survivors in each litter). Thus, at the end of the first year there will be 12 wolves (6 male and 6 female). At the end of the next year, there will be 36 wolves (18 male and 18 female), and so on.

a. In what ways does this seem a reasonable simulation of the population growth? What modeling assumptions seem unlikely to be accurate?

b. Make a table showing the number of wolves at each stage (assume no deaths).

Stage	0	1	2	3	4	5	6	7	8
Wolf Count	4	12	36						

c. Use a calculator or computer to find both linear and exponential models for the data in your table. Compare the fit of the two models to the data pattern. Explain which you feel is the better model.

d. What patterns of change will occur in the graph and in the table of values of a linear model? Of an exponential model? How do those typical patterns help you to decide which model is best in part c?

e. Why does the wolf population grow at a faster rate as time passes?

f. How would the numbers in your table change if you assumed that wolves lived only 5 years? How does that affect the growth rate of the population?

4. In a study of ways that young people handle money, four high school students were given $200 at the start of a school year. They were asked to keep records of what they did with that money for the next 10 months.

– Cheryl put the money away for safe keeping and worked so she could add 10% to the total every month.

– James put his money in a box at home and added $10 each month.

– Jennifer put her money in a box at home and spent $10 each month.

– Delano put his money in a box at home. At the start of each month, he took out 10% of his balance for spending in that month.

a. The following four graphs show possible patterns for the savings of the students over time. Match each student's saving or spending pattern to the graph that best fits it. Explain your reasoning.

i.

ii.

iii.

iv.

b. Match each graph from part a to the type of rule you would expect to produce it, $y = a + bx$ or $y = a(b^x)$. Then explain what you can expect for values of a and b in each rule.

5. If x is a whole number, calculations like 2^x, 3^x or $\left(\frac{1}{2}\right)^x$ involve many multiplications. For example, $2^{10} = 2 \times 2 \times 2 \times 2 \times 2 \times 2 \times 2 \times 2 \times 2 \times 2$. On a calculator you can reduce the number of operations by using an exponential key such as $\boxed{\wedge}$ or $\boxed{y^x}$. What could you do on a basic four-function calculator that has no exponential key? Answer parts a through d assuming you have only number keys, an = (ENTER) key, and the multiplication key ($\boxed{\times}$).

a. How could you calculate 2^{10} with fewer than nine $\boxed{\times}$ keystrokes (no addition allowed)?

b. How could you use the fact that $2^{10} = 1024$ to calculate 2^{20} with only one $\boxed{\times}$ keystroke?

c. How could you use the fact that $2^{10} = 1024$ and $2^5 = 32$ to calculate 2^{15} with only one $\boxed{\times}$ keystroke?

d. How could you calculate 3^{12} in several different ways with only the $\boxed{\times}$ key?

e. How could you calculate $3^{12} \times 3^8$ with only an exponential key?

f. Look back at the results of your work on parts a through e for a pattern that will complete calculations of this type: $2^m \times 2^n = 2^?$ for any nonnegative, whole-number values of n and m. Explain the rule your group invents using the meaning of exponents.

g. Explain why the rule you came up with in part f also applies when the base 2 is replaced by 3 or 6 or 1.5 or any other positive number.

Checkpoint

Exponential models can be used to solve problems in many different situations.

ⓐ In deciding whether an exponential model will be useful, what hints do you get from

- the patterns in data tables?

- the patterns in graphs or scatterplots?

- the nature of the situation and the variables involved?

ⓑ Exponential models, like linear models, can be expressed by an equation relating x and y values and by an equation relating *NOW* and *NEXT* y values.

- Write a general rule for an exponential model, $y = \ldots$.

- Write a general equation relating *NOW* and *NEXT* for an exponential model.

- What do the parts of the equations tell you about the situation being modeled?

ⓒ How can the rule for an exponential model be used to predict the pattern in a table or graph of that model?

ⓓ How are exponential models different from linear models?

ⓔ What real situations would you use to illustrate exponential change for someone who did not know what those patterns are like and used for?

✓ *Be prepared to share your ideas, equations, and examples with the whole class.*

Chapter **7** *Simulation Models*

1 *Simulating Chance Situations*

In some cultures it is customary for brides to go live with their husband's family. Couples who have no sons and whose daughters all marry will have no one to care for them in their old age.

Customs of a culture and the size of its population often lead to issues that are hard to resolve. China had a population of over 1,200,000,000 in 1993. In an effort to reduce the growth of its population, the government of China instituted a policy to limit families to one child. The policy has been very unpopular among rural Chinese who depend on sons to carry on the family farming. This situation raises many interesting mathematical questions as well as societal ones.

Think about this situation

a In a country where parents are allowed to have only one child, what is the probability that their one child will be a son? What is the probability they will not have a son? What assumption(s) are you making when you answer these questions?

b If each pair of Chinese parents really had only one child, do you think the population would increase, decrease, or stay the same? Explain your reasoning.

c Describe several alternative plans that the government of China might use to control population growth. For each plan, discuss how you might find the answers to the following questions.

– What is the probability that parents will have a son?

– What will happen to the total population of China?

– What will rural couples think about your plan?

Investigation  **1.1** How Many Children?

In part c of "Think about this situation" on the previous page, you shared different ways to examine the effects of your population policy. In real life, it is hard to gather data that easily show the effects of a policy on the population. It may take several generations to see the long term effects. To counteract this drawback, you can *simulate* the situation in a way that allows informative data to be gathered more easily and quickly. In this investigation you will simulate situations by flipping a coin.

1. Suppose China implements a new policy that allows each family to have two children.

   a. Explain how to use a coin to simulate the birth of *one* child. What did a head represent? What did a tail represent? What assumption(s) are you making?

   b. Explain how to use a coin to simulate the births of *two* children to a family. What are the possible outcomes?

   c. When you simulate a family of two children by flipping a coin twice and recording the results, you have conducted one **trial**. To be sure you have a reasonable estimate of what two-child families look like, it is necessary to conduct many trials. Conduct 200 trials simulating two-child families. Share the work among the groups in your class. Make a frequency table like the one below to record the results of your 200 trials.

Type of Family	Frequency
Two Girls	
Older Girl and Younger Boy	
Older Boy and Younger Girl	
Two Boys	
Total Number of Trials	200

d. Use your frequency table to estimate the probability that a family of two children will have *at least one* boy.

e. Estimate the probability that a family of two children will have at least one boy using a mathematical method other than simulation. Explain your other method.

f. Do the four types of families—two girls, older girl and younger boy, older boy and younger girl, two boys—appear to be **equally likely**? Describe the meaning of *equally likely* for a friend who is not in this class.

g. What is the total number of children in the 200 trials in part c? What is the total number of girls? Of boys?

Here is one plan for reducing population growth that your class may have discussed.

Allow parents to continue to have children until a boy is born. Then no more children are allowed.

For most of the remainder of this investigation, you will examine this plan. You will begin by making your best prediction about the effects of such a policy. Then you will use simulation techniques to improve your estimates.

2. Suppose that in rural China all parents continue having children until they get a boy. After the first boy, they have no other children. In your group, discuss each question below. Write your best prediction of the answer to each question.

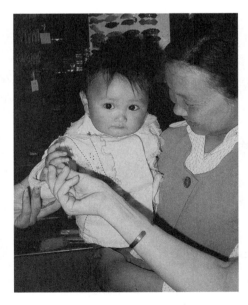

a. Will more boys or more girls be born in rural China?

b. What will be the average number of children per family in rural China?

c. Will the population of rural China increase, decrease, or stay the same?

d. What percentage of families will have only one child?

e. What percentage of families will have four children or more?

f. What percentage of the children in rural China will belong to single-child families?

To get a good estimate of the answers to these questions, your group could simulate the situation. To do this, design a **simulation model** that imitates the process of parents having children until they get a boy.

3. a. Explain how to use a coin to conduct one trial that models a family having children until they get a boy.

   b. Carry out one trial for your simulation of having children until a boy is born. Make a table like the following one. Make a tally mark (/) in the frequency column opposite the number of tosses it took to get a "boy".

Number of Tosses to Get a "Boy"	Frequency	Number of Tosses to Get a "Boy"	Frequency
1		7	
2		8	
3		9	
4		10	
5		*etc.*	
6		**Total Number of Trials**	50

4. Repeat the trial of having children until a boy is born. Stop when you have a total of 50 "families". Divide the work among the members of your group. Record your results in the frequency table. Add as many additional rows to the table as you need.

   a. How many of your 50 families had four children or more?

   b. How many boys were born in your 50 families?

   c. How many girls were born in your 50 families?

5. a. Use your frequency table to estimate answers to the six questions posed in activity 2.

   b. Compare your estimates with your original predictions. For which questions did your initial prediction vary the most from the simulation estimate? (If most of your original predictions were not accurate, you are in good company. Most people aren't very good at predicting the answers to probability problems.)

   c. Write several misconceptions that you or others in your group originally had about this situation.

6. Now make a histogram of your group's frequency table on a graph like the one shown below or on your calculator or computer.

   a. Describe the shape of this distribution.

   b. What is the largest family size? The smallest?

   c. On the histogram, locate the median and the lower and upper quartiles of the distribution.

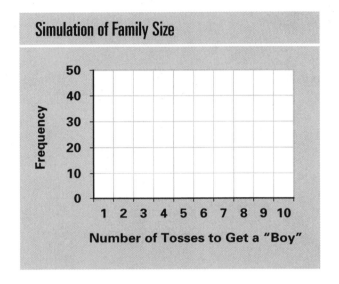

7. a. Each group should reproduce their histogram on the handout "Simulation of Family Size" or on the chalkboard.

   b. Describe any similarities in the histograms.

   c. Describe any differences in the histograms. Explain why the differences occurred.

   d. Combine the frequency tables from all of the groups in your class into one frequency table on the overhead projector or chalkboard.

   e. Make a histogram of the combined frequency table. How are the histograms from the individual groups similar to this one? How are they different?

   f. Reproduced below and on the next page are the questions from activity 2. Estimate the answers to these questions using the combined frequency table of part d.

   – Will more boys or more girls be born in rural China?

   – What will be the average number of children per family in rural China?

   – Will the population of rural China increase, decrease, or stay the same?

   – What percentage of families will have only one child?

– What percentage of families will have four children or more?

– What percentage of the children in rural China will belong to single-child families?

g. Should you have more confidence in the estimates from part f or in the estimates from your group? Explain your reasoning.

8. In "Think about this situation" on page 478, your class proposed several alternative plans for reducing population growth in China.

a. As a class, choose a plan different from the one where parents have children until they get a boy, and design one trial of your plan.

b. Perform at least 200 trials, sharing the work among groups in the class. Place your results in a frequency table.

c. Under your plan, what is the probability that parents will have a son? How did you calculate the probability?

d. Will the population of China increase, decrease, or remain the same under your plan? Explain your reasoning.

Checkpoint

ⓐ Describe, in your own words, what a *simulation model* is. Why is it important to conduct a large number of trials?

ⓑ Why is it always a good idea to make a histogram of the results of a simulation?

ⓒ Describe a way to simulate the have-children-until-you-get-a-boy plan that does not use coins.

ⓓ Is it possible to design a plan for flipping coins so that more heads are flipped than tails? Is it possible to design a plan for families having children so that a given child is more likely to be a girl than a boy?

✓ *Be prepared to share your descriptions and thinking with the class.*

Simulation is a good way to estimate the answer to a probability problem. The greater the number of trials, the more likely it is that the estimated probability is close to the actual probability. In our complex world, simulation is often the only feasible way to deal with a problem involving chance. Simulation is an indispensable tool to scientists, business analysts, engineers, and mathematicians.

"I've had it! Simulated wood, simulated leather, simulated coffee, and now simulated probabilities!"

On Your Own

When asked in what way chance affected her life, a ninth-grader in a very large Los Angeles co-educational city high school noted that students are chosen randomly to be checked for weapons. Suppose that when this policy was announced, a reporter for the school newspaper suspected that the students would

not be chosen randomly, but that boys would be more likely to be chosen than girls. The reporter then observed the first search and found that all ten students searched were male.

a. If a student is in fact chosen randomly, what is the probability that the student will be a boy?

b. Write instructions for conducting one trial of a simulation that models selecting 10 students at random and observing whether each is a boy or a girl.

c. What assumptions did you make in your model?

d. Perform 20 trials using your simulation model.

e. Report the results in a frequency table showing the number of boys selected.

f. Write an article for a school paper describing your simulation, its results, and your conclusion. Include a histogram in your article.

Modeling Organizing Reflecting Extending

Modeling

1. A new plan to control population growth in rural China is proposed. Parents will be allowed to have at most three children and must stop having children as soon as they get a boy.

   a. Describe how to conduct one trial that models one family that follows this plan.

   b. Conduct 5 trials. Copy the following frequency table which gives the results of 195 trials. Add your results to the frequency table so that there is a total of 200 trials.

Type of Family	Frequency
First Child is a Boy	97
Second Child is a Boy	50
Third Child is a Boy	26
Three Girls and No Boy	22
Total Number of Trials	

   c. Estimate the percentage of families that would not have a son.

   d. Make a histogram of the results in your frequency table.

   e. How does the shape of this histogram differ from that of the have-children-until-you-get-a-boy plan? Explain why you would expect this to be the case.

   f. What is the average number of children per family? Will the total population increase or decrease under this plan or will it stay the same?

   g. In the long run, will this population have more boys or more girls or will the numbers be about equal? Explain your reasoning.

2. Jeffrey is taking a ten question true-false test. He didn't study and doesn't even have a reasonable guess on any of the questions. He answers "True" or "False" at random.

   a. With your group, decide how to conduct one trial that models the results of a true-false test.

   b. Conduct 50 trials. Share the work. Record your results in a frequency table that gives the number of questions Jeffrey got correct in each trial.

c. Make a histogram of the results in your frequency table. Describe its shape.

d. Use your frequency table to estimate, on average, the number of questions Jeffrey will get correct. Theoretically, what is the number of questions that he should expect to get correct using his random guessing method?

e. If 70% is required to pass the test, what is your estimate of the probability that he will pass the test?

3. The winner of the World Series of baseball is the first team to win four games.

a. What is the fewest number of games that can be played in the World Series? What is the greatest number of games that can be played in the World Series? Explain.

b. Suppose that the two teams in the World Series are evenly matched. Describe how to conduct one trial simulating a World Series.

c. Use your simulation model to determine the probability that the series lasts seven games. Conduct 5 trials. Construct a frequency table similar to the one shown below and add your 5 results so that there is a total of 100 trials.

Number of Games Needed in the Series	Frequency
4	11
5	21
6	30
7	33
Total Number of Trials	

d. Make a histogram of the results in your frequency table.

e. What is your estimate of the probability that the series will go seven games?

4. According to the U.S. Department of Education report, *The Condition of Education 1993* (page 68), about 50% of high school transcripts in the United States show that the student has taken a chemistry course.

a. Describe how to conduct one trial of a simulation model to answer the following questions.

- Would it be unusual to find that only 12 students of a randomly selected group of 30 had taken chemistry?

- Would it be unusual to find that all 30 randomly selected students had taken chemistry?

b. Conduct five trials using your simulation model. Copy the frequency table below that shows the results of 195 trials. Add your results to the table.

Number of Students Who Have Taken Chemistry	Frequency	Number of Students Who Have Taken Chemistry	Frequency
6	1	15	28
7	0	16	18
8	1	17	24
9	6	18	13
10	5	19	7
11	9	20	5
12	19	21	3
13	29	22	1
14	26		

c. Identify a particular group of seniors at your school such as band members, yearbook staff, football players, *etc*. Select 30 members of this group and survey them to determine how many are taking or have taken chemistry. Is the number unusual? If so, what are possible reasons for this?

d. Suppose you survey a senior class selected at random in your school and find that all 30 of the students in the class have taken or are taking chemistry. List as many reasons as you can why this could occur.

e. Ask the chemistry teachers in your high school how many students are enrolled in each of their chemistry classes. Estimate the percentage of students in your high school who take a chemistry course.

Organizing

1. a. Make a scatterplot of the (*number of tosses to get a "boy", frequency*) data for your class frequency table from part d of activity 7 on page 482.

 b. Would a line be a reasonable model of the relationship between number of tosses and frequency? Why or why not?

2. In 1993 China had a population of approximately 1,200,000,000. Assume parents were not following the one-child-per-family policy and the population of China continued to grow at about 1.3% per year.

 a. At that rate, how many people would have been added to the population of China in 1994? Compare this number to the population of your state.

 b. Assume the growth rate of 1.3% per year continues. Make a table of the year-end populations of China from 1993 to 2003.

  – Is the relationship a linear one? Explain your reasoning on the basis of your table.

  – What is the percent increase in China's population from 1993 to 2003?

 c. Make a scatterplot of the data in your table.

  – Find an equation that fits this data well.

  – Use your equation to predict when the population of China will exceed 1.5 billion people.

3. Suppose that during first period, Central High School has 95 classes of 30 students each and 5 classes of 100 students each.

 a. What is the average first period class size as reported by the high school?

 b. Suppose each student writes the size of his or her first period class. What is the average class size from the students' point of view?

 c. How are these questions similar to activity 2, parts d and f of Investigation 1.1?

4. a. How could a cube be used to simulate the birth of a child—either boy or girl?

 b. Could you use a regular tetrahedron to simulate the birth of a child? Explain your procedure.

 c. Identify other geometric shapes that could be used as the basis for a simulation model of births.

5. A circle with radius 6 inches is inscribed in a square as a model of a dart board. Suppose a randomly thrown dart hits the board.

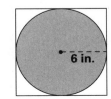

 a. What is a reasonable estimate of the probability the dart will land in the circle? Explain your reasoning.

b. Describe a simulation that could be used to estimate the probability.

c. Why might throwing darts at the board not be a good simulation?

d. How could you use the results of your simulation in part b to estimate π?

Reflecting

1. Is there any difference in the following three questions? Explain your position.

a. In a country where parents are allowed to have only one child, what percentage of couples will have a daughter?

b. In a country where parents are allowed to have only one child, what is the probability that a couple, selected at random, will have a daughter?

c. In a country where parents are allowed to have only one child, what fraction (proportion) of couples will have a daughter?

2. a. Suppose you toss a penny four times and get heads each time. What is the probability you will get a head on the fifth toss?

b. If a family has four boys in a row, what is the probability the next child will be a girl? How is this question different from the one in part a? How could you find the answer to this question?

3. Do some library research to find information about one of the following questions. Prepare a brief written report on your findings.

a. In what cultures of the world is there a strong preference for male children? For female children? What effect does this have on children of the opposite gender in these cultures?

b. Does a preference for male or female children exist in the United States? How do we know whether or not this is the case? If there is a preference for a particular gender in the United States, what might be some possible reasons for this preference?

4. A school is selling magazine subscriptions to raise money. A group wants to simulate the situation of asking ten people if they will buy a magazine. Jason proposes that the group flip a coin ten times and count the number of heads since a person either buys a magazine (heads) or doesn't buy a magazine (tails). Is Jason's simulation model a reasonable one? Explain your position.

5. In part c of activity 1 of Investigation 1.1, you simulated the situation of counting the number of girls and boys in a family that has two children. Does it matter if you flip *one* coin twice or flip *two* coins once? Explain your reasoning.

Extending

1. You have studied four plans in this lesson for population planning.

   – Each family has only one child.

   – Each family has exactly two children.

   – Each family has children until they have a boy (or girl).

   – Each family has at most three children, stopping when they get a boy (or girl).

   Suppose that all people marry at the age of 20 and have children immediately. Assume the first generation consists of an imaginary population of 32 twenty-year-old men and 32 twenty-year-old women. How many children can we expect to be in the fifth generation under each one of the four plans above? (Assume that in every generation there are an equal number of males and females.)

2. If a student guesses on every question of a 10 question true-false test, how many questions would you expect that student to get correct? What percentage is this? Devise a method of scoring a true-false test so that a student who guesses on every question would expect to get a 0% on the test and a student who knows all of the answers gets 100%.

3. In 1974, 48 male bank supervisors were each given one personnel file and asked to judge whether the person should be promoted or the file held and other applicants interviewed. The files were identical except that half of them indicated that the file was that of a female and half indicated that the file was that of a male. Of the 24 "male" files, 21 were recommended for promotion. Of the 24 "female" files, 14 were recommended for promotion. Design and carry out a simulation to evaluate how likely it is that a difference this large could occur just by chance. After conducting your simulation, do you believe that the bank managers were discriminating or do you believe the different numbers promoted could reasonably have happened just by chance?

   Source: B. Rosen and T. Jerdee, "Influence of Sex Role Stereotypes on Personnel Decisions," *Journal of Applied Psychology*, Volume 59, 1974, pages 9–14.

4. **a.** Look up the records of past World Series. Make a histogram of the number of games actually played per series.

   b. How does the shape of the histogram of the real data compare to the one of your simulated data in part d of Modeling task 3?

   c. Does it appear to you that the teams tend to be evenly matched?

5. For some rock concerts, audience members are chosen randomly to be checked for cameras, food, and other restricted items. Suppose that in the search of the first 25 boys and 25 girls to enter a concert, all ten people chosen to be searched were male.

a. How is this situation mathematically different from the one in "On Your Own" on page 484?

b. Describe a simulation model for this situation. What assumptions did you make in your model?

c. Conduct at least 20 trials of your simulation. Record the results in a frequency table showing the number of boys selected.

d. Is your conclusion different from your conclusion in the "On Your Own" activity? Explain.

6. One of the sequences below is the result of actual flips of a coin. The other was written by a student trying to avoid doing the actual flips.

Sequence I

THHHHTTTTH	HHHTHHHHHH	HHTTTHHTTH	HHHHTTTTTT
HHTHHTHHHT	TTHTTHHHHT	HTTTHTTTHH	TTTTHHHHHH
TTTHHTTHHH	THHHHHTTTT	THTTTHHTTH	TTHHTTTHHT
TTHHTHHTHH	TTTTTHHTHH	HHHHTHTHTT	HTHTTHHHTT
HHTHTHHHHH	HHHTTHTTHH	HTHHTTHTTT	TTTHHHTHHH

Sequenc+e II

THTHTTTHTT	HTTHTHTTTH	TTHHHTHHTH	THTHTTTTHH
TTHHTTHHHT	HHHTTHHHTT	THHHTHHHHT	TTHTHTHHHH
THTTTHHHTH	HTHTTTHHTH	HHTHHHHTTH	THHTHHHTTT
HTHHHTHHTT	THHHTTTTHH	HTHTHHHHTH	TTHHTTTTHT
HTHTTHTHHT	THTTTHHTTT	HHHHTHTHHH	TTHHTHTTHH

a. Which sequence do you think is the real one? Why did you select this one?

b. Flip a coin 200 times, being sure each time that the coin spins many times in the air. Record the sequence of results.

c. Does your sequence of actual coin flips look more like the first sequence or more like the second sequence?

2 *Estimating Expected Values and Probabilities*

Cheerios, a popular breakfast cereal, once included one of seven magic tricks in each box.

**Collect All 7 and
Put On Your Own Magic Show!**

MONEY CLIP TRICK
Make two clips magically
join together!

MIND-READING TRICK
Guess the color your friend
secretly picked!

VANISHING CARD TRICK
Make a card magically
disappear!

MAGIC ROPE TRICK
Make the rope magically
pass through solid tube!

DISAPPEARING COIN TRICK
Make a coin magically
disappear and reappear!

SURPRISE 4'S
Turn two blank cards into
two 4's!

MULTIPLYING COIN TRICK
Turn two coins into three!

Think about this situation

a Why do manufacturers include "surprises" in the packages with their product? What other products often have a "gift" in the package?

b What is the least number of boxes you could buy and get all seven magic tricks?

c What is your prediction of the average number of boxes of Cheerios a person would have to buy to get all seven magic tricks?

d Describe at least one way to simulate this situation.

Investigation 2.1   Simulation Using a Table of Random Digits

In the first lesson, you flipped a lot of coins to simulate situations. Fortunately, you won't have to flip coins any more. Calculators and computers will do the work for you. You can get strings of **random digits** either from your calculator or from a random digit table produced by a computer.

1. Examine this table of random digits between 0 and 9 inclusive generated by a computer.

2	4	8	0	3	1	8	6	5	6	4	2	0	0
7	6	8	6	3	0	5	6	8	2	5	0	7	5
0	9	5	8	1	7	3	0	9	9	8	7	7	7
0	2	6	8	6	2	5	5	4	1	5	9	8	0
4	1	2	9	0	8	6	7	0	3	3	8	2	1
1	5	8	0	9	5	7	3	5	6	5	0	2	3
9	7	6	2	5	9	2	6	3	5	0	3	1	3
2	1	0	9	6	0	1	8	5	5	2	2	6	6

a. How many digits are in the table? About how many 6s would you expect to find? How many are there? Choose another digit and determine its frequency.

b. About what percentage of digits in a large table of random digits from 0 to 9 will be even?

c. About what percentage of the 1s in a large table of random digits from 0 to 9 will be followed by a 2?

d. About what percentage of the digits in a large table of random digits from 0 to 9 will be followed by that same digit?

2. Refer to the table of random digits in activity 1 when describing simulation models for the situations below.

a. Explain how you could use the random digits to simulate whether a newborn baby is male or female. Describe a second way of using random digits for the same simulation.

b. Explain how you could use the random digits to simulate tossing a die. (Disregarding particular digits won't affect the results.)

c. Explain how you could use the random digits to simulate checking a box of Cheerios for which of seven magic tricks it contains. Does your plan require that you disregard some digits? Why or why not?

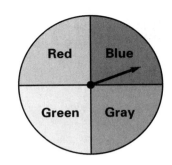

d. Explain how you could use the random digits to simulate spinning the spinner shown here.

e. Explain how you could use the random digits to simulate selecting three students at random out of a group of ten students. What does it mean to select students "at random?"

3. The Table of Random Digits supplied by your teacher contains one thousand random digits.

   a. Explain how you could use this table to simulate the random selection of three students from a group of seven students. Perform one trial.

   b. Explain how you could use this table to simulate the experiment of rolling a die until you get a six. Perform one trial.

   c. Explain how you could use this table to simulate tossing two coins until both tosses are heads. Perform one trial.

4. Refer back to the description of magic tricks in Cheerios at the beginning of this lesson.

   a. If you buy one box of Cheerios, what is the probability that you will get a multiplying coin trick? To get your answer, what assumptions did you make about the tricks?

   b. Suppose you want to find the number of boxes of Cheerios you will have to buy before you get all seven magic tricks. Describe a simulation model for this. Describe how to conduct one trial using the Table of Random Digits.

   c. Compare your group's simulation model with that of other groups. Then as a class, decide on a simulation model that all groups will use.

   d. Have each member of your group perform one trial using the agreed upon simulation model. How many "boxes" did each person in your group have to buy? Put these numbers in a frequency table such as the following one.

Number of Boxes to Get All 7 Tricks	Frequency	Number of Boxes to Get All 7 Tricks	Frequency
7		13	
8		14	
9		15	
10		16	
11		*etc.*	
12		**Total Number of Trials**	200

e. Complete a total of 200 trials of this simulation by sharing the work among the groups in your class. Complete a frequency table for the class data. Add additional rows if they are needed.

f. Find the average number of boxes purchased to obtain a complete set of the seven tricks. Use the frequency table and your calculator or computer, as needed. How does this estimate compare with the prediction you gave in part c of "Think about this situation" on page 498?

g. If you didn't use simulation, how else could you estimate the average number of boxes needed? Which method is preferable? Why?

h. Make a histogram of the information in your frequency table. Explain how your histogram verifies that your answer to part f is reasonable.

i. Describe the shape of your histogram. Is the shape of this distribution similar to any others you have constructed in this chapter? If so, identify the situations related to those histograms.

Checkpoint

a What is a table of random digits? How is it used in simulation?

b What are the advantages of using random digits in a simulation?

c To boost sales, tie-ins with popular movies are used by many types of manufacturers. As a tie-in to the animated film *The Hunchback of Notre Dame*, plastic figurines shaped like characters in the movie were distributed randomly in Cheerios boxes. Each box contained one of five different figurines. How would you modify your simulation model to study this new situation?

✓ *Be prepared to share your group's descriptions and thinking with the entire class.*

In this investigation, you have explored the properties of random digits and learned how to use them in designing a simulation.

On Your Own

A teacher notices that of the last 20 single-day absences in her class, 10 were on Friday. She wants to know if this can be attributed reasonably to chance or if she should look for another explanation.

a. Assuming that absences are equally likely to occur on each day of the school week, describe how to conduct one trial simulating the days of the week for 20 single-day absences using a table of random digits.

b. Conduct 10 trials. Place the results in a frequency table showing the number of absences that are on Friday.

c. Based on your simulation, what is your estimate of the probability of getting 10 or more absences out of 20 on Friday just by chance? What should the teacher conclude?

d. What is your estimate of the average number of absences on Friday, assuming that the 20 absences are equally likely to occur on each day of the week?

e. How could you get better estimates for parts c and d?

Investigation 2.2 Simulation Using a Random Number Generator

A table of random digits is a convenient tool to use in conducting simulations. Regular polyhedra models with numbered faces and playing cards are sometimes useful. However, a most versatile tool is a calculator or computer software with a *random number generator*.

1. Investigate the nature of the numbers produced by the random number generator on your calculator or computer software. On some calculators, the generator is abbreviated "rand". The "Technology Tip" handout may be helpful.

a. How many decimal places do the numbers usually have? Do some have one fewer place? If so, why?

b. Between what two whole numbers do all the random numbers lie?

c. Generate random numbers of the form "6 rand" (or "6 × rand"). Between what two whole numbers do all the random numbers lie?

d. Between what two whole numbers do the random numbers lie when "rand" is multiplied by 10? By 36? By 100?

e. Generate several numbers using the command "int 6 rand".

- What random numbers are generated by this function?

- What is the effect of the "int" function?

f. To simulate rolling a die, you need a random digit selected from the set 1, 2, 3, 4, 5, 6. In part e, you generated random digits from the set 0, 1, 2, 3, 4, 5.

- How could you modify the command "int 6 rand" to produce the numbers on the faces of a die? Try it.

- Generate a list of 10 digits randomly selected from the set 1, 2, 3, 4, 5, 6.

2. a. What random digits are generated by the command "int 10 rand + 1"?

b. Modify the command in part a to generate random digits from the set:

- 1 to 23 inclusive
- 1 to 100 inclusive
- 1 to 52 inclusive
- 0 to 6 inclusive

Test your modified commands.

3. a. Explain how you could use the random number generator to simulate the flips of a fair coin.

b. Explain how you could use the random number generator to select three students at random from a group of seven students. Perform one trial of this simulation.

c. Explain how you could use the random number generator to select six students at random from a group of 50 students. Perform one trial of this simulation.

d. Explain how you could use the random number generator to simulate the experiment of rolling a die until you get a six. Perform one trial of this simulation.

e. Explain how you could use the random number generator to simulate checking a box of Cheerios for which magic trick it contains. Perform one trial of this simulation.

f. Explain how you could use the random number generator to simulate the experiment of drawing a card from a well-shuffled deck of 52 playing cards and checking if it is an ace. Perform one trial of this simulation.

4. Software for computers and calculators has been developed to help you quickly conduct many trials of a simulation. This activity will illustrate how you can use such software to implement your simulation model for the Cheerios problem. (The calculator software AACOLECT is an example of this software.)

a. Use such software to conduct 25 trials of collecting the seven magic tricks.

b. Study a histogram of the results of your 25 trials. What do the bars in the display represent?

c. Compare your histogram with those of other members of your group. Are they the same? If not, what accounts for the differences?

d. With the AACOLECT program, you can use the arrow keys to explore the histogram. What do the "min =," "max =," and "n =" mean? (Remember that the number between two bars belongs in the bar to the right of the number.)

e. What is your estimate of the average number of boxes of cereal you would have to buy before you obtained all 7 tricks? (With AACOLECT, press ENTER from the histogram screen. This information will be displayed.)

f. Have each member of your group use the software to conduct different numbers of trials (for example, 50, 75, or 99). Record and compare your results.

g. Suppose the cereal manufacturer modified its marketing scheme. It randomly packaged one of six differently colored pens in each box of cereal. Use the software to help you estimate the number of boxes of Cheerios to be purchased in order to get a complete set of the six pens.

Checkpoint

When using a calculator or computer to generate random numbers,

a how can you control the size of these numbers?

b how can you ensure they will be integers?

✓ *Be prepared to share your group's thinking with the class.*

On Your Own

Lynn is taking a ten question multiple-choice test. Each question offers four possible choices for the answer. She didn't study and doesn't even have a reasonable guess on any of the questions. For each question, Lynn selects one of the four possible answers at random.

a. Describe how to conduct one trial simulating a 10-question test. Use the random number generator on your calculator or computer.

b. Conduct 20 trials and place the results in a frequency table.

c. What is your estimate of the probability that Barbara will pass the test with a score of 70% or more?

Modeling **O**rganizing **R**eflecting **E**xtending

Modeling

1. Cracker Jack, the caramel corn-peanut snack, traditionally gives a prize in each box. At one time, it offered five different prizes.

    a. Describe how to conduct one trial of a simulation model for estimating the number of boxes of Cracker Jack you would have to buy before you get all five prizes. What assumptions are you making?

    b. Conduct five trials. Copy the following frequency table, which has the results from 195 trials. Add the results from your five trials to the table.

Number of Boxes Purchased	Frequency
5	6
6	15
7	23
8	18
9	21
10	18
11	15
12	15
13	11
14	11
15	10

Number of Boxes Purchased	Frequency
16	6
17	6
18	8
19	1
20	2
21	4
22	0
23	0
24	1
25	2
26	0

Number of Boxes Purchased	Frequency
27	1
28	0
29	0
30	0
31	0
32	0
33	0
34	0
35	0
36	1

   c. What is the average number of boxes purchased in the 200 trials to get all five prizes?

   d. Make a histogram of the (*number of boxes purchased, frequency*) data. Describe the shape of the histogram.

   e. Explain how you can use the histogram to verify the average you found in part c.

2. Toni doesn't have a key ring and so just drops her keys into the bottom of her backpack. Her four keys—a house key, a car key, a locker key, and a key to her bicycle lock—are all about the same size.

   a. If she reaches into her backpack and grabs the first key she touches, what is the probability it is her car key?

If the key drawn is not her car key, she holds onto it. Then, without looking, she reaches into her backpack for a second key. If that key is not her car key, she holds on to both keys drawn and reaches in for a third key.

   b. Do the chances that Toni will grab her car key increase, decrease, or remain the same on each grab? Explain your reasoning.

c. Describe how to conduct one trial of a simulation model to estimate the probability that Toni has to grab all four keys before she gets her car key. Use a table of random digits, a calculator, or a computer to conduct the trial.

d. Conduct 10 trials. Copy the frequency table below and add your results so that there is a total of 1000 trials.

Number of Keys Toni Needs to Grab to Get Her Car Key	Frequency
1	253
2	250
3	233
4	254
Total Number of Trials	

e. What is your estimate of the probability that Toni has to grab all four keys before she gets her car key?

f. From the frequency table, it appears that the numbers of keys needed are equally likely. Explain why this is the case.

3. One cereal promotion offered one of four items for little girls: a comb, a mirror, a barrette, or a bracelet. The catch was that each item came in four colors: yellow, pink, blue, and lavender. Suppose that María wants a complete set, all in lavender.

a. Describe how to use a table of random digits or a random number generator to conduct one trial simulating the number of boxes María's parents will have to buy. What assumptions are you making?

b. Conduct five trials. Add your results to a copy of the stem-and-leaf plot at the right. There will be a total of 50 trials.

c. What is your estimate of the probability that more than 15 boxes of cereal must be purchased to get a complete set all in lavender?

```
1 | 0 4 4 6 6 8 8 9
2 | 0 1 2 2 3 4 4 6 6 7 7 8 8 9 9
3 | 1 3 3 3 4 4 5 7 8
4 | 0 1 4 5 6
5 | 0 0 1 6 7 8 8
6 | 6
```
2|4 represents 24

d. What is your estimate of the average number of boxes that must be purchased?

e. Will the median number of boxes be more or less than the average? Find the median to check your prediction.

4. Suppose Whitney also knows about the promotion described in Modeling task 3. She wants a complete set in one color, but any color is okay.

 a. Describe how to use a table of random digits or a random number generator to conduct one trial simulating the number of boxes Whitney's parents will have to buy. What assumptions are you making?

 b. Conduct 10 trials. Combine your results with those from other members of your group. Place the results in a frequency table.

 c. What is your estimate of the probability that more than 15 boxes of cereal must be purchased to get a complete set all in the same color?

 d. What is your estimate of the average number of boxes that must be purchased?

5. The card below shows a McDonald's-Atari Asteroids® scratch-off game. All of the asteroids were originally covered. The instructions say:

> *Start anywhere. Rub off silver asteroids one at a time. Match 2 identical prizes BEFORE a "ZAP" appears and win that prize. There is only one winning match per card.*

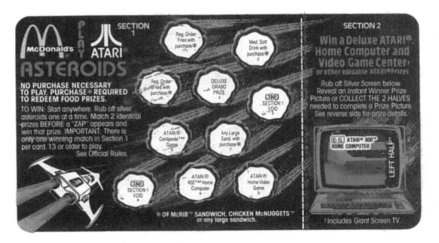

 a. Describe how to conduct one trial of a simulation to determine the probability of winning the prize in the scratch-off game. Share your instructions of how to perform a trial with your group. Modify the sets of instructions to reach a consensus on the model.

 b. Exchange your instructions with another group. Conduct 20 trials using the other group's model.

 c. Combine the results from all of the groups in your class and estimate the probability of winning the prize.

Organizing

1. a. Make a box plot of the data from the 200 trials simulating the Cheerios problem (part e of activity 4, page 501). How does the shape of the box plot reflect the shape of the histogram you prepared for part h of that activity? In which direction are the plots skewed?

   b. Complete this sentence about the distribution of boxes purchased to get all 7 magic tricks: *Half of the time, a person who wanted all seven magic tricks would have to buy at least _____ boxes of Cheerios.* Does this statement refer to the average number of boxes or the median number of boxes?

2. Make a box plot of the distribution in one of the Modeling tasks you completed. Compare this box plot to the one you made in Organizing task 1. Do the two plots have the same basic shape? Explain.

3. Suppose different cereal companies have packaged in their boxes the number of different prizes given below. Carry out simulations to estimate the average number of boxes that would have to be purchased to get all of the prizes in each case. (The software you used for activity 4, Investigation 2.2, would be helpful.)

   a. 2 different prizes   **b.** 3 different prizes

   c. 5 different prizes   **d.** 8 different prizes

   e. 20 different prizes

   f. Create a table with column headings "Number of Prizes" and "Average Number of Boxes Purchased". Fill the table with your responses to parts c and d of activity 4 in Investigation 2.2 and your data for this task (parts a through e). Make a scatterplot of the (*number of prizes, average number of boxes purchased*) data.

     – Does a linear model fit these data reasonably well? If so, find the regression line. If not, describe the shape of the graph.

     – About how many additional boxes must be purchased if one more type of prize is added to the boxes?

4. Toni's key selection problem (Modeling task 2) is one that depends on *order—* the order in which she chooses the keys. One way to model the problem would be to list all the possible orders in which the keys could be selected. An ordering of a set is called a **permutation** of the objects. For example, the permutations of the letters A, B, and C are:

ABC   ACB   BAC   BCA   CAB   CBA

   a. In what special sequence are the permutations above listed?

   b. List all of the permutations of the letters A and B. How many are there?

c. List all of the permutations of the letters A, B, C, and D. How many are there?

d. Look for a pattern relating the number of permutations to the number of letters.

e. How many permutations do you think there are of the letters A, B, C, D, and E? Check your conjecture by listing all of the permutations or by using the permutations option on your calculator or computer software. (For most calculators, you need to enter "5 nPr 5". This means the number of permutations of 5 objects taken 5 at a time.)

f. How many orders are there for Toni's four keys? What is the probability that all four keys have to be drawn before Toni gets her car key?

R*eflecting*

1. You have conducted simulations by coin flipping and by using random digits from a table, calculator, or computer.

a. Which of these simulation tools is easiest for you to understand?

b. Which tool is the most flexible in simulating a variety of situations?

c. Which tool do you find easiest to use?

2. A deck of playing cards can be used to simulate some situations.

a. How could you use cards to conduct one trial in a simulation of collecting Cheerios tricks?

b. How could you use cards to generate a table of random digits?

3. a. How can you tell the nature of the random numbers generated by looking at the expression "int 12 rand + 1"?

b. Give an example of a real life situation which might lead to a simulation model involving use of this calculator or computer command.

4. Do you think it is faster to do a simulation using a table of random digits or using a calculator to generate random digits? Design and carry out an experiment to answer this question. Write a brief summary describing your experiment and findings.

5. The AACOLECT software will conduct up to 99 trials of certain simulations. Suppose you need 200 trials simulating a collecting problem. How could you use the software to help you?

Extending

1. There is some evidence that either there were more of some of the Cheerios magic tricks than others, or the magic tricks weren't put into the boxes randomly. (This might happen, for example, if all of the boxes containing the disappearing coin trick were sent to California.) Suppose you are more likely to get some magic tricks than others. Will the average number of boxes purchased in order to get all seven magic tricks be more, the same, or less than if each trick is equally likely? Design and carry out a simulation to answer this question.

2. Suppose your class is having a holiday gift exchange. The name of each student is written on a card. The cards are placed in a hat, mixed up, and each student draws one. One of your classmates wonders how many students will draw their own names.

   a. Describe one trial of a simulation of this situation. Use cards or a table of random digits.

   b. Conduct 50 trials. Place the results in a table that shows the number of students who got their own name.

   c. What is your estimate of the probability that at least one student will get his or her own name?

   d. What is your estimate of the average number of students who will get their own names?

3. In Extending task 2, you answered these two questions:

   – What is the probability that at least one student will get his or her own name?

   – What is the average number of students who will get their own names?

   Will the answers to these two questions change with larger or smaller class sizes than yours? Design and carry out simulations to test your prediction. Write a summary of your findings.

4. One type of CD player will hold five CDs. The player can be set so that it selects a CD at random and plays a song on that CD. It then continues selecting CDs at random from all five CDs and playing songs. Describe one trial of a simulation to estimate the probability that there is at least one song from each of the five CDs among the first ten songs played.

5. Imagine ten people in a room.

    a. What is your estimate of the probability that two of them have the same birthday?

    b. Describe a simulation model to determine the probability that two people out of a group of 10 people have the same birthday.

    c. Conduct 100 trials, sharing the work with other members of your class.

    d. From your simulation, what is your estimate of the probability? Are you surprised?

    e. Investigate the probability that two people will have the same birthday if there are 20 people in the room. Repeat for cases when there are 30, 40, 60, and 80 people in the room.

    f. People often make too much of coincidences. Write an explanation of the following Drabble cartoon for a child who doesn't "get it."

3 *Simulation and the Law of Large Numbers*

In 1985, Major League Baseball switched from a best-of-five league playoff series to a best-of-seven league playoff series. In a best-of-five series, the team that first wins three games wins the series.

Think about this situation

> The winners of the league playoffs represent the National and American Leagues in the World Series. This event is also a best-of-seven series.
>
> **a** How many games do you have to win to be victorious in a best-of-seven series?
>
> **b** Why do you think Major League Baseball went from a five-game to a seven-game championship series?

Investigation 3.1 How Many Games Should You Play?

In this investigation, you will explore playoff series of various lengths. If the teams are evenly matched, each team has a probability of $\frac{1}{2}$ of winning. In reality, teams of all sorts often compete, and they are seldom evenly matched.

1. The Cyclones are playing the Hornets for the softball championship. Based on their history, the Cyclones have a 60% chance of beating the Hornets in any one game.

   a. Suppose the championship series were only one game long. What is the probability that the better team (Cyclones) would win?

   b. Suppose the Cyclones and the Hornets were to play 100 games. About how many games would you expect the Cyclones to win? The Hornets? Explain your reasoning.

c. Describe how you would design one trial of a simulation model for a one-game series. Use a table of random digits or a random number generator. How will you split the numbers so that the Cyclones have a 60% chance of winning and the Hornets have a 40% chance of winning?

d. Why isn't it appropriate to use a coin flip in your model to determine which team wins a game?

2. Should an even number of games be used for a playoff series? Explain your reasoning.

3. Suppose the Cyclones and the Hornets play a three-game series. A three-game series ends after one team wins two games.

a. Describe how to conduct one trial of a simulation model for a three-game series.

b. Describe how you could use 200 trials of your simulation model to estimate the probability that the better team (Cyclones) will win a best-of-three game series.

c. Conduct 200 trials. Share the work among the groups in your class. Record your data in a frequency table like the one below.

Number of Games Won by the Cyclones in a Best-of-Three Game Series	Frequency
0	
1	
2	
Total Number of Trials	200

d. Which rows represent a win of the championship series by the Cyclones? By the Hornets?

e. What is your estimate of the probability that the Cyclones will win a best-of-three series?

4. Next explore the idea of a five-game series between the same two teams.

a. Describe how to conduct one trial of a simulation model for a best-of-five series.

b. Describe how you could use your simulation model to estimate the probability that the Cyclones will win a best-of-five game series.

c. Conduct 200 trials by sharing the work among the groups in your class. Record your data in a frequency table where the number of games won by the Cyclones goes from 0 to 3. Why do you only need numbers up to 3?

d. What is your estimate of the probability that the Cyclones will win a best-of-five series?

5. Now explore the idea of a seven-game series for the same teams.

    a. Describe how to conduct one trial of a simulation model for a seven-game series.

    b. Describe how you could use your simulation model to estimate the probability that the Cyclones will win a best-of-seven game series.

    c. Conduct 200 trials. Share the work among the groups in your class. Place your results in a frequency table showing the number of games won by the Cyclones.

    d. What is your estimate of the probability that the Cyclones will win a best-of-seven series?

6. a. Complete the table below using the results from activities 1 part a, 3, 4, and 5.

Type of Series	Estimate of Probability the Cyclones Win
One game	
Best-of-three	
Best-of-five	
Best-of-seven	

    b. What pattern do you observe in the table? Which team, the Cyclones or the Hornets, would have the better chance to win a best-of-nine game series? Estimate the probability of their winning.

    c. Improve your estimate in part b by carrying out a simulation.

    d. From a mathematical point of view, why do you now think that Major League Baseball went from a five-game to a seven-game championship series?

7. Make histograms of your frequency tables from activities 3–5. How are these histograms alike? How are they different?

8. Tennis players have two chances to make a legal serve. Monica makes about 50% of her *first* serves. If she has to try a *second* serve, Monica makes about 80% of those.

    a. Describe how to use a table of random digits to conduct one trial simulating this situation.

    b. Describe how to use a random number generator to conduct one trial simulating this situation.

c. Conduct one trial of your simulation model and record the result in a frequency table. Your frequency table should have three rows: makes first serve, misses first serve and makes second serve, and double-faults (misses both serves).

d. Conduct 50 trials.

e. Estimate the probability that Monica double-faults.

In the previous situations, the percentages of *success*—winning a game or making a serve—were multiples of 10. In those cases, you may have used single digits from your random digits table or from your calculator. Often, as in the next two situations, the percentages are not as "nice."

9. A survey of high school seniors found that 29% had seen a movie in the previous two weeks.

a. Describe how to conduct one trial of a simulation to estimate the number of recent movie-goers in a randomly selected group of 20 seniors.

b. Conduct 10 trials, placing the results on a number line plot that shows the number of recent movie-goers in each group of 20 randomly selected students.

10. In the almost 50-year history of National Basketball Association playoffs, the home team has won about 67% of the games. Suppose that the Los Angeles Lakers are playing the Phoenix Suns in the NBA playoffs. The two teams are equally good, except for this home team advantage. The playoffs are a best-of-seven series. The first two games will be played in Phoenix, the next three (if needed) in Los Angeles, and the final two (if needed) in Phoenix.

a. What is the probability that the Suns will win a game if it is at home? What is the probability that the Suns will win a game if it is played in Los Angeles? What is the probability the Suns will win the first game of the series? The second game? The third game? The fourth game? The fifth game? The sixth game? The seventh game?

b. Describe how to conduct one trial to simulate a play-off series.

c. Conduct 200 trials by sharing the work among the groups in your class. Place the results in a frequency table like the following one.

Number of Games Won by the Suns	Frequency
0	
1	
2	
3	
4	
Total Number of Trials	200

d. What is your estimate of the probability that the Suns win the playoffs?

e. Suppose that, to cut travel costs, the NBA schedules three games in Los Angeles followed by four in Phoenix.

  – Design a simulation model to determine the probability that the Suns win the playoffs in this situation.

  – Conduct 200 trials of your model. Share the work with other groups.

  – What is your estimate of the probability that the Suns win this series?

f. Compare the probabilities in parts d and e. What is your conclusion?

Checkpoint

ⓐ In playoff series, what is the advantage of a longer series over a shorter one?

ⓑ How can random numbers be used in simulations when the two outcomes are not equally likely?

ⓒ Sheila has a 55% chance of winning a table tennis game against Bobby. Describe a simulation model for estimating the probability that Sheila wins a best-of-nine series of table tennis games against Bobby. Should Bobby prefer a best-of-three series?

✓ *Be prepared to share your group's thinking and simulation model with the class.*

In this investigation, you have explored a variation of the **Law of Large Numbers**. The Law of Large Numbers says, for example, that if you roll a die more and more times, the proportion of fives tends to get closer to $\frac{1}{6}$. The Cyclones have a 60% chance of winning each game. For a very long series, the Law of Large Numbers says that the percentage of games the Cyclones win tends to be close to 60%. (So the Cyclones are almost sure to win a long series.)

On Your Own

Recall that in Major League Baseball, the World Series is a best-of-seven games series. In Modeling task 3 on page 492, you estimated the probability that the World Series will go seven games if the teams are equally matched. That probability is actually 0.3125.

a. Suppose the two teams aren't evenly matched. Do you think the World Series is more likely to go seven games or less likely to go seven games than if the teams are evenly matched? Why?

b. Suppose that the teams are not evenly matched and that the American League team has a 70% chance of winning each game. Describe how to conduct one trial of a best-of-seven series for this situation.

c. Conduct 5 trials. Add your results to a copy of the frequency table below so that there is a total of 100 trials.

Number of Games Needed in the Series	Frequency
4	24
5	30
6	24
7	17
Total Number of Trials	

d. What is your estimate of the probability that the series will go seven games in this case? Is this probability of a seven-game series more or less than when the teams are evenly matched?

Modeling **O**rganizing **R**eflecting **E**xtending

Modeling

1. About 60% of high school graduates in the United States are enrolled in a college or university the fall after graduation.

   a. Describe how to conduct one trial of a simulation model to estimate the number of college enrollees from a randomly selected group of 20 high school graduates.

   b. Conduct 5 trials. Add your results to a copy of the frequency table below so there is a total of 400 trials.

Number Who Enroll in College	Percentage Who Enroll in College	Frequency
6	30	3
7	35	2
8	40	17
9	45	39
10	50	51
11	55	53
12	60	80
13	65	66
14	70	39
15	75	29
16	80	13
17	85	3
Total Number of Trials		

   c. Make a histogram of these results. Place "Percentage Who Enroll in College" on the horizontal axis.

   d. When 20 students are randomly selected, what is your estimate of the probability that fewer than half will enroll in college?

2. The following histogram shows the result of 400 trials of a simulation. The situation modeled is the same as in task 1 except that 80 high school graduates were randomly selected.

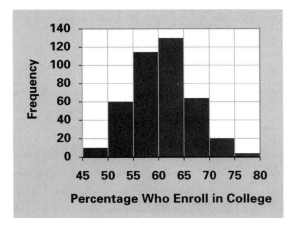

a. Estimate the probability that fewer than half of 80 randomly selected students will enroll in college.

b. Why do you think the probabilities in part d of Modeling task 1 and part a above are different?

c. Describe how the histograms from Modeling tasks 1 and 2 are different. Why would you expect this to be the case? How do these histograms illustrate the Law of Large Numbers?

d. Estimate the probability that fewer than half of a random selection of 320 students will enroll in college. Explain your reasoning.

3. Several years ago, a survey found that 25% of American pet owners carry pictures of their pets in their wallets.

a. Assume this percentage is true. Describe how to simulate determining if a randomly chosen American pet owner carries a picture of his or her pet. Use a calculator, computer, or table of random digits in your simulation.

b. Describe how to conduct one trial that models how many people in a random sample of 20 American pet owners carry pictures of their pets.

c. Perform 10 trials of your simulation model. Add your results to a copy of the following frequency table so that there is a total of 100 trials.

Number of People with a Picture of Their Pet	Frequency
0	0
1	2
2	6
3	12
4	17
5	18

Number of People with a Picture of Their Pet	Frequency
6	15
7	10
8	5
9	3
10	1
11	1
Total Number of Trials	

d. Take a survey of 20 American pet owners to see how many carry pictures of their pets in their wallets. Do you have any reason to doubt the reported figure of 25%?

4. Tri is planning a birthday party and would like to have as many of her friends attend as possible. Her parents say that she can have a maximum of 25 people at her party. Tri estimates that people will decide independently whether or not to come and that for each person there is an 80% chance that he or she will decide to come.

a. If Tri invites 30 people, how many does she expect will actually show up? Is it possible that all 30 will show up?

b. How many people should Tri invite if she expects 25 to show up? Is it possible that if Tri invites this many, more than 25 people will show up?

c. Suppose Tri decides to invite 30 people to her party. Describe one trial in a simulation of this situation.

d. Conduct 5 trials. Add your results to a copy of the frequency table below so that there is a total of 55 trials.

Number of People Who Show Up	Frequency
19	0
20	1
21	2
22	3
23	5
24	8

Number of People Who Show Up	Frequency
25	9
26	9
27	7
28	4
29	2
30	0
Total Number of Trials	

e. Make a histogram of the results of this simulation. Describe the shape of your histogram.

f. Suppose Tri invites 30 people. Based on your simulation, estimate the probability that more than 25 people show up. Is 30 a reasonable number to invite? Should Tri invite fewer or could she get away with inviting more?

g. What assumption made in this simulation is different from the real-life situation being modeled?

Organizing

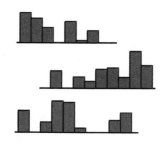

1. Examine all of the histograms that you have made in this chapter. Group them according to their general shape. What observations can you make about the shapes and kinds of probability situations associated with them? For example, which kinds of situations give distributions that have line symmetry?

2. **a.** Explain why it is important to conduct as many trials as you can in a simulation.

   Suppose you want to be 95% sure that a probability estimate from a simulation is within a certain *margin of error* of the actual probability. The formula

$$n = \frac{1}{E^2}$$

gives the number of trials n needed in order to estimate within a margin of error E.

   For example, suppose you want to estimate the probability that a bent coin comes up heads. You want to be 95% sure your estimated probability is within $E = 0.1$ (10%) of the actual probability. You need to perform

$$n = \frac{1}{(0.1)^2} = \frac{1}{0.01} = 100$$

trials of the simulation.

   Being "95% sure" means that out of every 100 simulations you perform, you expect that in 95 of them your estimated probability is within E of the actual probability.

   b. Suppose you want to estimate a probability in a simulation and be 95% sure that your estimated probability is within 5% of the actual probability. How many trials should you perform?

   c. In some of the simulations in this chapter, you performed 200 trials. What is the margin of error associated with 200 trials of a simulation?

   d. What is the margin of error associated with 1000 trials of a simulation?

3. Use your graphing calculator to investigate the graph of the *number-of-trials* function given in Organizing task 2.

   a. Should x or y on the calculator represent the number of trials? What does the other variable represent?

   b. Set Xmin = 0.01 and Xmax = 0.15. What are reasonable choices for Xscl, Ymin, Ymax, and Yscl?

   c. Describe the shape of the graph of this function, including any symmetry.

   d. Use the trace function to estimate the number of trials needed for a margin of error of 2%, 3%, and 8%.

   e. How could you answer part d using the table-building capability of your calculator or computer software?

4. a. In Organizing task 2 you saw that with 100 trials, there is a margin of error of 10%. How many trials would you need to cut this margin of error in half?

   b. With 625 trials there is a margin of error of 4%. How many trials would you need to cut this margin of error in half?

   c. In general, to cut a margin of error in half, how must the number of trials change?

Reflecting

1. The Law of Large Numbers tells you that if you flip a coin repeatedly, the percentage of heads tends to get closer to 50%.

   a. Does the following table illustrate the Law of Large Numbers? Why or why not?

   b. Do you see a surprising result in the following table? Explain why you find it surprising.

Number of Tosses	Number of Heads	Percentage of Heads	Expected Number of Heads	Excess Heads
10	6	60%	5	1
100	56	56%	50	6
1,000	524	52.4%	500	24
10,000	5140	51.4%	5000	140

2. Suppose your class is planning a checkers tournament and you are sure you are the best player in the class. What kind of tournament rules would you propose? Explain your reasoning.

3. One simulation method, called the *Monte Carlo method*, was developed during World War II at Los Alamos, New Mexico to solve problems that arose in the design of atomic reactors. Investigate this history and prepare a brief report.

4. You have now used simulation extensively to estimate answers to problems involving chance.

   a. What advantages do you see in using simulation?

   b. What disadvantages do you see in using simulation?

5. The mathematician Pierre Simon, Marquis de Laplace (1749–1827), once said:

   "It is remarkable that a science which began with the consideration of games of chance should have become the most important object of human knowledge. ... The most important questions of life are, for the most part, really only problems of probability."

   What do you think Laplace meant by the last statement?

   Do you agree with him?

   Why or why not?

Extending

1. **Acceptance sampling** is one method that industry uses to control the quality of the parts they use. For example, a recording company buys blank cassette tapes from a supplier. To ensure the quality of these tapes, the recording company examines a sample of the tapes in each shipment. The company buys the shipment only if 5% or fewer of the tapes in the sample are defective. Assume that 10% of the tapes actually are defective.

   "By a small sample we may judge the whole piece."

   Miguel de Cervantes

a. Suppose the recording company examines a sample of 20 tapes from each shipment. Design and carry out a simulation of this situation. What is your estimate of the probability that the shipment will be accepted?

b. Suppose the recording company examines a sample of 100 tapes from each shipment. Design and carry out a simulation of this situation. What is your estimate of the probability that the shipment will be accepted?

2. For a farmer, it is important that the energy and resources (such as water and fertilizer) invested in a crop produce as high a yield as possible. Laboratory tests indicate that when planted properly, 6% of a particular type of seed fail to germinate. This means that out of every 100 seeds planted according to instructions, on the average 6 do not sprout. The laboratory has been developing a new variety of the seed in which only 1% fail to germinate. Suppose that in an experiment, 10 seeds of each type are planted properly.

a. For each type of seed, make a prediction of the probability that at least one seed out of the 10 will fail to germinate.

b. Design and carry out a simulation to estimate the chance that if 10 of the seeds with the 6% rate are planted, at least one will fail to germinate.

c. Design and carry out a simulation to estimate the chance that if 10 of the new variety of the seed are planted, at least one will fail to germinate.

d. Compare the estimates from your simulations to your predictions in part a. What have you learned?

3. One example of an old gambling system is the Martingale. At first glance, it looks like a winner. Here's how it would work for a player betting on red in roulette. The roulette wheel has 38 spaces; 18 of these spaces are red. On the first spin of the wheel, the player bets $1. If red appears, he collects $2 and leaves. If he loses, he bets $2 on red on the second spin of the wheel. If red appears, he collects $4 and leaves. If he loses, he bets $4 on red on the third spin of the wheel, and so on. The player keeps doubling his bet until he wins.

a. If the player wins on his first try, how much money will he be ahead? If the player wins on his third try, how much money will he be ahead? If the player finally wins on his tenth try, how much money will he be ahead?

b. From a gambler's point of view, what are some flaws in this system?

c. Design and carry out a simulation to test the Martingale system on roulette.

d. Write a report on this system for a school newspaper.

4 *Looking Back*

In this chapter you have used simulation models to help solve problems involving chance. An important feature of all your models was the use of coins, dice, or random numbers to produce random outcomes. In each case, the outcomes had the same mathematical characteristics as those in the original problem.

Almost any problem involving probability or an expected value can be solved using simulation models. This final lesson of the chapter provides three more such problems to help you pull together the ideas you have developed and increase your confidence in using simulation methods.

1. About 10% of the adult population of the United States are African-American.

   a. Jurors are selected for duty in their city or town. Consider a city which has an African-American population representative of the U.S. population. Design a simulation model to determine the probability that a randomly selected jury of twelve people would have no African-American members. Write instructions for performing one trial of your simulation. Exchange instructions with another group.

   b. Do the other group's instructions model the situation well? If necessary, modify the instructions and then conduct five trials. Add your results to a copy of the following frequency table so that there is a total of 200 trials.

Number of African-Americans on the Jury	Frequency
0	56
1	73
2	45

Number of African-Americans on the Jury	Frequency
3	16
4	4
5	1
Total Number of Trials	

c. Make a histogram of the results in your frequency table.

d. What is your estimate of the probability that a randomly selected jury of twelve people would have no African-American members?

e. A *grand jury* decides whether there is enough evidence against a person to bring him or her to trial. A grand jury generally consists of 24 people. Do you think the probability that a randomly selected grand jury would have no African-American members is more, less, or the same as your answer to part d? Why?

f. Describe a simulation to find the probability that a randomly selected grand jury would have no African-American members. Conduct five trials of your simulation model.

2. This roller coaster has seven cars. Ranjana stands in a long line to get on the ride. When she gets to the front, she is directed by the attendant to the next empty seat. No one has any choice of seats, but must take the next empty one in the coaster. Ranjana goes through the line ten times. She likes to sit in the front car.

a. What is the probability Ranjana will get to sit in the front car each time she goes through the line? Do you think Ranjana has a good chance of sitting in the front car at least once in her 10 rides? Explain your reasoning.

b. Describe how to conduct one trial simulating this situation. Use your calculator or computer or a table of random digits.

c. Perform 15 trials. Place the results in a frequency table that lists the number of times out of the 10 rides that Ranjana gets to sit in the front car.

d. From your simulation, what is your estimate of the probability that Ranjana will get to sit in the front car at least once?

e. How could you get a better estimate for part d?

nursery hours
2-4

3. The chance that a newborn baby will be a girl is about $\frac{1}{2}$. Suppose that in one large hospital, 20 babies are born each day. In a smaller hospital nearby, 5 babies are born each day.

a. Do you think the size of the hospital affects the number of days in which 60% or more of the babies born are girls? If so, do you think this would happen more often in the large hospital or the small one? Explain your reasoning.

b. Describe how to conduct one trial of a simulation model to find the number of girls born on one day in the large hospital. Describe a similar model for the small hospital.

c. Conduct 20 trials of a simulation for both the large and the small hospital to test the conjecture you made in part a. Be sure to make a histogram of your results.

d. Are the results of your simulations different from your conjecture? What should you conclude?

e. Shown below are responses to the question in part a by a group of college undergraduates.

small hospital	large hospital	no difference
17	15	48

Why do you think so many undergraduates believed the size of the hospital would not make a difference?

f. How is this problem related to your work in the previous lesson on the best length for a play-off series?

Checkpoint

ⓐ Summarize the steps involved in using a simulation model to solve a problem involving chance.

ⓑ Will a simulation give you an "exact" answer? Explain your reasoning.

ⓒ What does the Law of Large Numbers say about how many trials should be done in a simulation?

ⓓ A letter to the *Washington Post* on May 11, 1993 suggested that China has more boys born than girls because if the first child is a boy then the parents tend to stop having children. Based on your work in this chapter, do you think this is likely to be the case? Write a response to the author of this letter explaining your reasoning.

✓ *Be prepared to share your summary and explanations with the entire class.*

Planning a Benefits Carnival

In this course you have built useful mathematical models—including linear, exponential, geometric, simulation, and graph models. You have used these models to solve important problems in many different settings. You have investigated patterns in data, change, chance, and shape. And you have learned how to make sense of situations by representing them in different ways

using physical representations, words, graphs, tables, and symbols. In this Capstone, you will pull together many of the important concepts, techniques, and models that you have learned and use them to analyze one big project.

Think about this situation

Many schools organize fund-raising events to raise money for improving their programs. The event might be a dance, a bike-a-thon, a book sale—anything that gets the community involved in raising money for the school. One event that is common for elementary schools is a benefits carnival. Suppose that a local elementary school is considering such a carnival. Your class has offered to plan the event and prepare a full report for the school's principal. (In return, your class will get part of the proceeds to use for yourselves!)

a Make a list of all the things that need to be done to plan, carry out, and clean up following such a carnival.

b Make a list of the kinds of booths or activities that might be good to have at the carnival. Think of as many as you can.

Investigation 1 — Lots of Math

Mathematics can be used in many different ways to help you organize the carnival. Think about the mathematics you have studied in each of the chapters in this course. The chapters are listed below. As a group, brainstorm and then write two ways the mathematics in each chapter could be used in the carnival project.

1. *Patterns in Data*
2. *Patterns of Change*
3. *Linear Models*
4. *Graph Models*
5. *Patterns in Space and Visualization*
6. *Exponential Models*
7. *Simulation Models*

Checkpoint

a For each chapter, compare and discuss the ideas from different groups.

b Are there any big mathematical ideas or topics from this course that have not been applied to the carnival project? If so, is there any way they could be applied?

✓ *Be prepared to share your group's thinking with the whole class.*

At the end of this Capstone, you will write an individual report for the principal of the elementary school. In this report, you need to explain how you used mathematics to help plan the carnival. To assist in the preparation of the reports, your group will complete three of the following investigations. Each group will present an oral report to the class on one of them. (Guidelines for the group report are given on page 544.)

As a group, examine Investigations 2 through 8 and choose three to complete. Confirm your choices with your teacher, and then start investigating!

Investigation 2 Careful Planning

Careful planning is necessary to make the carnival a success. An important part of planning is identifying and scheduling all the tasks that need to be done.

1. Some of the tasks and task times for the carnival project might be building the booths (5 days), laying out the floor plan (2 days), designing a carnival logo (1 day), publicity (10 days), and finding a location (2 days). Write at least two more tasks that will need to be done. Estimate the times needed to complete these tasks.

2. Use the tasks from activity 1 to do the following:

   a. Construct a prerequisite table showing the tasks, the task times, and the immediate prerequisites.

   b. Draw a project digraph.

   c. Find the critical tasks and the earliest finish time for the whole project.

   d. Set up a schedule for completing all the tasks. Your schedule should show earliest start times, earliest finish times, and slack times.

3. Committees must be formed to work on each of the tasks. Since some students will be on more than one committee, it is impossible for all the committees to meet at the same time. Assume there are five committees, each of which has a member in common with at least two other committees.

a. Construct a vertex-edge graph model that shows the five committees and which committees share members. (You decide which committees share members.)

b. What is the fewest number of meeting times needed so that all committees can meet? Explain how you can use the graph model from part a to answer this question.

4. Make a neat copy of your project digraph, showing the critical tasks and earliest finish time. Also make a copy of the graph model for the committee scheduling problem, showing the graph coloring.

a. File these two graphs at the location in the classroom designated by your teacher. Examine the graphs filed by other groups and compare their graphs to those from your group.

b. Write a question to at least one group asking them to explain something about their work that you found interesting or did not understand. Answer any questions your group receives.

Investigation ③ Booths and Floor Plans

In this investigation you will sketch a floor plan for the carnival and build a scale model of a booth.

1. Assume that the carnival will be held in a rectangular-shaped gym with dimensions 40 meters by 30 meters. Using centimeter graph paper, with one centimeter corresponding to 1 meter, sketch a floor plan for the carnival. Your floor plan should show the placement of the following items:

– The ticket and information booth. This booth is hexagonal-shaped so that during peak times customers can line up at six windows to get information or tickets. Two sides of the booth have length 1 m and the other sides have length 2.24 m. The booth is to be placed in the center of the gym.

– The game booths. There are ten game booths to be arranged along the sides of the gym. Eight of them are U-shaped, 1.5 m × 2 m × 1.5 m. The 2 m side faces out. The other two are triangular-shaped—two sides are the same length and the third side, which faces out, is 2 m long.

   – Concessions. Six tables, each of which has a 2 m × 1 m table top, are placed in a U-shape to serve as the area where food is sold.

   – Decide on one other feature of the floor plan. Describe it and add it to your plan.

2. Now consider the ticket booth in more detail.

   a. Build a model of the ticket booth frame using a scale of 10 cm to 1 m. The ticket booth has base dimensions as described in activity 1. The vertical walls of the booth are 2 m high.

   b. Design a tent-like canopy for the booth.

   c. Make a careful sketch of the ticket booth.

   d. How much canvas will be needed to cover the booth, including the canopy?

3. Deposit your floor plan and your ticket booth model and sketch at the location in the classroom designated by your teacher. Study the floor plans, models, and sketches filed by other groups and compare to your group's work. Write a question to at least one group asking them to explain something about their work that you found interesting or did not understand. Answer any questions your group receives.

Investigation 4 — Carnival Tee-Shirts

To help promote the carnival and raise more money, tee-shirts will be designed and sold.

1. Design a logo for the carnival, to be used on the tee-shirts as well as on other promotional materials. The logo might include the name of the school or a message of some sort. It could be an abstract design or a picture of something related to the carnival. It can be whimsical or serious. Be creative! The only requirement is that the logo must be symmetrical in some way.

a. Describe the symmetry shown in your logo.

b. Briefly explain why you chose your particular design and explain its meaning.

2. The price list for a tee-shirt shop is shown below.

Midwest Athletic Supply and Screen Printing

Set-up

$17.50 for one color $12.50 for each additional color

Art

$25 per hour

Tees

Prices for shirts with one color:

1–15	$6.55 ea.	63–147	$5.75 ea.
16–31	$6.25 ea.	148–	$5.40 ea.
32–62	$5.95 ea.		

Add $0.30 per shirt for each additional color

---

a. Suppose you decide to go with a deluxe four-color design that requires two hours of artwork from the shop's designers. Complete a table like the one at the right.

b. Suppose that you buy more than 150 of the shirts. Using *NOW* for the cost to buy a given number of shirts and *NEXT* for the cost to buy one more, write an equation showing the relationship between *NOW* and *NEXT*.

Cost of Four-color Tee-shirts

Number of Tee-shirts Purchased	Total Cost
1	
10	
100	
200	
201	
202	

   c. Using T for the number of tee-shirts purchased and C for the total cost, write an equation showing the relationship between T and C for any number $T > 150$.

3. You plan to sell the tee-shirts and make a profit. What price should you set for the shirts? Write a brief analysis justifying your choice of selling price. Your analysis should include the following:

   – An equation and graph showing the relationship between profit P and number of tee-shirts sold T, where $T > 150$

   – An explanation of how to use the profit equation and graph to find the number of shirts you must sell to break even

   – An estimate of the profit you expect to make

   – A summary of why you chose your selling price

4. File a copy of your logo, an explanation of the symmetry it exhibits, and your profit analysis at the location in the classroom designated by your teacher. Examine the logos and solutions filed by other groups and compare to your group's work. Write a question to at least one group asking them to explain something about their work that you found interesting or did not understand. Answer any questions your group receives.

Investigation  5   Money Made and Money Spent

The main purpose of the carnival is to make money in a fun way. Both organizers and customers are concerned about the money aspect. The organizers want to know how much money the carnival will make. The customers want to know how much money they will spend.

1. Customers will buy tickets and then pay for the games using one or more tickets per game. Each ticket costs 25¢. This year, parents who buy tickets in advance

can specify that the money paid goes to purchase equipment for their child's classroom. Parents are asking, "About how many tickets will I use at the carnival?" For the last three years, 25 parents were randomly chosen and asked how many tickets they used. These data are shown in the following table.

Number of Game Tickets Used by Sample of Parents at the Last Three Carnivals

3 Years Ago		2 Years Ago		Last Year	
26	20	20	32	6	8
20	30	48	24	4	10
20	18	36	12	4	12
16	25	16	11	20	10
4	8	16	36	8	18
21	15	44	40	8	20
20	14	24	8	8	12
20	48	40	12	24	28
26	16	8	42	7	26
10	10	8	12	12	24
16	16	18	22	22	20
20	35	10	14	18	12
34	—	44	—	16	—

a. Make a box plot of each year's data. Divide the work among your group. Draw all three box plots on the same axis.

b. Write a brief summary of the information shown in each box plot. Describe how patterns of ticket use vary from year to year.

c. What other graphs or statistics might be useful to help you inform parents about how many tickets they will need?

d. When a parent asks you, "How many tickets will I use?" what will you say? Explain the reasoning behind your response.

2. Someone suggests the carnival can do more than support the school for the current year. The class agrees to set up a fund that will grow and support the school in future years. Your goal is to put $800 of the carnival profits into a savings account for the school. The account pays 5% interest compounded yearly.

   a. How much money will be in the account when you graduate, assuming no withdrawals?

   b. Write equations that will allow you to calculate the balance of this account

      – for any year, given the balance for the year before.

      – after any number of years x.

   c. Use the equations from part b to make a table and a graph showing the growth of this account.

   d. Describe the pattern of growth in the savings account over a 10-year period.

   e. Think about how fast the account grows:

      – Is the account growing faster in year 5 or year 10? How can you tell?

      – What would the graph look like if the account were growing at a constant rate of change?

   f. Suppose that the school wants to buy a new computer for the library. A local manufacturer has offered to give the school a great price. The computer is expected to cost about $1000. How long will it be before there is enough in the account to buy the computer?

3. Make a neat copy of your work on this investigation, including graphs, plots, tables, and explanations. File the copy at the location in the classroom designated by your teacher. Check the solutions filed by other groups and compare to your group's work. Write a question to at least one group asking them to explain something about their work that you found interesting or did not understand. Answer any questions your group receives.

Investigation 6   Ring-Toss Game

The most important part of a carnival is, of course, the games. Suppose that you are setting up a ring-toss game. A number of two-liter bottles of soda are lined up. The goal of the game is to toss a ring around the top of one of them. If a player hooks one of the bottles (which is called getting a "ringer"), then she gets to keep it. Your task is to design this game. You need to consider how large the rings should be, how far back the players should stand, and what the cost to play the game should be.

1. Examine the following data collected from a ring-tossing experiment. The data show the average number of ringers per 100 tosses at a distance of 1 meter from the bottles, for rings of varying diameters.

Sample Ring-toss Data for 1-meter Tosses

Diameter of Ring (in centimeters)	Average Number of Ringers per 100 Tosses
4	3
5	6
6	8
7	11
8	14
9	19
10	22
11	27
12	32

a. Make a scatterplot of the data.

b. Describe and explain any patterns or unusual features of the data.

c. Notice that when the ring diameter doubles, the number of ringers increases by a factor of about four. Can you suggest any explanation for this pattern in terms of the size of the circular rings?

2. Data collected from another ring-tossing experiment are shown in the following table. These data show the average number of ringers per 100 tosses with rings of diameter 12 cm, for players standing at varying distances from the bottles.

Sample Ring-toss Data for 12-cm Diameter Rings	
Distance from the Bottles (in meters)	**Average Number of Ringers per 100 Tosses**
1	32
2	15
3	8
4	4
5	1

a. Make a scatterplot of the data.

b. Describe any patterns you see in the data.

c. Suppose *NOW* is the average number of ringers at one of the distances in the table and *NEXT* is the average number of ringers for a distance 1 meter farther away. Write an equation that approximates the relationship between *NOW* and *NEXT*.

3. It is important to charge enough to play the game so that the income from ticket sales for the game is greater than the cost of the prizes given away. For this activity, assume that a ring with diameter 12 cm is used and players stand 2 meters away from the bottles.

a. Suppose that a local merchant offers to support the carnival by loaning you all the soda you need to set up your game. The merchant will charge you 60¢

for every bottle you give away as a prize. You decide to charge 25¢ for a toss. Based on the data in the tables, you expect 15% of the tosses to be ringers. Use T for the number of tosses by customers and P for your profit from the game. Write an equation that shows the relationship between P and T.

b. Given the arrangement with the local merchant in part a, what is the least you can charge for a toss and still make a profit?

c. Suppose you have no sponsor and must pay the usual retail price for the soda. For stores near where you live, what is a reasonable price for a two-liter bottle of soda? In this situation, what is the least you can charge for a toss at a distance of 2 meters and still make a profit?

d. Based on the data in activity 2, how would your profit-modeling equation in part a change if players tossed rings at a distance of 3 meters? In this situation, what is the least you can charge for a toss and still make a profit?

e. As designers of fun, profitable games, would your group recommend a 2-meter toss or a 3-meter toss? Explain your reasoning.

4. Make a neat copy of your work on this investigation, showing graphs, equations, and other answers. File this "solution sheet" at the location in the classroom designated by your teacher. Study the solutions filed by other groups and compare them to your solutions. Write a question to at least one group asking them to explain something about their work that you found interesting or did not understand. Answer any questions your group receives.

Investigation  **7** **Free-Throw Game: Beat the Pro**

Games of skill, especially those involving sports, are always popular at carnivals. Suppose that you are in charge of setting up a basketball free-throw game where a challenger pits his or her skill against a pro. In this case, the pro is the top free-throw shooter from the girls' basketball team. The challenger and the pro each shoot ten free-throws. If the challenger makes more baskets than the pro, then he or she wins a prize. Your job is to decide how much to charge to play the game and what prizes should be awarded to winners.

1. You know from the basketball season's statistics that the pro makes about 85% of her free-throws. What about the challenger's percentage of successful free-throws? You cannot know the shooting percentage of every challenger that might play the game. However, it would be helpful to get some information to help you decide on the price to charge and prizes to award. One of your friends, who likes basketball and is a pretty good shooter, agrees to help you gather some data by being a sample challenger. He completes 50 trials of 10 free-throws and records the number of baskets for each trial. These data are shown in the following table.

Number of Free-Throws Made (Out of 10) for 50 Trials by One Sample Challenger									
8	8	9	6	7	8	7	6	8	7
8	8	10	9	8	7	7	8	5	5
7	5	6	10	6	8	9	8	9	10
8	7	8	9	8	5	8	6	8	7
7	6	9	4	9	6	8	10	7	6

a. Construct a histogram for these data. Describe and explain any patterns in the distribution.

b. Based on the data, about what percent of free-throws does the sample challenger make? Explain using a statistical measure.

c. Does he appear to be a fairly consistent shooter? Justify your answer by using an appropriate plot and summary statistics.

2. To help make good decisions about the amount you should charge and the value of prizes, you can simulate a game between the sample challenger and the pro.

a. What is a reasonable estimate for the probability that the pro will make a particular free-throw?

b. Explain why 0.75 is a reasonable estimate for the probability that the sample challenger will make a particular free-throw.

c. Using the probabilities above, design a simulation to estimate the probability that the challenger wins the game.

d. Conduct 5 trials of your simulation. Add your results to the Simulated Beat The Pro Game table so there is a total of 100 trials. (The table can be obtained from your teacher.)

3. Now examine the simulation table you completed in activity 2.

    a. Construct a histogram of the difference between the number of free-throws made by the challenger and the number made by the pro. Describe the shape of the distribution. Interpret the shape in terms of outcomes of the "Beat The Pro" game.

    b. What is your estimate of the probability that the challenger wins? Remember that the challenger wins only if he makes more of the 10 free throws than the pro does.

4. A local sporting goods store will support the carnival by selling you top-quality basketballs for winning prizes. The balls will cost $8 each.

    a. Based on the simulation data and your analysis in activity 3, determine how much you should charge the sample challenger to play the game. Remember, you want to keep the game affordable and yet ensure a profit over the course of many games.

    b. The actual game will be played with many different challengers, not just the one sample challenger. What do you think is a good price to charge for the actual game?

5. Would the pro be more likely to beat a 75% free-throw shooter in a game with 20 shots or one with 10 shots? Explain your reasoning.

6. Make a neat copy of your work on this investigation. File it at the location in the classroom designated by your teacher. Examine the work filed by other groups in the class and compare to your work. Write a question to at least one group asking them to explain something about their work that you found interesting or did not understand. Answer any questions your group receives.

Investigation **8** **Further Analysis**

In Investigations 2 through 7 you analyzed a variety of situations related to planning the carnival. Of course, there are other things to consider as well. Choose one of your ideas from Investigation 1 or from "Think about this situation" at the beginning of this Capstone. Carry out a brief mathematical analysis of the idea. Specifically, you should formulate and answer at least two questions related to your idea. For example, you might design and analyze another game, as is done in Investigations 6 and 7, or you might collect and analyze data on what kinds of games are most popular. File a copy of your analysis at the location designated by your teacher.

R E P O R T S : Putting It All Together

Finish this Capstone by preparing two reports, one oral group report and one individual written report as described below.

1. Your group should prepare a brief oral report on one of the investigations you have completed. You will present the report as if you are reporting to the principal of the elementary school that is planning to have the carnival. Your teacher will play the role of the principal. Your report should meet the following guidelines.

   – Choose one of the investigations you have completed. Confirm your choice with your teacher before beginning to prepare your report.

   – Examine the work that other groups have filed on your chosen investigation. Compare your work to theirs and discuss any differences with them. Modify your solutions, if you think you should.

   – Begin your presentation with a brief summary of your work on the investigation.

   – Convince the principal that your solutions are correct and should be adopted.

   – Be prepared to discuss alternative solutions, particularly those proposed by other groups that also worked on the same investigation.

   – Be prepared to answer any questions from the "principal" or your classmates.

2. On your own, write a two-page report summarizing how the mathematics you have learned in this course can be used to help plan a school carnival.

Checkpoint

In this course you have investigated important mathematics and you have gained valuable experience in thinking mathematically. Look back over the investigations you completed in this Capstone and consider some of the mathematical thinking you have done. Describe, if possible, an example where you did each of the following:

a Search for patterns

b Formulate or find a mathematical model

c Collect, analyze, and interpret data

d Make and check conjectures

e Describe and use an algorithm

f Visualize

g Simulate a situation

h Predict

i Experiment

j Make connections—between mathematics and the real world and within mathematics itself

k Use a variety of representations—like tables, graphs, equations, words, and physical models

✓ *Be prepared to share your examples and thinking with the entire class.*

Index

Mathematical Topics

Contexts

Technology

Photo Credits